PROBLEMATIZING LAW, RIGHTS, AND CHILDHOOD IN ISRAEL/PALESTINE

In this book, Hedi Viterbo radically challenges our picture of law, human rights, and childhood, both in and beyond the Israel/Palestine context. He reveals how Israel, rather than disregarding international law and children's rights, has used them to hone and legitimize its violence against Palestinians. He exposes the human rights community's complicity in this situation, due to its problematic assumptions about childhood, its uncritical embrace of international law, and its recurring emulation of Israel's security discourse. He examines how, and to what effect, both the state and its critics manufacture, shape, and weaponize the categories "child" and "adult." Bridging disciplinary divides, Viterbo analyzes hundreds of previously unexamined sources, many of which are not publicly available. Bold, sophisticated, and informative, *Problematizing Law, Rights, and Childhood in Israel/Palestine* provides unique insights into the ever-tightening relationship between law, children's rights, and state violence, at both the local and global levels.

HEDI VITERBO is Lecturer in Law at Queen Mary University of London. Previously, he was Lecturer in Law at the University of Essex, a Leverhulme Early Career Fellow at SOAS, University of London, a visiting scholar at Harvard Law School, and a visiting researcher at Columbia University. Dr Viterbo's previous publications include *The ABC of the OPT: A Legal Lexicon of the Israeli Control over the Palestinian Territory* (co-authored with Orna Ben-Naftali and Michael Sfard, 2018).

PROBLEMATIZING LAW, RIGHTS, AND CHILDHOOD IN ISRAEL/PALESTINE

HEDI VITERBO

Queen Mary University of London

CAMBRIDGE
UNIVERSITY PRESS

Shaftesbury Road, Cambridge CB2 8EA, United Kingdom

One Liberty Plaza, 20th Floor, New York, NY 10006, USA

477 Williamstown Road, Port Melbourne, VIC 3207, Australia

314–321, 3rd Floor, Plot 3, Splendor Forum, Jasola District Centre, New Delhi – 110025, India

103 Penang Road, #05–06/07, Visioncrest Commercial, Singapore 238467

Cambridge University Press is part of Cambridge University Press & Assessment, a department of the University of Cambridge.

We share the University's mission to contribute to society through the pursuit of education, learning and research at the highest international levels of excellence.

www.cambridge.org
Information on this title: www.cambridge.org/9781009011556

DOI: 10.1017/9781009019842

First published 2021
First paperback edition 2023

A catalogue record for this publication is available from the British Library

Library of Congress Cataloging-in-Publication data
Names: Viterbo, Hedi, author.
Title: Problematizing law, rights, and childhood in Israel/Palestine / Hedi Viterbo, Queen Mary University of London.
Description: Cambridge, United Kingdom ; New York, NY : Cambridge University Press, 2021. | Based on author's thesis (doctoral–London School of Economics and Political Science, 2012) issued under title: The legal construction of childhood in the Israeli-Palestinian conflict. | Includes bibliographical references and index.
Identifiers: LCCN 2021024874 (print) | LCCN 2021024875 (ebook) | ISBN 9781316519998 (hardback) | ISBN 9781009011556 (paperback) | ISBN 9781009019842 (epub)
Subjects: LCSH: Children–Legal status, laws, etc.–Israel. | Children–Legal status, laws, etc.–West Bank. | Children–Legal status, laws, etc.–Gaza Strip. | Arab-Israeli conflict–Law and legislation.
Classification: LCC KMK1475 .V58 2021 (print) | LCC KMK1475 (ebook) | DDC 342.569408/772–dc23
LC record available at https://lccn.loc.gov/2021024874
LC ebook record available at https://lccn.loc.gov/2021024875

ISBN   978-1-316-51999-8   Hardback
ISBN   978-1-009-01155-6   Paperback

CONTENTS

ACKNOWLEDGMENTS

This book is the culmination of fourteen years of research. Its first incarnation was a doctoral study conducted at the London School of Economics and Political Science (LSE) under the supervision of Nicola Lacey, Emily Jackson, and Jenny Kuper. My heartfelt gratitude goes to Niki, Emily, and Jenny for their invaluable guidance and their rock-steady support. I am also indebted to many others who have kindly provided helpful feedback, advice, and assistance along the way. Key among them are (in alphabetical order of surnames): Mimi Ajzenstadt, Shulamit Almog, Jonathan Alschech, Shira Atsmoni, Daphne Barak-Erez, Elizabeth Bartholet, Orna Ben-Naftali, Smadar Ben-Natan, Netanel Benischou, Shani Benkin, Jacqueline Bhabha, Brenna Bhandar, Michael Birnhack, José Brunner, Eric Cheyfitz, Hagai Elad, Elizabeth Emens, Itay Filiba, Michael Freeman, Shelley Gavigan, Yuval Ginbar, Neve Gordon, Aeyal Gross, Dafna Hacker, Lisa Hajjar, Hamed Hamdan, Ariel Handel, Fahim Hasson, Sharif Hasson, Dorit Itzhak, Sarah Joseph, Felicity Kaganas, Lisa Kelly, Tobias Kelly, Duncan Kennedy, Laleh Khalili, Coel Kirkby, Yitzhak Klein, Martti Koskenniemi, Hagar Kotef, Khaled Kuzmar, Nicolas Lamp, Gaby Lasky, Jennifer Leaning, Darryl Li, Terri Libesman, Assaf Likhovski, Jinee Lokaneeta, Alex Lubin, Orly Lubin, Kate Malleson, Brinkley Messick, Sarit Michaeli, Sabine Michalowski, Steven Mintz, Iyad Misk, Daniel Monk, Leslie Moran, Linda Mulcahy, Dianne Otto, K-Sue Park, John Parry, Roy Peled, Noam Peleg, Andrew Poe, Alain Pottage, Nery Ramati, Ronald Ranta, Maya Rosenfeld, Sue Ruddick, Ilan Saban, Ahmad Sa'di, Dana Salmon, Austin Sarat, Elizabeth Scott, Michael Sfard, Hamutal Shamash, Richard Sherwin, Yehoshua Shohat Gurtler, Ronen Shor, Lana Tatour, Kendall Thomas, Charles Tripp, Ilias Trispiotis, Lorenzo Veracini, Robert van Krieken, Sonja van Wichelen, Jane Wright, Dan Yakir, Shai Yaniv, Adi Youcht, Eyal Zisser, Kamel Ziyan, and the two anonymous reviewers for Cambridge University Press. Finally, I am grateful to Nadav Eden for his dedicated and competent research assistance in the late stages of working on this book; to Selihom Yuhannes for her technical assistance with the footnotes; to Stephen Pigney for his superb copyediting; and to Finola O'Sullivan for shepherding this book through the publication process. Apologies to anyone I have omitted. The research on which this book is based was made possible thanks to the generous support of the Leverhulme Trust, the LSE Law Department, the LSE Middle East Institute, the Queen Mary University of London School of Law, Essex University Law School, the Emile Zola Chair of Human Rights in the College of Management, and the Anglo-Israeli Association.

ABBREVIATIONS

ACRI	Association for Civil Rights in Israel
AdminA	Administrative Appeal
AdminC	Administrative Case
AppR	Appeal Request
CivA	Civil Appeal
CivC	Civil Case
CMA	Court-Martial Appeal
CMC	Court-Martial Case
COGAT	Coordinator of Government Activities in the Territories
CRC	Convention on the Rights of the Child
CrimA	Criminal Appeal
CrimC	Criminal Case
Ct.	Court
DCIP	Defence for Children International–Palestine
DisC	Disciplinary Case
Dist.	District
GA	UN General Assembly
HCJ	High Court of Justice
IDF	Israel Defense Forces (the Israeli military)
IPS	Israel Prison Service (Israel's national prison service)
Jer/Jer.	Jerusalem
MAG	Military Advocate General
Mag.	Magistrates'
MilA	Military Appeal
MilC	Military Case (involving noncitizen Palestinian defendants)
MP	Member of Parliament
MPD	Military Judgments, as collated and published by the Military Advocate General ("PD" is short for Piskei Din – the Hebrew term for judgments – which is commonly used to cite non-military Israeli judgments)
PCATI	Public Committee Against Torture in Israel
PTSD	Post-Traumatic Stress Disorder

SC	UN Security Council
UN Doc	United Nations Document
UNCAT	UN Committee Against Torture
UNCRC	UN Committee on the Rights of the Child
UNICEF	UN Children's Fund

Conceptual and Theoretical Foundations

1.1 Challenging Dominant Discourses

The Israeli legal system's handling of young Palestinians has been a subject of global debate. To mention just three examples touched on in this book: bills were introduced in the US Congress, requiring "that United States funds do not support military detention, interrogation, abuse, or ill-treatment of Palestinian children"; a delegation of lawyers commissioned by the British government published a high-profile report on the "treatment of Palestinian children under Israeli military law"; and Israel's detention of a 16-year-old Palestinian attracted worldwide media coverage[1] as well as condemnation from UN bodies, international celebrities, and a petition signed by 1.7 million people.[2] At the same time, in Israel, the legal system's treatment of Jewish settler youth has also been a matter of concern, with one lawmaker warning that the prosecution of young protestors could "stain them for life" and thus destroy "the lives of hundreds of young guys, the salt of the earth."[3]

---

[1] The US Congress bills are addressed in Chapter 5, Section 5.4 ("The Right to Childhood"); the report by the delegation of British lawyers is discussed in Chapter 2, Section 2.7 ("Israel's Human Rights Critics") and Chapter 4, Section 4.4.1 ("The Pitfalls of Child Law"); and Israel's detention of the 16-year-old Palestinian is explored, from various angles, in Chapters 2 (Section 2.4, "The Military Court System"), 4 (Section 4.4.3, "Confining Palestinian Minds"), 5 (Section 5.5.1, "Overlooking Young People's Accounts"), and 6 (Sections 6.1, "Introduction," and 6.3.2, "Denial").

[2] See, e.g., Office of the UN High Commissioner for Human Rights, "UN Rights Experts Alarmed by Detention of Palestinian Girl for Slapping Israeli Soldier" (February 13, 2018), www.ohchr.org/EN/NewsEvents/Pages/DisplayNews.aspx?NewsID=22654&LangID=E; +972 Magazine staff, "Prominent Actors, Musicians, and Authors Demand Ahed Tamimi's Release," +972 *Magazine* (February 12, 2018), https://972mag.com/prominent-actors-musicians-and-authors-demand-ahed-tamimis-release/133119; Middle East Monitor staff, "1.7m Sign Online Petition for Ahed Tamimi's Release," *Middle East Monitor* (February 7, 2018), www.middleeastmonitor.com/20180207-1-7m-sign-online-petition-for-ahed-tamimis-release/.

[3] See Chapter 7, Section 7.3.2 ("Israeli Settler Children as Soldiers in the Making").

Three claims recur in such debates: first, that Israel flouts international law and human rights; second, that law and rights offer the remedies for Israel's wrongs; and, third, that young people have distinct characteristics and needs, inherently different from those of their elders. As will soon become apparent, this book radically challenges all three claims. The British delegation thus asserted, quoting the UN Convention on the Rights of the Child (CRC): "The child by reason of physical and mental immaturity 'needs special safeguards.' . . . International law, international humanitarian law and the [CRC] . . . should be fully and effectively implemented [by Israel]. The international legal principle of the best interests of the child should be the primary consideration in all actions concerning children."[4] Similarly, the US bills note: "Children are entitled to special protections . . . under international human rights law and international humanitarian law." Citing reports by UN bodies and human rights NGOs, the bills maintain that Israel "violates international law and internationally recognized standards of human rights," including those enshrined in the CRC and in international humanitarian law.[5] As for settler youth in conflict with the law, one Israeli NGO emphasized the "need to remember that these minors have rights . . . [which] must be upheld."[6]

For some, it is not only the well-being of young Palestinians or Israelis that is at stake, but the very survival of childhood and child rights. This narrative, too, is brought into question in this book. "It is impossible to assess the . . . harm caused to [Palestinian] children [by the Israeli military's actions]," the Special Rapporteur of the UN Commission on Human Rights once warned, adding: "Many have simply lost their childhood." According to the British section of Amnesty International, "[c]hildren's rights [are] killed amid lawlessness" in the Gaza Strip. Using a similar rhetoric, the Public Committee Against Torture in Israel has

---

[4] S. Sedley et al., *Children in Military Custody: A Report Written by a Delegation of British Lawyers on the Treatment of Palestinian Children under Israeli Military Law* (Foreign and Commonwealth Office, June 2012), pp. 9, 32, www.childreninmilitarycustody.org.uk/wp-content/uploads/2012/03/Children_in_Military_Custody_Full_Report.pdf (emphasis removed).

[5] Promoting Human Rights by Ending Israeli Military Detention of Palestinian Children Act, H.R. 4391, 115th Cong. (2017), pp. 2, 8–9, www.congress.gov/115/bills/hr4391/BILLS-115hr4391ih.pdf; Promoting Human Rights for Palestinian Children Living under Israeli Military Occupation Act, H.R. 2407, 116th Cong. (2019), pp. 2, 10–12, https://nwttac.dci-palestine.org/hr2407_full_text.

[6] See Chapter 8, Section 8.1 ("Introduction: Law, Human Rights, and Young Israeli Settlers").

legitimized the more severe abuse of Palestinians classified as adults: "Childhood is not a Privilege but a Right! ... Torture Destroys Childhood ... [T]he threshold in which an act of abuse would be considered torture in the situation of an adult must be lowered when it comes to children."[7] Similarly, within legal scholarship, Israel has been described as "stripping [Palestinian] children of their childhood," "evicting children from childhood," and violating their "right to childhood." "The Israeli legal and political apparatus," the claim goes, "does not treat Palestinian children as children. ... [Consequently,] the children's rights discourse disappears."[8]

This book, while critical of Israel's conduct, also poses a radical challenge to these and other prevailing narratives. It problematizes law, rights, and childhood – that is, it unsettles and disrupts common ways of thinking about them, about the problems each of them presents, and about the solutions to these problems, in and beyond the Israel/Palestine context.[9] As laid bare in this and the following chapters, both law and rights lend themselves to divergent uses, including those operating in the service of state domination and violence. Further, rights and law, partly due to their reliance on abstractions and generalizations, are frequently applied without sufficient sensitivity to the context at hand. Child law (the sum of legal mechanisms relating directly to those defined as children) and child rights are premised on a specific abstraction: a supposedly universal and natural model of childhood, which in reality often marginalizes young people, legitimizes harshness toward older people, and suppresses valuable forms of life and thought. Combined, the malleability of law and rights, their problematic conceptualization of childhood, and their context-insensitivity often beget harm to disempowered communities, young and old alike.

[7] See, respectively, Chapter 5, Section 5.3.1 ("Lost Childhood"); Amnesty International UK, "Occupied Territories: Children's Rights Killed amid Growing Lawlessness" (December 12, 2006), www.amnesty.org.uk/press-releases/occupied-territories-childrens-rights-killed-amid-growing-lawlessness; Chapter 5, Section 5.4 ("The Right to Childhood").

[8] N. Shalhoub-Kevorkian, *Incarcerated Childhood and the Politics of Unchilding* (Cambridge and New York: Cambridge University Press, 2019), pp. 20, 25–26, 44, 50, 52, 54, 100, 103, 107, 111–12, 116–18, 121–22, 124, 126, 128–30, 132, 136–37. For my criticism of this scholarly narrative, see Chapter 4, Section 4.3.3 ("The Blind Spots of the Human Rights Community") and Chapter 5, Section 5.4 ("The Right to Childhood").

[9] This definition of "problematization" draws on A. Terwiel, "Problematization as an Activist Practice: Reconsidering Foucault" (2020) 23:1 *Theory & Event* 66, 67.

Drawing on cross-disciplinary literature, this book also takes as its point of departure that neither "children" nor "adults" are merely pre-existing groups to be served, regulated, or governed by law and human rights. Rather, each is in large part a socially manufactured category, one that is delineated, reinforced, challenged, and weaponized by historically and geographically contingent forces. Key among these forces are practices and discourses relating to law and human rights, whose role in shaping the meaning, nature, effects, and uses of childhood is a central concern of this book. Also examined in the following chapters is the intertwining of law and human rights with various other forces at both the local and global levels, including visual technologies and images, the mental health disciplines, militarism, and everyday acts of resistance.

Accordingly, and contrary to allegations by the human rights community, Israel neither simply erodes childhood nor disregards legal and human rights norms. Instead, as brought to light in this book, Israeli authorities have pursued a more sophisticated course of action: deploying law, rights, and childhood in general – and increasingly embracing international child rights law in particular – to entrench, perfect, and launder Israel's oppressive control regime. Law and rights have thus aided Israel in its efforts to subjugate Palestinian minds, bodies, and interactions; to confine Palestinians to a legally enshrined model of childhood that works to their detriment; to discipline older Palestinians through their young; to conceal and justify state violence; to portray abusive soldiers as children deserving of compassion; to expand the Jewish settlement project while dispossessing Palestinians; and much of this, supposedly, in the name of "the child's best interests."

Also put on trial in this book, along with the Israeli state, are its liberal human rights critics – NGOs (both local and international), UN bodies, and scholars. Not only have such critics repeatedly failed to recognize how the child rights framework ends up harming Palestinians, but they have also, in multiple ways, contributed to this harm. Moreover, throughout the chapters that follow, the liberal human rights community is revealed to have much more in common than is generally believed with Israeli authorities, as well as with Israeli settlers. One commonality, increasingly shared by all of them, is the language of law and rights. Another is the way in which human rights actors have emulated or even endorsed the Israeli depiction of Palestinians as a national security risk, as well as Israel's use of age distinctions as tools of control. The ever-tightening relationship between law, child rights, and state violence is a common thread throughout the book's chapters. It stems from various factors, including some of the characteristics of the human rights community, specifically: its questionable conception of childhood; its uncritical embrace of international law; its ignorance, misunderstanding, and misrepresentation of crucial legal and political issues; its need to keep donors and lay audiences interested in local issues that are both complex and contentious; and, on occasion, its assessment of human rights violations in isolation from their structural causes.

The main objects of inquiry of this book, then, are the Israeli legal system and Israel's human rights critics. I investigate how, and to what effect, they all conceptualize, shape, and utilize childhood. The inquiry unfolds within a multitude of contexts (as detailed in the last section of this chapter): the mass prosecution, incarceration, surveillance, abuse, and killing of Palestinians, both suspected lawbreakers and others; state policies and practices in relation to various areas, including Israeli rules of engagement, restrictions on Palestinians' movement and food consumption, the monitoring of unsuspected young Palestinians, the severing of Palestinian family ties, the use of human shields, and military hazing; the Israeli legal system's handling of Jewish settler youth who throw stones or participate in legally proscribed protests; and the multiple roles human rights organizations play across these settings, including as legal argument-makers, as disseminators of child-related imagery and truth claims, and as providers of legal counsel. Across these various contexts, I bring to light previously unexplored elements, effects, and pitfalls of legal and human rights discourses and practices.

Hundreds of hitherto unexamined legal and human rights sources are analyzed in this book, many of which are not publicly available. Among their institutional authors are the Israeli military, its legal advisors, its courts for noncitizen Palestinians, and its courts-martial for soldiers. I also scrutinize documents and actions of other Israeli authorities, primarily those of the government, parliament, and the state's nonmilitary legal arms, including the judiciary (from lower courts to the supreme court), the state attorney's office, the police, and the national prison authority. Also examined is a wide range of human rights publications by international, Palestinian, and Israeli organizations. Further information on the various types of sources under examination is provided in the penultimate section of this chapter.

Broader contexts – local and global – are considered throughout the book. Locally, I shed new light on the Israeli control regime, its transformation over time, and its under-researched features, including: its use of childhood, uncertainty, and visual images as modes of governance; its heavy reliance on law; its hierarchization of different types of evidence; and its interconnected modes of violence against different populations in different territories. Beyond the local context, I highlight under-examined pitfalls and characteristics of laws, policies, and social attitudes, both internationally and within various countries, while drawing comparisons and connections with Israel/Palestine. These laws, policies, and attitudes (past and present) span a wide range of issues, key among which are those concerning young people, their rights, and their legal status; armed conflict and counterinsurgency; and the (mis)treatment of colonized peoples, racialized minorities, and noncitizens. This simultaneous contextualization, at both the local and global levels, yields insights beyond this book's primary focus.

This book's contribution, then, is fivefold: conceptual, theoretical, methodological, thematic, and contextual. Conceptually, this study problematizes law, human rights, and childhood, thereby calling into question dominant assumptions in and beyond the Israel/Palestine context. Theoretically, it bridges disciplinary boundaries and brings into dialogue previously separate bodies of scholarship, including childhood studies, critical legal studies, critical human rights scholarship, and literature on Israel/Palestine. Methodologically, it dissects a wide array of legal and human rights materials, almost none of which have previously been studied, and many of which are not in the public domain. Among these materials, as detailed later in this chapter, are hundreds of military judgments and statutes – a central area of Israeli law that no academic book has thus far examined. Thematically, this study reframes various issues deserving of attention and, in so doing, provides new ways to address them. This includes casting light on subjects that have so far received little to no scholarly attention, such as the trials of Israeli soldiers, the prosecution of settlers, Israel's use of child law to govern and disempower Palestinian adults, and commonalities between the Israeli legal system and its human rights critics.[10] Contextually, this book brings to light parallels, connections, and tensions between the local and

[10] The limitations and dearth of legal scholarship on this book's following subjects of inquiry are discussed as follows: on Israeli military law, see Chapter 2, Section 2.4 ("The Military Court System"); on Israel's handling of soldiers charged with abusing Palestinians, see Chapter 6, Section 6.1 ("Introduction"); on young Israeli settlers, see Chapter 8, Section 8.1 ("Introduction: Law, Human Rights, and Young Israeli Settlers"); on the law applied by Israel to young noncitizen Palestinians, see Chapter 2, Section 2.4 ("The Military Court System"); and on childhood and law generally, beyond the Israel/Palestine context, see Section 1.2.1 ("Problematizing Childhood") in this chapter.

the global, and between past and present, thereby offering broader lessons applicable beyond Israel/Palestine. Rather than rehashing familiar tropes, this book offers a unique perspective from which alternative avenues for thinking and acting can be developed.

Unlike an expanding plethora of human rights and academic publications, I do not profess to represent the experiences and perspectives of young Palestinians. Though valuable, such discourse suffers from significant shortcomings (as explained in detail in Chapter 5).[11] My focus is not so much on the actions of "children" as on unexplored aspects of the legal and human rights forces that construct, conceptualize, and deploy childhood. This framing, however, is not intended to indicate that the book's protagonists – the Israeli legal system and the human rights community – necessarily succeed in their attempts to govern childhood. Nor does it mean that those whose lives are affected lack agency. Quite the opposite. Throughout the chapters that follow, I highlight wide-ranging forms of Palestinian resistance: exiting enclosed territories, in violation of Israel's movement restrictions, by misrepresenting one's age; developing critical political consciousness while in Israeli prisons; smuggling sperm from prison in defiance of Israel's ban on conjugal visits; using stones as weapons and thus destabilizing the power imbalance; committing to returning to what is deemed the stolen homeland; self-empowerment through protest; and using cameras and visual imagery to expose state violence. In addition, I demonstrate that young Jewish settlers have been at the forefront of political activism and, when detained, have refused to disclose their ages and identities. To adequately contextualize these actions, the following chapters also draw on and engage with a broad array of both Palestinian and settler sources.

In the remainder of this chapter, I establish the book's theoretical and conceptual foundations. Section 1.2 offers a rethinking of deep-rooted notions (including those mentioned so far) about each of the subjects to be examined: childhood, law, and human rights. This sets the stage for understanding how and why this study departs from dominant legal and human rights discourses, and what conceptual alternatives it offers. Section 1.3 then places the examined issues in their political context by outlining the varying modes and degrees of control that Israeli authorities exercise over the different parts of Israel/Palestine. Section 1.4

---

[11] See specifically Chapter 5, Section 5.5 ("Lost Voices").

discusses my methodology and sources. Finally, an outline of the book's chapters is provided.

1.2 Problematizing Childhood, Law, and Rights

1.2.1 Problematizing Childhood

This book lays bare the various ways in which legal and human rights discourses and practices, rather than simply regulating or responding to pre-existing children, are heavily implicated in the social production of childhood. This directly challenges two problematic views that tend to dominate social, legal, and human rights thinking about childhood: essentialism and what can be termed "developmentality." The former is the belief that a type of person or thing (in this case, the child or the adult) has a true, intrinsic, constitutive, and invariant nature.[12] The categories "children" and "adults," and the ostensible differences between the groups they designate, are thus understood as self-evident, natural, and universal. Developmentality is the conception of human life as a linear and cumulative development, and of childhood in particular as a distinct stage, or a sequence of standard stages, of development (cognitive and emotional) and socialization.[13]

Thus, through ageist generalizations and abstractions,[14] the prevailing essentialism and developmentality contrast childhood with adulthood. While this dichotomy brims with contradictions and indeterminacies, the archetypal child and adult tend to be diametrically opposed. The

---

[12] This is a somewhat crude definition. As Diana Fuss notes, essentialism has various iterations and forms. See D. Fuss, *Essentially Speaking: Feminism, Nature and Difference* (New York and London: Routledge, 1989), pp. xii, 2.

[13] As suggested by Lynn Fendler (whose definition of "developmentality" is slightly different from mine), this term alludes to Michel Foucault's widely cited concept "governmentality." L. Fendler, "Educating Flexible Souls: The Construction of Subjectivity through Developmentality and Interaction," in K. Heltqvist and G. Dahlberg (eds.), *Governing the Child in the New Millennium* (New York and London: Routledge, 2001), p. 120. On "governmentality," see G. Burchell, C. Gordon, and P. Miller (eds.), *The Foucault Effect: Studies in Governmentality* (Chicago: University of Chicago Press, 1991).

[14] On the ageism in thinking that young people of the same age are identical, see C. Breen, *Age Discrimination and Children's Rights: Ensuring Equality and Acknowledging Difference* (Leiden: Martinus Nijhoff, 2005); R. Pain, "Theorising Age in Criminology: The Case of Home Abuse" (1997) 2 *British Criminology Conferences: Selected Proceedings* 1, 5.

former is assumed to be relatively dependent, vulnerable, incomplete, developing, unreliable, ignorant, impulsive, and, therefore, in need of protection and supervision. The latter, in contrast, is considered relatively autonomous, competent, informed, responsible, fixed, and fully formed.[15]

This prevalent notion of childhood, however, is historically and culturally specific. As social constructs, childhood and adulthood have varied considerably across time and place. Although scholarship on the subject is well established, legal and human rights discourses have largely failed to engage with it. Therefore, it is worth mentioning that as early as 1928, Margaret Mead's *Coming of Age in Samoa*, the best-selling anthropological book for nearly four decades after its publication, paved the way for the presumed naturalness of young people's traits to be questioned. This ethnographic study found that teenage rebellion – perceived by many in the Global North as a universal phenomenon – was, by and large, absent in the Samoan Islands, where the transition to adulthood appeared to be relatively smooth and calm. Mead attributed this to cultural differences, including the coherent and stable values to which young Samoans were exposed (as opposed to mixed messages and expectations in the Global North), the non-concealment from young Samoans of supposedly adult information on issues such as sexuality and death, and the acceptance and approval among Samoans of adolescent sexuality.[16]

Later anthropological studies found a similar absence of teenage rebellion in other societies, as well as a stark contrast to dominant Western attitudes toward childhood sexuality. For example, the Canela, an Amerindian group in Brazil, were reported to encourage their young to have frequent, early, premarital sex – a practice neither the young nor their elders regarded as abuse or neglect. Certain communities in Papua New Guinea were found to gradually initiate boys into manhood through a series of ritualized homosexual oral sex, which the boys reportedly

---

[15] See, e.g., D. Kennedy, *The Well of Being: Childhood, Subjectivity, and Education* (Albany: State University of New York Press, 2006); N. Lee, *Childhood and Society: Growing Up in an Age of Uncertainty* (Buckingham: Open University Press, 2001); V. Zelizer, *Pricing the Priceless Child: The Changing Social Value of Children* (Princeton: Princeton University Press, 1985).

[16] M. Mead, *Coming of Age in Samoa: A Psychological Study of Primitive Youth for Western Civilisation* (New York: William Morrow & Co., 1928).

came to enjoy.[17] To contemporary Western eyes, such practices are likely to seem perverse, to say the least.

Also influential has been historian Philippe Ariès's 1960 book, *L'Enfant et la vie familiale sous l'Ancien Régime* (translated into English as *Centuries of Childhood*). Shifting the focus to Europe, Ariès contended that childhood, as a distinct stage separate from adulthood, is an invention of modernity – a provocative albeit not entirely unprecedented claim.[18] In premodern times, he argued,

> the idea of childhood did not exist; this is not to suggest that children were neglected, forsaken or despised. The idea of childhood is not to be confused with affection for children: it corresponds to an awareness of the particular nature of childhood, ... which distinguishes the child from the adult ... In medieval society, this awareness was lacking.[19]

Accordingly, in medieval Europe those we would now define as "children" mixed freely with "adults," worked from a fairly young age, played the same games as their elders, and were exposed to the same sights and information.

Admittedly, such academic studies do not merely observe social reality; rather, they partake in its construction, including the construction of childhood.[20] Further, childhood studies do not speak in a single voice,[21]

---

[17] For a useful overview of some of these studies, see H. Montgomery, *An Introduction to Childhood: Anthropological Perspectives on Children's Lives* (Malden and Oxford: Wiley-Blackwell, 2008), pp. 203–05, 209–10; M. J. Kehily and H. Montgomery, "Innocence and Experience: A Historical Approach to Childhood and Sexuality," in M. J. Kehily (ed.), *An Introduction to Childhood Studies*, 2nd ed. (Maidenhead and New York: Open University Press, 2009), pp. 79–81.

[18] In 1939, the sociologist Norbert Elias observed that, in medieval Europe, "[t]he distance [in behavior] between adults and children ... was slight." Quoted in H. Cunningham, *Children and Childhood in Western Society Since 1500*, 2nd ed. (London and New York: Routledge, 2005), p. 4.

[19] P. Ariès, *Centuries of Childhood: A Social History of Family Life*, R. Baldick (trans.) (London: Jonathan Cape, 1962), p. 128.

[20] On some of the ways in which childhood studies shape childhood, see P. Kelly, "Youth as an Artefact of Expertise: Problematizing the Practice of Youth Studies in an Age of Uncertainty" (2000) 3 *Journal of Youth Studies* 301; A. S. Benzaquén, "Childhood, History, and the Sciences of Childhood," in H. Goelman et al. (eds.), *Multiple Lenses, Multiple Images: Perspectives on the Child Across Time, Space, and Disciplines* (Toronto: University of Toronto Press, 2004), p. 14.

[21] See, e.g., K. H. Federle, "Rights Flow Downhill" (1994) 2 *International Journal of Children's Rights* 343, 349 (noting that both proponents and opponents of child rights find support for their assertions in sociology and psychology).

nor are they – including the works of Mead[22] and Ariès[23] – immune to criticism. These caveats notwithstanding, the insight about the culturally and historically contingent nature of childhood is invaluable, and has been refined and developed in later academic work.

Nevertheless, contemporary society clings to what historian Steven Mintz has called the "myth of progress," viewing "the history of child-hood as a story of steps forward over time."[24] Similarly, communities and individuals that diverge from the dominant ideal of childhood are often judged to be inadequate, unevolved, or even perverse. What this socially prevalent mindset overlooks, as I demonstrate in Chapters 4 and 5, is the systematic disempowerment of those defined as children and the exten-sive harm caused to people of all ages in the name of child-related norms.

Today's legal and social distinctions between "children" and "adults" tend to be taken for granted and hence are rarely accounted for. When justifications are provided, they typically rest on one of two argumen-tative strategies. The first is to offer, as supporting evidence, examples of toddlers and preteens. What this convenient framing ignores is that the general definition of "child" or "minor," in international,[25] Israeli,[26] and many other domestic legal systems, more broadly encompasses anyone up to the age of 18 years. According to this wide definition, every other person in the West Bank and Gaza Strip is a child[27]

---

[22] On the strengths and limitations of Mead's work, see P. Shankman, *The Trashing of Margaret Mead: Anatomy of an Anthropological Controversy* (Madison: University of Wisconsin Press, 2009).

[23] On the strengths and limitations of Ariès's thesis, see D. Gittins, "The Historical Construction of Childhood," in Kehily (ed.), *An Introduction to Childhood Studies*, pp. 35–49; C. Heywood, "Centuries of Childhood: An Anniversary – and an Epitaph?" (2010) 3:3 *Journal of the History of Childhood and Youth* 341; R. T. Vann, "The Youth of Centuries of Childhood" (1982) 21:2 *History and Theory* 279.

[24] S. Mintz, *Huck's Raft: A History of American Childhood* (Cambridge, MA and London: Harvard University Press, 2004), p. 3.

[25] Article 1 of the Convention on the Rights of the Child, November 20, 1989, 1577 UNTS 3 [hereinafter throughout the book: CRC].

[26] For the current law concerning noncitizen Palestinians in the West Bank, see Article 136 of the Order Concerning Security Provisions (Integrated Version) (Judea and Samaria) (No. 1651), 2009 [hereinafter: Order 1651] (amended in 2011 by Article 3 of the Order Concerning Security Provisions (Judea and Samaria) (Amendment No. 10) (No. 1676), 2011). Regarding Israelis and others, see Article 1 of the Youth Law (Adjudication, Punishment, and Modes of Treatment), 1971 [hereinafter: Youth Law]. Beyond the criminal law context, see, e.g., Article 3 of the Law of Legal Competence and Guardianship, 1962.

[27] For estimates of the age composition of Palestinians, see UN Office for the Coordination of Humanitarian Affairs, *2014 Strategic Response Plan* (November 2013), p. 4, https://

(making the local population far younger than those of the world as a whole,[28] the Global North,[29] and Israel "proper" within its pre-1967 borders[30]). Palestinian defendants classified as children, in particular, are normally above the age of criminal responsibility, which Israeli law sets at 12 years[31] (for this reason, I will usually be referring to them as "youth" rather than "children"). To invoke the very young to generalize about all under-18-year-olds renders them, in linguist John Lakoff's terms, a "social stereotype" standing for the entire group with which it is associated.[32]

A second and perhaps even more common argumentative strategy cites young people's perceived differences – physical, mental, psychological, and experiential – as if they are pregiven and entirely natural. Contrary to this view, such differences do not simply dictate that society must be divided into children and adults. Rather, as childhood came to be thought of as distinct from adulthood, so the bodies, minds, and experiences of those defined as children came to be regarded and shaped as other than those of their older counterparts. Further, each young person potentially differs, often significantly, from her or his peers.

docs.unocha.org/sites/dms/CAP/SRP_2014_oPt.pdf; Palestinian Central Bureau of Statistics, *The Status of the Rights of Palestinian Children 2014* (April 2015), p. 7, www.pcbs.gov.ps/Downloads/book2147.pdf. For an estimate that nearly half of Israeli settlers are under-18s, see Central Bureau of Statistics, "Selected Data for the International Child Day 2018" (October 18, 2018), p. 3 [Hebrew], www.cbs.gov.il/he/mediarelease/DocLib/2018/340/11_18_340b.pdf.

[28] A third of the world's population is estimated to be under the age of 18 years. See J. Wall, "Human Rights in Light of Childhood" (2008) 16 *International Journal of Human Rights* 523, 523.

[29] For data concerning the USA and UK populations, see, respectively, US Census Bureau, *Age and Sex Composition in the United States* (2018), www.census.gov/data/tables/2018/demo/age-and-sex/2018-age-and-sex-composition.html; Office for National Statistics, *2011 Census: Population Estimates by Single Year of Age and Sex for Local Authorities in the United Kingdom* (March 27, 2011), www.ons.gov.uk/peoplepopulationandcommunity/populationandmigration/populationestimates/datasets/2011censuspopulationestimatesbysingleyearofageandsexforlocalauthoritiesintheunitedkingdom.

[30] About a third of the Israeli population is aged under 18. See Central Bureau of Statistics, "Selected Data for the International Child Day 2018," p. 1.

[31] On issues concerning the age of criminal responsibility for Palestinians and Israelis under Israeli law, see, respectively, Chapters 3 (Section 3.2, "Age on Trial") and 8 (Sections 8.2.1, "Stone Throwing," and 8.3, "Age, Silence, and Infantilization").

[32] G. Lakoff, "Cognitive Models and Prototype Theory," in U. Neisser (ed.), *Concepts and Conceptual Development: Ecological .and Intellectual Factors in Categorization* (Cambridge and New York: Cambridge University Press, 1987), pp. 63, 76–77.

And similarities between some young and older people eclipse those within each of these cohorts. It is society that attaches importance to, enhances, and sometimes even creates certain physical differences while treating others as meaningless.[33] Similar realizations regarding other social groups are widely accepted in gender, sexuality, race, and disability studies.

Frequently, claims about age-based differences cite developmental theories, specifically developmental psychology and brain development studies. This brings to mind how mainstream science once supported racism, patriarchy, classism, and other forms of essentialist and infantilizing domination. However, critical literature has pointed out the reductive, totalizing, universalistic, deterministic, and essentialist tendencies of developmental psychology, as well as its concern less with actual "children" than with a mythical childhood. This discipline, the criticism goes, is part of a Western, liberal, class-specific project of turning "others" into rational subjects in the interest of existing power relations.[34] Neurodevelopmental studies have also been shown to suffer from myriad epistemological and methodological shortcomings. The evidence on which such studies hinge – the assumptions they make about brain activity and the equipment in use – is contested and ever-changing. Time and again, neuroscientists generalize on the basis of studies with relatively few participants, often from particular cultural or class backgrounds. Countless variables and phenomena that may influence the brain are ignored. Testing in a lab setting has limitations. Experiments exclude participants who are labeled as mentally abnormal. Moreover, brain maps are simplified (from numbers to color areas) to make them accessible to the media and public, and are normalized for statistical "significance," thereby failing to do justice to the messy and complex data.[35] At a more fundamental level, neurological development

---

[33] Cf. A. James, C. Jenks and A. Prout, *Theorizing Childhood* (Cambridge: Polity Press, 1998), pp. 147, 150–51; C. Castañeda, *Figurations: Child, Bodies, Worlds* (Durham, NC and London: Duke University Press, 2002).

[34] See, e.g., E. Burman, *Deconstructing Developmental Psychology*, 3rd ed. (London: Routledge, 2016); J. R. Moss, *Growing Critical: Alternatives to Developmental Psychology* (London and New York: Routledge, 1996); R. Stainton Rogers and W. Stainton Rogers, *Stories of Childhood: Shifting Agendas of Child Concern* (New York and London: Harvester Wheatsheaf, 1992).

[35] See J. Bessant, "Hard Wired for Risk: Neurological Science, 'the Adolescent Brain' and Developmental Theory" (2008) 11:3 *Journal of Youth Studies* 347–60; P. Kelly, "The Brain in the Jar: A Critique of Discourses of Adolescent Brain Development" (2012) 15:7 *Journal of Youth Studies* 944–59; A. Cox, "Brain Science and Juvenile Justice: Questions

is greatly affected by the information and experiences to which an individual is, or is not, exposed.[36] In modern society, such external stimuli have become highly age-specific. With so-called "non-age-appropriate" experiences and knowledge being withheld from young people, no wonder they appear to be less developed.

In a marked departure from most of the existing legal and human rights literature,[37] I analyze childhood from a social constructionist perspective.[38] Such a viewpoint, as sociologists Allison James, Chris Jenks, and Alan Prout explain, "rejects any idea that childhood rests on some pregiven essential nature and contends that notions of childhood, indeed the very term and concept itself, are a way of looking, a category of thought, a representation. The idea of childhood, in this view, came into being through discourses that created their own objects."[39] In line with this perspective, I generally avoid using the essentialist categories "children" and "adults" in this book, opting instead for phrases such as "young people" and "those over the age of majority" respectively.

1.2.2   Problematizing Child Law

Much of childhood, in its modern form, is law's doing. Law prescribes and enforces norms, confers entitlements and duties, informs language and social perceptions, and is thus among the key social forces shaping childhood, adulthood, and child–adult relations. At the hands of modern law and other social forces, childhood has become, according to sociologist Nikolas Rose, "the most intensively governed sector of personal existence."[40] "If children per se are governed closely," criminologists

---

for Policy and Practice," in W. T. Church et al. (eds.), *Juvenile Justice Sourcebook*, 2nd ed. (Oxford and New York: Oxford University Press, 2014), pp. 123–48.

[36] C. M. Bennett and A. A. Baird, "Anatomical Changes in the Emerging Adult Brain: A Voxel-Based Morphometry Study" (2006) 27:9 *Human Brain Mapping* 766–77; C. Fine, D. Joel and G. Rippon, "Eight Things You Need to Know About Sex, Gender, Brains, and Behavior" (2019) 15:2 *S&F Online*, http://sfonline.barnard.edu/neurogenderings/eight-things-you-need-to-know-about-sex-gender-brains-and-behavior-a-guide-for-academics-journalists-parents-gender-diversity-advocates-social-justice-warriors-tweeters-facebookers-and-ever.

[37] See discussion in the next section.

[38] On social constructionism, see, e.g., K. J. Gergen, *An Invitation to Social Construction*, 3rd ed. (London and Thousand Oaks: Sage, 2015).

[39] James, Jenks and Prout, *Theorizing Childhood*, pp. 139–40.

[40] N. Rose, *Governing the Soul: The Shaping of the Private Self*, 2nd ed. (London and New York: Free Association Books, 1999), p. 121.

Barry Goldson and Gordon Hughes argue, "those who ... transgress normative boundaries and/or breach the criminal law ... tend to be governed most closely of all."[41] These, indeed, are the sort of young people at the heart of the discourses and practices I will be examining.

The legal delineation and governing of childhood's boundaries take place, perhaps first and foremost, along age and spatial lines. Spatially, law's demarcation of childhood includes trying young people in special courts, incarcerating them separately, requiring them to attend school, and excluding them from the world of work and civic life. This spatial separation, in turn, is age-based, resting on the legal ages of criminal majority, compulsory education, employment, enlistment, voting, and eligibility for election, as well as on legal terms such as "minors," "children," and "youth." Statutory minimum ages – such as those for driving, drinking, contractual capacity, tort liability, sexual consent, marriage, social media use, and criminal responsibility – provide additional means for setting and regulating the moral, behavioral, and temporal boundaries of childhood and adulthood. With the assistance of these modern legal creations, a fairly age-homogeneous society has been erected and maintained, in which different sites, experiences, and actions are reserved for rigidly delineated age groups. By enshrining these norms and mechanisms in international law and human rights, this particular (and primarily Western) model of the child has been, to varying degrees, globalized.[42] Law's spatial and age-regimented construction of childhood is a central theme of this book, as is the interaction between global and local norms.

Until well into the nineteenth century, the legal state of affairs was profoundly different. For example, age-related legislation was rare and mostly unenforced. There were no universal compulsory education laws,

[41] B. Goldson and G. Hughes, "Sociological Criminology and Youth Justice: Comparative Policy Analysis and Academic Intervention" (2010) 10:2 *Criminology & Criminal Justice* 211, 211–12.

[42] On the globalization of childhood by international law and the human rights community, see, e.g., J. Boyden, "Childhood and the Policy Makers: A Comparative Perspective on the Globalization of Childhood," in A. James and A. Prout (eds.), *Constructing and Reconstructing Childhood: Contemporary Issues in the Sociological Study of Childhood*, 2nd ed. (London: Routledge, 2003), pp. 190–229; A. T. Imoh, "The Convention on the Rights of the Child: A Product and Facilitator of Global Childhood," in A. T. Imoh and R. Ame (eds.), *Childhoods at the Intersection of the Local and the Global* (Basingstoke and New York: Palgrave Macmillan, 2012), pp. 17–33; K. Cregan and D. Cuthbert, "The Convention on the Rights of the Child and the Construction of the Normative Global Child," in their *Global Childhoods: Issues and Debates* (Los Angeles and London: Sage, 2014), pp. 55–74.

and schools (where they existed) had mixed-age classrooms. A change in a person's social status normally occurred gradually, or through rites of passage, not through legal age thresholds.[43] Neither courts nor prisons separated by age; in England, prisoners were initially separated on the basis of their character, the severity of their offense, and their criminal record (or lack thereof).[44] And the minimum age of marriage for girls was set at 12 years, as was the age of sexual consent, on the assumption that from that point onward they were sufficiently mature to be sexually active.[45] To this day, similar laws and practices persist in certain parts of the world, evoking anxious censure from the international legal and human rights community.

Child law has been the subject of extensive and ever-growing scholarship. However, this literature, like the legal practice it addresses, has tended to regard both childhood and law as self-evident facts, whose nature and social construction warrant no discussion. Preoccupied with how "law" treats or should treat "children," this academic discourse largely disregards the historical and cultural specificity of childhood, the critical insights of childhood studies, and the broader lessons that can be drawn from legal scholarship's questioning of other social categories (such as gender, race, sexuality, and disability).[46] Studies of the legal construction of childhood are scarce and mostly short. The handful of books on the subject are valuable but, in various respects, limited.[47]

Departing from most of the existing child-centered legal scholarship, the present book calls into question conventional wisdom about both

---

[43] See, e.g., in relation to the United States, H. P. Chudacoff, *How Old Are You: Age Consciousness in American Culture* (Princeton and Oxford: Princeton University Press, 1989), pp. 10, 16–17, 19.

[44] M. May, "Innocence and Experience: The Evolution of the Concept of Juvenile Delinquency in the Mid-Nineteenth Century" (1973) 17:1 *Victorian Studies* 9–11.

[45] Kehily and Montgomery, "Innocence and Experience," pp. 71, 74–75.

[46] On these characteristics of child-focused legal literature, see A. R. Appell, "The Pre-Political Child of Child-Centered Jurisprudence" (2009) 46:3 *Houston Law Review* 703, 724–27; A. R. Appell, "Accommodating Childhood" (2013) 19:3 *Cardozo Journal of Law & Gender* 715, 715. On how the idea that children are incompetent overlooks contradictory empirical evidence, see M. C. Arce, "Towards an Emancipatory Discourse of Children's Rights" (2012) 20:3 *International Journal of Children's Rights* 365, 392–93.

[47] A case in point is M. King and C. Piper, *How the Law Thinks About Children*, 2nd ed. (Aldershot: Ashgate, 1995), which insightfully analyzes the child as a legally constructed semantic artifact. The authors' theoretical framework – social systems theory – has major shortcomings, as discussed, for example, in H. Rottleuthner, "A Purified Sociology of Law: Niklas Luhmann on the Autonomy of the Legal System" (1989) 23:5 *Law & Society Review* 779.

childhood and law. Further, my analysis rethinks child law in two additional respects. First, I systematically demonstrate how child law is no less concerned with older people and adulthood than with young people and childhood. Among the "adults" with which this area of law is preoccupied are not only those directly responsible for young people – parents, teachers, social workers, and so forth – but also countless others without such direct responsibility. I thus reveal the Israeli judiciary's attempt to use the punishment of Palestinians under the age of majority as a deterrent to older Palestinians (Chapters 3 and 6), as well as Israel's efforts to limit the influence of imprisoned Palestinians aged 18 and over by separating them from their younger counterparts (Chapter 4). This shows child law to be much wider in scope and effect than the existing child-centered legal literature would suggest.

Second, and more broadly, I seek to delineate how law's relationship with childhood extends beyond child law. The few books on law's conception or configuration of "childhood" deal exclusively with the law concerning under-18s and their carers.[48] Representative examples include two insightful books – Michael King and Christine Piper's *How the Law Thinks About Children* and David Archard's *Children: Rights and Childhood*[49] – as well as the collection *Legal Concepts of Childhood*, whose editor, Julia Fionda, states that "[a]n identification of legal concepts of *childhood* can offer many insights into our treatment of *children*."[50] In contrast to such reductive framing, the legal and social category "childhood" is not applied exclusively to those legally defined as "children."[51] Instead, childhood connotes behaviors and personality traits, elicits particular emotions and moral judgments, warrants certain

---

[48] A noteworthy exception, in this regard, is E. R. Meiners, *For the Children? Protecting Innocence in a Carceral State* (Minneapolis: University of Minnesota Press, 2016). Two other exceptions focus not on contemporary child law, but on the early modern period: H. Brewer, *By Birth or Consent: Children, Law, and the Anglo-American Revolution in Authority* (Chapel Hill: University of North Carolina Press, 2005); B. Premo, *Children of the Father King: Youth, Authority, and Legal Minority in Colonial Lima* (Chapel Hill: University of North Carolina Press, 2005).

[49] King and Piper, *How the Law Thinks About Children*; D. Archard, *Children: Rights and Childhood*, 3rd ed. (Abingdon and New York: Routledge, 2015).

[50] J. Fionda, "Legal Concepts of Childhood: An Introduction," in J. Fionda (ed.), *Legal Concepts of Childhood* (Oxford and Portland: Hart Publishing, 2001), p. 5 (emphases added).

[51] On the difference between "childhood" and "children," see, e.g., D. T. Cook, "Introduction: Interrogating Symbolic Childhood," in D. T. Cook (ed.), *Symbolic Childhood* (New York and Oxford: Peter Lang Publishing, 2002), pp. 1, 2–4, 7; C. Jenks, *Childhood*, 2nd ed. (New York: Routledge, 2005), p. 61.

modes of control, and, as I have described, draws spatiotemporal boundaries, thereby making itself readily applicable to people of all ages.[52] One manifestation of these issues I examine in this book is infantilization – the portrayal or treatment of adults, in the legal sense of the word, as children. Specifically, I lay bare the infantilization of two political players: soldiers and the Israeli legal system. The former, as I argue in Chapter 7, have been repeatedly characterized as children or childish, including in those rare cases where soldiers were convicted of abusing or killing young Palestinians. The latter, as I explain in Chapter 8, has been likened to a child for its purported rigidity toward settler youth.

1.2.3   Problematizing Law

The proposed problematization of law does not stop at its relationship with childhood. Israeli authorities and their human rights critics often diverge, even among themselves, in their interpretations of the law. The legal targets of their criticism also vary: Israeli authorities have repeatedly portrayed certain international legal bodies as rigged, politicized, or inept, whereas human rights organizations have leveled similar accusations at Israel's legal system. Such differences notwithstanding, a common conception of law prevails across legal and human rights discourses, and it is one that requires reconsideration. This is the notion that law, or at least specific legal norms and mechanisms, constitute a logical and scientific-like apparatus, that they are relatively autonomous and apolitical, significantly impartial and just (or at least a lesser evil), and embodied in specialized institutions, texts, and individuals.

Over the past two centuries, this view has been roundly criticized from various angles by, among others, legal realists,[53] socio-legal scholars,[54]

---

[52] See also E. Burman, *Fanon, Education, Action: Child as Method* (Boca Raton: Routledge, 2018), p. 2 (calling for analyses of "how rhetorics or mobilisations of appeals to notions of child (including abstract conceptions of 'childhood' as well as discussion of specific children) perform particular and significant ideological work").

[53] On (US) legal realism, see W. W. Fisher, M. J. Horwitz, and T. A. Reed (eds.), *American Legal Realism* (Oxford and New York: Oxford University Press, 1993); J. Zremby, *Legal Realism and American Law* (New York and London: Bloomsbury, 2013).

[54] On "law and society" studies, see D. Cowan, L. Mulcahy, and S. Wheeler (eds.), *Law and Society* (London: Routledge, 2013); A. Sarat and P. Ewick (eds.), *The Handbook of Law and Society* (Malden and Oxford: Wiley, 2015).

poststructuralists,[55] Marxists,[56] and other critical legal scholars.[57] A detailed overview of these criticisms is beyond the scope of this chapter. It is sufficient to note that the conception of law as an autonomous, coherent order – with defined and transparent concepts, rules, and precedents dictating particular outcomes through logical reasoning – stems from a highly contested formalist tradition.[58] In addition, the respect for the rule of law, and the belief in legal reform and rights as cornerstones of progressive social change, derive from a problematic mindset discussed in Chapter 2: legalism – the fetishization of legal arguments and institutions. Similarly, the tendency to equate law with legal institutions, texts, and professionals overlooks the crucial role of ostensibly nonlegal factors and players in animating and shaping law.

Building on and contributing to a rich body of critical scholarship, I set out to deconstruct and challenge these conceptions of law through, and in relation to, the materials and issues I will be examining. Among other things, this necessitates reflecting on the nature of language. After all, it is largely through words and terminological distinctions – such as "peacetime" versus "war," "children" versus "adults," and, perhaps first and foremost, "legal" versus "illegal" – that law operates.[59] However, such concepts, like countless others ("proportionality," "necessity," "torture" – the list could go on), are not self-evident givens. Rather, they are innately fluid and elusive, readily lending themselves to multiple interpretations,

---

[55] See, e.g., C. Douzinas, *Postmodern Jurisprudence: The Law of Text and the Texts of Law* (London and New York: Routledge, 1991); D. Cornell, "Post-Structuralism, the Ethical Relation, and the Law" (1988) 9:6 *Cardozo Law Review* 1587–628; D. C. Hoy, "Interpreting the Law: Hermeneutical and Poststructuralist Perspectives" (1985) 58:1–2 *Southern California Law Review* 135–76.

[56] See, e.g., C. Mieville, *Between Equal Rights: A Marxist Theory of International Law* (Leiden: Brill, 2005); S. Marks (ed.), *International Law on the Left: Re-examining Marxist Legacies* (Cambridge and New York: Cambridge University Press, 2008).

[57] On critical legal theory, see E. Christodoulidis, R. Dukes, and M. Goldoni (eds.), *Research Handbook on Critical Legal Theory* (Cheltenham and Northampton: Edward Elgar, 2019); C. Douzinas and C. Perrin (eds.), *Critical Legal Theory* (London: Routledge, 2011); I. Ward, *Introduction to Critical Legal Theory*, 2nd ed. (Abingdon and New York: Routledge Cavendish, 2004).

[58] For an overview of legal formalism, see, e.g., S. Veitch, E. Christodoulidis, and M. Goldoni, "Formalism and Rule-Scepticism," in their *Jurisprudence: Themes and Concepts*, 3rd ed. (Abingdon and New York: Routledge, 2018), pp. 167–81.

[59] On law as revolving around the production of distinctions, see, e.g., N. Luhmann, "Operational Closure and Structural Coupling: The Differentiation of the Legal System" (1988) 15:5 *Journal of Law and Society* 153.

including those operating in the service of state violence.[60] Even ostensibly watertight terms can be malleable, as I demonstrate in Chapter 3 regarding the statutory category "minor." Whereas human rights organizations tend to depict Israel as either obeying or violating any given law, it seems that law's inherent flexibility makes it amenable to a variety of competing interpretations.

Further, if legality is an ever-changing product of discourse, imagination, and practice – as prominent jurists have long observed[61] – then law extends far beyond the institutions, professionals, and texts with which it is typically associated: the judiciary, the legislature, jurists, statutes, and the like. With potent yet porous and elastic boundaries, law is neither truly separate nor distinguishable from other imagined fields of knowledge and power, such as the media, culture, and politics.[62] Accordingly, among those actively participating in its construction are lay people,[63] including, in the present context, Palestinians and settlers of all ages, as well as Israeli soldiers.

Law's violence is also overlooked by dominant discourses. Violence is, by no means coincidentally, part and parcel of law's operation, of every legal interpretation and decision.[64] Law realizes itself through physical and symbolic violence, it occasions violence, and it justifies certain forms of violence while proscribing others. In defining what counts as violence in the first place, part of law's function is to deny and thus launder its

---

[60] On these aspects, see, e.g., C. Jochnick and R. Normand, "The Legitimation of Violence: A Critical History of the Laws of War" (1994) 35:1 *Harvard International Law Journal* 49; D. Kennedy, "Lawfare and Warfare," in J. Crawford and M. Koskenniemi (eds.), *The Cambridge Companion to International Law* (Cambridge: Cambridge University Press, 2012), p. 158; I. Hurd, *How to Do Things with International Law* (Princeton and Oxford: Princeton University Press, 2017).

[61] See, e.g., R. M. Cover, "The Supreme Court 1982 Term – Foreword: Nomos and Narrative" (1983) 97:1 *Harvard Law Review* 4; R. M. Cover, "Violence and the Word" (1986) 95:8 *Yale Law Journal* 1601. On law as subject to an endless "deference of meaning," see J. Derrida, "Before the Law," in J. Derrida and D. Attridge (eds.), *Acts of Literature* (London: Routledge, 1991).

[62] See, e.g., P. Schlag, "The Dedifferentiation Problem" (2009) 42 *Continental Philosophy Review* 35; N. Rose and M. Valverde, "Governed by Law?" (1998) 7:4 *Social & Legal Studies* 541, 545–46.

[63] P. Ewick and S. S. Silbey, *The Common Place of Law: Stories from Everyday Life* (Chicago: University of Chicago Press, 1998), pp. 43–46.

[64] W. Benjamin, "Critique of Violence," in P. Demetz (ed.), *Reflections: Essays, Aphorisms and Autobiographical Writings* (Berlin: Schocken, 1986), pp. 227, 284; Cover, "Violence and the Word." For further discussion, see, e.g., A. Sarat (ed.), *Law, Violence and the Possibility of Justice* (Princeton: Princeton University Press, 2001); A. Sarat and T. R. Kearns (eds.), *Law's Violence* (Ann Arbor: University of Michigan Press, 1993).

own violent nature,[65] in an attempt to monopolize the use of violence.[66] Violent as well as plastic, law thus provides a framework not only for restricting but also for enabling, legitimizing, and expanding state violence.

Complicity in state violence is not limited to states' own legal systems. As I argue in Chapters 2–4 and 7, international law is also implicated. Among other things, Israel's military legal system has long incorporated international law into its self-legitimating rhetoric,[67] as evidenced by its following claim: "While various complaints have been made about [Israel's] ... administration of law generally ..., and regarding [Palestinian] minors specifically, it is important to emphasize [Israel's] conformity with international law."[68]

International law's utility for Israeli authorities largely stems from the elasticity of what are commonly described as its two key elements. The first, international *treaty* law, involves endless struggles over the interpretation of treaties due to the inevitable indeterminacy of legal (and all) language. The second, *customary* international law, is commonly understood to derive from state practice; this potentially enables states to reshape customary international law by engaging, consistently and with enough companions, in what was once deemed a violation of the law.[69] A testament to the Israeli military's awareness of this idea of legalization through violation is a remark by one of its top lawyers: "If you do something for long enough, the world will accept it. The whole of

---

[65] E. Grosz, "The Time of Violence: Deconstruction and Value" (1998) 2:2–3 *Cultural Values* 190, 193–94.

[66] Cf. M. Stirner, *The Ego and Its Own* (D. Leopold ed., Cambridge and New York: Cambridge University Press, 1995), p. 176 ("The State ... calls its violence 'law'; that of the individual, 'crime'."); M. Weber, "Religious Rejections of the World and Their Directions," in H. H. Gerth and C. W. Mills (eds. and trans.), *From Max Weber: Essays in Sociology* (New York: Oxford University Press, 2009), pp. 323, 334 (discussing the state's desire to monopolize violence).

[67] H. Viterbo, "Lawfare" and "Violence," in O. Ben-Naftali, M. Sfard, and H. Viterbo, *The ABC of the OPT: A Legal Lexicon of the Israeli Control over the Occupied Palestinian Territory* (Cambridge and New York: Cambridge University Press, 2018), pp. 246–50, 257, 259–60, 436–39.

[68] Military Courts Unit, "The Legal Treatment of Malak Ali Yussef Khatib's Case," *IDF* (February 11, 2015), ¶ 23 [Hebrew], https://web.archive.org/web/20150921111312/http://www.law.idf.il/163-7111-he/Patzar.aspx.

[69] D. Kennedy, *Of War and Law* (Princeton: Princeton University Press, 2006); Kennedy, "Lawfare and Warfare"; E. Weizman, "Legislative Attack" (2010) 27:6 *Theory, Culture & Society* 11, 19.

international law is now based on the notion that an act that is forbidden today becomes permissible if executed by enough countries."[70]

1.2.4 Problematizing Human Rights

As a language and a praxis, human rights have significant parallels with law. They, too, have come to figure prominently in contemporary public rhetoric. Like law, they assume varied shapes, meanings, and effects within different settings, due in part to their intrinsic plasticity, ambiguities, and contradictions. For these and other reasons, human rights readily lend themselves, as does law, to divergent uses.[71] This includes providing states – Israel (as this book shows) and many others – with a useful vocabulary for justifying their controversial conduct while maintaining their self-image as law-abiding.[72]

Doubtless, human rights can help highlight and confront certain instances of inequality, exclusion, and oppression. However, in their current institutional and ideational configuration, they tend to focus on technical violations and remedial solutions, without systematically exposing – let alone challenging – the root political and economic causes of injustice.[73] In the process, intentionally or not, they can end up

[70] Quoted in Y. Feldman and U. Blau, "Consent and Advise," *Haaretz* (January 29, 2009), www.haaretz.com/consent-and-advise-1.269127.
[71] C. Bob, *Rights as Weapons: Instruments of Conflict, Tools of Power* (Princeton and Oxford: Princeton University Press, 2019); C. Douzinas, *Human Rights and Empire: The Political Philosophy of Cosmopolitanism* (London: Routledge, 2007), pp. 8–14; T. Evans, "International Human Rights Law as Power/Knowledge" (2005) 27:3 *Human Rights Quarterly* 1068; J. Curtis, *Human Rights as War by Other Means: Peace Politics in Northern Ireland* (Philadelphia: University of Pennsylvania Press, 2014); D. Kennedy, "The International Human Rights Movement: Part of the Problem?" (2002) 15 *Harvard Human Rights Journal* 101, 116–17 [hereinafter: "Part of the Problem?"]; N. Perugini and N. Gordon, *The Human Right to Dominate* (New York: Oxford University Press, 2015), pp. 16, 19.
[72] C. Douzinas, *The End of Human Rights: Critical Legal Thought at the Turn of the Century* (Oxford: Hart, 2000); Bob, *Rights as Weapons*; A. Bogain, "Security in the Name of Human Rights: The Discursive Legitimation Strategies of the War on Terror in France" (2017) 10:2 *Critical Studies on Terrorism* 1; Kennedy, "Part of the Problem?," p. 119; D. Kennedy, "The International Human Rights Regime: Still Part of the Problem?," in R. Dickinson et al. (eds.), *Examining Critical Perspectives on Human Rights* (Cambridge and New York: Cambridge University Press, 2012), pp. 19, 19, 30–31.
[73] K. Marx, "On the Jewish Question," in R. C. Tucker (ed.), *The Marx-Engels Reader*, 2nd ed. (New York: W. W. Norton, 1978), pp. 26–46; Douzinas, *Human Rights and Empire*, pp. 108–10; Evans, "International Human Rights Law as Power/Knowledge," p. 1067; Kennedy, "Part of the Problem?," p. 118; S. Marks, "Human Rights and Root Causes"

marginalizing more radical emancipatory discourses, whether by making such alternatives appear too "political," "ideological," and "subjective," or by engrossing public attention, resources, and imagination at their expense.[74]

In large part, this state of affairs stems from, and contributes to, the legalism of human rights. It is predominantly in legal terms that the dominant human rights discourse of today, and the associated human rights scholarship, frame harm and solutions.[75] For most liberal human rights organizations, the panacea seems to lie specifically in international law. For instance, a UNICEF report on young noncitizen Palestinians in Israeli custody, which garnered extensive media coverage both in Israel[76] and abroad,[77] "considered whether the [Israeli] military detention system is in conformity with the ... Convention on the Rights of the Child," and "whether the legal safeguards in place ... are in line with the norms, guarantees and safeguards found in international law." The report adds: "Ill-treatment of Palestinian children in the Israeli military detention system appears to be widespread, systematic and institutionalized ...., in violation of international law." Typically of the genre, the report "concludes by recommending ... measures to improve the protection of children within the system, in line with applicable international

(2011) 74:1 *Modern Law Review* 57, 70–72; R. West, "Tragic Rights: The Rights Critique in the Age of Obama" (2011) 53:2 *William and Mary Law Review* 713, 720–21.

[74] W. Brown, "'The Most We Can Hope For...': Human Rights and the Politics of Fatalism" (2004) 103:2 *South Atlantic Quarterly* 451–63; Kennedy, "Part of the Problem?," pp. 108, 115; Perugini and Gordon, *The Human Right to Dominate*, p. 17; R. Williams, *The Divided World: Human Rights and Its Violence* (Minneapolis and London: University of Minnesota Press, 2010), p. xvii. See also J. R. Slaughter, "Hijacking Human Rights: Neoliberalism, the New Historiography, and the End of the Third World" (2018) 40:4 *Human Rights Quarterly* 735.

[75] Evans, "International Human Rights Law as Power/Knowledge," pp. 1046–47, 1067; Kennedy, "Part of the Problem?," pp. 109–10, 116–17, 125; Perugini and Gordon, *The Human Right to Dominate*, p. 130.

[76] J. Khouri, "UNICEF: Israel Abuses Palestinian Children," *Haaretz* (March 7, 2013) [Hebrew], www.haaretz.co.il/news/politics/1.1953252; Ynet Staff, "UNICEF: Israel Humiliates Palestinian Child Detainees," *Ynet* (March 6, 2013) [Hebrew], www.ynet.co.il/articles/0,7340,L-4353138,00.html; A. Valdman, "UN Report: Israel Systematically Abuses Palestinian Children," *Channel 2 News* (March 6, 2013) [Hebrew], www.mako.co.il/news-military/israel/Article-22d64aafd4f3d31004.htm.

[77] BBC Staff, "Palestinian Children 'Mistreated' in Israeli Detention," *BBC News* (March 6, 2013), www.bbc.co.uk/news/world-middle-east-21683420; Reuters, "U.N. Finds Israeli Military Abuses Young Palestinians," *New York Times* (March 6, 2013), www.nytimes.com/2013/03/07/world/middleeast/un-finds-israeli-military-abuses-young-palestinians.html.

standards."[78] The legitimacy and morality of international law, its effi-
cacy, and its complicity in structures of domination – none of these are
called into question in such human rights texts.[79]

Further, human rights have all too often been applied without due
sensitivity to the social, political, and even legal specificity of the context
at hand. This, it appears, is no mere accident. The prevailing human
rights discourse promotes and rests on generalizations and abstractions:
it holds an overly abstract concept of the human being, articulates rights
in a one-size-fits-all manner, groups individuals into crude categories,
and reduces sociopolitical complexity to the fairly simplistic terms it
deploys.[80]

Children's rights – the joint offspring of human rights[81] and child
law – exhibit all of these traits. Riddled with ambiguities and contradictions, children's rights invite various, and potentially competing, interpretations and applications. Illustrating this equivocality of children's
rights is the question, dealt with in Chapter 4, of whether to separate
and rehabilitate young Palestinians in Israeli custody. On the one hand,
the separation and rehabilitation of young inmates are rights enshrined,
in various formulations, in the CRC and the International Covenant
on Civil and Political Rights,[82] as well as in several UN General
Assembly resolutions.[83] On the other hand, according to most of these
legal documents, these (and other) child rights should be implemented

---

[78] UNICEF, *Children in Israeli Military Detention: Observations and Recommendations*
(February 2013), pp. 1–2, 13–14, www.unicef.org/oPt/UNICEF_oPt_Children_in_
Israeli_Military_Detention_Observations_and_Recommendations_-_6_March_2013
.pdf.

[79] Evans, "International Human Rights Law as Power/Knowledge," pp. 1046–47; Perugini
and Gordon, *The Human Right to Dominate*, pp. 132–33.

[80] Kennedy, "Part of the Problem?," pp. 111–12.

[81] On the centrality of human rights organizations in the history of child rights, see P. S.
Fass, "A Historical Context for the United Nations Convention on the Rights of the
Child" (2011) 633 *Annals of the American Academy of Political and Social Science* 17.

[82] Article 37(c) of the CRC; Articles 10.2.(b), 10.3, 14(4) of the International Covenant on
Civil and Political Rights, opened for signature December 16, 1966, 999 UNTS 171
(entered into force March 23, 1976).

[83] Articles 13.4, 24.1, 26.3 of the GA Resolution 40/33: Standard Minimum Rules for the
Administration of Juvenile Justice (adopted: November 29, 1985,) UN Doc A/RES/40/33
[hereinafter: Beijing Rules]; Articles 27, 29, 32 of the UN Rules for the Protection of
Juveniles Deprived of their Liberty, GA Res 45/113, UN Doc A/RES/45/113 (December
14, 1990) [hereinafter: Havana Rules]. See also Articles 4, 11, 88, 91–94, 96, 98, 104,
112 of the UN Standard Minimum Rules for the Treatment of Prisoners (the Nelson
Mandela Rules), Annex, UN Doc A/RES/70/175 (December 17, 2015).

only when they serve children's "best interests" and enhance their "well-being."[84] What these open-ended phrases – "best interests" and "well-being" – actually entail, however, remains unresolved.

In its preoccupation with how best to implement and monitor international legal norms, the child rights discourse offers little to no critical consideration of their legitimacy and benefit. Time and again, this legalism – combined with the abstractions and claim to universality of the child rights discourse,[85] the cultural specificity of the childhood envisioned by children's rights,[86] and the broader conceptual limitations of rights – leads to decontextualization[87] in the form of giving precedence to international legal norms over the particular conditions in which those classified as children live, or even overlooking those conditions altogether. Thus, in Chapter 4 I argue that reforms made by the Israeli military regarding young Palestinians, which were advocated by most of the human rights community without due attention to the context at hand, are actually detrimental to Palestinians, young and old alike. In Chapter 5, I likewise show how the human rights framing of young Palestinians' plight disregards the realities and views of those in whose name it purports to speak.

1.3   Reframing Israel/Palestine

In public debates, including those on law and human rights, "Israel" tends to be treated as a separate entity to the "Palestinian territory" (or "territories"). Zionist discourses, in particular, reserve the term "Palestine" exclusively for pre-Israeli-statehood eras.[88] In line with a growing body of academic writing, however, I employ the concept

[84] Articles 3, 37(c) of the CRC; Articles 1.1, 5.1, 14.2, 17.1(d) of the Beijing Rules; Articles 2, 29, Annex – Articles 1, 28 of the Havana Rules.
[85] See, e.g., E. Burman, "Local, Global or Globalized? Child Development and International Child Rights Legislation" (1996) 3:1 *Childhood* 46–47.
[86] See, e.g., A. T. Imoh, "The Convention on the Rights of the Child"; T. Kaime, *The Convention on the Rights of the Child: A Cultural Legitimacy Critique* (Groningen: Europa Law, 2011).
[87] On the decontextualization and technicalization of child rights, see D. Reynaert, M. Bouverne-de-Bie, and S. Vandevelde, "A Review of Children's Rights Literature Since the Adoption of the United Nations Convention on the Rights of the Child" (2009) 16:4 *Childhood* 528.
[88] J. Alloul, "Signs of Visual Resistance in Palestine: Unsettling the Settler-Colonial Matrix" (2016) 25:1 *Middle East Critique* 23, 29–35; Julie Peteet, "Words as Interventions: Naming in the Palestine-Israel Conflict" (2003) 26:1 *Third World Quarterly* 153, 163.

"Israel/Palestine" to convey the intricate relation between these territories, whose overall population is divided almost evenly between Palestinians (mostly noncitizens) and Israelis. On the one hand, the slash in this phrase denotes the separation and exclusion, attempted or actual, of certain Palestinian territories and populations from Israel "proper" (the latter being delimited by its pre-1967 borders). On the other hand, by placing "Israel" and "Palestine" together, this phrase calls attention to the inextricable ties between the territories subject to Israeli control: Israel "proper," most of the West Bank, East Jerusalem, and the Gaza Strip.[89] The varying, albeit interrelated, modes and degrees of control that Israeli authorities exert over Palestinians in these territories are the subject of this section.

1.3.1   Israel "Proper" (Within Its Pre-1967 Borders)

A fifth of Israeli citizens (around 1.9 million) are Palestinian.[90] As in other contexts, the terminology surrounding them is paramount. In contemporary Zionist discourse, they are commonly called "Israeli Arabs."[91] This term might, however, deny their Palestinian identity,[92]

---

[89] Some scholars characterize Israel's control over these territories as amounting to apartheid, (settler) colonialism, or both. See, e.g., J. Dugard and J. Reynolds, "Apartheid, International Law, and the Occupied Palestinian Territory" (2013) 24:3 *European Journal of International Law* 867; L. Veracini, *Israel and Settler Society* (London and Ann Arbor: Pluto Press, 2006). Israel has also controlled the Golan Heights since 1967, in a manner condemned by the UN Security Council and General Assembly as "null and void and without legal effect." See SC Res 497, UN Doc S/RES/497 (December 17, 1981); GA, 64th Meeting, UN Doc GA/10794 (December 5, 2008).

[90] Israeli Central Bureau of Statistics, "Population of Israel on the Eve of 2019 – 9.0 Million" (December 31, 2018), www.cbs.gov.il/he/mediarelease/DocLib/2018/394/11_18_394e.pdf.

[91] Polls differ considerably regarding the proportion of those in this group who self-identify as "Arabs" or "Palestinian." See, e.g., D. Scheindlin, "+972 Poll: Joint Arab List Would Raise Voter Participation," *+972 Magazine* (December 24, 2014), https://972mag.com/972-poll-joint-arab-list-would-raise-voter-participation/100442/; A. S. Muhammad, M. Khatib and S. R. Marjieh, *Palestinians in Israel: The 5th Socio-Economic Survey – 2017 – Abstract* (Shefa-'Amr: The Galilee Society, April 2018), www.gal-soc.org/en/the-5th-socioeconomic-survey-on-palestinians-in-israel.

[92] D. Rabinowitz, "Oriental Nostalgia: The Transformation of the Palestinians into 'Israeli Arabs'" (1993) 4 *Theory & Critique* 141 [Hebrew]; H. Rashed et al., "Nakba Memoricide: Genocide Studies and the Zionist/Israeli Genocide of Palestine" (2014) 13:1 *Holy Land Studies* 1, 15–17.

in addition to overlooking the Arab origin of many Jewish citizens.[93] Another term in use, the "'48 Palestinians," distinguishes this group from the noncitizen "'67 Palestinians" of the West Bank and Gaza Strip.[94]

In the first two decades following its establishment in 1948, Israel placed most Palestinian citizens under military rule. Thousands were tried and convicted in military courts, primarily for failing to carry proper permits or exceeding travel restrictions. Military governors and their staff outlawed political organizations, censored the media, placed Palestinian political activists in "administrative detention" (incarceration without charge or trial) or under house arrest, and confiscated lands on a massive scale in an overt effort to "Judaize" the country. Undercover security agents were deployed, and some Palestinians were recruited as informants and collaborators through a combination of incentives and disincentives. The military regime came to an end a few months before Israel seized control in the West Bank and Gaza Strip. These practices have, however, remained in use toward noncitizen Palestinians,[95] as I show throughout the book. Moreover, from 1967 to 2000, a military court continued to operate within Israel's pre-1967 borders, in which dozens and sometimes hundreds of Palestinian citizens were tried annually.[96]

With limited exceptions, Jewish and Palestinian citizens live in separate communities and attend separate state-run schools with different curricula taught in different languages.[97] Most Palestinian citizens, unlike their (non-ultraorthodox) Jewish counterparts, are not conscripted into

---

[93] Y. Shenhav, *The Arab Jews: A Postcolonial Reading of Nationalism, Religion, and Ethnicity* (Stanford: Stanford University Press, 2006); E. Shohat, "Rupture and Return: Zionist Discourse and the Study of Arab Jews" (2003) 21:1 *Social Text* 49.

[94] See, e.g., G. Burton, "Building Ties Across the Green Line: The Palestinian 15 March Youth Movement in Israel and Occupied Palestinian Territory in 2011" (2017) 38:1 *Third World Quarterly* 169.

[95] H. Viterbo, "Outside/Inside," in Ben-Naftali, Sfard, and Viterbo, *The ABC of the OPT*, pp. 305–08.

[96] S. Ben-Natan, "Citizen-Enemies: Palestinian Citizens and Military Courts in Israel and the Occupied Territories, 1967–2000," in A. Jamal (ed.), *The Politics of Inclusion and Exclusion in Israeli-Palestinian Relations* (Tel Aviv: University of Tel Aviv Press, 2020), pp. 47–78 [Hebrew].

[97] I. Abu-Saad, "State-Controlled Education and Identity Formation Among the Palestinian Arab Minority in Israel" (2006) 49:8 *American Behavioral Scientist* 1085; Y. T. Jabareen, "Law and Education: Critical Perspectives on Arab Palestinian Education in Israel" (2006) 49:8 *American Behavioral Scientist* 1052.

the military.[98] Though they enjoy formal equality with Jewish citizens in many areas of life, Palestinian citizens are systematically discriminated against,[99] a reality acknowledged and harshly lambasted by a government-appointed Israeli commission in the early 2000s.[100] Moreover, in certain areas – such as land acquisition, education, and immigration – Israeli law either explicitly denies Palestinian citizens the rights afforded to their Jewish counterparts or lays the foundation for exclusionary state policies.[101]

The country's longest-serving prime minister, Benjamin Netanyahu, affirmed in 2019: "Israel is not a state of all its citizens. [It] is the nation-state of the Jewish people – and them alone."[102] Judging from polls conducted around that time, his view largely aligns with those of Jewish Israelis at large: about 80 percent object to their daughters being friends with "an Arab boy," 50 percent oppose having "an Arab resident in their building," and 48 percent deny the very existence of a Palestinian people.[103]

1.3.2   The West Bank, Excluding East Jerusalem

Prior to Israel's capture of the West Bank in 1967, the law in this territory was an amalgamation of remnants from the Ottoman, British Mandate, and Jordanian periods, as well as Islamic law. Some of this earlier

---

[98] Palestinian and ultraorthodox Jewish citizens are exempt from military conscription under Articles 26b–26x, 36, 40 of Defense Service Law (Integrated Version), 1986.

[99] See, e.g., N. Rouhana (ed.), *Israel and Its Palestinian Citizens: Ethnic Privileges in the Jewish State* (Cambridge and New York: Cambridge University Press, 2017).

[100] *Report of the Commission of Inquiry into the Clashes between Security Forces and Israeli Citizens in October 2000* (Jerusalem, 2003) [Hebrew], http://uri.mitkadem.co.il/vaadat-or.

[101] See, e.g., M. Masri, *The Dynamics of Exclusionary Constitutionalism: Israel as a Jewish and Democratic State* (Oxford and Portland: Hart, 2017).

[102] Haaretz staff, "'Israel Is the Nation-state of Jews Alone': Netanyahu Responds to TV Star Who Said Arabs Are Equal Citizens," *Haaretz* (March 10, 2019), www.haaretz.com/israel-news/.premium-israel-belongs-to-jews-alone-netanyahu-responds-to-tv-star-on-arab-equality-1.7003348.

[103] Guttman Center for Public Opinion and Policy Research, "Survey: Attitudes toward the Other," *The Israel Democracy Institute* (December 12, 2018) [Hebrew], www.idi.org.il/media/11758/%D7%A1%D7%A7%D7%A8-%D7%A2%D7%9E%D7%93%D7%95%D7%AA-%D7%9B%D7%9C%D7%A4%D7%99-%D7%94%D7%90%D7%97%D7%A8.pdf; D. Scheindlin, "Poll: Most Israelis Have Positive View of Jewish-Arab Relations," *+972 Magazine* (April 4, 2019), https://972mag.com/poll-israelis-positive-view-jewish-arab-relations/140846/.

legislation remains in effect to date, including emergency laws kept in force by Israel across both sides of its 1967 borders.[104] Israel has operated two separate legal systems, along ethnic lines, concurrently in this territory. On the one hand, the Palestinian population, numbering more than 2.7 million,[105] have been subject to Israeli military law and are usually tried in Israeli military courts. With international law and the Israeli supreme court attracting most of its attention,[106] legal scholarship on Israel's control over the West Bank and Gaza Strip has, for the most part, neglected this military legal system, an issue discussed in Chapter 2. Breaking new ground, this book is the result of an analysis of, among other materials, hundreds of military judgments, together with military statutes. Such an analysis of Israeli military legal documents is unprecedented, both in scope and in its theoretically informed approach.

On the other hand, Israeli settlers, numbering nearly 400,000,[107] have been extraterritorially placed under the non-military Israeli law[108] and are tried in civil courts, which I examine in Chapters 7 and 8. Notwithstanding some similarities between these two ethnically aligned legal systems, some of which are brought to light in Chapter 4, their overall disparity is considerable. The result, as I argue in Chapter 8, is a substantially broader array of rights and protections being given to Israeli settlers. Human rights organizations, the Israeli military, and others have reported not only this institutionalized discrimination[109] (which some

---

[104] See, e.g., Y. Mehozay, *The Rule of Law and State of Emergency: The Fluid Jurisprudence of the Israeli Regime* (Albany: State University of New York Press, 2016).

[105] Central Intelligence Agency (CIA), *The World Factbook – Middle East: The West Bank* (last accessed on July 25, 2018), www.cia.gov/library/publications/the-world-factbook/geos/we.html (data referring to July 11, 2018) [hereinafter: CIA Factbook].

[106] See, e.g., A. Gross, *The Writing on the Wall: Rethinking the International Law of Occupation* (Cambridge and New York: Cambridge University Press, 2017); S. M. Akram et al. (eds.,), *International Law and the Israeli–Palestinian Conflict: A Rights-Based Approach to Middle East Peace* (New York and Abingdon: Routledge, 2011); D. Kretzmer, *The Occupation of Justice: The Supreme Court of Israel and the Occupied Territories* (Albany: State University of New York Press, 2002).

[107] CIA Factbook (data referring to July 11, 2018).

[108] The term "non-military" is used in this book due to the inadequacy of alternative terms. "Civil law" might be confusing given the present focus on criminal law. "Domestic law" fails to capture the legal and political porosity of the boundaries between the supposedly domestic territory of Israel "proper" and the territories Israel conquered in 1967. On this porosity, see Viterbo, "Outside/Inside."

[109] See, e.g., ACRI, *One Rule, Two Legal Systems: Israel's Regime of Laws in the West Bank* (October 2014), https://law.acri.org.il/en/wp-content/uploads/2015/02/Two-Systems-of-Law-English-FINAL.pdf; M. Schaeffer Omer-Man, "IDF Admits Discriminating against Palestinian in Home Demolitions," *+972 Magazine* (April 6, 2016), http://972mag.com/

legal scholars describe as apartheid),[110] but also poor standards of law enforcement when settlers harm Palestinians.[111]

Alongside these Israeli legal systems, the Palestinian Authority, established in the mid-1990s, operates its own courts in regions under its jurisdiction. The Israeli military retains jurisdiction over Palestinians' offenses in these regions,[112] while allowing the Palestinian Authority courts to adjudicate cases involving internal Palestinian matters. In 2014, for instance, Israel transferred to Palestinian Authority custody 18 percent of arrested Palestinians below the age of 18.[113] At the same time, Israel denies Palestinian courts any jurisdiction over Israelis who commit offenses within Palestinian Authority territory.[114]

Israeli authorities' position on the applicability of international law to the West Bank has been controversial and, at times, confused. Initially, on the day it entered the West Bank and Gaza Strip, the Israeli military published an ordinance decreeing that its courts would abide by the Fourth Geneva Convention (widely regarded as the principal international treaty concerning belligerent occupation).[115] At the time, the

idf-admits-discriminating-against-palestinians-home-demolitions/118434; C. Levinson, "Precedent: Military Court Acquits Palestinians Discriminated Compared to Settlers," *Haaretz* (January 2, 2014) [Hebrew], www.haaretz.co.il/news/politics/.premium-1 .2206078.

[110] See, e.g., Dugard and Reynolds, "Apartheid, International Law, and the Occupied Palestinian Territory."

[111] See, e.g., Z. Stahl, *Mock Enforcement: The Failure to Enforce the Law on Israeli Civilians in the West Bank* (Tel Aviv: Yesh Din, May 2015), www.yesh-din.org/userfiles/Yesh% 20Din_Akifat%20Hok_%20English.pdf; V. Azarov, *Institutionalised Impunity: Israel's Failure to Combat Settler Violence in the Occupied Palestinian Territory* (Ramallah: Al-Haq, 2013), www.alhaq.org/publications/institutionalised-impunity.pdf; A. Strashnov, *Justice Under Fire* (Tel Aviv: Yedioth Ahronoth, 1994), pp. 40–41 [Hebrew].

[112] Articles 10(d)–10(e) of Order 1651; MilA 3924/06 *Sa'adi* v. *Military Prosecutor* (October 17, 2007); MilA 2016/07 *Issa* v. *Military Prosecutor* (May 16, 2007); MilA 1628/13 *John Doe* v. *Military Prosecution* (June 10, 2013). For discussion, see S. Weill, "The Judicial Arm of the Occupation: The Israeli Military Courts in the Occupied Territories" (2007) 89 *International Review of the Red Cross* 395, 407–09.

[113] A. Laor and R. Jaraisy, *Arrests, Interrogations and Indictments of Palestinian Minors in the Occupied Territories: Facts and Figures for 2014* (Tel Aviv: ACRI, February 2016), p. 11, www.acri.org.il/en/wp-content/uploads/2016/02/arrests-minors-OPT2014-ENG .pdf.

[114] I. Zertal and A. Eldar, *Lords of the Land: The War over Israel's Settlements in the Occupied Territories* (New York: Nation Books, 2005), pp. 372–73.

[115] Articles 5 and 35 of the Order Concerning Security Provisions (West Bank), 1967.

military referred to itself as an "occupying military" and to the newly captured territories, accordingly, as "occupied."[116] Shortly thereafter, however, this ordinance was rescinded. Nevertheless, military officials have continued invoking the Convention as a legal basis for the country's military court system. During the first two years following the rescinding of the ordinance, a similar inconsistency prevailed, whereby Israeli military courts continued holding the Geneva Convention applicable to the newly acquired territory. In Chapter 3, I bring to light these and other legal inconsistencies and uncertainties, as well as their effects on Palestinians.

Using legal interpretations roundly rejected by most of the international community – including many human rights organizations,[117] the International Court of Justice,[118] UN treaty monitoring bodies,[119] and most international law scholars[120] – Israeli governments have come to maintain that the West Bank is not occupied, a view shared by nearly two-thirds of Israeli Jews.[121] Instead, Israeli governments refer to this

---

[116] See, e.g., IDF General Staff, *Capturing Occupied Territories and Military Government* (June 1969) [Hebrew], www.akevot.org.il/article/aims-and-means-3-file-gl-17005-6-the-reordering-of-control-over-palestinian-citizens-of-israel-at-the-late-stages-of-the-mili tary-government/#popup/26e10ef6471eb29068949c449e6342cc.

[117] See, e.g., petition in HCJ 8092/20 *Bejawi* v. *Military Commander in the West Bank* (November 22, 2020) [Hebrew], ¶¶ 78–85, 97, 106, 108, www.hamoked.org.il/files/1664680.pdf.

[118] *Legal Consequences of the Construction of a Wall in the Occupied Palestinian Territory*, Advisory Opinion, 2004 ICJ 136 [hereinafter: ICJ Wall Opinion].

[119] See, e.g., UNCAT, Consideration of Report Submitted by States Parties Under Article 19 of the Convention – Israel: Concluding Observations, UN Doc CAT/C/ISR/CO/4 (May 14, 2009), ¶ 11, www2.ohchr.org/english/bodies/cat/docs/cobs/CAT.C.ISR.CO.4 .pdf; UNCRC, Consideration of Reports Submitted by States Parties Under Article 8 of the Optional Protocol to the Convention on the Rights of the Child on the Involvement of Children in Armed Conflict – Concluding Observations: Israel, UN Doc CRC/C/OPAC/ISR/CO/1 (January 29, 2010), ¶ 4, www2.ohchr.org/english/bodies/crc/docs/CRC-C-OPAC-ISR-CO-1.pdf.

[120] See, e.g., Kretzmer, *The Occupation of Justice*; O. Ben-Naftali and Y. Shany, "Living in Denial: The Application of Human Rights in the Occupied Territories" (2003) 37:1 *Israel Law Review* 17; A. Imseis, "On the Fourth Geneva Convention and the Occupied Palestinian Territory" (2003) 44:1 *Harvard International Law Journal* 65; A. Roberts, "Prolonged Military Occupation: The Israeli-Occupied Territories since 1968" (1990) 84:1 *American Journal of International Law* 44.

[121] E. Yaar and T. Hermann, *Peace Index: May 2017* (June 4, 2017), www.peaceindex.org/indexMonthEng.aspx?num=322.

territory as "administered"[122] and "disputed,"[123] terminology also used by the Israeli supreme court.[124] According to Israel's claim, this means that international treaties it has ratified do not apply to the West Bank, including not only the Fourth Geneva Convention but also the CRC, the Convention Against Torture, and the International Covenant on Civil and Political Rights, among others. While avowing to act in accordance with the "humanitarian provisions" of the Geneva Convention, Israeli governments have never specified these provisions. And the supreme court, despite referring to the Convention time and again in its rulings, has never determined its applicability.[125] Israeli military courts and courts-martial, for their part, have occasionally mentioned international humanitarian law or the CRC when adjudicating cases involving young Palestinians, but they have insisted that these legal frameworks have no binding force over Israel's actions in the West Bank.[126]

Israel's relation to the West Bank can be summed up as one of duality. On the one hand, it has effectively, if not entirely formally, annexed this territory.[127] In tandem with the mass settlement project and Israel's

---

[122] This formal Israeli position was developed in Y. Z. Blum, "The Missing Reversioner: Reflections on the Status of Judea and Samaria" (1968) 3:2 *Israel Law Review* 279; M. Shamgar, "The Observance of International Law in the Administered Territories" (1971) 17 *Israel Yearbook on Human Rights* 262.

[123] See, e.g., Israel Ministry of Foreign Affairs, "Israel, the Conflict and Peace: Answers to Frequently Asked Questions" (December 30, 2009), https://mfa.gov.il/MFA/ ForeignPolicy/Issues/Pages/FAQ_Peace_process_with_Palestinians_Dec_2009.aspx.

[124] See, e.g., HCJ 9518/16 *Harel* v. *Israeli Knesset* (September 5, 2017), ¶ b of deputy chief justice Rubinstein's leading opinion.

[125] See, e.g., HCJ 591/88 *Taha* v. *Minister of Defense* (1991) 45(2) PD 45, 53 [Hebrew]; HCJ 1661/05 *Coast of Gaza Regional Council* v. *Israeli Knesset* (2005) 59(2) PD 481, ¶ 4 of the majority opinion. Israel's position regarding the Hague Regulations (which, among other things, define the occupying power's responsibilities) has been different: the HCJ has affirmed their applicability and enforceability in the West Bank, and Israeli governments have not rejected this position. See Kretzmer, *The Occupation of Justice*.

[126] For such references to international humanitarian law, see, e.g., MilA 41867/01 *Military Prosecutor* v. *Abu Esh-Shabab* (April 7, 2003); MilA 1/07 *Meshbaum* v. *Military Prosecutor* (January 29, 2007); MilA 3335/07 *Dar-Halil* v. *Military Prosecutor* (May 29, 2008); CMC (South) 400/04 *Military Prosecutor* v. *Captain R.* (November 15, 2005). For references to the CRC, see, e.g., MilA 128/02 *Kudsi* v. *Military Prosecutor* (December 23, 2002); MilA 346/03 *Military Prosecutor* v. *Jawadra* (July 1, 2004); MilC (Judea) 4941/08 *Military Prosecutor* v. *Draj* (August 6, 2009).

[127] See, e.g., N. Kadman, *Acting the Landlord: Israel's Policy in Area C, the West Bank* (Jerusalem: B'Tselem, June 2013), www.btselem.org/download/201306_area_c_report_ eng.pdf; Z. Stahl, *From Occupation to Annexation: The Silent Adoption of the Levy Report on the Retroactive Authorization of Illegal Construction in the West Bank* (Tel Aviv: Yesh Din, February 2016), https://s3-eu-west-1.amazonaws.com/files.yesh-din.org/%D7%9E

application of its non-military law to settlers, there has also been an ongoing diffusion of practices from Israel "proper" to the West Bank and vice versa, as I demonstrate in Chapter 4. Accompanying this has been the Israeli government's symbolic annexation of the territory: though Israeli officials initially referred to it as "the West Bank," a conscious decision was quickly made to change its formal name to "Judea and Samaria,"[128] a biblical term now commonly used by Jewish Israelis.[129] The military legislation disambiguates: "The term 'Judea and Samaria Area' carries the same meaning . . . as the term 'West Bank Area'."[130] On the other hand, Israeli authorities generally view and treat Palestinian noncitizens as foreigners. The Israeli supreme court, for instance, has referred to prisoners from the West Bank, including residents of Area C (where Israel retains full authority over security and civil matters according to the Oslo peace accords of the 1990s), as "foreign prisoners" residing "outside the borders of the State of Israel."[131] Similarly, the supreme court, military courts, and some human rights NGOs have distinguished the military law applied by Israel to Palestinians in the West Bank from "Israeli law," as if the former is somehow external to the latter.[132]

1.3.3   East Jerusalem

After assuming control over the West Bank in 1967, Israel formally annexed East Jerusalem (the territory's largest urban center) and applied its non-military law there – an act considered unlawful by the

---

%D7%9B%D7%99%D7%91%D7%95%D7%A9+%D7%9C%D7%A1%D7%99%D7%A4%D7%95%D7%97/From+Occupation+to+Annexation+English+Yesh+Din.pdf.

[128] Recently declassified government documents on the subject from 1967 to 1968 are available at Akevot staff, "Linguistic Move," *Akevot* (n.d., last accessed on May 27, 2019), www.akevot.org.il/en/article/linguistic-move.

[129] Peteet, "Words as Interventions," pp. 158–59, 163; M. Billig and U. Lebel, "Introduction: Judea and Samaria Jewish Settlers and Settlements – Cultural Sociology of Unsettled Space" (2015) 21 *Israel Affairs* 309, 310.

[130] Article 1a of Order 1729 Concerning Interpretation (Integrated Version) (Judea and Samaria), 2013.

[131] HCJ 4644/15 *Ra'ee* v. *Prison Service* (June 15, 2016), ¶ 1 of justice Vogelman's leading opinion. For a publication of Israel's national prison authority using the same terminology, see D. Valk, "We and the World – Incarceration Figures in Israel and Other Countries" (2012) 33 *Seeing Shabas* 27 [Hebrew], http://shabas.millenium.org.il/Items/04434/33.pdf.

[132] Viterbo, "Outside/Inside," pp. 301–02.

overwhelming majority of the international community.[133] Consequently, if charged with an offense, Palestinians residing in East Jerusalem are usually tried under non-military Israeli law in civil courts – a major difference to the situation in the rest of the West Bank.

At the same time, Palestinian residents, numbering nearly 300,000,[134] are not citizens, unlike the 200,000 or so Israeli Jewish settlers in East Jerusalem. Approximately 15,000 Palestinians have also had their residency revoked by Israel, a practice some critics link to Israeli governments' stated aim of "maintaining a solid Jewish majority in the city."[135] Further, depending on where an offense is alleged to have been committed, Palestinians from East Jerusalem, unlike Israeli citizens, can also be tried in military courts.[136]

1.3.4   The Gaza Strip

Currently home to around 1.8 million Palestinians,[137] the Gaza Strip first came under Israeli military control not in 1967, but in 1956, following Israel's war with Egypt. Over the course of its subsequent one-year occupation of the territory, Israel instituted a military tribunal, detained political activists, and replaced the local police with Israeli police officers. Two agricultural army settlements were also established, and additional reforms were introduced with the aim of permanent Israeli presence. Eventually, intense international pressure forced Israel to withdraw from the occupied territory.[138] Nevertheless, this short-lived belligerent occupation laid the groundwork for the country's later control of the West Bank and Gaza Strip, as the military advocate general acknowledged in 1967.[139]

---

[133] See, e.g., SC Res 298, UN Doc S/RES/298 (September 25, 1971); SC Res 478, UN Doc S/RES/478 (August 20, 1980); ICJ Wall Opinion.

[134] CIA Factbook; United Nations Relief and Work Agency for Palestine Refugees in the Near East, "West Bank & Gaza Strip: Population Census of 2007" (January 2010), www.unrwa.org/userfiles/2010012035949.pdf.

[135] Human Rights Watch, "Israel: Jerusalem Palestinians Stripped of Status" (August 8, 2017), www.hrw.org/news/2017/08/08/israel-jerusalem-palestinians-stripped-status.

[136] See, e.g., Addameer, *In the Shadow of the 2014 Gaza War: Imprisonment of Jerusalem's Children* (2016), pp. 52, 65–66, www.addameer.org/sites/default/files/publications/imprisonment_of_jerusalems_children_2016.pdf.

[137] CIA Factbook.

[138] Viterbo, "Outside/Inside," pp. 308–09.

[139] Constitution, Law, and Justice Committee, 6th Knesset – Transcript 126 (July 5, 1967) [Hebrew], https://fs.knesset.gov.il//6/Committees/6_ptv_425043.PDF.

For nearly four decades since 1967, the legal status of Gazans resembled that of their West Bank brethren. In 2005, however, Israel unilaterally withdrew its armed forces from the Gaza Strip and evacuated all Israeli settlers, numbering about 8,000 and including around 3,400 under the age of 18.[140] The following year, the Hamas party won the local elections, remaining in power ever since. In 2007, Israel declared the Gaza Strip an "enemy entity," and it has subsequently carried out several large-scale military offensives, resulting in thousands of Palestinian fatalities, including hundreds of under-18s.[141] Gaza's local justice system currently comprises the following: sharia courts dealing with personal status matters; administrative, civil, and criminal courts adjudicating other civilian issues; and, for "security" matters, military courts.[142]

Israeli law and public discourse refer to the formal pullout as "the disengagement."[143] Its aim, according to the Israeli Ministry of Foreign Affairs, was to "dispel the claims regarding Israel's responsibility for the Palestinians in the Gaza Strip."[144] In actuality, Israel continues to actively, if remotely, regulate and take Gazans' lives in ways amounting to a more sophisticated mode of engagement.[145] Among the areas over which Israel retains control are: the entry and export of goods; the supply of electricity; the entry of fuel, building materials, and medical and communications equipment; travel and access by land, sea, and air, including travel to and from the West Bank; and the permissible fishing areas. Following decades of economic de-development under direct

---

[140] Knesset Research and Information Centre, *The Governmental Treatment of the Children of those Evacuated from Gush Katif – A Follow-up Report* (June 22, 2009), p. 3 [Hebrew], https://fs.knesset.gov.il/globaldocs/MMM/87546b58-e9f7-e411–80c8–00155d010977/2_87546b58-e9f7-e411–80c8–00155d010977_11_8594.pdf.

[141] Between January 19, 2009 and May 31, 2018, the Israeli security forces reportedly killed 3,283 Palestinians, of whom 2,865 were from the Gaza Strip. Of the fatalities, 764 were under the age of 18, including 643 from the Gaza Strip. In addition, 29 Palestinians were reportedly killed by Israeli civilians, and 7 others by an unknown Israeli party. During this period, 91 Israeli security force personnel and 84 Israeli civilians were reportedly killed by Palestinians. B'Tselem, "Fatalities Since Operation Cast Lead" (n.d., last accessed on September 17, 2018), www.btselem.org/statistics/fatalities/after-cast-lead/by-date-of-event.

[142] Human Rights Watch, *Abusive System: Failures of Criminal Justice in Gaza* (September 2012), pp. 8–23, www.hrw.org/sites/default/files/reports/iopt1012ForUpload_0.pdf.

[143] See, e.g., Disengagement Plan Implementation Law, 2005.

[144] Quoted in M. Luft, "Living in a Legal Vacuum: The Case of Israel's Legal Position and Policy towards Gaza Residents" (2018) 51:2 *Israel Law Review* 193.

[145] Cf. L. Bhungalia, "Im/Mobilities in a 'Hostile Territory': Managing the Red Line" (2012) 17:2 *Geopolitics* 256.

Israeli rule, Gaza's population is now forbidden to build a seaport or to rebuild their airport.[146]

Not only does the closure limit Gazans' life chances and inflict mass suffering, it also brings about actual loss of lives. Among the contributing causes of death are: Israel's rejection of applications for permits to receive lifesaving treatment in the West Bank; the prevention of medical teams from traveling between Gaza and the West Bank; the frequent electricity shortage and its ramifications for hospital equipment and refrigerated medicine; and the lack of adequate water and sanitation.[147] Israeli armed forces have also conducted multiple military incursions,[148] occasionally taking Gazans into detention in Israel. These detainees are either interrogated and then tried in civil courts (under civil security legislation),[149] or they are held in "administrative detention" without trial. Despite Israeli claims to the contrary, many have therefore concluded that Israel's control over the Gaza Strip has not fully terminated.[150]

Israel has thus come to deploy two modes of control in the Palestinian territories outside its pre-1967 borders, depending on the presence or

---

[146] See, e.g., M. Niezna, *Hand on the Switch: Who's Responsible for Gaza's Infrastructure Crisis?* (Tel Aviv: Gisha, January 2017), http://gisha.org/UserFiles/File/publications/infra structure/Hand_on_the_Switch-EN.pdf; Human Rights Watch, "Unwilling or Unable: Israeli Restrictions on Access to and from Gaza for Human Rights Workers" (April 2, 2017), www.hrw.org/report/2017/04/03/unwilling-or-unable/israeli-restrictions-access-and-gaza-human-rights-workers; M. Abo Arisheh, *#Denied: Harassment of Palestinian Patients Applying for Exit Permits* (Physicians for Human Rights – Israel, June 2015), http://cdn3.phr.org.il/wp-content/uploads/2015/06/Denied.pdf. On the de-development of Gaza under Israeli control, see S. Roy, "The Gaza Strip: A Case of Economic De-Development" (1987) 17:1 *Journal of Palestine Studies* 56.

[147] Viterbo, "Violence," pp. 440–43.

[148] The Israeli military made at least 262 known ground incursions and operations between 2015 and 2018, according to data obtained from the UN Office for Coordination of Humanitarian Affairs. See H. Chacar, "Israeli Incursions into Gaza Are the Rule, Not the Exception," *+972 Magazine* (November 13, 2018), https://972mag.com/israeli-incur sions-in-gaza-are-the-rule-not-exception/138600.

[149] See, e.g., G. Cohen and A. Hass, "Israel Holding Unknown Number of Palestinians Captured in Gaza Strip," *Haaretz* (July 25, 2014), www.haaretz.com/news/diplomacy-defense/.premium-1.607185; Y. Yagna, "Palestinian from Gaza Detained by Israel for 'Security Crimes'," *Haaretz* (July 10, 2013), www.haaretz.com/news/diplomacy-defense/palestinian-from-gaza-detained-by-israel-for-security-crimes.premium-1.534999.

[150] See, e.g., S. Darcy and J. Reynolds, "An Enduring Occupation: The Status of the Gaza Strip from the Perspective of International Law" (2010) 15:2 *Journal of Conflict and Security Law* 211; I. Scobbie, "Gaza," in E. Wilmshurst (ed.), *International Law and the Classification of Conflicts* (Oxford: Oxford University Press, 2012), p. 280; N. Stephanopoulos, "Israel's Legal Obligations to Gaza after the Pullout" (2006) 31 *Yale Journal of International Law* 524.

absence of Israeli inhabitants. In areas predominantly populated by Palestinians – the Gaza Strip and Palestinian Authority territories in the West Bank – Israel has effectively "outsourced" responsibility over Palestinian lives to non-state Palestinian actors, while maintaining control over issues seen as affecting fundamental Israeli interests. Rather than being a permanent military presence on the ground, Israel conducts intermittent incursions and also, in the case of Gaza, exercises control through closure and airstrikes. In contrast, most of the West Bank, apart from Palestinian Authority regions, is populated by both Israeli settlers and Palestinians, and therefore has Israeli security forces, legal institutions, and administrative authorities operating regularly and extensively on the ground. Israel's rule over the West Bank combines the not entirely coherent mix detailed earlier: annexation, formally for East Jerusalem and effectively for other parts of the West Bank, in tandem with exclusion and separation.[151]

1.4   Methodology and Sources

This book is largely based on my analysis of hundreds of texts[152] collected between the years 2007 and 2020, whose authors are the Israeli legal system and its human rights critics, local and international. Hardly any of these documents have thus far been studied, and many of them are not in the public domain. Israel has a record of preventing access to such sources, especially, though not exclusively, to non-Israeli scholars.[153] My being identified as Israeli and Jewish, coupled with being a former soldier, may well have been instrumental to getting hold of these and other unpublished Israeli legal documents.

[151] For related analyses, see L. Allen, "The Scales of Occupation: 'Operation Cast Lead' and the Targeting of the Gaza Strip" (2012) 32:3 *Critique of Anthropology* 261; A. Cohen, "Israel's Control of the Territories – An Emerging Legal Paradigm" (2016) 21:3 *Palestine-Israel Journal* 102.

[152] By "text" I am mostly referring to written documents but also, for Chapters 6–8, visual materials. On visuality as discourse, see, e.g., H. Piper and J. Frankham, "Seeing Voices and Hearing Pictures: Image as Discourse and the Framing of Image-Based Research" (2007) 28:3 *Discourse: Studies in the Cultural Politics of Education* 373.

[153] See, e.g., Gisha, "Military Changes Procedure in Order to Justify Its Refusal to Allow a British Student to Enter the Gaza Strip" (February 25, 2014), http://gisha.org/updates/2690; L. Hajjar, *Courting Conflict: The Israeli Military Court System in the West Bank and Gaza* (London: University of California Press, 2005), pp. 16–17; C. A. Jones, "Frames of Law: Targeting Advice and Operational Law in the Israeli Military" (2015) 33:4 *Environment and Planning D: Society and Space* 676, 678.

The documents under scrutiny can be divided into three main groups. The first consists of human rights publications, mostly obtained from relevant human rights organizations, their websites, and mailing lists. The second, analyzed in Chapters 6–8, contains materials concerning Israelis in conflict with Israeli law. The documents included in, and absent from, this latter group require some explanation. Only a few criminal court cases concerning settlers under the age of 18 are included, all of which, for various reasons, were heard in adult courts. The reason is that hearings involving Israeli defendants in that age group are normally held in youth courts, behind closed doors,[154] and the civil court administration refused my requests to access them, despite my offer to redact any identifying details and cover the redaction costs. As in other countries,[155] the (non-military) youth justice system thus remains out of public sight and scrutiny.[156] The Police Prosecution, which handles some charges against under-18s, also refused my freedom of information requests, claiming that tracing the information would be too time-consuming. This book also analyzes transcripts of Israeli parliamentary debates relating to young settlers, obtained from the website of the Israeli parliament, the Knesset. To some extent, these transcripts may help compensate for the inaccessibility of youth court judgments. Also examined are Israeli judgments involving soldiers who were, uncharacteristically, charged with abusing young Palestinians. Of these cases, those involving border police soldiers (who are under civil jurisdiction) were heard in either civil courts or police disciplinary tribunals, whereas those involving other soldiers were heard in courts-martial.

The third and largest group of Israeli legal materials concerns Palestinians in conflict with Israeli law. Among them are some non-military legal documents: police and prison regulations and publications, statutes, and supreme court judgments, as well as lower civil court decisions regarding young residents of East Jerusalem (who are subject to Israel's non-military law). However, the vast majority of these

---

[154] Article 9 of the Youth Law.

[155] See, e.g., G. Geis, "Publicity and Juvenile Court Proceedings" (1957) 30:2 *Rocky Mountain Law Review* 101; J. L. Trasen, "Privacy v. Public Access to Juvenile Court Proceedings: Do Closed Hearings Protect the Child or the System" (1995) 15:2 *Boston College Third World Law Journal* 359.

[156] On some of the ramifications in the Israeli context, see T. Morag, "The Effect of the Commission for Examination of the Basic Principles Concerning the Child and the Law on the Israeli Case Law's Underlying Conceptions" (2010) 3 *Family in Law* 68, 74 [Hebrew].

documents comprises hundreds of military law documents: judgments and statutes.[157] Though Israeli military judgments are not formally secret,[158] one of the challenges for researchers is that most of them are not publicly accessible. In the first four decades of its rule over the West Bank and Gaza Strip, the military published, every two years or so, only a meager number of "select" judgments.[159] I have analyzed all the cases in these compilations that are identifiable as involving defendants below the age of 18. Moreover, until the second decade of the twenty-first century, not only military judgments but also the military statutes in force were difficult to obtain; thereafter, however, the military codified its numerous and ever-changing statutes, and has published updated compendiums from time to time.

Since 2008, the military has also been routinely sending new military court of appeals judgments to the Israeli online commercial legal database Nevo, in which I found relevant cases through several keyword searches over the past few years. However, earlier decisions by the military court of appeals usually remain unpublished. No less crucially, also unpublished are first-instance judgments, which (as detailed in Chapter 2) constitute the overwhelming majority of military court decisions. In 2010, following two years of attempts to get hold of unpublished military court decisions, I gained from the military court administration access to several dozen unpublished military cases from the years 1993–2009.[160] Under surveillance by specially assigned soldiers, I was allowed to read some of the requested cases at the Ofer military court, located near the city of Ramallah in the West Bank. Time and resource constraints required me to photocopy only the documents that seemed most relevant.

---

[157] In addition to military statutes and judgments, I attempted to obtain records of internal military deliberations over military legislation from the 1960s. To this end, I turned to the military archive (which is separate and much larger than the military court archive described shortly), but was told by the staff that there was no relevant information there. Regrettably, a meager 0.4 percent of files in the military archive are available to the public. Akevot, "State of Access to Israeli Government Archives – Data Sheet" (September 2017), pp. 1–2, https://akevot.org.il/wp-content/uploads/2017/09/Akevot-State-of-Access-to-Govt-Archives-2017-09-Eng.pdf.

[158] Military courts, unlike civil ones, are not required (though they are authorized) to hold hearings involving under-18s behind closed doors, as detailed in Chapter 2, Section 2.4 ("The Military Court System").

[159] Hajjar, *Courting Conflict*, p. 59.

[160] I had gleaned the details of these cases through two sources: other documents in legal databases, and acquaintances with ties to the military legal system.

I deliberately avoid treating the sources under examination as a gateway into either "reality" or the intentions of their authors. Indeed, that they cannot be taken at face value will become patently evident throughout this book. It will thus become clear that Israeli state documents, legal and other, are often inconsistent not only with compelling evidence (Chapters 6 and 7) but also with one another (Chapter 2). Similarly, I will show that human rights reports evince repeated misunderstanding, and hence misrepresentation, of Israeli military law (Chapter 3) as well as of young Palestinians' voices (Chapter 5). Further, while most military and youth court judgments are inaccessible, the many other Israeli state documents I have obtained conceal as much as they reveal. They lack clear, consistent information about Palestinians in Israeli custody (Chapter 2) and systematically cover up violence toward young Palestinians (Chapters 6 and 7). Military judgments, in particular, will be shown to reflect neither the actual court hearings (Chapter 2) nor the military statutes that formally bind them (Chapter 3). In this book, I take as my subjects of inquiry not only what is visible or said about the issues under examination, but also what is, or at least seems to be, out of sight, excluded, or silenced. Such omissions and invisibilities, I will demonstrate, are part and parcel of the relationship between law, human rights, and childhood in Israel/Palestine.

As for intentions, it may seem tempting to attribute them to documents, assertions, and actions, be they those of Israeli authorities or of human rights organizations. This, ostensibly, would advance the analysis further. However, doing so would be problematic in three key respects: analytically, epistemologically, and normatively. First, from an analytical standpoint, claims to unearth supposedly "invisible" or "underlying" motives tend to resort to questionable causal or structural explanations.[161] If such explanations are supported by nothing other than one's preconceived theories, a disservice is likely to be done to the complex issues in question. Second, epistemologically, to treat statements or deeds as indicative of intents is to make untenable assumptions about the transparency, knowability, and even existence of intentions. Regardless of whether a certain legal or human rights actor acts (or believes it acts) strategically, one's motivations and interests are never fully transparent

---

[161] M. Valverde, *Law's Dream of a Common Knowledge* (Princeton: Princeton University Press, 2003), pp. 12–14. See also M. Foucault, *Power/Knowledge: Selected Interviews and Other Writing, 1972–1977* (Colin Gordon et al. trans., New York: Pantheon Books, 1980), p. 97.

to oneself, nor, obviously, are the implications of one's words and actions. Finally, from a normative perspective, conceptualizing contentious practices in terms of intentions might inadvertently help those who, by describing them as unintentional, seek to legitimize them. A sounder course of analysis, in all three respects, is to focus on the content of the available sources, while constantly questioning and problematizing it, confronting it with and contextualizing it within its surrounding sociopolitical environment and developments.

For these reasons, rather than equating texts and practices with either reality or intentions, I concentrate on their available content, as well as on their effects, both symbolic and material. When carefully inspected, these sources are thus revealed to be of great value in two key respects. First, they advance understanding of the ethos of Israeli authorities and their human rights critics, shedding light on the stories – about themselves and about the world in which they operate – these actors tell themselves and others. Second, when examined within their sociopolitical context, these sources lay bare the ways in which the language, narratives, and framings of law and human rights govern knowledge, imagination, and conduct regarding childhood in Israel/Palestine, with real-life consequences for Palestinians and Israelis of all ages.

Complementing my discourse analysis is a quantitative analysis of military court files. In late 2010, I gained access to the so-called archive (a small and cluttered portable cabin) of the Salem military court, on the West Bank's northern border. The files there were from the years 2008–09, and 155 of them had been classified by the military as involving defendants under the age of 18. In Chapter 2, I provide the findings of a quantitative analysis of these 155 files, such as the conviction rate, sentencing averages, and the defendants' average age. At the same time, unlike the proclivity of some quantitative researchers to reduce representativeness to numbers and size,[162] my quantitative analysis of the 155 military court files does not profess to be any more representative of "reality" than the non-quantitative analysis of other materials (including hundreds of other military court decisions). Further, statistics and quantification are anything but politically neutral. Among other things,

---

[162] On the potential misuses and limitations of statistics, see, e.g., J. Best, *Damned Lies and Statistics: Untangling Numbers from the Media, Politicians and Activists* (Berkeley and London: University of California Press, 2001); D. Huff, *How to Lie with Statistics* (New York: W. W. Norton & Co., 1954).

they provide states with instruments of governance[163] and means of promoting particular forms of knowledge.[164] In Israel/Palestine, where statistics with political implications are hotly contentious,[165] the military has also repeatedly dismissed empirically based criticism by the human rights community as statistically unrepresentative, including a report based on more than 800 military court observations.[166]

Also informing this book are observations I made while attending hearings at the Ofer military court, as well as my other experiences at both Ofer and Salem military courts. For example, several scholars have observed Israel's attempts to legitimize its control over the Palestinian territory by presenting it as temporary.[167] In visits to the military courts, I was able to witness an emblem of this semblance of temporariness: the makeshift appearance of the military courts' architecture. Thus, the military makes use of portable cabins not only for its so-called archive (in which I analyzed files), but also for most of the courtrooms themselves. Despite criticism by senior state officials in and outside the military, the military announced in 2018 that constructing permanent court buildings is not a priority in the coming years.[168]

---

[163] See, e.g., Burchell, Gordon, and Miller, *The Foucault Effect*; C. Shore and S. Wright, "Governing by Numbers: Audit Culture, Rankings and the New World Order" (2015) 23:1 *Social Anthropology* 22.

[164] On tensions between political and military actors who seek to promote specific forms of knowledge – statistical versus qualitative – about war, see L. Khalili, "The Uses of Happiness in Counterinsurgencies" (2014) 32:1 *Social Text* 23.

[165] On political disputes over demographic statistics in Israel/Palestine, see, e.g., I. S. Lustick, "What Counts Is the Counting: Statistical Manipulation as a Solution to Israel's 'Demographic Problem'" (2009) 67:2 *Middle East Journal* 29.

[166] IDF Spokesperson, "Response to the Yesh Din Report Draft: Backyard Proceedings," *Yesh Din* (November 12, 2007), ¶¶ 14–18 [Hebrew], https://s3-eu-west-1.amazonaws .com/files.yesh-din.org/%D7%9E%D7%A9%D7%A4%D7%98%D7%99%D7%9D+%D7% 91%D7%97%D7%A6%D7%A8+%D7%94%D7%90%D7%97%D7%95%D7%A8%D7% 99%D7%AA/BackyardProceedings+IDF+Response+ENG.pdf. For similar dismissals, see IDF Spokesperson, "Response to B'Tselem Report," *B'Tselem* (June 22, 2015), pp. 1, 9 [Hebrew], www.btselem.org/download/20150622_presumed_guilty_idf_response_heb .pdf; P. Greenwood, "Israel Furious at UN Report Detailing Torture of Palestinian Children," *The Telegraph* (June 21, 2013), www.telegraph.co.uk/news/worldnews/mid dleeast/israel/10135157/Israel-furious-at-UN-report-detailing-torture-of-Palestinian-chil dren.html.

[167] See, e.g., O. Ben-Naftali, "Temporary/Indefinite," in Ben-Naftali, Sfard, and Viterbo, *The ABC of the OPT*, pp. 406–13; Zertal and Eldar, *Lords of the Land*, pp. 352–62.

[168] State Comptroller and Ombudsman of Israel, *Annual Report 69B* (2019), p. 2352 [Hebrew], www.mevaker.gov.il/sites/DigitalLibrary/Documents/69b/2019-69b-504-Aiosh-Mishpat.pdf.

Empirical research, qualitative and quantitative, is often equated with objectivism and structuralism.[169] This book, in contrast, makes no claim to "uncover" an objective "truth" through its analysis.[170] Instead, the aim is to offer a rich and hopefully reflexive interpretation of the materials at hand.

1.5   Outline of Chapters

Having presented the conceptual and methodological framework of this study, I introduce in Chapter 2 the book's two institutional protagonists: the Israeli legal system and its human rights critics. I outline their key characteristics, examine their shared legalism, describe the intricate dynamic within and between them, and identify issues and trends in their approaches to noncitizen Palestinians below the age of 18. The chapter expands on the mass prosecution and incarceration of Palestinians, the military court system, the mechanisms for judicial review of military actions, and Israel's repeated invocation of international law, with special attention to the effects and manifestations of each of them in relation to young Palestinians. At the forefront of my analysis are the importance, characteristics, blind spots, and silences of legal and human rights texts. Accordingly, my entry point into the subject matter are extensive quotes from two documents – an Israeli military court file and a human rights report – both of which concern Palestinians convicted of stone throwing. As this is the most common charge against noncitizen Palestinians under 18, it is also a common thread through the chapter.

With these theoretical and factual foundations in place, each of the following chapters delves deeper into specific areas and dimensions of the childhood–law–rights triad. Chapter 3 investigates the constitutive role of age in marking and shaping Palestinians' lives, with a focus on four

---

[169] D. M. Trubek and J. Esser, "'Critical Empiricism' in American Legal Studies: Paradox, Program, or Pandora's Box?" (1989) 14:1 *Law & Social Inquiry* 3, 12. On the different meanings attributed to empiricism in critical legal studies, see D. M. Trubek, "Where the Action Is: Critical Legal Studies and Empiricism" (1984) 36:1 *Stanford Law Review* 575, 579–88. On objectivism, see, e.g., R. J. Bernstein, *Beyond Objectivism and Relativism: Science, Hermeneutics, and Praxis* (Philadelphia: University of Pennsylvania Press, 1983). On structuralism, see, e.g., E. Kurzweil, *The Age of Structuralism: From Lévi-Strauss to Foucault* (New York: Columbia University Press, 1980).

[170] Cf. Valverde, *Law's Dream of a Common Knowledge*, pp. 12–14.

areas: military court trials, Israel's open-fire regulations (rules of engagement), food quotas for the Gaza Strip, and impediments to Palestinian movement. Starting with the first of these areas, military judges are required, under the Israeli law that formally binds them, to consider a Palestinian defendant's young age. By closely inspecting the actual implementation of this statutory requirement, I bring to light previously unknown findings that run contrary to assertions by both Israel and its human rights critics. Some judges, I demonstrate, have deliberately treated young age not as a mitigating factor but, rather, as grounds for harsher punishment, aiming to send a deterrent message to other Palestinian youth as well as to their adult environment. I argue that this judicial view reflects two Israeli traditions: the portrayal of Palestinians as weaponizing their young, and the desire to discipline older Palestinians through their younger counterparts. I show how others in the judiciary have sentenced Palestinians based on their bodily appearance, taking into account not their chronological but their apparent age. Further, the military judiciary has exhibited inconsistency on all these matters, as well as on the meaning of seemingly precise statutory age terms, such as "minor." These findings, I suggest, offer lessons regarding both Israel's apparatus of governing through uncertainty and the inherent fluidity of childhood and age. To further contextualize the statutory age categories that Israel applies to Palestinians, I trace their origin to colonial British law and compare them to laws enacted elsewhere in the British Empire.

From military sentencing, the chapter turns its gaze to three areas where age potentially determines if and how Palestinians get to live. First under examination are legal disputes over Israel's open-fire regulations. In principle forbidding shooting at under-14s, these regulations have been interpreted to authorize firing at younger Palestinians whom Israeli forces perceive to be dangerous or older. I then cast a critical light on the logic guiding the biological warfare on Gazans in the form of age-based food and calorie quotas, as well as on Israel's attempts to justify this warfare in humanitarian and legal terms. Next, I interrogate Israel's deployment of age as a risk management tool within the movement restrictions that curtail Palestinians' access to medical treatment, work, resources, their families, their communities, and their territories. Palestinians, for their part, do not let these measures go unchallenged. The chapter hence concludes by casting light on their resort to deception about their chronological age to circumvent Israel's movement restrictions.

Age, I have noted, operates in tandem with space to demarcate and construct childhood. Shedding light on their interaction, Chapter 4 turns to the age and spatial boundaries of Palestinian childhood, as perceived, negotiated, and transformed by discourses and practices of law and human rights. Whereas the previous chapter brought to the fore childhood's fluidity, my test case here is a series of reforms in the first two decades of the century, which represented, for both Israel and the human rights community, the opposite: fixing childhood's boundaries in line with international child rights law, non-military Israeli law, and Israel's national security interests. Key among these reforms were the separation of incarcerated Palestinians under 18 from their adult counterparts; the establishment of the world's only "military youth court"; raising the age of majority under military law; and assessment of the rehabilitation chances of Palestinian youth.

Contrary to claims by Israeli officials and their human rights critics, I reveal that some reforms have made little to no actual difference, while others have served to fragment, monitor, and suppress Palestinian interactions, bodies, and minds. Age-based segregation and "rehabilitation" behind bars, in particular, have been designed to prevent intergenerational knowledge transfer among Palestinians and to undo such knowledge as already exists. Neither exceptional nor unique, Israel's reforms and the rhetoric surrounding them exemplify five broader issues that I discuss in turn: the blind spots of human rights actors (NGOs and scholars alike); the long-standing complicity of child law and children's rights in the oppression of disempowered communities around the globe; the growing convergence between military and non-military Israeli law; the multiple forms of separation Israel imposes on Palestinians, which, like their age-based segregation in prison, operate to divide and conquer them; and Israel's attempts at confining Palestinian minds beyond the prison walls. In the process of examining Israel's modes of control, I also call attention to Palestinian acts of resistance: running study groups in prison, smuggling sperm of incarcerated men, and conducting readings and discussions in public protests.

Continuing the critical assessment of the child rights discourse, Chapter 5 tackles four interrelated interpretive frameworks recurring in human rights publications: a mental health discourse of childhood trauma and loss; a depiction of Palestinian childhood as lost or stolen; talk of a "right to childhood"; and a claim to represent young Palestinians' voices. I call into question their essentialist and developmentalist assumptions, reveal their pitfalls, and reflect on their omissions, all of which I link to wider issues at both the global and the local levels.

Specifically, I demonstrate how the mental health language of trauma and loss individualizes, and thus potentially decontextualizes, the issues it supposedly conveys; how it pathologizes young Palestinians; and how it casts them as a future threat to Israel's security. Next, I argue that the stolen-childhood narrative portrays Palestinians as both an exception to normal childhood and an epitome of a worldwide demise of childhood, without sensitivity to the actual sociopolitical circumstances. Further, I look at how human rights texts tie the loss of childhood to another loss – that of the Palestinian homeland – and how this linkage depicts Palestinians' collective past, present, and future. Turning to the notion that Palestinians have a "right to childhood," I explain how it perpetuates two harmful tendencies of the dominant children's rights discourse: the exclusion of those under the age of majority (or their inclusion only on older people's terms) and the legitimation of apathy and harshness toward those defined as adults. Finally, and contrary to what human rights organizations claim to be doing, I point to several ways in which they obscure rather than simply represent the voices of young Palestinians: prioritizing older people's voices; excluding youth from the writing and editing process; omitting crucial information relating to the quoted testimonies; ignoring witnesses' nonverbal expressions; and overlooking the inseparability of the human voice from the messy social fabric.

In a shift from the verbal to the visual, Chapter 6 takes as its subject the legal and political forces that determine the visibility, knowability, and experience of Israeli state violence against Palestinian under-18s. After outlining the impact of visual technologies and imagery, I zoom in on three ways in which Israel subjects Palestinians to its gaze or pressures them to internalize it: putting up posters with threats accompanied by photographs of Palestinian youth or their parents – a disciplinary visual tool presented by Israel as serving the best interests of young Palestinians; taking pictures of unsuspected Palestinian youth at home and on the street, who are presumed potential rather than actual wrongdoers; and soldiers filming their abuse of young Palestinians.

At the same time, where such visibility is deemed jeopardizing to the state and to its agents, concealment comes into play. I lay bare a number of mutually complementary Israeli practices serving this function in cases of violence against young Palestinians: the destruction of potentially incriminating evidence; the prevention of such violence from being

witnessed in real time; restrictions on publishing unflattering information about Israel's conduct toward Palestinians; the failure to record
interrogations, either in whole or in part; the resort to torture tactics that
leave no marks on the body; and legally sanctioned secrecy across a range
of areas. Also analyzed are the de facto impunity of alleged perpetrators;
their depiction by the Israeli judiciary as a few rotten apples unrepresentative of either Israel or its military; and other discursive techniques
employed by state authorities to deny, dismiss, and downplay
Palestinian complaints. Against this backdrop, the chapter concludes by
offering an alternative approach to evidence, visual and other. The Israeli
legal system and its human rights critics alike tend to privilege two forms
of evidence: video footage and state agents' testimonies. In so doing, they
ultimately validate both Israel's dismissal of uncorroborated Palestinian
allegations and its "rotten apples" narrative. I argue that alternative
images – specifically pictures of absence, reenactment photographs, and
sketches – bring to the fore the representation and mediation at work
and, for this reason, possess the unique evidentiary potential to highlight
the invisibility shrouding both state violence and young witnesses.

Whereas the spotlight up to this point has been on Palestinian childhood, the final two chapters bring into the picture Israeli childhood as
well. At the heart of Chapter 7 are two characteristics of the dominant
Israeli legal and human rights discourse. One is its infantilization of
soldiers (its portrayal of them as children), particularly in court cases
concerning either soldiers' violence against Palestinians or military
hazing. I pay special attention to the conjuring up, in judgments involving violence against Palestinians under the age of 18, of two potentially
conflicting childhoods: that of the violent soldier, who is not formally a
child yet tends to be perceived as such; and that of the young Palestinian,
who, by the applicable statutory definitions, is an actual "minor." In
addition, I call into question the Israeli legal system's insistence that
soldiers' acts of violence, whether against their comrades or
Palestinians, are no more than isolated transgressions. As I contend,
the military has a long record of internal violence, and the resemblance
between this violence and that of soldiers against Palestinians may well
be no mere coincidence. The other discursive feature I examine is the
militarization of young Israelis and Palestinians – that is, their characterization or treatment in military terms. Regarding young Israelis, specifically those evacuated from settlements in the Gaza Strip, I analyze their
depiction as soldiers in the making, as well as the judiciary's consideration of their future military service as a mitigating factor when they

come into conflict with the law. Regarding young Palestinians, I discuss their use (alleged or actual) as human shields, as well as Israeli contentions that they are trained for combat from an early age. I cast light on the double standards in such Israeli accusations and call into question the claim that, whereas Palestinians use their young as weapons, Israel wages war to protect its young.

The chapter inspects how, across these contexts, state and human rights actors invoke, shape, and challenge what I explain are two problematic versions of the child/soldier dichotomy: first, international law's categorization of people below certain ages as protected civilians (as opposed to non-protected combatants), and, second, the international legal ban on recruiting underage soldiers. I discuss the role militarism and childhood play in this respect, as well as the political consequences for both Palestinians and Israelis.

Finally, Chapter 8 delves deeper into the legal construction of young settlers' childhood, revisiting in the process key themes and insights from all the previous chapters. The greater rights and preferential treatment enjoyed by settlers under 18, compared with those of same-age Palestinians (be they citizens of Israel, residents, or nonresident-noncitizens), are explored in this chapter, at the levels of both statute and state practice. My two test cases are stone throwing by settler youth and the question of whether to detain settlers aged under 18 separately from their elders. The former, I reveal, has been subject to several trends: lax law enforcement on settler youth; lenient sentencing; soldiers' abuse of Palestinian victims of stone throwing; the Israeli judiciary's rejection of selective enforcement claims by Palestinian stone-throwers, contrasted with its acceptance of such claims by their settler counterparts; the courts' consideration of settlers' military service as a mitigating factor; and convictions only where Palestinian complaints are corroborated by Israeli witnesses. In the second test case, I look at the Israeli policy of jointly detaining settlers under and above the age of 18 who protested the Gaza pullout – a policy contrary to Israel's age-based separation of incarcerated Palestinians.

At the same time, the childhood–law–rights triad is not reducible to such disparities between Israelis and Palestinians, important though they are. Accordingly, the chapter expands its scope of inquiry to interrogate, first, what critics have described as Israel's childish response to the refusal of detained settler girls to disclose their ages. From this dynamic, I draw broader lessons about age, voice, and infantilization. Second, I shed light on the operation, effects, and interaction of two modes of representation that figured centrally in parliamentary debates on the impact of the Gaza pullout on young Jewish evacuees: a mental health language of trauma and loss, and visual imagery.

Running throughout these chapters are several meta-themes, key among which are: the malleability of childhood as a legal-political construct; the pitfalls of child law and children's rights, including their operation as means of domination; the human rights industry, its shortcomings, and its commonalities with the state; the preoccupation of seemingly child-focused law with those not formally classified as children; the modes of operation of the Israeli control regime, including its legalism; the practices shaping what can be known and seen about the issues under examination; the perceptions and roles of Israeli armed forces on the ground; the resistance and collective imaginary of Palestinians, as well as of Jewish settlers; the intersection of childhood with other identity categories; and the inextricable connections, parallels, and tensions between the global and the local, and between the past and present.

Casting the First Stone: The Israeli Legal System, Its Human Rights Critics, and Their Approaches to Young Palestinians

2.1 Another Day in Court

February 26, 2004 saw yet another young Palestinian from the West Bank convicted of stone throwing in an Israeli military court. Previously unavailable to the public,[1] the court transcript, quoted in full below, contains the case details, identifies the individuals present in the courtroom, provides the parties' concluding statements, and delivers the military judge's decision. My translation from Hebrew is designed to be as faithful as possible to the original language and form, though I have omitted the defendant's identifying details to protect his privacy (with each omission marked by three consecutive hyphens). My comments appear in square brackets (with my initials, "HV"), to distinguish them from the original text.

Date: 26 February, 2004   Case no.: 1019/04

4 Adar, 5764 [HV: The Jewish date]

Military Court
Judea
- Transcript -

Hearing on date: 26/02/04   The presiding Deputy President: Major Zvi Lekah

Prosecutor: Lieutenant Sergei Morin

Defense attorney: Adv. Ahlam Haddad – present

---

[1] Such first-instance military court decisions are not publicly available, nor are most appeals decisions from before 2008, as explained in Chapter 1, Section 1.4 ("Methodology and Sources").

Defendant: ---   ID: --- / IPS [HV: Acronym for the Israel Prison Service – Israel's national prison authority] **- present**
Transcriber: Private Marrie-Anne Gurevitz
Interpreter: Corporal Ibbad Nasralladin

- The Presiding Judge opens the proceeding and identifies the defendant -

The course of the proceeding

<u>Military prosecutor</u>**:** We have reached a plea agreement under which the defendant would plead to the charge as would be amended in the charge sheet.

<u>Defense attorney</u>: I confirm the prosecutor's statement. I have read the amended charge to my client, explained its content to him, he understands it and pleads to the offense attributed to him.

The Court clarifies to the defendant and the parties that it is not bound by their plea agreement. The prosecutor amends the charge sheet.

<u>Defendant</u>: I confirm my attorney's statement, and plead to the amended charge.

Verdict

On the basis of his admission of guilt, I convict the defendant of the offense attributed to him in the amended charge sheet.

Delivered and announced today, 26/02/2004, publicly and in the presence of the parties.

Zvi Lekah
Deputy President

<u>The parties</u>: No evidence regarding the sentence.

<u>The prosecutor concludes</u>: We have reached a plea agreement under which we ask that the following penalties be imposed on the defendant:

a. 3 months and a day imprisonment to be counted from the day of his arrest.

b. A suspended sentence at the discretion of the Court.

c. A 1,000 NIS [HV: Acronym for New Israeli Shekels – the Israeli currency] fine to be paid as a condition for the defendant's release from prison.

I ask that this agreement be accepted and that the defendant be treated leniently, given his tender age, his clean record, and his admission in court.

The defense attorney concludes: I ask that the plea agreement be accepted. I echo the prosecutor's statement. This is an eighth-grade student. I ask that he be allowed to return to school.

The defendant's concluding statement: I have nothing to say.

Sentence

The defendant has been convicted, based on his admission, of the offense of throwing objects at a vehicle, seeing that he hurled stones at military jeeps during the months of August–September 2003.

This is a minor under the age of 14 years, who was about 13 and a half when committing the offense attributed to him. Under these circumstances, the plea agreement presented by the parties is appropriate and fitting, and the defendant will hopefully learn the lesson, return to school and to routine life.

I therefore impose on the defendant the following penalties:

a. 3 months and a day imprisonment to be counted from the day of his arrest.

b. A suspended sentence of two and a half months, with the condition that within 3 years of the day of his release from prison he will not violate Article 53a of the 1970 Order Concerning Security Provisions. [HV: This, at the time, was the provision that prohibited stone throwing].

c. A 1,000 NIS fine or a month imprisonment instead. Payment of the fine is a condition for the defendant's release from prison.

A right to appeal within 30 days.

Delivered and announced today, 26/02/2004, publicly and in the presence of the parties.

Zvi Lekah

Deputy President

The amended charge sheet, mentioned in the judgment, reads as follows, with strikes (each accompanied by the prosecutor's signature) indicating withdrawn or revised charges:

Israel	Defense	forces

At the Military Court of
J u d e a
A single judge presiding

	Court case:	**1019**/04
	Prosecution case:	30/04
	C.R. [HV: Acronym for Charge Record] case:	27/04
		2713/04

The parties:

The Military Prosecutor   **The prosecutor**

- versus -

This charge sheet was received on 27.01.04 and registered [no date appears]

[HV: the prosecutor's signature appears here]

---.

ID ---, born on 10.03.90, resident of ...

Detained since 06.01.04   **The defendant**

Amended Charge Sheet 26.1.04

Amended 26.2.04
[HV: Prosecutor's signature]

The above defendant is hereby charged with committing the following offenses:

First charge:
[HV: Prosecutor's signature]

The essence of the offense: Throwing objects at a driving vehicle, constituting an offense under Article 53a(3) of the 1970 Order No. 378 Concerning Military Provisions (Judea and Samaria).

The details of the offense: The above defendant, in the region, during the year 2003 or thereabout, threw an object, including a stone, at a driving vehicle, with the purpose of hitting it or the driver, namely:

The defendant, in the aforesaid period, in … [HV: The omitted text is the name of the defendant's village] or nearby, on about thirty occasions, hurled stones at driving vehicles on Route 443 near his village, with the purpose of harming them or their passengers.

(C.R. – 2713/03)

First charge:

The essence of the offense: Throwing objects at a driving vehicle, constituting an offense under Article 53a(3) of the 1970 Order No. 378 Concerning Military Provisions (Judea and Samaria).

The details of the offense: The above defendant, in the region, during the months of August–September 2003 or thereabout, threw an object, including a stone, at a driving vehicle, with the purpose of hitting it or the driver, namely:

During the aforesaid period, in … [HV: The omitted text is the name of the defendant's village] or nearby, ~~on about ten occasions,~~ the defendant hurled ~~about six~~ stones ~~on each occasion~~ at military jeeps, with the purpose of harming them or their passengers. ~~On one of these occasions, the defendant succeeded in hitting one of the military jeeps.~~ [HV: Prosecutor's signature]

The Prosecution's witnesses:

1. Sergeant Major ---, P.N. [HV: Acronym for Personal Number] --- , Benjamin Station [HV: This is an Israeli police station] (who obtained the defendant's statement).

2. ---, ID --- (arrested, P.C. [HV: Acronym for Prosecution Case] ---)

3. ---, ID --- (arrested, P.C. ---)

4. ---, ID --- (arrested, P.C. ---)

Rani Amer,	**Lieutenant**
Military	**Prosecutor**

Date: 26.01.04

Mark: 30-04

Of the hundreds of materials I have analyzed, these military court case documents, like the human rights report quoted later in this chapter, have not been chosen for their uniqueness. Quite the opposite: in many respects, these documents resemble countless others (including more recent ones, which are the majority of the analyzed materials). It is precisely the absence of anything particularly atypical that makes these documents all the more valuable for understanding wider issues concerning the Israeli legal system, the human rights community, and their approaches to young noncitizen Palestinians.

In particular, these documents offer a window into six broad issues, each of which I will examine in turn: (a) stone throwing – the charge in this specific case and also, crucially, the most common charge against noncitizen Palestinians under the age of 18 years; (b) Israel's mass incarceration of Palestinians, with a focus on so-called security prisoners; (c) the Israeli military legal system – its structure, activity, impact, and main players; (d) the silences of military court case documents, including about the legal drama outside the courtroom; (e) Israel's legalism, of which incarceration and the military legal system are but part; and (f) the human rights community and its relationship with Israeli authorities.

By investigating each of these issues, I will lay the foundations and context, legally and politically, for the chapters that follow. In the process, I will highlight how the method in use – namely, harnessing texts as entry points into the subject matter – is itself part of the book's message about the centrality of language and texts in relation to law, rights, and childhood.

2.2 The Children of the Stones

Young Palestinians have played key roles, symbolically and practically, throughout the sociopolitical history of Israel/Palestine.[2] Their involvement at the forefront of Palestinian political activity dates back to at least the 1910s,[3] but it was during the Intifada (popular Palestinian uprising) of 1987–93 that their presence in the political arena garnered

---

[2] See, e.g., B. K. Barber, "Political Violence, Social Integration, and Youth Functioning: Palestinian Youth from the Intifada" (2001) 29:3 *Journal of Community Psychology* 259; J. Kuttab, "The Children's Revolt" (1988) 17:4 *Journal of Palestine Studies* 26; J. Høigilt, "The Palestinian Uprising That Was Not: The Youth and Political Activism in the Occupied Palestinian Territories" (2013) 35:4 *Arab Studies Quarterly* 343.

[3] D. Rosen, *Armies of the Young: Child Soldiers in War and Terrorism* (New Brunswick and London: Rutgers University Press, 2005), pp. 2, 91–93, 96–131; J. Collins, *Occupied by*

unprecedented public attention, locally and globally. Much of the attention focused on stone-throwing boys and girls, whose key role in the uprising made them its public face. These "children of the stones," as they were often called, were portrayed as impassioned heroes, modern Davids fighting an Israeli Goliath, or, alternatively, as lawbreakers, security threats, and terrorists.[4]

For Israeli authorities, these young Palestinians posed a serious challenge. In the words of the former military advocate general (Israel's chief military legal officer), stone throwing was

> the most dominant and impactful phenomenon in the Intifada. . . . It was impossible [for Israel] to remove and hide all the stones in Judea, Samaria, and Gaza, [and thus Palestinians] . . . could easily . . . throw them at a person or a driving vehicle . . . Is there anything easier to do? Is there anything harder to prevent? . . . A considerable proportion of the stone-throwers were youth and children.[5]

Stone throwing, however, did not begin in the Intifada, nor did it end there. My analysis of military court rulings reveals that as early as 1968 – a year after taking over the Palestinian territory – the military detained, tried, and convicted three Palestinian girls for pelting stones at a military vehicle during a demonstration in Gaza.[6] In the early 1980s, military judgments lamented what they described as a surge in stone throwing.[7] From the 1990s onward, judgments have repeatedly noted that it is under-18s who usually commit these acts.[8]

Memory: The Intifada Generation and the Palestinian State of Emergency (New York and London: New York University Press, 2004), pp. 17–20.

[4] M. Hasian, Jr. and L. A. Flores, "Children of the Stones: The Intifada and the Mythic Creation of the Palestinian State" (1997) 62:2 *Southern Communication Journal* 89, 94–99; Collins, *Occupied by Memory*, pp. 2, 13–14; Rosen, *Armies of the Young*, pp. 115–16; B. K. Barber et al., "Whither the 'Children of the Stones'? An Entire Life under Occupation" (2016) 45 *Journal of Palestine Studies* 77, 78–79 [hereinafter: "Whither the 'Children of the Stones'?"]; G. Usher, "Children of Palestine" (1991) 32 *Race & Class* 1, 2.

[5] A. Strashnov, *Justice Under Fire* (Tel Aviv: Yedioth Ahronoth, 1994), pp. 29–31 [Hebrew].

[6] MilA 21/69 *Military Prosecutor v. Kattiba* (1969) 1970(1) MPD 96, 96–98.

[7] MilA 1075/83 *Military Prosecutor v. Sabih* (1983) 1987(6a) MPD 442, 452; MilA 4069/83 *Military Prosecutor v. Sahluv* (1983) 1987(6a) MPD 495, 498.

[8] See, e.g., MilA 4581/90 *Military Prosecutor v. Awad* (1993) 1994 MPD 482, 505; MilA 275/95 *Military Prosecutor v. Kamil* (1995) 1996 MPD 38, 40; MilA 58/00, quoted (without further details) in MilA 225/01 *Military Prosecutor v. Samhan* (November 15, 2001); MilA 71/04 *Military Prosecutor v. Fakiyah* (2004) (March 31, 2004); MilA 2891/06 *Military Prosecutor v. Hashem* (August 13, 2006); MilA 1261/09 *Military Prosecution v. Elfaroukh* (February 23, 2009).

To this day, young stone-throwers, such as the defendant in the previously quoted military case, remain a central preoccupation of the Israeli legal system. Accordingly, they form a common thread throughout this chapter. In recent years, stone throwing has been the most common charge against noncitizen Palestinians under the age of 18. Of the military court cases I quantitatively analyzed, nearly two in three – 63 percent – had the young defendant charged with stone throwing. Usually (in 82 percent of these cases), this was the sole charge. Other common charges were: membership of, or activity in, proscribed associations (30 percent of cases); Molotov cocktail throwing (17 percent); and possession, trade, or use of firearms (25 percent).[9] Though understandable, the public focus on seemingly more dramatic cases – such as those involving young Palestinians who attempt suicide bombings or who are photographed clashing with the military – might distract from these far more common circumstances in which young Palestinians find themselves in Israeli custody.

Under Israeli military law, "throwing an object, including a stone" is an offense punishable by up to 10 years, or up to 20 years if perpetrated against a moving vehicle.[10] Usually, prison sentences of several months are imposed,[11] with the maximum sentences being reserved for fatal incidents.[12] Since 2016, the military law also requires minimum

---

[9] Similar figures appear in human rights publications, sometimes based on information reported by Israeli authorities. See, e.g., A. Laor and R. Jaraisy, *Arrests, Interrogations and Indictments of Palestinian Minors in the Occupied Territories: Facts and Figures for 2014* (Tel Aviv: ACRI, February 2016), p. 6, www.acri.org.il/en/wp-content/uploads/2016/02/arrests-minors-OPT2014-ENG.pdf [hereinafter: *Arrests, Interrogations and Indictments*]; N. Baumgarten-Sharon, *No Minor Matter: Violation of the Rights of Palestinian Minors Arrested by Israel on Suspicion of Stone-Throwing* (Jerusalem: B'Tselem, July 2011), pp. 3, 17, www.btselem.org/download/201107_no_minor_matter_eng.pdf; GA, Situation of Human Rights in the Palestinian Territories Occupied since 1967, UN Doc A/71/554 (October 19, 2016), p. 9, www.ohchr.org/Documents/Countries/PS/A_71_554_en.pdf.

[10] Article 212 of the Order Concerning Security Provisions (Integrated Version) (Judea and Samaria) (No. 1651), 2009 [hereinafter: Order 1651]. However, as explained in Chapter 3 (Section 3.2.3, "Age Categorization: Origins and Judicial Inconsistency"), defendants below the age of 14 at the time of their sentencing – as in the case that opens this chapter – cannot be sentenced to more than 6 months in prison.

[11] Data obtained from the Israeli military suggests that, of Palestinians convicted of stone throwing between 2005 and 2010, 13.5 percent of those aged 14–15 and 1.2 percent of those aged 16–17 were given sentences greater than a year (though these figures include suspended sentences). Baumgarten-Sharon, *No Minor Matter*, pp. 21–22.

[12] For an example of young Palestinians sentenced to 15 years in prison for throwing stones at a moving car and, consequently, killing an Israeli settler baby, see Channel 2 News Staff, "Youths Who Killed Adele Bitton Sentenced to 15 Years," *Channel 2 News* (January

sentences for Palestinians aged 18 and over convicted of stone throwing: two years or, where stones are hurled at a moving vehicle, four years.[13]

As explained in the previous chapter, the legal status of Palestinians in East Jerusalem differs from that of their brethren in the rest of the West Bank. For decades, the law Israel applied to Palestinians in East Jerusalem made no reference, unlike the military law, to stone throwing. It also set the minimum age for custodial sentences at 14 years, rather than the military law's minimum of 12 years. But in 2015, following riots and a surge in stone throwing in East Jerusalem, Israel made two amendments, along the line of the military law, to its non-military law. First, stone throwing was criminalized specifically, with a maximum penalty of 20 years' imprisonment. And, second, incarceration in secure juvenile facilities was permitted from the age of 12.[14] Although the amendments were formally applicable to all Israeli residents, prime minister Benjamin Netanyahu made it no secret that they were specifically aimed to act "aggressively against ... stone-throwers" and "return quiet and security to every part of Jerusalem."[15] Following his lead, an Israeli judge, in a ruling concerning a young Palestinian from East Jerusalem, described stone throwing as Jerusalem's "calamity."[16] Modeling such provisions after the military law is another item in the extensive evidence of Israel's de facto annexation of the West Bank, an issue discussed in the previous chapter. An additional element of Netanyahu's 2015 "war on stone-throwers" (to use his words) was granting Israel's armed forces greater

---

28, 2016) [Hebrew], www.mako.co.il/news-law/legal-q1_2016/Article-f6186796e2a82510 04.htm.

[13] Articles 1–3 of the Order Concerning Security Provisions (Judea and Samaria) (Amendment No. 51) (No. 1771), 2016 (amending Articles 168, 210a, 201b, 212 of Order 1651).

[14] See, respectively, Articles 1, 3 of Penal Code (Amendment No. 119), 2015; Article 1 of the Youth Law (Adjudication, Punishment, and Modes of Treatment) (Amendment 22 – Temporary Order), 2016.

[15] B. Ravid and J. Lis, "Netanyahu's Cabinet Backs Bill to Jail Stone-Throwers Up to 10–20 Years," *Haaretz* (November 2, 2014), www.haaretz.com/news/national/.premium-1 .624039; Jerusalem Post Staff, "In Move to Restore Order to Jerusalem: Up to 20 Years in Jail for Stone-Throwers," *Jerusalem Post* (November 2, 2014), www.jpost.com/Israel-News/In-move-to-restore-order-to-Jerusalem-Up-to-20-years-in-jail-for-stone-throwers-380528.

[16] CrimC (Jer. Dist.) 40049-05-15 *State of Israel v. John Doe* (November 3, 2015), ¶ 18 of judge Marzel's opinion.

latitude to fire live ammunition at stone-throwers, including those classified as children.[17]

2.3 Mass Incarceration and "Security Prisoners"

The defendant whose case appears at the beginning of this chapter is one of an estimated 880,000 noncitizen Palestinians, including more than 41,000 under the age of 18, taken into Israeli custody since 1967.[18] This equates to about one-fifth of the current noncitizen Palestinian population.[19] During the Intifada of 1987–93, the West Bank and Gaza Strip had the world's highest incarceration rate by far: about 1 percent of all Palestinians,[20] and – more astonishingly – over 2 percent of (or 1 in every 50) Palestinians under the age of 18.[21] This mass incarceration mirrors the transformation of the Palestinian territory into, in effect, a colossal prison, or rather a disjointed network of prisons,[22] owing to Israel's severe restriction of Palestinian movement within, between, from, and into the West Bank and Gaza Strip (an issue discussed in the previous chapter as well as in the next two).

It is estimated that, in the first decade and a half of the twenty-first century, Israeli authorities took between 8,500 and 12,000 young

[17] P. Beaumont, "Israel Relaxes Live-Fire Rules against Palestinian Stone-Throwers," *The Guardian* (September 25, 2015), www.theguardian.com/world/2015/sep/25/israel-live-ammunition-measures. On Israel's open-fire regulations, see Chapter 3, Section 3.4.1 ("Age in Israel's Open-Fire Regulations").

[18] Military Court Watch, *Monitoring the Treatment of Children Held in Israeli Military Detention – Annual Report 2018/19* (June 24, 2019), p. 3, www.militarycourtwatch.org/files/server/MCW%20ANNUAL%20REPORT%20(2019).pdf.

[19] See United Nations Relief and Work Agency for Palestine Refugees in the Near East (UNRWA), *West Bank & Gaza Strip: Population Census of 2007* (January 2010), www.unrwa.org/userfiles/2010012035949.pdf.

[20] Human Rights Watch, *Prison Conditions in Israel and the Occupied Territories* (April 1991), p. 1, www.hrw.org/sites/default/files/reports/Israel914.pdf.

[21] J. Graff, *Palestinian Children and Israeli State Violence* (Toronto: Near East Cultural and Educational Foundation of Canada, 1991), p. 110, cited in L. Hajjar, *Courting Conflict: The Israeli Military Court System in the West Bank and Gaza* (London: University of California Press, 2005), p. 286.

[22] A. Korn, "The Ghettoization of the Palestinians," in R. Lentin (ed.), *Thinking Palestine* (London and New York: Zed Books, 2008), pp. 116–30; A. Bornstein, "Military Occupation as Carceral Society: Prisons, Checkpoints, and Walls in the Israeli-Palestinian Struggle," in A. Waterston (ed.), *An Anthropology of War: Views from the Frontline* (New York: Berghahn Books, 2008), pp. 106–30.

noncitizen Palestinians into custody.[23] On average, upwards of 1,100 under-18s have been arrested annually (about a fifth of whom Israel transfers to the Palestinian Authority), and 520 have been tried in military courts, according to data obtained from Israeli authorities.[24] None of these figures, however, include East Jerusalem – the West Bank's largest urban area – where the number of arrests of young noncitizen Palestinians has recently ranged from 800 to 1,138 per year.[25] NGO estimates, taking into account the entire West Bank, suggest that some 1,332 young Palestinians were arrested in 2016 alone, including 757 from East Jerusalem.[26] Most young noncitizen Palestinians in Israeli custody are 16 or 17 years old.[27] Accordingly, while my quantitative analysis of 155 military court cases reveals that defendants ranged in age from 12.3 to 19.1 years (in files that specified their ages), the average age was 16.8 years at the time of arrest and around 17 years at the time of sentencing.

My repeated resort to estimates stems not only from conflicting figures reported by different sources, but also from the absence of clear,

---

[23] See, respectively, DCIP, Madaa Silwan Creative Center, YMCA East Jerusalem, and War Child Holland, *Israel's Compliance with the International Covenant on Civil and Political Rights—Shadow Report to the Fourth Periodic Report of Israel, 112th Session of the Human Rights Committee* (September 12, 2014), http://tbinternet.ohchr.org/Treaties/ CCPR/Shared%20Documents/ISR/INT_CCPR_CSS_ISR_18219_E.docx; Addameer, *The Right of Child Prisoners to Education* (October 2010), www.addameer.org/sites/default/ files/publications/addameer-report-the-right-of-child-prisoners-to-education-october-2010-en.pdf.

[24] Addameer, "Joint Annual Report: Around 6500 Arrests in 2018" (December 31, 2018), www.addameer.org/publications/joint-annual-report-around-6500-arrests-2018; N. Alyan and S. Slutzker Amran, "Arrest and Detention of Palestinian Minors in the Occupied Territories – 2015 Facts and Figures" 2, 5–6 (Tel Aviv: ACRI, March 2017), www.acri.org .il/en/wp-content/uploads/2017/03/Arrest-of-Palestinian-Minors-.pdf [hereinafter: "Facts and Figures"]; Laor and Jaraisy, *Arrests, Interrogations and Indictments*, p. 11.

[25] For the figure of 800 arrests, see N. Alyan and M. Russo, *Arrested Childhood: The Ramifications of Israel's New Strict Policy toward Minors Suspected of Involvement in Stone Throwing, Security Offenses, and Disturbances* (Tel Aviv: ACRI, February 2016), www.acri.org.il/en/wp-content/uploads/2016/02/Arrested-Childhood0216-en.pdf (referring to 2014 and based on information provided by the Israeli police). For the figure of 1,138 arrests, see Addameer, "Born a Target: The Arrest and Prosecution of Jerusalem's Palestinian Children" (April 22, 2018), www.addameer.org/publications/born-target-arrest-and-prosecution-jerusalems-palestinian-children-1 (referring to 2017).

[26] Addameer, "Joint Report Estimates that 6440 Palestinians Arrested in 2016" (January 2, 2017), www.addameer.org/news/joint-report-estimates-6440-palestinians-arrested-2016.

[27] B'Tselem, "Statistics on Palestinian Minors in the Custody of Israeli Security Forces" (n.d., last accessed on March 4, 2019), www.btselem.org/statistics/minors_in_custody [hereinafter: "Statistics on Minors in Custody"].

aggregate, and complete official data. Indeed, the UN Committee on the Rights of the Child, various NGOs, Israel's own state comptroller, and even top Israeli officials have all criticized Israeli authorities for not gathering or publishing clear and precise information about Palestinians – including under-18s – in Israeli custody.[28] The limited information made available by Israeli authorities is sometimes self-contradictory, with discrepancies, for example, between police reports on the number of arrests. Prison publications likewise provide conflicting accounts of the number of Palestinian "security prisoners" (a classification explained shortly), with the figure for the year 2006 ranging from 8,606 to 9,628, and the figure for 2007 from 8,933 to 9,528. Different methodologies cannot account for such inconsistencies, as some of these reports have identical figures for certain years but not for others.[29]

Further, publicly available information may vanish: over the years, I repeatedly encountered the disappearance from state websites of official publications and data that had previously been available online. This might not always have been the result of an intentional act. However, former officials have admitted to authorizing, witnessing, or participating in the concealment of politically sensitive state documents, including formerly public ones, in what they describe as a deliberate attempt to protect Israel's reputation, prevent Palestinian unrest, and discredit critical scholars.[30] Like the inaccessibility of court documents described in

---

[28] See, e.g., petition in HCJ 8092/20 *Bejawi v. Military Commander in the West Bank* (November 22, 2020) [Hebrew], www.hamoked.org.il/files/1664680.pdf; UNCRC, Consideration of Reports Submitted by States Parties Under Article 8 of the Optional Protocol to the CRC on the Involvement of Children in Armed Conflict – Concluding Observations: Israel, UN Doc CRC/C/OPAC/ISR/CO/1 (January 29, 2010), ¶ 16, www2 .ohchr.org/english/bodies/crc/docs/CRC-C-OPAC-ISR-CO-1.pdf; Baumgarten-Sharon, *No Minor Matter*, pp. 17, 19, 51–52, 55, 67; Military Court Watch, "Do Official Israeli Prison Service Figures Present the Full Picture?" (January 19, 2015), www .militarycourtwatch.org/page.php?id=K2oXKCH88oa472647A1GWNWZR63k; State Comptroller and Ombudsman of Israel, *Annual Report 65c* (2015) [Hebrew], p. 354, www.mevaker.gov.il/he/Reports/Report_290/d3f96279-8933-4fdb-b1ec-a03e9692d40a/ 65C-204-ver-3.pdf.

[29] On the police reports, see Y. Kubovich, "How Many Arrests Did the Police Conduct in 2013? Depends Which Report One Reads," *Haaretz* (June 11, 2015) [Hebrew], www .haaretz.co.il/news/law/.premium-1.2657662. For the prison authority's conflicting reports, see Office of the IPS Spokesperson, *Annual Report – 2008* (2009), p. 53 [Hebrew]; Office of the IPS Spokesperson, *Annual Report – 2013* (2014), p. 19 [Hebrew]; IPS, "Statistical Figures – Prisoners" (last accessed on November 27, 2016; no longer available online) [Hebrew].

[30] H. Shezaf, "Burying the Nakba: How Israel Systematically Hides Evidence of 1948 Expulsion of Arabs," *Haaretz* (July 4, 2019), www.haaretz.com/israel-news/.premium.MAGAZINE-

Chapter 1, such concealment of information, coupled with the lack of clear information, plays a crucial role in restricting what can be known, said, and done regarding Israel's handling of Palestinians (young and old). Thus, these knowledge-governing factors, as well as others examined in Chapters 3 and 6,[31] shape, and are themselves part of, the relationship between law, human rights, and childhood in Israel/Palestine.

The available information, though limited, brings into relief the uniqueness of the Israeli–Palestinian situation. For the sake of comparison and perspective, the number of young Palestinians in Israeli detention in a single year exceeds the total number of inmates held by the United States at the (in)famous Guantánamo prison since 2002.[32] The child detention per capita rate in the United Kingdom – another illustrative reference point – is about three times lower than the rate for young noncitizen Palestinians in Israeli custody.[33] Moreover, these figures do not take into account the thousands of young Palestinians in conflict with Palestinian authorities. In 2014, for example, 2,457 Palestinians aged under 18 reportedly came into conflict with the Palestinian Authority's

how-israel-systematically-hides-evidence-of-1948-expulsion-of-arabs-1.7435103;   Akevot, *Silencing: DSDE's Concealment of Documents in Archives* (July 2019), www.akevot.org.il/wp-content/uploads/2019/07/Silencing-Akevot-Institute-Report-July-2019.pdf.

[31] Chapter 3 (Section 3.2, "Age on Trial") reveals the previously unknown discrepancy between Israeli military legislation and judgments, while Chapter 6 (Section 6.3, "State-Induced Invisibility") examines Israel's concealment and denial of its violence against Palestinians.

[32] Since January 11, 2002, the US Department of Defense has held a total of 779 men at Guantánamo. See American Civil Liberties Union, "Guantánamo by the Numbers" (last updated in May 2018; last accessed on March 4, 2019), www.aclu.org/issues/national-security/detention/guantanamo-numbers?redirect=infographic/guantanamo-numbers.

[33] In 2011, there were 15,098,000 people aged 19 or under in the United Kingdom– nearly seven times the number of noncitizen Palestinians aged 18 or under. See, respectively, Office for National Statistics, *2011 Census* (n.d.), www.ons.gov.uk/census/2011census; Palestinian Central Bureau of Statistics, *The Status of the Rights of Palestinian Children 2014* (April 2015), p. 7, www.pcbs.gov.ps/Downloads/book2147.pdf. However, in April 2016, the number of under-18s detained in the United Kingdom (906) was only about twice the number of young noncitizen Palestinians in Israeli detention (445). See, respectively, HM Inspectorate of Prisons, *Children in Custody 2015–16: An Analysis of 12–18-Year-Olds' Perceptions of Their Experiences in Secure Training Centres and Young Offender Institutions* (2016), p. 14, www.justiceinspectorates.gov.uk/hmiprisons/wp-content/uploads/sites/4/2016/11/Children-in-Custody-2015-16_WEB.pdf; B'Tselem, "Statistics on Minors in Custody."

law in the West Bank, while in 2006, Palestinian courts in Gaza and the West Bank tried nearly 1,120 under-18s.[34]

Pursuant to Israeli law and regulations, all common charges against noncitizen Palestinians aged under 18 – chief among which is stone throwing – are considered "security offenses." The regulations of the Israel Prison Service (IPS), the Israeli prison authority, apply this term to several specific offenses, as well as, more vaguely, to any offense that is "by its nature or circumstances a security offense."[35] In recent years, between one-quarter and one-half of Israel's overall prison population,[36] and between one-third and one-half of inmates under the age of 18,[37] have been classified as security prisoners. This term is rejected by many of the imprisoned Palestinians, who self-identify as political prisoners and freedom fighters instead.[38] Those classified as security prisoners are held separately and denied many of the rights granted to other inmates, in matters including welfare, education, and family visits.[39]

The nationality and gender composition of the so-called security prisoner population is revealing. According to IPS figures, 96 percent are Palestinians, a mere 0.2 percent are Israeli Jews, and the rest are foreign Arab nationals. Most (89 percent) of the Palestinians classified by Israel as security prisoners are from the West Bank, including 4 percent from East Jerusalem. About 7 percent are Gazans (including some captured in military incursions since Israel's 2005 pullout), and nearly

---

[34] See, respectively, M. M. Qafisheh, "Palestine," in S. H. Decker and N. Marteache (eds.), *International Handbook of Juvenile Justice*, 2nd ed. (Switzerland: Springer, 2017), p. 497; V. Trojan, *Child Rights – Situation Analysis: Right to Protection in the Occupied Palestinian Territory – 2008* (Ramallah and Jerusalem: DCIP and Save the Children – Sweden, December 2008), pp. 45–46, https://reliefweb.int/sites/reliefweb.int/files/resources/B1A832D8C0A3681FC125755C00455B58-Full_Report.pdf.pdf.

[35] Article 3–4, Appendices A–B of IPS Commission Ordinance 04.05.00: The Definition of Security Prisoner, May 1, 2001.

[36] IPS, "Statistical Figures – Prisoners."

[37] Knesset Research and Information Center, *Children in Israel: Select Issues Concerning Rights, Needs, and Services* (May 28, 2015) [Hebrew], http://main.knesset.gov.il/Activity/Info/MMMSummaries19/Children.pdf.

[38] While valuable, the resistant term "political prisoners" might erroneously imply that crime and punishment are otherwise apolitical. See H. Viterbo, "Security Prisoners," in O. Ben-Naftali, M. Sfard, and H. Viterbo, *The ABC of the OPT: A Legal Lexicon of the Israeli Control over the Occupied Palestinian Territory* (Cambridge and New York: Cambridge University Press, 2018), p. 386.

[39] Articles 1b, 4a of IPS Commission Ordinance 03.02.00: Guidelines Regarding Security Prisoners, March 15, 2002, www.gov.il/BlobFolder/policy/030200/he/03.02.00%20-%20כללים%20ביחס%20לאסירים%20בטחוניים.pdf.

4 percent are Palestinian citizens of Israel.[40] More than 99 percent of Palestinian "security prisoners" aged 18 and over are men, and nearly 99 percent of those under 18 are boys.[41] Therefore, it is of little surprise that not a single one of the 155 military court cases I quantitatively analyzed involved a girl as defendant.[42] Thus, notwithstanding their active involvement in the national struggle,[43] most Palestinian girls and women encounter the Israeli legal system not as detainees or prisoners but as, among other things, daughters, sisters, wives, or mothers of prisoners. Nonetheless, the cumulative number of women and girls incarcerated during the decades of Israeli control adds up to several thousand by some estimates.[44]

Also amounting to substantial numbers are the 3 percent or so of incarcerated Palestinians held in "administrative detention"[45] – imprisonment without charge or trial. Their incarceration is based on classified materials undisclosed to them or their attorneys,[46] routinely consisting of allegations by anonymous Palestinian informants.[47] Subject to military judicial review every six months, such incarceration can be extended with no set limit and without independent judicial verification of the alleged evidence.[48]

---

[40] Adalah, "Statistics on Detainees and Prisoners in Israeli Prisons" (April 2013), www .adalah.org/Public/files/English/Newsletter/103-April2013/PalestianPoliticalPrisoners-Statistics-April-2013.pdf [hereinafter: "Statistics"].

[41] See, respectively, Addameer, "Statistics" (last accessed on September 12, 2016), www .addameer.org/statistics (referring to 2014–16); Military Court Watch, "Statistics – Palestinian 'Security' Prisoners in Israeli Detention" (last accessed on July 20, 2018), www.militarycourtwatch.org/page.php?id=J5V0bQevz8a19020AWwFbv7lxv2   (data obtained from the IPS, referring to 2008–17).

[42] A few other cases I was able to trace and analyze, however, did involve Palestinian girls.

[43] See, e.g., T. M. Ricks, "In Their Own Voices: Palestinian High School Girls and Their Memories of the Intifadas and Nonviolent Resistance to Israeli Occupation, 1987 to 2004" (2006) 18:3 *National Women's Studies Association Journal* 88, 90–93.

[44] Miftah, "Palestinian Prisoners – Fact Sheet" (June 2012), p. 2, www.miftah.org/Doc/ Factsheets/Miftah/English/Prisoners.pdf; Addameer, *Annual Violations Report: Violations of Palestinian Prisoners' Rights in Israeli Prisons – 2015* (2016), p. 84, www .addameer.org/sites/default/files/publications/website.pdf.

[45] Adalah, "Statistics."

[46] Articles 290–91 of Order 1651.

[47] H. Cohen and R. Dudai, "Human Rights Dilemmas in Using Informers to Combat Terrorism: The Israeli-Palestinian Case" (2005) 17 *Terrorism and Political Violence* 229–43, 233–36.

[48] H. Viterbo, "Future-Oriented Measures," in Ben-Naftali, Sfard, and Viterbo, *The ABC of the OPT*, p. 131.

2.4   The Military Court System

Military courts – where Israel tries the vast majority of detained non-citizen Palestinians[49] – are the judicial arm and keystone of Israel's rule in the West Bank. Thousands of Palestinians are brought to trial each year. In 2006 alone, there were, according to the military, about 42,000 first-instance court and 267 appeal proceedings,[50] while 2015 saw 28,343 first-instance court and 1,851 appeals decisions.[51] As a result, most Palestinians in the West Bank have had some experience with the military legal system, if not personally then through the detention of others – relatives, friends, or colleagues. Other countries have tried under-18s in military tribunals, usually only very occasionally,[52] yet nowhere outside Israel/Palestine is an entire population's youth automatically and routinely prosecuted in military courts.[53]

These courts are entrusted with implementing the military's thousands of constantly changing[54] enactments, key among which is the voluminous Order Concerning Security Provisions, cited in the documents that

---

[49] L. Yavne, *Backyard Proceedings: The Implementation of Due Process Rights in the Military Courts in the Occupied Territories* (Tel Aviv: Yesh Din, December 2007), p. 25, www .hamoked.org/files/2012/8521_eng.pdf.

[50] See, respectively, IDF Spokesperson, "Response to the Yesh Din report Draft: Backyard Proceedings," *Yesh Din* (November 12, 2007) [Hebrew], https://s3-eu-west-1.amazonaws .com/files.yesh-din.org/%D7%9E%D7%A9%D7%A4%D7%98%D7%99%D7%9D+%D7% 91%D7%97%D7%A6%D7%A8+%D7%94%D7%90%D7%97%D7%95%D7%A8%D7%99% D7%AA/BackyardProceedings+IDF+Response+ENG.pdf; MAG, *Annual Activity Report – 2010* (2011), p. 71 [Hebrew], www.idf.il/media/32542/%D7%94%D7%95%D7%A8%D7% 93%D7%AA-%D7%94%D7%93%D7%95%D7-%D7%9C%D7%A9%D7%A0%D7% AA-2010.pdf.

[51] IDF Spokesperson, *IDF Annual Report 2015* (2016), p. 65 [Hebrew], www.idf.il/media/ 5662/%D7%93%D7%95%D7-%D7%A9%D7%A0%D7%AA%D7%99-2015.pdf.

[52] See, e.g., D. J. R. Frakt, "Muhammed Jawad and the Military Commissions of Guantánamo" (2011) 60 *Duke Law Journal* 1368; Human Rights Watch, "Egypt: Children on Trial" (March 27, 2012), www.hrw.org/news/2012/03/27/egypt-children-trial; Human Rights Watch, "'It's Like We're Always in Prison': Abuses against Boys Accused of National Security Offenses in Somalia" (February 21, 2018), www.hrw.org/ report/2018/02/21/its-were-always-prison/abuses-against-boys-accused-national-secur ity-offenses; Thai Lawyers for Human Rights, "Demanding an Official Explanation Regarding Detention of a 14-Year-Old-Suspect and Military Detention must Be Stopped" (May 21, 2017), www.tlhr2014.com/?p=4302&lang=en.

[53] M. Bochenek, *Children Behind Bars: The Global Overuse of Detention of Children* (Human Rights Watch, 2016), p. 7, www.hrw.org/sites/default/files/childrenindetention .pdf.

[54] On the ever-changing nature of the military statutes, see S. Ben-Natan, *All Guilty! Observations in the Military Juvenile Court* (No Legal Frontiers, July 2011), p. 10, http://nolegalfrontiers.org/images/stories/report_2011/report_en.pdf.

open this chapter.[55] Over time, the military's enactments have extended its jurisdiction to nearly every facet of Palestinians' lives, including offenses considered unrelated to security.[56] The number of military courts has changed through the years, with two main ones currently in operation: the Ofer and Salem courts, the former located in the Ofer military base next to the Palestinian city of Ramallah (in the central West Bank) and the latter in the Salem military base (on the West Bank's northern border).[57] Israeli authorities, whose attempt to rhetorically annex the West Bank was described in the previous chapter, refer to these courts by the biblical names Judea and Samaria (Ofer and Salem, respectively), though these official names have not caught on.

Seven "players" can appear in military court case files such as those quoted at the start of this chapter: the judge, the prosecutor, the defense attorney, the defendant, the court interpreter, the interrogators, and other detained Palestinians. Military judges are military officers and, since the early 2000s, qualified lawyers.[58] Their number varies from one hearing to the next, depending on the type of proceeding and the severity of the charges.[59] The prosecutors are Israeli soldiers, whether officers or not, with a Bachelor's degree in law. The prosecution and the judiciary are closely tied: it is from the ranks of the military prosecutors that military judges normally come. For instance, the prosecutor signed on the charge sheet at the start of this chapter later became a military judge, hearing the sort of cases he had once prosecuted. The ties extend further, all the way up to the supreme court. For example, prior to their appointment as supreme court justices, Uri Shoham and Elyakim Rubinstein, both mentioned by name later in this book, held high-level positions in the military legal system, with Shoham even serving as the military advocate general and later as president of the military court of appeals.[60]

---

[55] Article 212 of Order 1651.

[56] On the distribution of offenses, as reported by the military, see IDF Spokesperson, *IDF Annual Report 2015*, p. 64 (referring to 2015); N. Baumgarten-Sharon and Y. Stein, *Presumed Guilty: Remand in Custody by Military Courts in the West Bank* (Jerusalem: B'Tselem, June 2015), p. 12, www.btselem.org/download/201506_presumed_guilty_eng .pdf (referring to the years 2008–13).

[57] A few courts also operate within Israel's pre-1967 borders, dealing primarily with remand proceedings of Palestinians interrogated by the Israeli General Security Service.

[58] M. Tamir and A. Dahan, "Side Judges: The Case of the Israeli Military Courts" (2012) 8 *Socio-Legal Review* 1.

[59] Articles 15–19 of Order 1651.

[60] Supreme Court of Israel, "Justice Elyakim Rubinstein: Curriculum Vitae," *Judicial Authority* (n.d.), http://elyon1.court.gov.il/eng/judges/doc/CvRubinstein.pdf; Supreme

Palestinian defendants are entitled by law to defense attorneys – Palestinian or Israeli. However, the limited access to most military judgments (as described in Chapter 1) has been criticized for compromising defense attorneys' ability to effectively fulfill their duty.[61] It has also – as I show in the next two chapters – kept human rights organizations unaware of crucial differences between the formal military law and actual military court practice.

Although Palestinians' mother tongue is Arabic, military court proceedings are usually conducted in Hebrew. There are soldiers who serve as court interpreters, but part of their function is to ensure the order and proper conduct of the proceedings. Most of the interpreters are Druze, a religious community that emerged from Islamism in the eleventh century. Native Arabic speakers, Israeli Druze learn Hebrew in school and, unlike most Israeli Arabs, are usually conscripted.[62] Those serving as interpreters in military courts reportedly receive no professional training in either translation or law prior to their enlistment, and their training during their service is often partial and unsystematic.[63]

Military courts are authorized – but, unlike youth courts for young Israelis, not required[64] – to hold hearings involving under-18s behind closed doors, for reasons that include the protection of the young defendant.[65] This discretionary procedure can, however, be used to prevent public and media scrutiny. Thus, in a high-profile case from 2018, a military judge closed the hearing and ejected the journalists, supposedly in order to protect the 17-year-old defendant's interests. This was done in

---

Court of Israel, "Justice Uri Shoham – Curriculum Vitae," *Judicial Authority* (n.d.) http://elyon1.court.gov.il/eng/judges/doc/CvShoham.pdf.

[61] C. Cook, A. Hanieh, and A. Kay (in association with DCIP), *Stolen Youth: The Politics of Israel's Detention of Palestinian Children* (London: Pluto Press, 2004), p. 25; Hajjar, *Courting Conflict*, p. 225; Yavne, *Backyard Proceedings*, p. 17.

[62] K. M. Firro, *The Druzes in the Jewish State: A Brief History* (Leiden: Brill, 1999); R. Kanaaneh, *Surrounded: Palestinian Soldiers in the Israeli Military* (Palo Alto: Stanford University Press, 2008); H. Frisch, "The Druze Minority in the Israeli Military: Traditionalizing an Ethnic Policing Role" (1993) 20:1 *Armed Forces & Society* 51.

[63] S. L. Lipkin, "Norms, Ethics and Roles Among Military Court Interpreters: The Unique Case of the Yehuda Court" (2008) 10:1 *Interpreting* 84; Yavne, *Backyard Proceedings*, pp. 146–47.

[64] As described in Chapter 1 (Section 1.4, "Methodology and Sources"), this disparity eventually enabled me to access military court decisions while being denied access to those of civil youth courts.

[65] Article 89(b) of Order 1651. The court is also authorized to prohibit publishing the names and identifying details of under-18s. Article 93 of Order 1651.

spite of an explicit request by her lawyer for the media to be present.[66] The military court of appeals upheld the decision, again citing what it described as the defendant's best interests, while disrespecting her express wishes.[67] A decade earlier, some Israeli human rights activists likewise reported how closed hearings were used to exclude them from observing military trials.[68]

A number of jurists have noted the scarcity of legal scholarship on Israel's military legal system.[69] Much of the existing literature on the subject consists of outdated publications by Israeli military lawyers (acting or retired), with little if any engagement with theory.[70] In contrast to the abundant academic attention to other areas of Israeli law, Israeli law schools rarely teach and research Israel's military law,[71] thereby producing one generation after another of scholars and practitioners unfamiliar with the law their country routinely applies to millions of Palestinians. Possible explanations for this state of affairs include the limited access to military judgments, restrictions placed on individuals wishing to observe military court hearings or to interview military officials,[72] and the prevalent perception in Israel (as described in Chapter 1) of the military law as external to Israeli law. It is perhaps for these reasons that some soldiers at the military courts voiced puzzlement at my academic interest in military rulings, while others mistook me for an NGO worker.

---

[66] O. Holmes, "Palestinian Teenager Ahed Tamimi's Trial Begins Behind Closed Doors," *The Guardian* (February 13, 2018), www.theguardian.com/world/2018/feb/13/palestin ian-teenager-ahed-tamimis-trial-begins-behind-closed-doors; L. Morris, "Israel's Decision to Put a Palestinian Teen on Trial Could Come Back to Bite It," *The Washington Post* (February 13, 2018), www.washingtonpost.com/world/israels-decision-to-put-a-palestinian-teen-on-trial-could-come-back-to-bite-it/2018/02/12/bf33b864-100f-11e8-a68c-e9374188170e_story.html.

[67] Y. Berger, "Military Court: Ahed Tamimi's Trial to Remain Confidential 'In Her Best Interest'," *Haaretz* (March 19, 2018) [Hebrew], www.haaretz.co.il/news/politics/1 .5914724.

[68] Machsom Watch, "Public Trial – Not Wanted" (n.d.), https://machsomwatch.org/en/ node/51718 (citing specific cases from 2008 and 2009).

[69] N. Benichou, "Criminal Law in the Regions of Judea, Samaria, and Gaza" (2004) 18 *Law & Military* 293, 294 [Hebrew] [hereinafter: "Criminal Law"]; Hajjar, *Courting Conflict*, pp. 8, 97 endnote 3; R. Harris, A. Kedar, P. Lahav, and A. Likhovsky, "Israeli Legal History: Past and Present," in Ron Harris et al. (eds.), *The History of Law in a Multicultural Society: Israel 1917–1967* (Dartmouth: Ashgate, 2002), pp. 1, 16; S. Weill, "The Judicial Arm of the Occupation: The Israeli Military Courts in the Occupied Territories" (2007) 89 *International Review of the Red Cross* 395, 396.

[70] On the latter issue, see Hajjar, *Courting Conflict*, p. 66 endnote 65.

[71] The few elective courses defined as dealing with "military law" tend to focus exclusively on the law applicable to Israeli soldiers in courts-martial.

[72] See Hajjar, *Courting Conflict*, pp. 16–17; Yavne, *Backyard Proceedings*, pp. 14, 83–88.

The only academic book on Israel's military court system heretofore – Lisa Hajjar's perceptive *Courting Conflict* – notes the inaccessibility of most military judgments (and, at the time, of military legislation too)[73] and instead relies primarily on interviews and observations completed in 2002. Similarly, one of the most expansive human rights reports on the military courts mentions the inaccessibility issue[74] and notes: "In the absence of research and regular, comprehensive review (by academics, civil society or others) . . . [the military courts operate] under a veil of darkness."[75] Public attention to the military courts has slightly increased in recent years, largely due to some high-profile cases, media reports, and, notably, the Israeli documentary *The Law in These Parts* (which contains interviews with former Israeli military judges), the winner of the 2012 Sundance Film Festival best documentary award.[76] Quoted in the Israeli state comptroller's 2019 annual report is a presentation by the military courts unit from 2011, which demonstrates the military's awareness of this trend: "the military courts' activity . . . has received growing exposure through . . . various international elements as well as the Israeli and foreign media."[77]

Scholarship on the Israeli law concerning young noncitizen Palestinians is equally scant, especially in comparison with studies of other aspects of their lives.[78] Like their elders, noncitizen Palestinians under the age of 18 have been affected by Israel's rule in virtually every area of life. However, more than in any other legal field, it is in criminal law that a separate set of laws has been created for them[79] – either within the Israeli military legal system or, for residents of Gaza (since the 2005 Israeli pullout) and East Jerusalem, the non-military legal system.

---

[73] Hajjar, *Courting Conflict*, p. 59.

[74] Yavne, *Backyard Proceedings*, pp. 14, 83–88.

[75] Ibid., p. 26.

[76] On this film, see L. Lambert, "Law as a Colonial Weapon: Review of 'The Law in These Parts' by Ra'anan Alexandrowicz," *Critical Legal Thinking* (November 2, 2013), http:// criticallegalthinking.com/2013/10/02/palestine-law-colonial-weapon/. For my critical analysis of the privileging of testimonies by Israeli officials and soldiers over those of Palestinians, see Chapter 6, Section 6.4.1 ("'Strong' Evidence and Its Pitfalls").

[77] State Comptroller and Ombudsman of Israel, *Annual Report 69B* (2019), p. 2351 [Hebrew], www.mevaker.gov.il/sites/DigitalLibrary/Documents/69b/2019-69b-504-Aiosh-Mishpat.pdf.

[78] Examples of the latter are A. Dwonch, *Palestinian Youth Activism in the Internet Age: Online and Offline Social Networks after the Arab Spring* (London and New York: I. B. Tauris, 2019) and S. Asthana and N. Havandjian, *Palestinian Youth Media and the Pedagogies of Estrangement* (London: Palgrave Macmillan, 2015).

[79] Family law proceedings, like most intra-Palestinian cases, are normally dealt with by Palestinian courts. See Chapter 1, Section 1.3 ("Reframing Israel/Palestine").

Partly for this reason, it is to this particular legal context that three of the following seven chapters pay most attention. Frequently absent from public and academic discussions is adequate attention to such everyday and routine forms of Israeli control, as opposed to high-profile incidents and large-scale outbursts of violence.[80]

2.5   The "Real" Trial

The importance of military court case documents, such as those quoted earlier, emanates as much from their silences, omissions, and exclusions as from what they say. One silence or exclusion concerns the words and actions of those present in the courtroom. Take, for example, the words attributed to the defendant by the quoted judgment: "I confirm the statement of my attorney, and plead to the amended charge." Rather than necessarily being his actual statement, this is a standard text appearing, in similar versions, in countless military court case documents. It is likewise possible that the laconic statements attributed to the prosecutor and the defense attorney do not accurately represent what they said in court. In fact, during my observations of military court proceedings, I witnessed how, despite their relevance, some of the things being said did not appear to be transcribed at all.[81]

Further, as illustrated by the quoted documents, military court case documents – particularly those of first-instance courts – tend to be restricted to the bare minimum: the charges, the sentences, the defendant's identity, and the like. Young Palestinians' ages, for instance, can potentially influence their sentencing and treatment (as analyzed in the next two chapters), yet in most cases the courts mention them only in passing, if at all. My quantitative analysis of military court cases concerning young defendants found verdicts to be less than a page long on average, and sentencing decisions to be slightly longer than a page.

Against this backdrop, I treat military court case documents not as a reflection of reality, but primarily as a window into the ethos and self-

---

[80] On this disregard of Israel's control over Palestinians generally, and young Palestinians specifically, see, respectively, H. Viterbo, "Violence," in Ben-Naftali, Sfard, and Viterbo, *The ABC of the OPT*, pp. 433–35, 440–44; J. Hart and C. Lo Forte, "Mandated to Fail? Humanitarian Agencies and the Protection of Palestinian Children" (2013) 37:4 *Disasters* 627, 631–32.

[81] For similar observations, see R. Smith, "'A Danger to the Region': Subaltern Geopolitics of Palestinians Detained in Israeli Prisons" (2013) 16:1 *Arab World Geographer* 75, 91 [hereinafter: "A Danger to the Region"].

image of the military courts. In so doing, I seek to enable their silences, omissions, and paraphrases to reveal – rather than merely conceal or skew – quite a lot about the workings of this legal system.

The brevity of military court documents goes hand in hand with hasty proceedings. Between 2006 and 2007, the Israeli NGO Yesh Din conducted observations of detention hearings in military courts. It reported the average length of these hearings to be as follows: 3 minutes and 4 seconds for remand for the purpose of interrogation prior to filing an indictment; 1 minute and 54 seconds for authorizing continued detention pending disposition; and 3 minutes and 20 seconds for detention hearings involving under-18s.[82]

The hastiness and brevity of the military court system can be attributed to several factors. The first is the rarity of full evidentiary trials: reportedly, witnesses give testimony, evidence is examined, and closing arguments are made in less than 1 percent of trials.[83] Illustrating this is the charge sheet quoted in this chapter: none of the four potential witnesses it mentions – the Israeli police interrogator and three detained Palestinians – were questioned in court. A second issue, also evident in the quoted judgment, is the prevalence of plea bargains. Defence for Children International – Palestine (DCIP), the biggest provider of legal counsel to young noncitizen Palestinians,[84] reports that almost all (99.3 percent) of the military court cases closed by its attorneys end in plea bargains.[85] In comparison, the plea bargain rate in criminal trials of Israelis is substantially lower: 68 percent.[86] A third potentially contributing factor, described in this and the previous chapter, is the relatively scant public and scholarly attention to the military courts. Finally, the

---

[82] Yavne, *Backyard Proceedings*, pp. 13, 160. See also Ben-Natan, *All Guilty*, pp. 27–28.

[83] Baumgarten-Sharon, *No Minor Matter*, pp. 52–53, 55; Yavne, *Backyard Proceedings*, p. 136.

[84] The NGO claims to represent 22–25 percent of young Palestinians in Israeli military courts and 60 percent of young Palestinians from East Jerusalem in the non-military courts. See, respectively, DCIP, *No Way to Treat a Child: Palestinian Children in the Israeli Military Detention System* (April 14, 2016), p. 18, https://d3n8a8pro7vhmx .cloudfront.net/dcipalestine/pages/1527/attachments/original/1460665378/DCIP_NWTTAC_ Report_Final_April_2016.pdf; DCIP, *Voices from East Jerusalem: The Situation facing Palestinian Children* (November 12, 2011), p. 41, https://d3n8a8pro7vhmx.cloudfront.net/ dcipalestine/pages/1297/attachments/original/1433986700/DCIP_east_jerusalem_final.pdf.

[85] DCIP, *No Way to Treat a Child*, p. 50 (referring to 297 cases closed between 2012 and 2015).

[86] State Attorney, *2015 Report* (August 2016), p. 23 [Hebrew], www.justice.gov.il/Units/ StateAttorney/Documents/2015AnnualReport.pdf (referring to 2015).

Israeli courts authorized to review the military's legislative and adminis-trative activities rarely accept appeals on decisions of the military court of appeals, thereby further shielding the military courts.[87]

With proceedings conducted rapidly and in Hebrew, it is no wonder that Palestinian former detainees, when interviewed about their encoun-ter with the Israeli legal system, tended to characterize their courtroom experience as one of exclusion, ignorance, and helplessness.[88] This, coupled with the settling of most charges outside the court through plea bargains, may explain why some Palestinian ex-detainees have described the interrogation room, rather than the military courtroom, as the site of their "real" trial. Indeed, it is during the crucial stage of interrogation that a confession – the basis for their conviction – is extracted.[89] As in the military courtroom, language is also an issue at this stage, with Palestinians aged under 18 reporting that they were commonly shown or made to sign documentation in Hebrew.[90]

There is an additional sense in which the "real" trial largely occurs in the pretrial stages of arrest and interrogation: once their military trial commences, Palestinians are as good as destined for conviction. According to the Israeli military, the conviction rate in its courts is 99.76 percent.[91] Moreover, in the military court of appeals that has operated since 1989,[92] the military prosecution's appeals to increase sentences are twice as likely to succeed as defendants' appeals.[93]

As for defendants under the age of 18, not a single one of the military court cases I quantitatively analyzed ended in an acquittal.[94] The prison

---

[87] See, e.g., HCJ 10285/07 *Abbad v. Military Prosecutor* (January 6, 2009); HCJ 8036/09 *Zuhara v. Judea and Samaria Area Military Court of Appeals* (October 12, 2009); HCJ 5145/10 *Hallef v. Judea and Samaria Area Military Court of Appeals* (July 20, 2010); HCJ 4224/16 *Asfur v. Military Court of Appeals* (December 1, 2016). For further discussion, see Section 2.6 ("Israel's Legalism").

[88] Hajjar, *Courting Conflict*, pp. 189–90.

[89] Ibid., pp. 188–90. See also Collins, *Occupied by Memory*, pp. 136–37.

[90] Military Court Watch, *Monitoring the Treatment of Children Held in Israeli Military Detention - Annual Report 2018/19*, p. 12.

[91] C. Levinson, "Nearly 100% of All Military Court Cases in West Bank End in Conviction, Haaretz Learns," *Haaretz* (November 29, 2011), www.haaretz.com/nearly-100-of-all-mili tary-court-cases-in-west-bank-end-in-conviction-haaretz-learns-1.398369 (referring to 2010) [hereinafter: "Nearly 100% of Cases End in Conviction"].

[92] Benichou, "Criminal Law," p. 296; Yavne, *Backyard Proceedings*, pp. 37–38.

[93] Levinson, "Nearly 100% of Cases End in Conviction."

[94] A few cases were closed or deleted for various reasons, without either a sentence or acquittal. For similar figures, see, e.g., Alyan and Slutzker Amran, "Facts and Figures," p. 2; Laor and Jaraisy, *Arrests, Interrogations and Indictments*, p. 8.

sentence rate was 93.55 percent, the suspended sentence rate was 98.71 percent, and fines were imposed in 96.77 percent of cases – indicating that most sentences include all three components: imprisonment, a suspended sentence, and a fine. The average prison sentence was 7.91 months, the average suspended sentence was 7.22 months (with an average probation period of 3.56 years),[95] and the average fine was 1,157 Israeli shekels – the equivalent of about three months' average income at the time.[96] In recent years, fines have reportedly been even higher.[97] This is but one of the burdensome payments Israel imposes on Palestinian defendants and petitioners; others include bail, fines, bonds, and litigation expenses.[98] As for the probation figures here, they indicate that young Palestinians are placed on probation for several years after their release from prison,[99] and hence remain subject to monitoring by the Israeli authorities. Palestinians' experience of continued Israeli control after release from prison often comes in the additional form of being denied work permits or having their movement within the West Bank restricted on the basis of possessing a criminal record. In a sense, then, the feeling of being incarcerated does not fully end upon completion of their prison sentences.[100]

Prior to their near-certain conviction, most Palestinian defendants are kept in detention until the end of their trial. My quantitative analysis found that 81.7 percent of defendants under the age of 18 were detained

---

[95] On the sentences the military courts impose on young Palestinians, see also Baumgarten-Sharon, *No Minor Matter*, pp. 19–22; DCIP, *Palestinian Child Prisoners: The Systematic and Institutionalised Ill-treatment and Torture of Palestinian Children by Israeli Authorities* (June 15, 2009), p. 98, https://d3n8a8pro7vhmx.cloudfront.net/dcipales tine/pages/1298/attachments/original/1433987832/DCIP_childprisoner_report.pdf? 1433987832 [hereinafter: *Palestinian Child Prisoners*].

[96] See World Bank, *Data: West Bank and Gaza* (n.d., last accessed on June 4, 2018), https:// data.worldbank.org/indicator/NY.GNP.PCAP.CD?locations=PS&view=chart.

[97] A. Hass, "In Three Years, Israeli Military Courts Have Fined Palestinians $16 Million," *Haaretz* (January 15, 2019), www.haaretz.com/israel-news/.premium-in-three-years-israeli-military-courts-have-fined-palestinians-16-million-1.6830009.

[98] On Israel's growing imposition of bonds and litigation expenses on Palestinian plaintiffs, see G. J. Bachar, "Access Denied – Using Procedure to Restrict Tort Litigation: The Israeli-Palestinian Experience" (2017) 92:3 *Chicago-Kent Law Review* 841, 849–51. On fines and bail as a way of economically exploiting Palestinians, see Addameer, *The Economic Exploitation of Palestinian Political Prisoners* (2016), pp. 42–43, www .addameer.org/sites/default/files/publications/final_report_red_2_0.pdf.

[99] For similar figures in human rights reports, see Alyan and Slutzker Amran, "Facts and Figures," pp. 1–2; DCIP, *No Way to Treat a Child*, pp. 52–53; Baumgarten-Sharon, *No Minor Matter*, p. 55; Ben-Natan, *All Guilty*, pp. 37, 44–46.

[100] Smith, "A Danger to the Region," p. 96.

pending disposition, while only 14.5 percent were released on bail.[101] As a result, even in rare cases of non-conviction, remand is likely to become a de facto punishment. This further incentivizes Palestinians and their lawyers to reach a plea bargain as soon as possible.[102] The extent to which remand (as opposed to release on bail) is the default was thrown into sharp relief during a military court hearing in 2018. Before the judge even announced her final decision, the court typist's computer screen was caught on camera by an Israeli human rights attorney, showing the following template text: "I order that the defendant be remanded for __ additional days, until __."[103] This entire state of affairs, as I show in detail in Chapters 7 and 8, stands in stark contrast to Israel's handling of its citizens.

2.6   Israel's Legalism

Israel, the country with the highest rate of lawyers per capita in the world,[104] has gone to remarkable lengths to shape and justify its conduct through legal institutions, arguments, and professionals.[105] As evident throughout this book, this legalism[106] – of which mass incarceration and military law are emblematic – is a long-standing earmark of the Israeli

---

[101] Some of the analyzed cases did not contain sufficient information. For similar figures in human rights reports, see Baumgarten-Sharon, *No Minor Matter*, p. 24; DCIP, *Palestinian Child Prisoners*, p. 97; DCIP, *No Way to Treat a Child*, p. 48. More recent data, provided by the military, shows slightly lower rates of detention pending disposition for young Palestinian defendants: 71 percent in 2014 and 72 percent in 2015. See, respectively, Laor and Jaraisy, *Arrests, Interrogations and Indictments*, pp. 7–8; Alyan and Slutzker Amran, "Facts and Figures," p. 1.

[102] Baumgarten-Sharon and Stein, *Presumed Guilty*, pp. 12–14, 40–42.

[103] For the photograph and a description of the circumstances in which it was taken, see A. Feldman, Facebook post (November 25, 2018) [Hebrew], www.facebook.com/avigdor .feldman/posts/10156081471734716.

[104] Y. Guetta, "2016 Law Firm Ranking: Which Is the Biggest?," *The Marker* (February 1, 2016) [Hebrew], www.themarker.com/law/1.2835927; T. Zarchin, "Israel First in World for Lawyers Per Capita, Study Finds," *Haaretz* (August 3, 2011), www.haaretz.com/ print-edition/news/israel-first-in-world-for-lawyers-per-capita-study-finds-1.376646.

[105] See also E. Playfair, "Playing on Principle? Israel's Justification for Its Administrative Acts in the Occupied West Bank," in E. Playfair (ed.), *International Law and the Administration of Occupied Territories* (Oxford: Clarendon Press Oxford, 1992); G. E. Bisharat, "Land, Law, and Legitimacy in Israel and the Occupied Territories" (1994) 43 *American University Law Review* 467.

[106] On the meaning(s) of legalism, see K. McEvoy, "Beyond Legalism: Towards a Thicker Understanding of Transnational Justice" (2007) 34:4 *Journal of Law & Society* 411, 414–24.

control regime, albeit with significant parallels in other countries.[107] According to the military's strategy document, which was made public in 2015, Israel's legalism is designed to garner domestic and international support for its actions:

> The [military's] primary efforts and capabilities [include] ... *carrying out effective legal and public diplomacy efforts* during and following combat in order to generate legitimacy for [military] operation. ... *The diplomatic, perception-shaping, and legal effort to preserve and enhance the operation's legitimacy* [is intended] ... to generate, preserve, and improve operation legitimacy in both Israel itself and the international community.[108]

As early as 1963, four years before Israel took over the West Bank and Gaza Strip, military lawyers began developing the legal infrastructure for a possible belligerent occupation. Meir Shamgar, the military advocate general at the time and later the attorney general and chief justice, described how military lawyers were equipped with "kits" containing "basic legal textbooks" and "a large set of precedents of military government proclamations and orders, vital at the initial stages of military government."[109] Senior military lawyers and officials also held meetings to discuss legal matters concerning the occupied territory, such as the possible establishment of military courts.[110]

In 1967, when Israeli brigades entered the West Bank and Gaza Strip, they were accompanied by the previously trained military lawyers, who were subsequently attached to the military's various regional headquarters.[111] Ever since, military lawyers have been at the forefront of Israel's

---

[107] On parallels with, and connections to, the legalistic state violence of the United States, see H. Viterbo, "Seeing Torture Anew: A Transnational Reconceptualization of State Torture and Visual Evidence" (2014) 50:2 *Stanford Journal of International Law* 281; H. Viterbo, "Export of Knowledge," in Ben-Naftali, Sfard, and Viterbo, *The ABC of the OPT*, pp. 95–117.

[108] IDF – Office of the Chief of the General Staff, *The IDF Strategy* (August 2015), pp. 17, 19 [Hebrew], www.idf.il/media/5679/%D7%90%D7%A1%D7%98%D7%A8%D7%98%D7% 92%D7%99%D7%99%D7%AA-%D7%A6%D7%94%D7%9C.pdf (emphases in the original). An English translation, as well as analysis, is available in A. S. Khalidi, "Introduction: On the Limitations of Military Doctrine" (2016) 45 *Journal of Palestine Studies* 127.

[109] M. Shamgar, "Legal Concepts and Problems of the Israeli Military Government – The Initial Stage," in M. Shamgar (ed.), *Military Government in the Territories Administered by Israel, 1967–1980: The Legal Aspects* (Jerusalem: Hebrew University, 1982), pp. 13, 25 [hereinafter: "Legal Concepts"].

[110] H. Viterbo, "Outside/Inside," in Ben-Naftali, Sfard, and Viterbo, *The ABC of the OPT*, pp. 310–11.

[111] Shamgar, "Legal Concepts," pp. 13, 24–25.

control over these territories. Currently numbering around 1,000, including 300 on active duty,[112] among their key functions, as they describe them, are "legal public relations" and "legitimacy maintenance."[113] Some of their efforts are directed toward international audiences. In 2009, for instance, a military spokesperson tried to ward off criticisms of Israel's offensive on the Gaza Strip by telling the foreign press: "We have international lawyers at every level of the command ... We don't think we have breached international law."[114] At other times, it is Israeli public opinion they target. Thus, the IPS has made a point of maintaining, on its Hebrew website, that so-called security prisoners "are held ... pursuant to law and international treaties," and that their "living conditions, obligations, and rights ... are legally defined ... in accordance with international legal definitions."[115] In a 2018 op-ed in the Israeli press, the former military advocate general made the following case for incorporating law into Israel's military apparatus:

> No military-tactical achievement will be translatable into a long-term political achievement if Israel is perceived as a pariah state of war criminals. Therefore, the legal counsel provided by [military lawyers] ... is a vital element in the IDF's might ... As the former military advocate general I can testify that the vast majority of [military] investigations into [incidents] ... with [Palestinian] casualties ended without a trial.[116]

The prosecution of Palestinians (in military courts) and soldiers (in courts-martial, as examined in Chapters 6 and 7) is among the military lawyers' key duties. Other responsibilities include: involvement in drafting military legislation; furnishing the military with legal advice and policy; planning and executing the military's operations; and

---

[112] M. N. Schmitt and J. J. Merriam, "The Tyranny of Context: Israeli Targeting Practices in Legal Perspective" (2015) 37 *University of Pennsylvania Journal of International Law* 53, 82.

[113] MAG, *Annual Activity Report – 2017* (2018), pp. 29, 34 [Hebrew], www.idf.il/media/ 34839/%D7%93%D7%95%D7%97-%D7%94%D7%A9%D7%A0%D7%AA%D7%99-% D7%A9%D7%9C-%D7%94%D7%A4%D7%A8%D7%A7%D7%9C%D7%99%D7%98 D7%95%D7%AA.pdf.

[114] C. McGreal, "Demands Grow for Gaza War Crimes Investigation," *The Guardian* (January 13, 2009), www.theguardian.com/world/2009/jan/13/gaza-israel-war-crimes.

[115] See, respectively, IPS, "Security Prisoners Incarcerated in the Israel Prison Service" (2007; last accessed on September 10, 2016; no longer available online) [Hebrew]; IPS, "About the Organization" (n.d.; last accessed on September 10, 2016; no longer available online) [Hebrew].

[116] L. Liebman, "Shooting Inside the APC," *Yedioth Aharonoth* (November 19, 2018) [Hebrew], www.yediot.co.il/articles/0,7340,L-5409624,00.html.

providing legal education and training to soldiers.[117] Their task, according to a former high-ranking military lawyer, is "not to tie down the army, but to give it the tools to win in a way that is legal."[118] Another top military lawyer described in an interview how, during an offensive on the Gaza Strip, commanders "thought it is not allowed to attack mosques, but I, the legal practitioner, tell them that it is allowed. You can attack, no problem."[119]

Another central piece of this legalistic puzzle has been judicial review of Israel's actions in the West Bank and Gaza Strip. In the early 1970s, the Israeli supreme court opened its doors to petitions against such actions. In 2018, jurisdiction over administrative decisions in the West Bank – concerning matters including entry and exit permits, building and planning permits, and freedom of information requests – was transferred to the Jerusalem district court in the first instance, with the supreme court's role now limited to that of an appeals court.[120] Such petitions and appeals have, however, rarely been successful.[121] For example, of 322 appeals on "administrative detention" heard by the supreme court between 2000 and 2010 – including appeals by Palestinians aged under 18[122] – not a single one resulted in a release order or in a rejection of the secret evidence.[123] A similar fate has befallen the hundreds of petitions

---

[117] A. Craig, *International Legitimacy and the Politics of Security: The Strategic Deployment of Lawyers in the Israeli Military* (Lanham: Lexington Books, 2013); M. Geva, *Law, Politics and Violence in Israel/Palestine: The Israeli Military International Law Department* (Cham: Springer International, 2016); C. A. Jones, "Frames of Law: Targeting Advice and Operational Law in the Israeli Military" (2015) 33:4 *Environment and Planning D: Society and Space* 676.

[118] U. Blau and Y. Feldman, "How IDF Legal Experts Legitimized Strikes Involving Gaza Civilians," *Haaretz* (January 22, 2009), www.haaretz.com/how-idf-legal-experts-legitim ized-strikes-involving-gaza-civilians-1.268598.

[119] Quoted in Geva, *Law, Politics and Violence in Israel/Palestine*, p. 175.

[120] Administrative Courts Law (Amendment No. 117), 2018.

[121] See, e.g., D. Kretzmer, *The Occupation of Justice: The Supreme Court of Israel and the Occupied Territories* (Albany: State University of New York Press, 2002); G. Harpaz and Y. Shany, "The Israeli Supreme Court and the Incremental Expansion of the Scope of Discretion under Belligerent Occupation Law" (2010) 43:3 *Israel Law Review* 514 [hereinafter: "Incremental Expansion"].

[122] For a case in which the appellant was 17 years old at the time of the judgment and 16 years old at the time of his arrest, see HCJ 9454/07 *Abu Matar v. IDF Commander* (December 20, 2007) 62(4) PD 77.

[123] S. Krebs, "Lifting the Veil of Secrecy: Judicial Review of Administrative Detentions in the Israeli Supreme Court" (2012) 45:3 *Vanderbilt Journal of Transnational Law* 639, 643.

against demolitions of Palestinian homes, all of which the supreme court has dismissed over the years.[124]

The few exceptional decisions in favor of noncitizen Palestinians, widely publicized by Israeli authorities, have had little to no long-term impact on Israel's conduct, aside from sometimes leading Israeli authorities to "legalize" or come up with new legal justifications for their contested practices. In some cases, perhaps in order to avoid a trial and the international scrutiny it may evoke, Israeli authorities respond to the threat of litigation by providing some remedies, but they tend to be modest and isolated.[125] Even rulings heralded as human rights victories have frequently contained loopholes that allow for continued violations, as shown later in this book.

Israel's legalism entails not only relying on its own legal system but also, as mentioned in the previous chapter, closely engaging with international law. Though Israel's critics repeatedly accuse it of flouting international law,[126] Israeli governments and courts invoke it repeatedly, albeit inconsistently.[127] For example, Israeli officials have justified the military court system by citing the Fourth Geneva Convention[128]

---

[124] Y. Stein, *Fake Justice: The Responsibility Israel's High Court Justices Bear for the Demolition of Palestinian Homes and the Dispossession of Palestinians* (Jerusalem: B'Tselem, February 2019), p. 22, www.btselem.org/sites/default/files/publications/201902_fake_justice_eng.pdf.

[125] Kretzmer, *The Occupation of Justice*; R. Shamir, "'Landmark Cases' and the Reproduction of Legitimacy: The Case of Israel's High Court of Justice" (1990) 24:3 *Law & Society Review* 781; Y. Dotan, "Judicial Rhetoric, Government Lawyers, and Human Rights: The Case of the Israeli High Court of Justice during the *Intifada*" (1999) 33:2 *Law & Society Review* 319; Harpaz and Shany, "Incremental Expansion"; D. Kretzmer, "The Law of Belligerent Occupation in the Supreme Court of Israel" (2012) 94 *International Review of the Red Cross* 207.

[126] See, e.g., UN Human Rights Council, "Human Rights Situation in the Occupied Palestinian Territory, Including East Jerusalem" UN Doc A/HRC/34/38 (March 16, 2017), ¶ 13, www.ohchr.org/en/hrbodies/hrc/regularsessions/session34/documents/a_hrc_34_38_auv.docx ("In the Occupied Palestinian Territory, Israel disregards the law of occupation").

[127] Exemplifying this inconsistency is the Israeli government's claim, in 2018, that "the Knesset [the Israeli parliament] is entitled to ignore directives of international law in any area it pleases." Government's Response to Petitioners' Follow-Up Arguments in HCJ 1308/17 *Silwad Municipality* v. *Knesset* (August 7, 2018), ¶ 4 [Hebrew], https://law.acri.org.il/he/wp-content/uploads/2018/08/bagatz2055–17-hoq-hahasdara-memshala-0818.pdf.

[128] See, e.g., Benichou, "Criminal Law," p. 295; Z. Hadar, "The Military Courts," in M. Shamgar (ed.), *Military Government in the Territories Administered by Israel – 1967–1980: The Legal Aspects* (Jerusalem: Hebrew University, 1982), pp. 173–75; Strashnov, *Justice Under Fire*, p. 37.

(despite also arguing, controversially, that Israel is under no legal obligation to apply the Convention to the Palestinian territory).[129] Referring to
the Israeli judiciary's use of international law, the former chief justice
Dorit Beinisch has remarked: "the international community does not
agree with the [Israeli supreme court's] interpretation ... of some of the
[Geneva] Convention's articles. ... Yet, [it is] ... a creative and original
interpretation of international law."[130]

At the same time, as I argued in Chapter 1, law is more than formal
legal mechanisms, documents, and practitioners. It also comprises, no
less importantly, other parties and factors, such as Israeli soldiers on the
ground. Though not professional lawyers, they too take part in shaping
what counts and is perceived as law. Illustrating this are testimonies of
former Israeli soldiers. Some of them have described the West Bank as
brimming with law, while trying to distance themselves from that law by
arguing that they were "just following orders." Others insist they not only
enforced but actually embodied the law, as evidenced when they told
Palestinians: "How dare you say no to me? I am the law!" There are also
those who claim that, in the West Bank, "there is no law, only Jewish
interests."[131] Notwithstanding the differences in these accounts, they are
all immersed in the distinction between "legal" and "illegal," thus operating, as explained in the previous chapter, within law's conceptual
confines.

2.7 Israel's Human Rights Critics

This book puts on trial not only the Israeli legal system but also its
human rights critics. In recent decades, human rights organizations have
burgeoned remarkably in Israel/Palestine,[132] perhaps partly as a conse-

---

[129] Y. Z. Blum, "The Missing Reversioner: Reflections on the Status of Judea and Samaria"
(1968) 3:2 *Israel Law Review* 279; Shamgar, "Legal Concepts," pp. 33–34.
[130] D. Beinisch, "The Rule of Law in Times of War" (2004) 17 *Law and Military* 19,
24–25 [Hebrew].
[131] These testimonies are quoted in M. Zagor, "'I am the Law!' – Perspectives of Legality and
Illegality in the Israeli Army" (2010) 43:3 *Israel Law Review* 551.
[132] According to one Palestinian source, Palestinian NGOs rose sharply in number from
79 in 1966 to 272 in 1987, then to 1,150 in 2001, and eventually to 2,775 in 2014.
M. Samara, "'The Observatory': 2770 NGOs Operating in Palestine," *Wattan* (October
22, 2014) [Arabic], www.wattan.tv/news/109870.html.

quence of Israel's combination of legalism and repression.[133] For these organizations, as seen throughout this book, childhood is a major concern. Indeed, it features prominently even for those not focused on child-related issues: in 2017, for instance, the three most watched reports on the website of Israeli human rights NGO B'Tselem all dealt with young Palestinians.[134]

The human rights organizations under examination are varied, ranging from UN bodies (such as the UN Human Rights Council), international children's rights NGOs (such as Save the Children), and foreign-based organizations (such as the Council for Arab-British Understanding), to local ones, both Palestinian (such as Addameer) and Israeli (such as Yesh Din). Whether child-focused or not, local or international, these organizations are, in one way or another, fully fledged legal actors. Among their key activities, which vary from one organization to another, are: reporting on Israel's human rights violations; pressing Israeli or foreign governments to bring an end to these violations by enforcing international law; submitting shadow reports to UN human rights treaty bodies; filing legal petitions and complaints; providing legal aid to Palestinians in Israeli custody; offering workshops to Palestinians on their rights under international law; and guiding tours that reveal the situation on the ground to legal professionals and organizations.[135] With many founders, leaders, and prominent members who are themselves lawyers,[136] human rights organizations have several legalistic features: they operate within and in response to the Israeli legal

---

[133] On Israel's combination of legalism and repression, see G. E. Bisharat, "Courting Justice? Legitimation in Lawyering under Israeli Occupation" (1995) 20:2 *Law & Social Inquiry* 349, 403–04 [hereinafter: "Courting Justice"].

[134] Two of the three reports focused exclusively on under-18s, and the third referred specifically to "children" in its title while also dealing with older Palestinians. B'Tselem, Email Update (February 7, 2018) [Hebrew] (on file with the author).

[135] L. Allen, *The Rise and Fall of Human Rights: Cynicism and Politics in Occupied Palestine* (Stanford: Stanford University Press, 2013), pp. 45, 63, 65; A. Levin, "The Reporting Cycle to the United Nations Human Rights Treaty Bodies: Creating a Dialogue between the State and Civil Society – the Israeli Case Study" (2016) 48 *George Washington International Law Review* 315, 352–55.

[136] G. Barzilai, "The Ambivalent Language of Lawyers in Israel: Liberal Politics, Economic Liberalism, Silence and Dissent," in T. C. Halliday et al. (eds.), *Fighting for Political Freedom: Comparative Studies of the Legal Complex and Political Liberalism* (Portland: Hart, 2007), pp. 247, 261–62.

system, produce truth-claims about it, rely on legal standards and sources, and avail themselves of international legal forums.[137]

The plethora of lengthy human rights reports stands in sharp contrast to the relative brevity of Israeli military judgments. While an example of such a report would be impossible to quote here in full, the following excerpt, from a 2009 DCIP publication, provides a window into some broader issues concerning the human rights community and its relationship with law and childhood. The excerpt – one of several "case studies" (as the report frames them) – concerns 17-year-old Mohammad who, like hundreds of young Palestinians every year, is reported to have been convicted of stone throwing:[138]

Name:	**Mohammad A.**
Date of arrest:	**26 November 2008**
Age at arrest:	**17**
Accusation:	**Throwing stones**

At around 2:00am on 26 November 2008, 17-year-old Mohammad from the West Bank city of Nablus, was arrested from his bed by Israeli soldiers. Mohammad had a pre-existing injury to his leg which made it difficult to walk. The soldiers tied and blindfolded him and forced him to walk several kilometres to a checkpoint.

When we reached Za'tara checkpoint, a military jeep came and one of the soldiers pushed me hard towards the jeep. My body banged into the jeep and another soldier standing nearby pushed my head into the jeep.

The soldiers then pushed me inside the jeep and made me sit on the floor. Four soldiers surrounded me and my head was between their feet. The jeep drove away. During the trip, the soldiers kicked me, shouted and insulted me. The trip lasted for about half an hour. ...[319]

[HV: The ellipsis here marks where the report splits this "case study" into two parts, which are separated by about 20 pages of text not directly related to the narrative.]

Eight days after being arrested and after being detained in Huwwara Interrogation and Detention Centre, I was transferred to Salem Interrogation and Detention Centre for interrogation. I was taken into a room in which an interrogator named 'Saleh Nasr' was sitting behind a desk. Saleh was tall and had green eyes. I was kept tied with plastic cords behind my back.

---

[137] On the legalism of Israeli human rights NGOs, particularly those dealing with issues concerning noncitizen Palestinians, see N. Berkovitch and N. Gordon, "The Political Economy of Transnational Regimes: The Case of Human Rights" (2008) 52 *International Studies Quarterly* 881; D. Golan and Z. Orr, "Translating Human Rights of the 'Enemy': The Case of Israeli NGOs Defending Palestinian Rights" (2012) 46 *Law & Society Review* 781, 791.
[138] DCIP, *Palestinian Child Prisoners*, pp. 40, 62 (emphases in the original).

Saleh began interrogating me by asking me questions about some persons of my age from my village. He said that they said I had participated in throwing stones and Molotov cocktails. I denied this. He began shouting at me and said: 'I will shoot you in the head if you don't confess and stick your head in a bucket full of water until you choke and die.' When he shouted another interrogator came into the room and threatened me. The other interrogator was tall and scary. He would raise his hand as if he wanted to slap me.

I was terrified and therefore asked them to let me write my statement on my own. Saleh dictated and I wrote as he spoke. I confessed, as he asked me to, that I threw stones. When he asked me to write that I threw Molotov cocktails, I refused and said: 'I won't do it even if you shoot me in the head.'

18 December 2008

Mohammad was charged with throwing stones and was sentenced by a military court to five months imprisonment and a fine of NIS 500 (US$125) after entering into a plea bargain. He served the majority of his sentence in Salem Interrogation and Detention Centre. He was released on 26 April 2009.

This framing seems to differ markedly from that of Israeli military court case documents. Among other things, the report containing this excerpt, unlike military judgments, discusses at relative length the drama taking place outside the courtroom – during arrest, detention, interrogation, and imprisonment (stages of the legal process examined in Chapters 4–7). Also unlike military judgments, the report presents itself (questionably, as I show in Chapters 4 and 5) as representing the authentic voices of Mohammad and others like him. Given such differences, Israel and its human rights critics may appear, to themselves and to others, as two opposite camps.

However, throughout the book, such a notion of opposite camps is shown to be misleading. To begin with, neither Israel nor the human rights community is truly a camp in the monolithic sense of the word. Time and again, the Israeli legal system has been inconsistent in interpreting and applying even ostensibly clear-cut legal provisions, as I reveal in the next chapter. There is some divergence between claims made by human rights organizations, and even by the same organization, as illustrated in Chapters 4 and 5. Hence, no fully univocal or coherent camps operate here.

Further, the approach of liberal human rights actors to Israeli authorities is far from simply antagonistic. Some organizations not only share Israel's legalism but also repeatedly cite the law Israel applies to its citizens as a model worthy of emulation. Some litigate in Israeli courts, file complaints with Israel's investigation mechanisms, and routinely communicate with Israeli legal officials.[139] There is also considerable convergence in how Israel and its human rights critics conceptualize childhood. More than once, Israel's critics even articulate the problems faced by young people in Israel/Palestine, as well the solutions, in terms nearly identical to those used in Israeli security and legal circles, as I show in subsequent chapters (particularly in Chapter 4). This messy dynamic, within and between Israel and the human rights community, cannot be encapsulated by the common yet simplistic idea of opposing camps.

One of Israel's additional commonalities with human rights organizations is its resort, increasingly and like other countries, to a human rights rhetoric.[140] As seen throughout this book, human rights actors repeatedly formulate their criticism of Israel in legal terms (as do critical media reports).[141] For Israel's part, its 2015 periodic report to the UN Committee Against Torture insisted that it had made "an honest attempt . . . [to adhere] to the rule of law and [to respect] . . . the human rights of all individuals in its territory," adding:

> When preparing its periodic reports to . . . UN Human Rights Committees, Israel makes a concerted effort to involve civil society in the process . . . Civil Society contributions are given substantial consideration during the drafting of the Report. In addition, the Ministry of Justice actively seeks data and information on the relevant NGOs' websites.[142]

At the same time, the Israeli Jewish public and its political representatives have shown growing animosity toward the human rights community in recent years. A poll conducted in 2016 found that nearly three in four Israeli Jews regarded human rights organizations as harmful to

---

[139] On the pitfalls and benefits of the participation of human rights organizations in the Israeli legal system, see H. Viterbo, "Lawfare," in Ben-Naftali, Sfard, and Viterbo, *The ABC of the OPT*, pp. 251–53.

[140] On the rise of human rights in contemporary political rhetoric, see Chapter 1, Section 1.2.4 ("Problematizing Human Rights").

[141] See, e.g., Al Jazeera News Staff, "Is Israel Breaking Laws by Abusing Palestinian Boys?," *Al Jazeera* (October 25, 2017), www.aljazeera.com/programmes/insidestory/2017/10/israel-breaking-laws-abusing-palestinian-boys-171025181053379.html.

[142] UNCAT, Consideration of Reports Submitted by States Parties Under Article 19 of the Convention Pursuant to the Optional Reporting Procedure: Fifth Periodic Reports of States Parties Due in 2013 – Israel, UN Doc CAT/C/ISR/5 (February 16, 2015), ¶¶ 48, 103, 232–33, 446–47, 450–51, http://docstore.ohchr.org/SelfServices/FilesHandler.ashx?enc=6QkG1d%2FPPRiCAqhKb7yhsmEKqNhdzbzr4kqou1ZPE787pA64z90a%2FZN18JHW%2Bkxawxy0ig%2FWuoddnyM%2BN7PHmuASmEY6ojM6VX3krxvNSVxPuoqb1FlsbvTHqntEyOT5.

Israel.[143] Recent Israeli governments have likewise introduced a host of legal initiatives designed to stigmatize liberal human rights NGOs and suppress their activities.[144] This is not an entirely new development: according to recently published documents, Israeli authorities used covert informants to monitor local human rights organizations in the 1960s and 1970s.[145] Israel's vehement opposition to its human rights critics may seem at odds with its proclaimed commitment to law and human rights. In fact, these are two sides of the same coin: Israel invokes law and human rights, and directs animosity toward those critics who challenge this invocation, in order to ensure its continued reliance on law and human rights as a means of achieving and legitimizing its military and political objectives.[146]

Notwithstanding conflicting assertions from Israeli authorities and officials, the military has on occasion professed responsiveness to, and engagement with, human rights organizations. Such organizations thus risk being used to legitimize Israel's actions.[147] In its 2012 annual report, for instance, the military advocate general, in the course of outlining the "central elements of . . . activity" of his office, remarked:

> there has been increased engagement, by human rights organizations, international organizations, and other international bodies, in the way the [Israeli] law enforcement authorities in the [West Bank] . . . treat [Palestinian] minor offenders. As a result, activity has taken place at headquarter level to examine and amend the relevant security legislation, with [military] prosecution officers even escorting a number of delegations to Israel and responding in writing to several international reports . . . on this matter.[148]

---

[143] In comparison, less than one in four Palestinian citizens expressed this view. T. Hermann et al., *The Israel Democracy Index – 2016* (Jerusalem: Israel Democracy Institute, 2017), p. 133, https://en.idi.org.il/media/7811/democracy-index-2016-eng.pdf.

[144] D. Gild-Hayo, *Overview of Anti-Democratic Legislation Advanced by the 20th Knesset* (Tel Aviv: ACRI, December 2017), https://law.acri.org.il/en/wp-content/uploads/2017/07/December-Overview-of-Anti-Democratic-Legislation-2017-1.pdf.

[145] L. Yavne and N. Hofstadter, "Appropriate Tools: Israeli Ministry of Foreign Affairs and Amnesty's Israel Section, 1969–1977," *Akevot* (March 17, 2017), http://akevot.org.il/en/article/appropriate-tools/.

[146] See Viterbo, "Lawfare," pp. 260–62.

[147] Bisharat, "Courting Justice"; M. Sfard, "The Price of Internal Legal Opposition to Human Rights Abuses" (2009) 1 *Journal of Human Rights Practice* 37.

[148] MAG, *Annual Activity Report – 2012* (2013), pp. 5–6 [Hebrew], www.idf.il/media/32430/%D7%93%D7%95%D7%97-2012.pdf.

Despite such claims, the actual impact of the human rights community on Israeli authorities is unclear.[149] A case in point, to which the military advocate general may have been alluding, involves a high-profile delegation of British lawyers that visited Israel/Palestine in late 2011 to evaluate the Israeli legal system's treatment of young Palestinians. Funded and facilitated by the British Foreign Office, and with members including the UK's former attorney general and a former court of appeals judge, the delegation's report in 2012 attracted media attention in both the United Kingdom and Israel.[150] The Israeli government, having refused to cooperate with UN delegations on a number of occasions,[151] nonetheless arranged for this particular delegation to meet with senior officials and lawyers. Among them were military judges and prosecutors, the deputy attorney general, the military's legal advisor in the West Bank, and the supreme court's chief justice.[152] Within no more than ten days of the delegation's return to the United Kingdom to compile its report, the Israeli military enacted and then widely publicized two reforms: first, it raised the age of criminal majority for Palestinians from 16 to 18 years

<hr>

[149] For various assessments of their impact, see G. Golan, "The Impact of Peace and Human Rights NGOs on Israeli Policy," in G. Golan and W. Salem (eds.), *Non-State Actors in the Middle East: Factors for Peace and Democracy* (London and New York: Routledge, 2013), pp. 28–41; Y. Levy, K. Michael, and A. Shapira, "Extra-Institutional Control of the Military: A Conceptual Framework" (2010) 4 *The Public Sphere* 45 [Hebrew]; P. Vennesson and N. M. Rajkovic, "The Transnational Politics of Warfare Accountability: Human Rights Watch versus the Israel Defense Forces" (2012) 26:4 *International Relations* 409.

[150] See, e.g., BBC Staff, "Israel 'Breaching UN Convention on Children's Rights'," *BBC News* (June 27, 2012), www.bbc.co.uk/news/world-middle-east-18608900; J. Rugman, "Israel 'Breaches Rights of Palestinian Children'," *Channel 4 News* (June 26, 2012), www.channel4.com/news/israel-regularly-breaches-rights-of-palestinian-children; Walla! News Staff, "Israel Detains Children in Violation of International Law," *Walla! News* (June 27, 2012) [Hebrew], http://news.walla.co.il/item/2544984; Ynet Staff, "Israel Detains Palestinian Minors Unconscionably," *Ynet* (June 28, 2012) [Hebrew], www.ynet.co.il/articles/0,7340,L-4247917,00.html.

[151] See, e.g., T. Adamson, "UNESCO Adopts Controversial Jerusalem Decision," *The Washington Post* (October 18, 2016), www.washingtonpost.com/world/middle_east/unesco-expected-to-adopt-controversial-jerusalem-resolution/2016/10/18/57d1993e-950e-11e6-9cae-2a3574e296a6_story.html; Associated Press, "UN's Gaza War Crimes Investigation Faces Obstacles," *Ynet News* (June 9, 2009), www.ynetnews.com/articles/0,7340,L-3728466,00.html.

[152] S. Sedley et al., *Children in Military Custody: A Report Written by a Delegation of British Lawyers on the Treatment of Palestinian Children under Israeli Military Law* (Foreign and Commonwealth Office, June 2012), www.childreninmilitarycustody.org.uk/wp-content/uploads/2012/03/Children_in_Military_Custody_Full_Report.pdf.

and, second, it made provision for the notification of Palestinian parents about their child's arrest.

Thus, continuing their long record of relying on legal mechanisms and arguments, Israeli authorities do more than simply contest or deny allegations that they violate international children's rights norms. What they also do, as these reforms illustrate, is develop new legal means to fend off the criticism. As I reveal in Chapter 4, however, these reforms, as well as others Israel has introduced in recent decades, have been mostly tokenistic, and in some respects have even been detrimental to Palestinians, young and old alike. Rather than flouting child rights law, then, Israeli authorities find ways to deploy it to their benefit, with harmful consequences for Palestinians.

Statements and publications disseminated by the military in recent years demonstrate this embracing of the language of law and children's rights. A leaflet distributed to foreign delegations since 2013 thus asserts that Israel's military courts "were established in accordance with international law," and that, as part of their "efforts to protect the rights of all defendants," these courts protect young Palestinians' "welfare and best interests."[153] Along similar lines, a 2015 public statement by the military legal system insisted that, despite "complaints ... about [Israel's] ... administration of law [in the West Bank] ... generally, and regarding [Palestinian] minors specifically, it is important to emphasize [its] conformity with international law and the law applicable [therein]."[154] This cosy and ever-tightening relationship between law, children's rights, and state violence is a key concern of the chapters to come.

---

[153] Military Courts Unit, "The Military Courts Unit (Judea and Samaria)" (April 2013), www .militarycourtwatch.org/files/server/IDF%20Military%20Court%20Briefing%20Paper.pdf.
[154] Military Courts Unit, "The Legal Treatment of Malak Ali Yussef Khatib's Case," *IDF* (February 11, 2015), ¶ 23 [Hebrew], https://web.archive.org/web/20150921111312/www .law.idf.il/163-7111-he/Patzar.aspx.

3

The Age of Governing: Young Age as a Means of Control

3.1   Introduction: Terms of Age

Building on the foundations laid in the previous two chapters, this chapter focuses on the childhood–law–rights triad through a specific prism: age. As noted in Chapter 1, it is first and foremost on an age basis that law defines and demarcates certain perceived life stages as inherently distinct and internally homogeneous. Age-based distinctions enshrined in law reinforce, intensify, and reshape society's developmentalist age norms.[1] This dynamic, however, plays out differently in different contexts, four of which are the subject of this chapter: Palestinians' trials in Israeli (and mostly military) courts; Israel's open-fire regulations (rules of engagement); food quotas imposed on Gazans; and restrictions on Palestinian movement. This chapter examines Israel's use of Palestinians' age as a means to control their lives in each of these four contexts.

Drawing on my analysis of hundreds of Israeli judgments, Section 3.2 provides previously unknown findings on the role Palestinians' ages play in their trials, with a focus on three elements. The first is the statutory requirement to consider age when sentencing young defendants. As I will reveal, the military's enforcement of this requirement has been inconsistent in a number of ways. My central object of inquiry here will be judgments that hold young age to be an aggravating rather than a mitigating factor when sentencing Palestinians – a judicial view that, as will be explained, reflects two Israeli traditions: the portrayal of Palestinians as weaponizing their young, and the desire to discipline

---

[1] On "developmentality," see Chapter 1, Section 1.2.1 ("Problematizing Childhood"). On the intensification of age norms in Western societies, see H. P. Chudacoff, *How Old Are You? Age Consciousness in American Culture* (Princeton and Oxford: Princeton University Press, 1989); N. Lesko, *Act Your Age!: A Cultural Construction of Adolescence* (New York and London: Routledge, 2001).

older Palestinians through their younger counterparts. The second element to be examined is Palestinians' apparent age. I will investigate how this factor, despite formally having no legal relevance, figures centrally in Israeli judges' sentencing and remand decisions. The third element is the statutory age classification applied to Palestinians. I will trace its origin to colonial British law, compare it to classifications enacted elsewhere in the British Empire, and bring to light military judges' competing definitions and uses of statutory age categories.

Inconsistency, vagueness, and uncertainty – characteristics recurrent in the analysis to this point – will be the subject of Section 3.3. My findings, as I will argue, speak to broader issues at both the local and global levels. Locally, the production of uncertainty and ambiguity is a hallmark of Israel's rule, enabling Israeli authorities to expand their discretionary powers while disorientating Palestinians. Globally, childhood and age, while rigidly constructed, are also inherently fluid, elusive, and flexible.

Section 3.4 will be dedicated to contexts in which Palestinians' ages determine whether and how they get to live. The first is Israel's open-fire regulations, which formally forbid shooting at under-14s. I will discuss Israeli officials' public licensing of firing at younger Palestinians and analyze, through court-martial and other judgments, legal disputes over the apparent ages of shooting fatalities. The second context is age-based food quotas imposed on the Gaza Strip. I will cast a critical light on the logic guiding this form of biopolitical warfare, as well as on Israel's attempts to justify it in humanitarian and legal terms. Third, I will investigate Israel's use of age as a risk management tool, as evidenced by the restrictions placed on Palestinians' movement.

At the same time, the power to utilize ages lies not only with Israel but also with Palestinians. In Section 3.5, I will lay bare Palestinians' attempts to resist and circumvent Israel's rule by lying about age. By inquiring into such performative acts, I will bring center stage not only the resistant potential of age, but also the anxieties evoked in both Israel and its human rights critics by the inability to ascertain Palestinians' ages.

3.2   Age on Trial

3.2.1   Youth as an Aggravating Factor

Since 1980, Israel's military legislation has required the military courts, when sentencing a Palestinian under the age of 16, "to take into consideration, among other things, his age at the time of offending."[2] For the Israeli military, appearing to bear in mind Palestinians' young age is crucial for fending off human rights criticism. Illustrating this mindset is a legalistic (albeit not legally binding) military brief, which became public in 2014, and which likewise instructs soldiers to handle arrested Palestinian "minors"

> with due sensitivity and in consideration of their young age. Such sensitivity is required ... by the [applicable] ... laws and legal norms ... In addition, ... international bodies and various NGOs have roundly criticized the handling of [Palestinian] minors ... – criticism [that] ... might substantially harm Israel's legitimacy and the legitimacy of its actions in the [West Bank].[3]

As explained in Chapters 6 and 7, numerous testimonies of young Palestinians paint Israeli arrests as entailing little if any of this professed leniency and "sensitivity." Nonetheless, the legalistic language is revealing.

The language of these documents may appear to reflect the modern association of young age with innocence,[4] irresponsibility, reduced rationality, and hence with a need for leniency. My research, however, unearths substantial inconsistencies in the implementation of the statutory requirement to treat young age as a sentencing consideration. The implications, as I will explain, are far-reaching.

On the one hand, some military judgments indeed cite the defendant's youth as a mitigating factor. This is particularly evident in cases of relatively young "minors" who have no prior criminal record, or are

---

[2] Article 1 of the Order Concerning the Adjudication of Young Offenders (Judea and Samaria) (Amendment No. 7) (No. 863), 1980, currently codified as Article 168(a) of the Order Concerning Security Provisions (Integrated Version) (Judea and Samaria) (No. 1651), 2009 [hereinafter: Order 1651].

[3] Office of the Legal Advisor to the IDF in the Judea and Samaria Region, *A Brief for the Commander and the Soldier – Arresting Minors* (n.d.) [Hebrew], www.militarycourtwatch. org/files/server/%D7%AA%D7%A9%D7%95%D7%91%D7%94%20%D7%9C%D7%91% D7%A7%D7%A9%D7%AA%20%D7%97%D7%95%D7%A4%D7%A9%20%D7%9E%D7% 99%D7%93%D7%A2%20%D7%9E%D7%93%D7%95%D7%91%D7%A8%20%D7%A6% D7%94%D7%9C.tif. An unofficial English translation by NGO Military Court Watch is available at www.militarycourtwatch.org/files/server/FOI%20-%20ARREST%20 PROCEEDURES.pdf.

[4] On this association, see, e.g., C. Jenks, *Childhood*, 2nd ed. (New York: Routledge, 2005), pp. 49, 58, 62–64, 75–76, 119, 124–25.

not accused of causing actual harm, or both.[5] Correspondingly, when trying Palestinians aged 18 and over, the military judiciary has sometimes presented their legal adulthood as an aggravating factor. It has done so by emphasizing that they are not minors, or by characterizing their offenses as "not a youthful folly," or by drawing other contrasts with under-18s.[6]

On the other hand, judgments concerning defendants aged under 16 frequently make no reference whatsoever to the youthfulness of the defendant.[7] When mentioned, it is often said to be overridden by other factors, two of which, in particular, recur. The first is the prevalence, real or imagined, of the defendant's offense among young Palestinians. This rationale has been used by the military courts to justify harsh punishment for youth convicted of stone throwing, Molotov cocktail throwing, or stabbing[8] (though the latter was hardly widespread among young Palestinians at the time, and no stabbing charges appeared in the 155 cases I quantitatively analyzed).[9] Non-military courts, including the supreme court, have applied the same rationale to young noncitizen Palestinians in East Jerusalem, where Israel applies its non-military law.[10] The other factor regarded as overriding the defendant's youth and warranting harsh sentencing has been an increase in Palestinian riots at the time of the trial.[11]

The military judiciary has been similarly inconsistent regarding Palestinian defendants aged 16 and 17, to whom the youth consideration

---

[5] See, e.g., MilA 63/02 *Military Prosecutor* v. *Hanawi* (February 9, 2003); MilC (Judea) 4415/10 *Military Prosecutor* v. *Za'akik* (November 22, 2010).

[6] For representative examples see, respectively, MilA 2168/15 *Aliya* v. *Military Prosecution* (June 30, 2015); MilA 4788/07 *Military Prosecution* v. *Tamiza* (December 27, 2007); MilA 1387/08 *Hajaj* v. *Military Prosecution* (April 23, 2009).

[7] For similar findings, see L. Yavne, *Backyard Proceedings: The Implementation of Due Process Rights in the Military Courts in the Occupied Territories* (Tel Aviv: Yesh Din, December 2007), p. 160, https://s3-eu-west-1.amazonaws.com/files.yesh-din.org/%D7%9E%D7%A9%D7%A4%D7%98%D7%99%D7%9D+%D7%91%D7%97%D7%A6%D7%A8+%D7%94%D7%90%D7%97%D7%95%D7%A8%D7%99%D7%AA/BackyardProceedings fullreportEng+full+report.pdf.

[8] For three representative examples, see, respectively, MilA 2261/09 *Military Prosecutor* v. *Zaul* (May 20, 2009); MilA 1413/06 *Military Prosecutor* v. *Sabih* (February 19, 2006); MilA 355/03 *Abiyat* v. *Military Prosecutor* (August 11, 2004).

[9] Six cases (3.9 percent) included a knife possession charge.

[10] See, e.g., CrimA 3572/16 *John Doe* v. *State of Israel* (January 3, 2017), ¶ t of deputy chief justice Rubinstein's leading opinion; CrimC (Jer. Dist.) 42595-06-15 *State of Israel* v. *Alian* (June 16, 2016), ¶ 12 of justice Carmel's opinion.

[11] See, e.g., MilA 14/01 *Military Prosecutor* v. *Abu-Hamad* (April 3, 2001); MilA 63/02; MilA 128/02 *Kudsi* v. *Military Prosecutor* (December 23, 2002); MilA 1553/07 *Karini* v. *Military Prosecutor* (November 21, 2007).

does not formally apply. On the one hand, military judgments have repeatedly maintained that, being "on the verge of adulthood," this age group deserves no such mitigation.[12] On the other hand, some of the military judgments analyzed later in this chapter will show judges applying the youth consideration to 16- and 17-year-olds.

Moreover, the military judiciary has occasionally gone a significant step further, by refusing to treat youth as a mitigating factor and deeming it an aggravating factor instead. Harsh treatment, judgments have argued, is necessary precisely because – not in spite – of young Palestinians' age. Such refusal to treat youth with leniency can be found in a judgment dating back to July 1967 – only a month after Israel's military conquest and more than a decade before the youth consideration was enshrined in military legislation. Military judge Abraham Pachter held the defendant's youth to be an aggravating factor, and reasoned that this would deter other young Palestinians from involvement in armed offenses. "Regarding the punishment of criminal terrorist activity involving the use of weapons, the defendants' young age works against them," he maintained, explaining that "for such roles and purposes youth are the best suited, and when they hold weapons to realize their intents they should be punished severely to prevent other same-age youth from being tempted by such adventures."[13] For this Israeli judge, Palestinian youth were harnessing their young age – and its emblem of innocence – in the service of terrorism. Their actions were, in this view, like Trojan horses of sorts, using their youth to undermine the rationale for youth-based leniency.

More than three-and-a-half decades later, in 2003, a similar position appeared in a decision by military judge Ori Egoz. Despite conceding that young age was, in principle, a mitigating factor, she stressed that, according to rulings by the military court of appeals, "the age consideration is an aggravating circumstance where minors are sent to perform missions precisely due to their [young] age, to prevent a stricter punishment being imposed on ... [their] sender should he take action [rather than recruiting them]." Egoz further warned: "Adopting a lenient

---

[12] See, e.g., MilA 1109/13 *John Doe v. Military Prosecution* (March 10, 2013); MilA 1854/12 *Military Prosecution v. Hajajle* (May 19, 2012).

[13] MilC (Nablus) 331/68 *Military Prosecutor v. Abd al-Mussa* (1968) – an abstract of the ruling appears in 1970(1) MPD 252–53. Some information on the case is unknown, since the only two publicly available documents are a court decision (regarding a defendant over the age of majority) and a summary of the judgment.

punitive approach might lead to the opposite of the desired result, encouraging the use of minors to harm public order and security. Young age cannot grant immunity to deterrent punishments ... [The] court is obligated to contribute to eliminating this phenomenon."[14]

Akin to other judges' previously mentioned depiction of certain offenses as endemic, Egoz justified her stance by supposing there to be an epidemic of Palestinians instrumentally utilizing their young for terrorist purposes. Harking back to the 1987–93 Intifada, she claimed that such use of "young children and youth spread during the violent rampages in the early 90s, when children were being sent to throw stones and Molotov cocktails and to partake in violent disorderly conducts." This, according to Egoz, was not merely a past event, but an ongoing issue: "Unfortunately, the circumstances of the case before us demonstrate that a similar negative phenomenon might also spread nowadays, though through much graver crimes."[15]

The following year, another military judge, Yoram Hani'el, adopted a similar stance:

> [E]xperience shows that the appellant's young age has a twofold consequence. On the one hand, we take his age into consideration ... However, on the other hand, his age also has an aggravating consequence, as it has become clear, time and again, that there is a directing hand in minors being sent by adults to actions that endanger their lives and the lives of others. Their objective is to receive a light sentence owing to the[ir] young age.[16]

Thus, while all three judges advocated treating youth as an aggravating factor in the interest of deterrence, they differed in their target audiences. For Pachter, the aim was to deter "other young people," whose transgressions he regarded as designed to "realize their [own] intents." Judges Egoz and Hani'el, in contrast, characterized young Palestinians not as active agents in their own right but, rather, as mere pawns. For both Egoz and Hani'el, the target was, therefore, older Palestinians,[17] whom they accused of taking advantage of law's expected leniency toward the young.

---

[14] MilC (Judea) 3900/03 *Military Prosecutor* v. *A-Nasirat* (November 17, 2003).

[15] Ibid.

[16] MilA 30/04 *Satita* v. *Military Prosecutor* (October 13, 2004).

[17] The military court of appeal, in its decision regarding Egoz's ruling, remarked: "the inclusion of minors in such offenses should indeed be discouraged, ... such deterrence should be achieved through punishing those *adults* who exploit minors in their activity, as harshly as possible." MilA 358/03 *A-Nasirat* v. *Military Prosecutor* (December 18, 2003) (emphasis in original).

Reverberating in the judgments of Egoz and Hani'el are two long-lived Israeli traditions. The first is the allegation that Palestinians ill-serve or even weaponize their young. Golda Meir, Israel's prime minister from 1969 to 1974, has thus been quoted as saying: "Peace will come when the Arabs will love their children more than they hate us."[18] More recently, prime minister Benjamin Netanyahu contended that, while "Israel facilitates the entry of humanitarian aid into Gaza, ... Hamas ... robs Palestinian children of that very aid."[19] Similarly, as detailed in Chapter 7, Israeli officials have accused Palestinians of hiding behind their young during combat, though it is Israel's soldiers who have repeatedly used Palestinians under the age of 18 as human shields. More than simply revisiting such allegations, military judges Egoz and Hani'el translated them into law in the form of an aggravating sentencing factor. Egoz's judgment reads:

> I am not happy to [make] this harsh assertion, from which derives reducing the relative weight that should be given to the offender's young age, however the current state of affairs in the region and the worry of an increase in such crimes make this assertion inescapable.[20]

The second tradition echoing in these rulings is Israel's attempt to discipline, utilize, or deter older Palestinians through their young. As early as the late 1970s, an Israeli human rights lawyer accused the military of exploiting arrests of Palestinian teenagers to pressure their parents into becoming informants.[21] In 1988, a year into the Intifada, a new military order authorized the imposition of financial sanctions on Palestinian parents based on the mere suspicion of their child's wrongdoing. A parent unable to pay could face a year's imprisonment.[22]

---

[18] Another saying attributed to Meir is: "When peace comes, we will perhaps in time be able to forgive the Arabs for killing our sons, but it will be harder for us to forgive them for having forced us to kill their sons." For both quotations, see G. Meir, *A Land of Our Own: An Oral Autobiography* (M. Syrkin ed., New York: Putnam, 1973), p. 242.

[19] Times of Israel Staff, "Netanyahu: I Care More about Palestinians Than Their Leaders Do," *Times of Israel* (August 11, 2016), www.timesofisrael.com/netanyahu-claims-to-care-more-about-palestinians-than-their-leaders/.

[20] MilC 3900/03.

[21] L. Tzemel, "Detention of Palestinian Youths in East Jerusalem" (1977) 6:2 *Journal of Palestine Studies* 206, 206.

[22] Articles 2, 5 of the Order Concerning Supervision Over Minors' Behavior (Imposition of Financial Guarantees) (Temporary Order) (Judea and Samaria) (No. 1235), 1988 [hereinafter: Order 1235].

Through this statute, Israel obtained millions of shekels from Palestinian parents, according to the military advocate general at the time.[23] The order was upheld by the supreme court in 1991,[24] but after the Intifada it was no longer considered necessary and was hence revoked. Currently, the military law authorizes only the imposition of "financial guarantees" on parents following their child's actual conviction.[25] Nonetheless, in 2014, this measure was revived in East Jerusalem, where Israel applies its non-military law.[26] The following year, another amendment to the non-military law denied state benefits to parents of youth convicted of "security offenses"[27] (a term encompassing most charges against young noncitizen Palestinians, as explained in the previous chapter). This practice – modeling non-military laws after military laws – was touched on in the previous chapter, and I will delve deeper into it in this chapter and the next. Somewhat similarly, house demolitions have been applied to Palestinian families on account of their children's involvement in terrorist attacks,[28] a practice approved by the supreme court in 2019.[29] In Chapter 6, I examine comparable examples, in which Israeli troops posted notices in the West Bank threatening Palestinian parents with punishments if their children violate Israeli law.

[23] A. Strashnov, *Justice Under Fire* (Tel Aviv: Yedioth Ahronoth, 1994), p. 34 [Hebrew].

[24] HCJ 591/88 *Taha* v. *Minister of Defense* (1991) 45(2) PD 45.

[25] Article 177 of Order 1651.

[26] N. Hasson, "Prosecution Imposes Fines on Rioters' Parents," *Haaretz* (October 31, 2014) [Hebrew], www.haaretz.co.il/news/politics/.premium-1.2472769.

[27] Article 3 of Penal Code (Amendment No. 120 and Temporary Order), 2015. At the time of writing, a petition against this amendment is pending before the supreme court: petition in HCJ 3390/16 *Adalah* v. *Knesset* (April 21, 2016) [Hebrew], www.adalah.org/uploads/Children_Allowances_Sawsan_April_2016.pdf.

[28] See, e.g., Channel 2 News, "IDF Preparing for House Demolition of Two Minor Terrorists," *Channel 2 News* (December 15, 2015) [Hebrew], www.mako.co.il/news-military/security-q4_2015/Article-4855ea03d54a151004.htm. On Israel's house demolitions practice generally, see M. Sfard, "House Demolitions," in O. Ben-Naftali, M. Sfard, and H. Viterbo, *The ABC of the OPT: A Legal Lexicon of the Israeli Control over the Occupied Palestinian Territory* (Cambridge and New York: Cambridge University Press, 2018), pp. 162–81.

[29] HCJ 8886/18 *Jabareen* v. *Military Commander in West Bank Area* (January 10, 2019). At the same time, two recent rulings held that a Palestinian mother may not be deported merely based on suspicion that her child committed a terrorist attack. AdminA (Jer. Dist.) 11930-07-18 *State of Israel* v. *Hatib* (January 3, 2019); AdminA (Jer. Dist.) 13708-03-20 *Hatib* v. *State of Israel* (July 8, 2020).

3.2.2   The Appearance of Age

Appearance, and apparent age specifically, heavily influence how society treats and judges its members.[30] Nevertheless, when it comes to age-based legal entitlements, the dominant belief (at least in societies with institutionalized birth registration) is that only chronological age, rather than apparent physical age, should be of relevance. As a case in point, whether one is legally a "minor" or an "adult" is normally seen as solely a matter of chronological age. Similarly, criminal responsibility is meant to be determined by a person's chronological age; hence, people under the age of criminal responsibility who are arrested merely because the arresting officer perceives them as older are unlikely to face prosecution.[31] It is mostly where chronological age is deemed unascertainable that physiology may come to bear on one's age-based status. For example, if asylum seekers without birth documentation self-identify as children, they are subjected to age assessment tests, in which their bodies serve as evidence of their supposedly "real" age.[32] Another example concerns suspected pedophilic pornography, in which the ages of those appearing in it, absent chronological information, are gauged by experts based on physical appearance.[33]

So far, I have shown the Israeli military courts to be inconsistent on two issues: first, the weight to be given to defendants' youth, and, second, whether youth is a mitigating factor at all. But my research reveals that the elusiveness of the youth consideration goes further. On a number of occasions, Israel's courts have defied the prevailing notion that physical appearance carries no legal bearing on determining age-based entitlements. They have done so even when there was no doubt over the young Palestinian's date of birth, and even when they deemed the apparent age different from, rather than evidence of, the chronological one.

---

[30] See, e.g., R. Ward and C. Hollad, "'If I Look Old, I Will Be Treated Old': Hair and Later-Life Image Dilemmas" (2011) 31:2 *Ageing & Society* 288; L. Amoore and M. de Goede, "Transactions After 9/11: The Banal Face of the Preemptive Strike" (2008) 33:2 *Transactions of the Institute of British Geographers* 173.

[31] An example outside Israel/Palestine is A. Travis, "More than 1,000 Children Under 10 Stopped and Searched in Five Years," *The Guardian* (July 1, 2014), www.theguardian.com/law/2014/jul/01/children-under-10-stop-search-police.

[32] P. Hopkins and M. Hill, "Contested Bodies of Asylum-Seeking Children," in K. Hörschelmann and R. Colls (eds.), *Contested Bodies of Childhood and Youth* (Basingstoke and New York: Palgrave Macmillan, 2010), pp. 141–44.

[33] C. Cattaneo et al., "The Difficult Issue of Age Assessment on Pedo-Pornographic Material" (2009) 183:1–3 *Forensic Science International* 21.

Citing among their considerations the young appearance of the defendants, judges have justified imposing sentences shorter than those requested by the military prosecution, or even shorter than the parties' plea bargain. One such judgment reached this conclusion while describing the defendant as "13+ years old, but physically he looks no older than 9 years."[34] Another, concerning a Palestinian aged 15 years at the time of his arrest, reads: "The defendant came across to me as genuinely remorseful, an impression intensified by his being a young child who, judging by his exterior appearance, looks much younger than his age, and is short, weak and undeveloped."[35] Though the military court of appeals later overturned both decisions and issued harsher sentences, it embraced the lower courts' remarks on the defendants' young appearance. In relation to the latter case especially, the appeals judge commented: "I too have been able to observe the appellee, and I must concur with the lower court's conclusions about his level of physical and mental development."[36] Yet another judgment likewise reads: "before me stands a defendant who has not yet turned 16 years old (and it should be noted that his appearance is even younger) ... In such a case, prolonged incarceration ... is likely to gravely harm his rehabilitation chances and, consequently, the public interest as well."[37] In addition to justifying shorter sentences, it has sometimes been held that a defendant's young appearance warrants, under certain restrictions, release from detention. One defendant was thus described by the court as "a 14 year old minor, of a minor body size, whom detention ... will not benefit to say the least,"[38] while another was said to be "under the age of 15, whose looks and appearance testify to his young age."[39]

Judicial remarks such as these – "his appearance is even younger" or "[he] looks much younger than his age" – demonstrate the power of childhood bodies to rival chronological age in influencing judicial sentencing. Childhood bodies offer the court a means to pronounce the defendant's "true" age based on notions of "normal" bodily development.

---

[34] MilC (Judea) 1506/06 *Military Advocate General v. Sabih* (February 14, 2006).

[35] MilC (Judea) 4668/06 *Military Prosecutor v. Halaf* (December 27, 2006).

[36] MilA 1350/07 *Military Prosecutor v. Halaf* (February 25, 2007). In the former case, the military court of appeals judge mentioned, uncritically, that "the first court reached ... [its] conclusion in reference to the ... [defendant's] exterior looks." MilC 1413/06.

[37] MilA 1261/09 *Military Prosecution v. al-Farukh* (February 23, 2009).

[38] MilC (Judea) 4380/08 *Military Prosecutor v. Hawajah* (September 16, 2008).

[39] MilA 1307/10 *Barakan v. Military Prosecution* (2010).

I use the phrase "childhood bodies"[40] here, as opposed to "children's bodies," to indicate how, by influencing the legal status or entitlements of a person classified as a child, it is the body that "owns" the so-called child, to an extent, rather than merely the other way around. Further, this phrase also highlights the complex power relations whereby the judicial gaze establishes the bodies in question as its ready-made visual evidence and thus, in a sense, as its property. Justice, as much as it is expected to be seen, also appears to need to see its subjects. Here, its gaze is largely through developmentalist eyes, representing society's broader desire to observe childhood bodies as bodies of evidence.[41]

Two additional judgments, both given by military court of appeals judge Moshe Tirosh on the same day in 2003, throw the judicial specta-torship of childhood bodies into sharp relief. On both occasions, Tirosh dismissed (either fully or partly) the military prosecution's appeals to increase the sentences of Gazan youth convicted of illegally entering Israel. In the first case, Tirosh decided to leave unchanged the prison sentence and the fine imposed by the lower court (while increasing the suspended sentence). He explained his decision as follows: "the court's eyes are in its head, and it can see before it three mere children, and despite the light moustache above their upper lip, their mother's milk has yet to dry upon their lips." Indeed, it is largely the "court's eyes" that, by weighing competing bodily markers of age, determine the defendants' true age. To this end, Tirosh appealed to developmental theory (as he understood it): "We would not be introducing any innovation to devel-opmental theory by saying that no 15- or 16-year-old is identical to another 15- or 16-year-old. At this age, some are adults and some still children. The appellees before us belong to the latter group." Having relied on developmental ideas in his inspection of the defendants' appearance, Tirosh concluded: "It could be said, jokingly, that they [the defendants] are not appellees, but rather mini-appellees ... [They are]

---

[40] This term is borrowed from A. Prout, "Childhood Bodies: Construction, Agency and Hybridity," in A. Prout (ed.), *The Body, Childhood and Society* (London: MacMillan Press, 2000), pp. 1–18.

[41] "Bodies of evidence" is a paraphrase of H. D'cruz, "The Social Construction of Child Maltreatment: The Role of Medical Practitioners" (2004) 4:1 *Journal of Social Work* 99, 105. On another type of gaze – Israeli authorities and their human rights critics alike capturing young Palestinians on camera and, subsequently, arguing over these visual materials – see Chapter 6, Sections 6.1 ("Introduction") and 6.2 ("The Visibility of State Violence").

not merely formally minors, but evidently immature."[42]

Later that day, the second case was heard. The defense attorney – the same one that represented the former defendant – cited Tirosh's earlier decision and reasoned: "I have nothing to add to what His Honor noted in that verdict. These youths appear smaller than their real age. The court described this eloquently ... The prison sentence imposed [on the defendants is appropriate] ... especially in light of ... [their] age [and] body structure."[43] Tirosh, dismissing the prosecution's appeal, concurred:

> Formally, the appellees are adults under the [military] law ... Nevertheless, the court is under the impression that their adulthood is but formal ... We find no reason to change the [lower court's] decision ..., given the required balance between the security of the area [i.e., the West Bank and Gaza Strip] and these appellees' age and physical and mental maturity, as they appeared to the [lower] court.[44]

Far from being exclusive to the military courts, such reasoning can be found in non-military Israeli judgments as well. As a case in point, a 2015 judgment concerning a 16-year-old noncitizen Palestinian from East Jerusalem notes: "A mitigating consideration is the fact of his being a minor ... The Probation Service observed in its assessment that the defendant appears younger than his age. This is indeed apparent, and such has also been the court's impression during the hearings."[45] As shown throughout this book, this is but one of many commonalities and parallels between Israel's military and non-military laws in relation to handling noncitizen Palestinians.

Whereas all these judgments illustrate the mitigating potential of young appearance, others, conversely, treat mature appearance as an aggravating factor. In one case, involving a Palestinian aged 17 years at the time of offending, the military court of appeals held that "the appellant's young age cannot justify a substantial reduction of his punishment, as he is ... a person who ... given his looks, should have understood well the severe consequences of his acts."[46]

---

[42] MilA 66/03 *Military Prosecutor* v. *Abu Safra* (July 28, 2003).

[43] MilA 65/03 *Military Prosecutor* v. *Abu Hagayar* (July 28, 2003).

[44] Ibid.

[45] CrimC (Jer. Dist.) 40049-05-15 *State of Israel* v. *John Doe* (November 3, 2015), ¶ 23 of judge Marzel's opinion.

[46] MilA 149/02 *Harbawi* v. *Military Prosecutor* (August 22, 2002).

At the same time, in a manner similar to its inconsistent treatment of chronological youth, the military judiciary has sometimes held young appearance to be an aggravating rather than mitigating factor. Judge Menashe Vahnish of the Bet El military court once invoked an 18-year-old Palestinian's young appearance as a basis for extending his detention pending disposition. A young-looking person, Vahnish ruled, was especially vulnerable to unwanted Palestinian influences outside Israeli custody. In his own interest, therefore, he ought to be kept in detention: "according to the evidence and a visual observation of the defendant's face, he is a young youth in his adolescence who appears to be influenced by others ... [R]eleasing him [from detention] ... might return him to the influence of those people."[47] Throughout the next three chapters, I bring to light similar instances of disempowerment, persecution, and domination being dressed as child protection.

3.2.3 Age Categorization: Origins and Judicial Inconsistency

Three months into its rule over the West Bank and Gaza Strip, the Israeli military enacted the Order Concerning the Adjudication of Young Offenders.[48] Deployed in this piece of military legislation was a developmentalist age classification that remains in force to this day.[49] It comprises three categories, two of which – "youth" (encompassing 12–13-year-olds) and "tender adult" (aged 14–15) – are accompanied by maximum sentence limits of six months and a year respectively (no limit exists for 16–17-year-olds, who constitute the majority of imprisoned Palestinian "minors"). Crucially, these statutory limits apply not to a defendant's age when breaking the law, but to how old they are at the moment of sentencing.[50] This results in a race against time: the longer the trial, the older the defendant. In my qualitative analysis of 155 military judgments involving under-18s, proceedings averaged 3.2 months in length, but some stretched beyond a year. As time passes, some defendants inevitably lose their "youth" or "tender adult" status and, consequently, are stripped of the maximum sentence limit

---

[47] MilC (Bet-El) 1173/03 *Military Prosecutor v. Sha'alan* (2003).
[48] Order Concerning the Adjudication of Young Offenders (West Bank Area) (No.132), 1967 [hereinafter: Order 132]. It was later incorporated into Order 1651.
[49] Article 1 of Order 132, currently codified as Article 1 of Order 1651.
[50] Articles 168(b) and 168(c), respectively, of Order 1651.

previously afforded to them. Indeed, some of those whose court cases I have analyzed experienced precisely this loss of status.[51]

The third category – "child" (defined as anyone aged under 12) – formally shields those who belong to it from both detention and prosecution.[52] In practice, Israeli forces have arrested numerous Palestinians as young as five without trying to ascertain their age,[53] and entire families with toddlers as young as two have been detained overnight.[54] In 2019, soldiers were also caught on camera disregarding pleas not to arrest an underage Palestinian on the grounds that "it doesn't matter what age [he is], he threw stones."[55]

Like other colonized territories (such as Pakistan, Malaysia,[56] and Cyprus[57]), Israel/Palestine inherited these age categories from British colonial law. With its establishment in 1948, Israel adopted all British Mandate law, including the Emergency Regulations, which have remained in force to maintain a never-ending state of emergency, as well as the Prison Ordinance, which became the country's key statute regarding incarceration.[58] Also absorbed into Israeli law was British

---

[51] See, e.g., MilC (Judea) 4407/03 *Military Prosecutor v. Harfush* (2004); MilC (Hebron) 1091/02 *Military Prosecutor v. Janam* (2003).

[52] Article 2 of Order 132, currently codified as Article 201 of Order 1651. The criminal impunity of under-12s was also enshrined in Article 4 of the Order Concerning Rules of Criminal Responsibility (Judea and Samaria) (No. 225), 1968.

[53] See, e.g., B'Tselem, "Video Footage: Soldiers Detain Palestinian Five-Year-Old in Hebron" (July 11, 2013), www.btselem.org/press_releases/20130711_soldiers_detain_5_year_old_in_hebron; B'Tselem, "Israeli Border Police Seize 6-Year-Old in Hebron, Drag Him to a Checkpoint, and Hold Him for an Hour" (December 12, 2018), www.btselem.org/video/20181212_border_police_detain_boy_aged_6_in_hebron.

[54] N. Hasson, "Palestinian Family Taken into Custody, Two-year-old Toddler Spends Four Hours in Jail," *Haaretz* (March 1, 2016), www.haaretz.com/israel-news/.premium-1.706354.

[55] M. Rapoport, "WATCH: Israeli Soldiers Break into Palestinian School, Arrest 10-Year-Old," *+972 Magazine* (March 21, 2019), https://972mag.com/israeli-soldiers-arrest-palestinian-child-in-school/140655.

[56] See, respectively, the term "youthful offender" in the Sindh Children Act, 1955; the Sharia Criminal Procedure (Federal Territories) Act, 1984. On these statutes, see N. Abiad ad F. Z. Mansoor, *Criminal Law and the Rights of the Child in Muslim States: A Comparative and Analytical Perspective* (London: British Institute of International and Comparative Law, 2010), pp. 63, 233–34.

[57] See the terms "child" (under 14 years) and "young adult" (14–15 years) in the Criminal Code of Cyprus (Juveniles Act, Cap. 157). On this statute, see A. Kapardis, "Juvenile delinquency and justice in Cyprus," in A. C. Baldry and A. Kapardis (eds.), *Risk Assessment for Juvenile Violent Offending* (Abingdon: Routledge, 2013), pp. 43, 49.

[58] See, respectively, Article 11 of the Governance and Law Organization Ordinance, 1948; Prison Ordinance [New Version], 1971.

legislation relating to "juvenile delinquency." The latter body of law introduced the youth court system to Palestine, alongside an array of regulations both for rehabilitating young people in trouble with the law and for dealing with deserted and "wayward" young individuals, thereby making Palestine the Empire's first territory with a probation system.[59]

Key among the local British legislation on youth offending was the Juvenile Offenders Ordinance. Enacted in 1922 and thoroughly amended in 1937, it divided "juvenile offenders" into the three subcategories that would later appear in Israel's military law, but with higher age thresholds: "child" (defined at the time as anyone aged under 14), "youth" (14–15-year-olds), and "tender adult" (16–17-year-olds).[60] These are literal translations of the categories in the Hebrew version of the ordinance, whereas the English version employed the terminology "child," "young person," and "juvenile adult" respectively. This age categorization resembled those deployed elsewhere in the British Empire: in India, for instance, the only difference was the use of the term "youthful offender" instead of "juvenile adult."[61] The law in Britain itself, in contrast, used only the two categories "child" and "young person," both of which were initially defined as in Palestine,[62] although the latter category was eventually extended to 16–17-year-olds[63] (who in Palestine were classified separately as "juvenile adults"). This disparity did not go unnoticed by the Executive Council of the British Government in Palestine, which nonetheless rejected a suggestion to adopt the categorization used in Britain.[64]

Israel's military law, as I have noted, conspicuously sets all three categories two years lower than the British Mandate legislation. For

---

[59] M. Ajzenstadt, "Constructing Juvenile Delinquency: The Socio-Legal Control of Young Offenders in Israel, 1920–1975," in A. Jokinen, K. Juhila, and T. Pösö (eds.), *Constructing Social Work Practices* (Hampshire: Ashgate Publishing, 1999), pp. 196–97; T. Razi, *Forsaken Children: The Backyard of Mandate Tel-Aviv* (Tel Aviv: Am Oved, 2009), pp. 219–20 [Hebrew].

[60] Article 2 of Juvenile Offenders Ordinance, 1937.

[61] Article 3 of the Madras Children Act, 1920; Article 3 of the Tamil Nadu Children Act, 1920; Section 3 of the Bengal Children Act, 1922; Article 3 of the Bombay Children Act, 1924.

[62] Article 131 of the Children and Young Persons Act (1908). Previously, the term "young person" applied, more broadly, to those aged 12–15 years: Article 48 of the Summary Jurisdiction Act (1897); Article 11 of the Youthful Offenders Act (1901).

[63] Article 107 of the Children and Young Persons Act (1933).

[64] Executive Council Held at the Government Offices, *Minutes of the 605th Meeting held at Jerusalem, on the 5th January, 1937 – art. 31, in* Government of Palestine – Executive Council Decisions (1937).

instance, the threshold between "child" and "youth" is only 12 years in the military law, as compared with 14 years under British Mandate law. My attempts to trace the reasoning for this change in the Israeli military archive bore no fruit. Nonetheless, the consequence of redrawing the statutory age lines is clear: it has facilitated harsher treatment of Palestinians at earlier ages.

In lowering the age thresholds, the military departed not only from pre-statehood British legislation but also from Israel's own non-military law, which until 1971 kept the original thresholds unchanged. This legalized discrimination is analogous to nineteenth-century Australia's minimum ages for removing young people from their parents, which were similarly set lower for young Indigenous people than for others.[65] In the next Chapter, I consider other parallels with settler–colonial[66] laws and policies, and in Chapter 8 I elaborate on Israel's ethnically and nationally differentiated law.

In 1971, Israel's non-military law replaced the three subcategories "child," "youth," and "tender adult" with a wider one: "minor," denoting all under-18s.[67] Military statutes, in contrast, offered no such overarching definition of "minor" for more than four decades. Only in a single context – release on bail – was the term used (since 1975) in reference to defendants aged 12–17.[68] For other purposes, the statutory military law applied the three subcategories, extending up to the age of 16 rather than 18. This, as I will now demonstrate, has had two consequences: first,

---

[65] See S. Swain, "Enshrined in Law: Legislative Justifications for the Removal of Indigenous and Non-Indigenous Children in Colonial and Post-Colonial Australia" (2016) 47 *Australian Historical Studies* 191, 196. On race-specific legislation in this context, see also ibid., pp. 200–01, 203–06.

[66] On the different meanings attributed to "settler colonialism," and how some conceptualizations can contribute to analyses of Israel/Palestine, see H. Viterbo, "Ties of Separation: Analogy and Generational Segregation in North America, Australia, and Israel/Palestine" (2017) 42:2 *Brooklyn Journal of International Law* 686, 731–39.

[67] The change was explicated in the 1970 Bill. See Youth Law (Adjudication, Punishment, and Modes of Treatment) draft, 1969, in *Government Bills*, vol. 825, p. 160 [Hebrew], https://fs.knesset.gov.il//6/law/6_ls1_289838.PDF. Only two statutes, concerning acquisition of evidence and police regulations respectively, define "children" as under-14s: Article 1 of the Law to Amend the Rules of Evidence (Protection of Children) 1955; Article 1 of the Police General Commissioner Ordinance No. 14.01.05 Concerning Police Handling of Minors, November 29, 2004.

[68] Article 181(a) of Order 1651. This provision was originally anchored in Article 7a(e) of the Order 132. A different definition temporarily appeared in a military order that was eventually annulled: "anyone who cannot be criminally prosecuted due to his age." Article 1 of Order 1235.

a discrepancy between military statute and judicial practice; and second, a misrepresentation of the military law by human rights critics, due to their unawareness of this discrepancy.

According to human rights organizations, the absence of a statutory definition of "minor," combined with the use of age subcategories for under-16s, set the age of majority for Palestinians under Israel's military law at 16.[69] This claim, which presumed conformity between judicial practice and military statute, was in fact inaccurate. My analysis finds that, absent a statutory definition, military judgments actually provided two competing definitions of "minor." While some indeed defined it as referring to Palestinians under 16,[70] numerous others classified and referred to older Palestinians – aged 16[71] and 17[72] – as minors. A 2003 military court of appeals judgment, for example, pronounced two 16-year-old defendants (at the time of offending) to be only "[f]ormally . . . adults according to the [military] law," and reiterated that "their adulthood is merely formal."[73]

In 2009, the military added an overarching definition of "minor" as anyone under 16,[74] while keeping in force the subcategories "child," "youth," and "tender adult." With the age of criminal majority now defined in military statute as 16 years, human rights organizations doubled down on their accusation that Israel set it two years lower for Palestinians than for Israelis.[75] Given the military's introduction of a

---

[69] See, e.g., Save the Children – Sweden, *Briefing Papers on the Situation and Rights of Palestinian Children in the Occupied Palestinian Territories* UN Commission on Human Rights (2005).

[70] See, e.g., MilA 2651/09 *Military Prosecution* v. *Hasnia* (July 22, 2009) (stressing that a 16-year-old is not legally a "minor"). There are many similar rulings.

[71] Representative examples are: MilC 1655/08 *Military Prosecution* v. *Jadallah* (April 30, 2008); MilA 1442/09 *Al-Kuwasma* v. *Military Prosecution* (February 25, 2009).

[72] Representative examples are: MilC (Samaria) 4080/08 *Military Prosecution* v. *Adwan* (2008); MilC (Judea) 4635/08 *Military Prosecution* v. *Abiat* (June 1, 2009).

[73] MilA 65/03.

[74] Article 1 of the Order Concerning Security Provisions (Temporary Order) (Amendment No. 109) (Judea and Samaria) (No. 1644), 2009.

[75] See, e.g., UNCRC, Consideration of Reports Submitted by States Parties Under Article 8 of the Optional Protocol to the CRC on the Involvement of Children in Armed Conflict – Concluding Observations: Israel, CRC/C/OPAC/ISR/CO/1 (January 29, 2010), ¶ 8, www2.ohchr.org/english/bodies/crc/docs/CRC-C-OPAC-ISR-CO-1.pdf; UNCAT, Consideration of Report Submitted by States Parties Under Article 19 of the Convention – Israel: Concluding Observations, UN Doc CAT/C/ISR/CO/4 (May 14, 2009), ¶ 27, www2.ohchr.org/english/bodies/cat/docs/cobs/CAT.C.ISR.CO.4.pdf; Yesh Din and ACRI, "Adequate Protection for Palestinian Minors Tried in Military Courts" (June 16, 2010), ¶¶ 9–10, 18–26, 28 [Hebrew], https://law.acri.org.il/he/2511.

statutory definition of "minor," one might assume that at this point human rights critics finally represented the situation accurately.

However, my findings suggest that the military judiciary's inconsistency persisted, with some judgments still labeling 16–17-year-olds – unequivocally adults under the statutory definition – as minors.[76] One representative case thus saw the military court of appeals describe a defendant aged 16 at the time of the alleged offenses as "a minor when committing the offenses."[77] Judges classifying Palestinians aged 16 and 17 as "minors" may have been influenced by Israel's non-military law. Such influence was acknowledged in some judgments, such as one in 2009 by the military court of appeals: "*a minor is a minor is a minor*, whether he lives where [the non-military] Israeli law fully applies to him, or elsewhere [namely, in the West Bank], where [the non-military] Israeli law indeed does not fully apply but there is a real influence of the [non-military] Israeli legal system."[78] Another judgment supporting such influence rightly noted that all military judges and lawyers, having received their legal education in Israel, are versed in the non-military law.[79] Though connections and mutual influences between Israel's two legal systems indeed exist, and are discussed in Chapter 4,[80] their precise nature and strength are sometimes vague, as evidenced by the military judiciary's inconsistency about whether to adopt the non-military law's definition of "minor."

This long-lived inconsistency in the meaning of "minor" is in some respects representative of, and in others dissimilar to, the military courts' record on the issues examined so far in his chapter. On the one hand, it represents the broader pattern of judicial inconsistency in applying and interpreting military statutes. On the other hand, contrary to most of the sentencing and remand issues I have investigated, the definition of "minor" is not formally open to judicial discretion. For instance, no precise statutory formula exists for the youth consideration, in contrast to the formally unambiguous statutory definition of "minor." There is,

---

[76] See, e.g., MilC (Samaria) 3291/09 *Military Prosecution v. John Doe* (2010); MilC (Samaria) 4770/09 *Military Prosecution v. Safadi* (2009).

[77] MilA 1528/09 *Massarwah v. Military Prosecution* (August 26, 2009).

[78] MilA 2912/09 *Military Prosecution v. Abu Rahma* (August 31, 2009) (emphasis in original). For critical discussion of this depiction of the military law as located outside Israeli law, see Chapter 1, Section 3.2 ("The West Bank, Excluding East Jerusalem").

[79] MilC (Judea) 3975/04 *Military Prosecution v. Nemer* (January 17, 2006).

[80] For broader analysis, see H. Viterbo, "Outside/Inside," in Ben-Naftali, Sfard, and Viterbo, *The ABC of the OPT*, pp. 312–24.

therefore, something particularly remarkable in the military court system's inconsistent application of an ostensibly unequivocal age category. While critics have repeatedly described Israel as violating international law, this finding makes evident a far less known yet equally consequential phenomenon: the Israeli judiciary's systematic breach of Israel's own, supposedly binding, statutes.

The inconsistency in the meaning of "minor" ended in 2011, as a statutory amendment (scrutinized in the next chapter) redefined this term to refer to under-18s, thus making it akin to the non-military law's definition. At the same time, the military judiciary's use of the other statutory age categories – "child," "youth," and "tender adult" – has been loose, thereby maintaining some degree of legal ambiguity. For example, my research found a judgment describing a 17-year-old defendant as "a tender adult" (a term formally applicable to 14–15-year-olds),[81] as well as judicial references to 14–15-year-olds (formally "tender adults") as "youth" and to 12–15-year-olds (formally "youth" or "tender adults") as "children."[82]

3.3 Vagueness, Control, and Childhood

As is by now evident, the Israeli military judiciary has shown inconsistency on a range of issues: whether and how to give weight to Palestinians' young age; whether youth is a mitigating or aggravating factor; whether and in what manner to consider defendants' young appearance; and how to define or use statutory age categories. These instances of legal inconsistency and vagueness cannot, however, be understood in isolation from their local and global contexts.

At the local level, Israel's control regime derives much of its power from constantly producing uncertainty. At the global level, ambiguity and fluidity are inherent to the legal and social construction of childhood. By contextualizing my findings locally and globally, this section challenges simplistic characterizations of Israel/Palestine either as an unparalleled exception or as a carbon copy of other political-legal regimes. Chapters 4 and 5 will develop this analysis further. On the one hand, I will link the findings of these chapters to global issues: colonial patterns,

---

[81] MilA 28/04 *Abu-A-Shabab* v. *Military Prosecutor* (July 14, 2004).
[82] For respective examples, see MilA 3647/05 *Military Advocate General* v. *Abu-Shama* (January 1, 2006); MilC (Judea) 3008/08 *Military Advocate General* v. *Alalu* (July 14, 2008).

the shortcomings of child law and children's rights, and contemporary conceptions of childhood. On the other hand, I will examine these findings in connection to local national narratives, as well as to features of the Israeli control regime: its legalism, its fragmentation of Palestinian society, its attempted confinement of Palestinian minds, and its increasingly overlapping military and non-military law.

3.3.1   Governing through Uncertainty

Legal inconsistency, ambiguity, and uncertainty have characterized Israel's rule over the West Bank and Gaza Strip since its inception. The very day the Israeli military entered these territories, it issued an order declaring the establishment of military courts that would observe the Fourth Geneva Convention,[83] the principal international treaty on belligerent occupation. The following month, the military advocate general boasted to a parliamentary committee of this statutory enshrining of the Convention.[84] But within a mere three months, the reference to the Convention was removed from the statute.[85] From then onward, Israeli governments abandoned their earlier secret strategy of "evading discussion ... of the applicability of the convention,"[86] and have instead controversially claimed not to be bound by it.[87]

Nonetheless, for two whole years following its own statutory amendment, the military continued instructing its soldiers that the Convention is binding.[88] Military judges likewise kept reasserting the Convention's applicability as well as its primacy over Israel's military law.[89] Thereafter,

---

[83] Articles 5 and 35 of the Order Concerning Security Provisions (West Bank), 1967.

[84] Constitution, Law, and Justice Committee, 6th Knesset – Transcript 126 (July 5, 1967) [Hebrew], https://fs.knesset.gov.il//6/Committees/6_ptv_425043.PDF.

[85] Articles 1, 8 of the Order Concerning Security Provisions (Amendment No. 9) (No. 144), 1967.

[86] Ministry of Foreign Affairs – Communication Department, "Classified Telegram to Israeli Embassy in Washington, D.C.," *Akevot* (March 3, 1968) [Hebrew], www.akevot .org.il/article/comay-meron-cable/.

[87] This position was articulated in Y. Z. Blum, "The Missing Reversioner: Reflections on the Status of Judea and Samaria" (1968) 3 *Israel Law Review* 279.

[88] General Staff, *Capturing Occupied Territories and Military Government* (June 1969) [Hebrew], www.akevot.org.il/article/aims-and-means-3-file-gl-17005-6-the-reordering-of-control-over-palestinian-citizens-of-israel-at-the-late-stages-of-the-military-govern ment/#popup/26e10ef6471eb29068949c449e6342cc.

[89] MilC (Ramallah) 144/68 *Military Prosecutor v. Bakis* (1968) 1970(1) MPD 371; MilC (Gaza) 1238/69 *Military Prosecutor v. Abu Janas* (1969) 1970(1) MPD 130.

the courts mostly aligned themselves with Israel's formal position.[90] However, on at least one later occasion, they exhibited further inconsistency: a 2002 military judgment held, yet again, that the customary international law of occupation – including provisions of the Geneva Convention – prevails over Israeli military law.[91] Despite the government's inapplicability claim, top military lawyers have also repeatedly cited the Convention as a legal basis for Israel's operation of military courts.[92]

Similar inconsistency has characterized the courts' enforcement of military legislation concerning protest: in determining the legality of demonstrations, some judgments have cited this legislation to the letter, whereas others have completely ignored it and imposed their own dissimilar tests instead.[93] The military judiciary has reportedly shown further inconsistency by issuing substantially different sentences for similar charges.[94] Indeed, the military court of appeals itself has admitted the inconsistency of military judgments on penalties and detention periods of young Palestinians.[95]

These inconsistencies all operate at two different levels. At the individual defendant's level, they leave open the possibility of a relatively lenient outcome. At a broader level, however, they prevent defense lawyers from predicting matters as basic as their clients' classification as minors/adults, the criteria for a demonstration's legality, the relevance of the Geneva Convention, and the range of likely sentence or detention periods. Consequently, increased uncertainty ensues.

Palestinian defendants are also likely to experience uncertainty about, and misunderstanding of, the course of their proceedings. This is not

---

[90] See, e.g., MilC (Bethlehem) 48/69 *Military Prosecutor* v. *Harufa* (1970) 1970(1) MPD 565; MilC (Bethlehem) 1114/72 *Military Prosecutor* v. *Scheinbeum* (1972) 1972(3) MPD 346, 354–57.

[91] MilC (Samaria) 5708/01 *Military Prosecutor* v. *Udda* (2002) 2002 MPD (13) 269, 277.

[92] See, e.g., N. Benichou, "Criminal Law in the Regions of Judea, Samaria, and Gaza" (2004) 18 *Law & Military* 293, 295 [Hebrew]; Z. Hadar, "The Military Courts," in M. Shamgar (ed.), *Military Government in the Territories Administered by Israel – 1967–1980: The Legal Aspects – Volume I* (Jerusalem: Hebrew University, 1982), pp. 173–75.

[93] R. Jaraisy and T. Feldman, *The Status of the Right to Demonstrate in the Occupied Territories* (ACRI, September 2014), pp. 38–39, www.acri.org.il/en/protestright/the-right-to-demonstrate.

[94] L. Hajjar, *Courting Conflict: The Israeli Military Court System in the West Bank and Gaza* (London: University of California Press, 2005), p. 256.

[95] MilA 355/03; MilA 4497/08 *Military Prosecution* v. *Hawajah* (September 25, 2008). In MilA 1261/09, the judge further described the military prosecution as inconsistent in the sentences it pursues for minors.

only due to the familiar issue of unintelligible legalese, but also for reasons detailed in the previous chapter: hearings are hasty, most Palestinian defendants speak Arabic but trials are conducted in Hebrew, and the court interpreters often lack sufficient training and are preoccupied with ensuring proper conduct in the courtroom.

Two unique uncertainties face so-called administrative detainees, whom Israel imprisons with no charge or trial. First, they are condemned to uncertainty about the alleged reasons for their incarceration. As mentioned in the previous chapter, "administrative detention" is reviewed by military judges behind closed doors, is unbound by the regular rules of evidence, and is typically based on secret materials not disclosed to the defense. Second, absent a fixed sentence, it is impossible for such incarcerated Palestinians to predict their release from prison and plan their lives accordingly. They are thus kept in a stressful cycle: hope toward each judicial review, followed by despair after each decision to extend their incarceration. Not even convicted Palestinians, serving a seemingly fixed sentence, are immune to such uncertainty: some have been placed in "administrative detention" immediately or shortly after their scheduled release, and have thus been kept behind bars with no known release date in sight.[96]

Deliberate or not, uncertainty thus operates as a mode of governance. Although not always fulfilling whatever intentions Israeli authorities may have, this mode of governing expands their discretion and the possibility of on-the-spot, flexible interpretations. Along with incarceration and military adjudication, Israel's control regime is rife with other uncertainty-inducing institutions and practices. Among them are Israel's constantly changing military legislation, the vagueness and contradictions in some guidelines of the Israeli security authorities, and the changing rules determining eligibility for permits to enter Israel or travel within the West Bank.[97]

3.3.2   Elusive Childhood

Fluidity, while feeding into Israel's uncertainty-inducing apparatus, is inherent to age and childhood. For example, judicial consideration of

---

[96] See H. Viterbo, "Security Prisoners," in Ben-Naftali, Sfard, and Viterbo, *The ABC of the OPT*, pp. 385–86.

[97] See H. Viterbo, "Military Courts," in Ben-Naftali, Sfard, and Viterbo, *The ABC of the OPT*, pp. 270–74.

young age as an aggravating rather than mitigating factor, as in Israeli military judgments, can also be found in some US supreme court rulings on the death penalty.[98] Similarly, the judicial preference to apparent age over chronological age appears in a US judgment that considered a defendant's large body as diminishing the mitigating weight of his young age.[99] Another example, to be discussed shortly, is the prosecution of legal adults for pretending to be under the age of majority, which has occurred not only in Israel/Palestine but across time and space.[100] Such legal practices reflect, inform, and, to some extent, create the broader social fluidity of childhood. Moreover, they also parallel seemingly removed social practices: for instance, the prioritization of young looks over chronological age, as found in the previously mentioned judgments, is also a key objective of practices such as plastic surgery, the digital manipulation of human images, and the application of cosmetic products.[101]

Other legal elements – at the international, regional, and national levels – further enhance childhood's fluidity. One is the coexistence of different statutory age limits for different purposes, such as drinking alcohol, driving, compulsory education, or medical consent. Another is the different definitions of the same age category (such as "youth") in different international legal documents.[102] Further, an age-based legal

[98] See T. R. Birckhead, "The Age of the Child: Interrogating Juveniles After Roper v. Simmons" (2008) 65 Washington & Lee Law Review 385, 395–406; E. F. Emens, "Aggravating Youth: Roper v. Simmons and Age Discrimination" (2006) 2005 Supreme Court Review 51, 51–52, 75.

[99] P. Williams, "Double Jeopardy," New Yorker (November 17, 2014), www.newyorker.com/magazine/2014/11/17/double-jeopardy-3.

[100] For two recent examples, see Associated Press, "Authorities Say 'Teen' Who Claimed to be Missing US Boy is 23," The Guardian (April 5, 2019), www.theguardian.com/us-news/2019/apr/04/us-police-illinois-timmothy-pitzen-teen; C. Drury, "Investigation Launched Into How Man Aged About 30 Could Be Enrolled at School as 15-Year-Old Pupil," The Independent (November 24, 2018), www.independent.co.uk/news/uk/home-news/asylum-seeker-uk-age-school-boy-ipswich-school-stoke-home-office-a8649696.html.

[101] See, e.g., M. Featherstone and M. Hepworth, "The Mask of Ageing and the Postmodern Life Course," in M. Featherstone, M. Hepworth and B. S. Turner (eds.), The Body: Social Process and Cultural Theory (London and Thousand Oaks: Sage, 1991); V. Sobchack, "Scary Women: Cinema, Surgery, and Special Effects," in K. Woodward (ed.), Figuring Age: Women, Bodies, Generations (Bloomington and Indianapolis: Indiana University Press, 1999).

[102] On the disparity in international legal definitions of "youth," see UN Department of Economic and Social Affairs, "Definition of Youth" (n.d.), www.un.org/esa/socdev/documents/youth/fact-sheets/youth-definition.pdf.

definition itself can often be loose. Such is the widely quoted definition of "child," in the UN Convention on the Rights of the Child, as "every human being below the age of 18 years unless, under the law applied to the child, majority is attained earlier."[103] The caveat – "unless ... majority is attained earlier" – renders the age threshold between childhood and adulthood flexible, while the absence of a starting age leaves the beginning of childhood unresolved.[104] The UN Standard Minimum Rules for the Administration of Juvenile Justice (commonly known as the "Havana Rules") allow for a similar country-by-country disparity in the definition of "juvenile," as does the African Union's Youth Charter in relation to the term "minor."[105] In addition, some countries extend the statutory meaning of "child" beyond the age of majority in certain contexts. Thus, UK law concerning the functions of the Children's Commissioner (a public body entrusted with promoting and protecting "children's rights") classifies some 18–24-year-olds as "children."[106]

The fluidity in question derives, in part, from the transitional nature of age and the perceived temporariness of childhood.[107] It also emanates from the multidimensionality of age – its amalgamation of chronological, physiological, apparent, performed, and other aspects, as evident throughout this chapter. In addition, it stems from competing ideas about childhood, such as perceptions of children as innocent or evil, ignorant or perceptive, at risk or risky. Further, childhood and adulthood in their modern forms, while socially constructed as two distinct opposites, constantly collapse into one another. And relatedly, the enforcement of age homogeneity takes place alongside competing processes, which increase age heterogeneity.[108] Legal children are sometimes attributed with ostensibly adult traits,[109] while some legal adults, as

---

[103] Article 1 of the CRC.
[104] J. Kuper, *International Law Concerning Child Civilians in Armed Conflict* (Oxford: Oxford University Press, 1997), pp. 8–9.
[105] See, respectively, Commentary to Rule 2.2 of GA Resolution 40/33: Standard Minimum Rules for the Administration of Juvenile Justice, UN Doc A/RES/40/33 (November 29, 1985); definitions section of African Youth Charter (adopted: July 2, 2006).
[106] Section 9 of The Children Act, 2004.
[107] See, e.g., K. Sánchez-Eppler, *Dependent States: The Child's Part in Nineteenth-Century American Culture* (Chicago and London: University of Chicago Press, 2005), pp. xxv–xxvi.
[108] See, e.g., M. W. Riley and J. W. Riley, "Age Integration: Conceptual and Historical Background" (2000) 40:3 *Gerontologist* 266, 267–68.
[109] See Jenks, *Childhood*, p. 112; G. Valentine, "Boundary Crossings: Transitions from Childhood to Adulthood" (2003) 1:1 *Children's Geographies* 37, 38.

discussed in Chapters 7 and 8, are characterized as children. Furthermore, especially since Freud, there has been considerable professional and cultural preoccupation with what is believed to be the "inner child" of every "adult."[110]

As discussed in Chapter 5, society, and the children's rights industry in particular, is rife with anxieties over the perceived disintegration, disappearance, or demise of childhood. The other side of these anxieties is the hope and supposition that, by somehow tracking down and repairing childhood, it could once again be made stable. However, against the backdrop I have outlined, the elusiveness of age and childhood in Israel/Palestine is by no means an instance of childhood or law going astray. Though the analyzed materials reveal features that are unique to the Israeli legal system, elusiveness is a defining feature of childhood and age – and also, as explained in Chapter 1, of law.

3.4 Age as a Life-and-Death Matter

So far, my focus has been on Palestinians' trials in Israeli military courts. It is within this context that I have investigated the relationship between age and childhood, and it is from this context that I drew out broader issues at both the local and global levels. And yet, a Palestinian's age has repercussions far beyond arrests, detention, and trials; it also determines who gets to live, and, for those spared death, what their lives would look like. In what follows, I focus on three areas where this is especially evident: Israel's open-fire regulations (the rules of engagement), restrictions on the entry of food into the Gaza Strip, and impediments to movement. How have each of these been articulated and interpreted? How have they been implemented and enforced? And, crucially, what roles do age and childhood – perceived, defined, and utilized as they have been – play in each of these contexts?

3.4.1 Age in Israel's Open-Fire Regulations

In its open-fire regulations, Israel lays down the rules for armed forces' use of firearms, including the permitted "targets." The military's open-fire regulations are, however, classified, and the police regulations are heavily redacted (an issue elaborated in Chapter 6). Consequently, their

---

[110] D. Kennedy, *The Well of Being: Childhood, Subjectivity, and Education* (Albany: State University of New York Press, 2006), pp. 12, 95.

precise content, including as regards young people and age, requires inference from a combination of Israeli sources. As early as 1969, the military issued guidelines to its troops with the instruction: "Do not open fire at women and children."[111] Over subsequent years, the prohibition became more age-specific. In 1984, the military's regulations forbade firing at "children (who appear to be under the age of 16)," whereas a 1990 version, reportedly published by the Israeli consulate in New York, proscribed shooting at "children under the age of 14 and women."[112] Currently, according to Israeli judgments, the open-fire regulations of both the military and the police refer to under-14s.[113]

Later, in this chapter and the next two, I will critically revisit such prioritizing (professed or actual) of those classified as children and women. My focus here, however, is on two complexities relating to the implementation of the formally conclusive age threshold of 14 years. The first is that the military and some of its officials, serving or retired, have openly licensed firing at younger Palestinians. A former brigadier commander thus remarked, in a 2018 interview, that any Palestinian in Gaza approaching the border with Israel, "even a child," must be shot dead.[114] Soldiers, serving and former, have also described witnessing actual incidents of unarmed Palestinians under 14 being shot and killed.[115] Moreover, customized shirts ordered by troops upon finishing their training courses or deployment periods have made light of shooting to kill children and women. Some shirts depicted targeted Palestinians caught in the crosshairs of a sniper's sight: an Arab woman holding a baby, with the caption "Kill them while they're young"; a pregnant Arab, with the legend in English "1 shot 2 kills"; and an armed child alongside

---

[111] Quoted in C. Levinson, "'A Letter to the Soldier in the Administered Territories' Provides a Peek into an Era of a Seemingly Proper Occupation," *Haaretz* (September 17, 2010) [Hebrew], www.haaretz.co.il/news/education/1.1221600.

[112] Quoted, respectively, in S. Gazit, *Trapped Fools: Thirty Years of Israeli Policy in the Territories* (London: Frank Cass Publishers, 2003), pp. 349–53; R. Talmor, *Shooting by Israeli Security Forces in the Territories* (Jerusalem: B'Tselem, July 1990), pp. 10–14 [Hebrew], www.btselem.org/sites/default/files2/ptykhh_bsh_l_ydy_kvkhvt_hbytkhvn_bshtkhym.pdf.

[113] See, regarding the military and police respectively, CMC (South) 400/04 *Military Prosecutor* v. *Captain R* (November 15, 2005), ¶ j(2); CivA 5604/94 *Hammed* v. *State of Israel* (2004) 58(2) PD 498, ¶¶ 19–20 of Chief Justice Barak's leading opinion.

[114] A. Abunimah, "Snipers Ordered to Shoot Children, Israeli General Confirms," *Electronic Intifada* (April 22, 2018), https://electronicintifada.net/blogs/ali-abunimah/snipers-ordered-shoot-children-israeli-general-confirms.

[115] See, e.g., the quote in A. Gvaryahu, "The Real Open-Fire Procedure," *Haaretz* (January 23, 2013) [Hebrew], www.haaretz.co.il/opinions/1.1913427.

the message "The smaller, the harder."[116] The second complexity is that, insofar as age does curb Israelis from firing at Palestinians, what matters is not chronological age but physical age, as perceived by the potential shooters. "Sometimes it's really difficult to tell [a Palestinian's age]," a former Israeli sniper said in 2020, adding: "You look at facial features, height, and mass. Clothing also provides some indication."[117]

Throwing both issues into sharp relief is the high-profile killing of the Palestinian girl Iman al-Hams near the southern border of the Gaza Strip in 2004. After al-Hams was injured by Israeli fire, the commander of the firing force, Captain R (as the courts and media would refer to him), shot her again at close range; later, he was accused by several of his subordinates of doing so to ensure she was dead.[118] He was brought to trial before a court-martial but, instead of being charged with homicide, faced more minor charges:[119] unlawful use of weapon, conduct unbecoming, obstruction of justice, and, lastly, breaching the open-fire regulations by instructing his subordinates, shortly after the killing, to fatally shoot "even a three-year-old" approaching the area.

The three-judge court-martial unanimously cleared Captain R of all charges. The judges accepted his argument that his instruction to kill "even a three-year-old" was neither meant nor taken literally, and therefore did not breach the open-fire regulations.[120] Among the mitigating circumstances described at length in the judgment are inadequacies and flaws in the military investigation into the matter. This line of argument – that Israel's own investigative flaws absolve soldiers who shoot and kill Palestinians – has been put forward in other judgments, as I show in Chapter 6. The judgment also mentions the defendant's claim to have "exhibited sensitivity toward the local [Palestinian] population" prior to the incident, "especially toward minors," noting that "one time he was even photographed handing candy to minors whose homes were about to

---

[116] U. Blau, "Dead Palestinian Babies and Bombed Mosques – IDF Fashion 2009," *Haaretz* (March 19, 2009), www.haaretz.com/1.5090720.

[117] H. Glazer, "You Sent Us to Fire Live Ammunition at 8,211 Protestors. Now Listen to Us," *Haaretz* (March 4, 2020) [Hebrew], www.haaretz.co.il/magazine/.premium-MAGAZINE-1.8625943.

[118] CMC 400/04, ¶ f.

[119] C. MCgreal, "Not Guilty. The Israeli Captain Who Emptied His Rifle into a Palestinian Schoolgirl," *The Guardian* (November 16, 2005), www.theguardian.com/world/2005/nov/16/israel2.

[120] CMC 400/04, ¶¶ n, o, q.

be demolished [by the military]."[121] Following his exoneration, the
commander remained in the military, and was later promoted to the
rank of major.[122]

The incident received extensive media coverage, both locally and
abroad.[123] This included, on the day of the indictment, an investigative
report appearing on Israel's most popular television channel. Following
his acquittal, the shooter successfully sued the program for slander, and
was awarded unusually high damages by district court judge Noam
Sohlberg,[124] a West Bank settler who would later be appointed to the
supreme court. In 2012, Sohlberg's decision was partly overturned by the
supreme court, which held that despite the program's slanderous nature,
the team behind it, having reported the truth as they perceived it at the
time, was entitled to the "substantial truth" defense. Nonetheless, the
supreme court awarded the shooter damages (albeit lower than the initial
ones) for the show's promo, which it described as tendentious and hence
slanderous.[125]

Presented in both the television program and the court-martial trial
was a recording of the soldiers' radio exchange, in which the indicted
commander is heard reporting, after the initial shooting: "I'm moving
closer ... to confirm the killing."[126] Former soldiers have long reported
that this phrase – "confirmation of killing," sometimes referred to as
"dead checking" – means shooting already neutralized (and thus harm-
less) combatants.[127] Polls conducted in 2015 and 2016 found that about
half of Jewish Israeli respondents supported such conduct.[128] The
defendant's account, accepted by the judges, was different. He insisted
he had operated on the assumption that al-Hams was a potentially

---

[121] Ibid., ¶ f(8).
[122] A. Bohbot, "Captain R Promoted and Returns to Fight in the Gaza Strip," *NRG* (January
       12, 2009) [Hebrew], www.makorrishon.co.il/nrg/online/1/ART1/838/812.html.
[123] See, e.g., BBC staff, "Israelis Probe Gaza Girl Shooting," *BBC News* (October 11, 2004),
       http://news.bbc.co.uk/1/hi/world/middle_east/3733638.stm; M. Moore, "A Girl's Chilling
       Death in Gaza," *The Washington Post* (November 28, 2004), www.washingtonpost.com/
       archive/politics/2004/11/28/a-girls-chilling-death-in-gaza/744bfdc9-bef3-40ec-89fb-d88
       1b0befa5c/?noredirect=on&utm_term=.a670edd3a110.
[124] CivC (Jer. Dist.) 8206/06 *Captain R* v. *Dayan* (December 7, 2009).
[125] CivA 751/10 *John Doe* v. *Dayan-Orbach* (2012) 65(3) PD 369.
[126] Quoted in CivC 8206/06, ¶ 1 of justice Sohlberg's opinion.
[127] See Breaking the Silence, "Testimonies – Confirmation of Killing" (n.d., last accessed on
       April 30, 2019), www.breakingthesilence.org.il/testimonies/?ci=154.
[128] M. Schaeffer Omer-Man, "Nearly Half of Israeli Jews Support Extrajudicial Killings, Poll
       Finds," *+972 Magazine* (September 14, 2016), https://972mag.com/nearly-half-of-israeli-
       jews-support-extrajudicial-killings-poll-finds/121904/.

dangerous combatant and, therefore, that what he meant by "confirming the killing" was the neutralization of a perceived threat.[129]

In support of the defendant's account, a brigadier commander told the court that soldiers indeed commonly attribute this meaning to the phrase in question. He added, evincing the ambiguity in implementing the ostensibly unequivocal age threshold in the open-fire regulations, that the military allows for "latitude for reasonable mistakes resulting from [a soldier's] incorrect identification" of a Palestinian's age. Moreover, while professing to condemn firing at children because "a child is a child is a child," the brigadier commander effectively justified such firing, thereby making the vagueness of the age-based prohibition all the more evident: "if someone arrives threatening and endangering the lives of our forces, then his age is irrelevant."[130]

This case symptomizes broader trends, including the culture of impunity for shooters specifically, and for Israeli state violence generally – an issue elaborated in Chapter 6. At the same time, what distinguishes this case from many other fatal shootings is how it revolved around the victim's age. More than most other factors, it was al-Hams' perceived age that has been invoked as a yardstick for assessing the reasonableness of the commander's "confirmation of killing." Heard in the soldiers' recorded exchange were competing views about al-Hams' age: the operations room officer's initial estimate that she was 10 years old; a later argument over her age, after firing ceased, between the defendant and the observation post soldiers; and the defendant's later estimate that she was 15–18 years of age. Conflicting accounts of her perceived age appeared in the court-martial as well. Two of the defendant's subordinates recalled having realized, upon spotting her, that she was "a girl." One of them recounted having reported this to the operations room and, when asked by them if she was 10 years old, replying that "she was aged 10–12." However, the court pronounced these two soldiers unreliable, primarily on account of alleged tensions between them and the defendant prior to the incident.[131]

---

[129] CMC 400/04, ¶¶ f-i, l(4).

[130] Ibid., ¶ j(2).

[131] Ibid., ¶¶ f(1)–f(3), g(2). The soldiers' tensions concerned the hierarchy between longer-serving and newer soldiers, with the former widely referred to as "veterans" and the latter as "youth." On this issue, see Chapter 7, Section 2.4 ("Infantilization in Military Hazing").

The defendant, in contrast, was deemed credible, and his conduct was described as "reasonable and logical." On his account, upon first spotting al-Hams running, he thought she was a "grown-up youth," not a "child." He denied having heard the observation post's report "that it was a 10-year-old girl who should not be killed," and remarked that "even had he heard the report he would not have behaved differently, because the observation post soldiers ... are not authorized ... [nor] equipped to identify beyond doubt whether it was an innocent child or a terrorist." He added that "within the short time of noticing the figure, he could not have recognized her as a girl, as she was a large figure wearing [the traditional Arab] Keffiyeh and Galabeya, a clothing atypical of children."[132] The association of different age groups with different clothes is not, in itself, extraordinary. Indeed, it is through age-specific clothing, among other things, that a child/adult dichotomy has been forged in modern times.[133] Treating clothing as an age marker, therefore, has become quite normal. But given that in some contexts supposedly age-inappropriate clothing can signify anything from acting and playing to rebellion, a risk, or even a fetish,[134] the shooter's testimony brings into sharp relief its potentially deadly nature.

The three courts dealing with the case likewise presented varying narratives regarding al-Hams' perceived age. In stark contrast to the brevity of military court decisions concerning Palestinian defendants, their judgments were 99 pages (the court-martial), 115 pages (the district court), and 74 pages (the supreme court) in length, allowing considerable space for discussing this and other matters. At the time of her death, al-Hams' age was 13 years and 10 months. The court-martial judgment, which acquitted her shooter, twice characterized the girl not as 13 years old but as "apparently aged about 14."[135] Similarly and more resolutely, district court judge Sohlberg, who awarded the shooter significant

---

[132] Ibid., ¶¶ f(8), g(5).

[133] See, e.g., S. Helvenston, "Advice to American Mothers on the Subject of Children's Dress: 1800–1920" (1981) 7:1 *Journal of the Costume Society of America* 30; R. Rubinstein, *Society's Child: Identity, Clothing, and Style* (Boulder: Westview Press, 1999).

[134] See, e.g., S. Wieder, "The Power of Symbolic Play in Emotional Development Through the DIR Lens" (2017) 37:3 *Topics in Language Disorders* 259; L. Tsaliki, *Children and the Politics of Sexuality* (London: Palgrave Macmillan, 2016), pp. 165–207; B. D. Zamboni, "A Qualitative Exploration of Adult Baby/Diaper Lover Behavior from an Online Community Sample" (2019) 56:2 *Journal of Sex Research* 191.

[135] MilC 400/04, ¶¶ b, l(1). Tentatively and parenthetically, the judgment adds: "the parties have informed us that, according to a Palestinian birth certificate not submitted to the court, her age at the time of the incident was 13 years and 10 months." Ibid., ¶ b.

damages, described her as "about fourteen years old,"[136] and criticized the allegedly slanderous television program for saying "she was thirteen years old." Judge Sohlberg further lambasted the program for only playing recordings of "a soldier ... calling her once 'a little girl,' ... another time 'a girl, about 10 years old,' ... [and later saying] 'it's a girl, aged ten or twelve,'" without also playing the defendant's later conjecture that she was aged 15–18. "Selectively citing [these] age estimates," Sohlberg concluded, misled the viewers "to believe that her real age was thirteen ... and that, in real time, she appeared to soldiers even younger. ... [T]he demarcation between an unsuspicious innocent girl and a potential terrorist adolescent lies precisely within this age range."[137] An alternative framing appeared in the supreme court's decision to reduce the damages. Never once did the supreme court use phrases such as "about 14 years old." Instead, the justices described al-Hams once as "thirteen years and ten months old" and later as "a 13-year-old girl,"[138] precisely the language criticized earlier by the lower court.

Although categorically forbidding shooting at those aged under 14, Israel's open-fire regulations have thus been interpreted as authorizing firing at younger Palestinians whom Israeli shooters perceive to be dangerous or older. The gap between formal age thresholds and actual state practice parallels that regarding arrests. As mentioned earlier, there have been numerous arrests of Palestinians far below the age of criminal responsibility. Despite their dramatically different ramifications, the two practices sometimes overlap: arrest can also cost lives, whether of suspected offenders or of bystanders. Thus, in 2019, Israeli troops shot a 16-year-old Palestinian whom they later claimed to have arrested for suspected stone throwing. Handcuffed and blindfolded, he was shot in both thighs while trying to flee. Thanks to treatment in a Palestinian hospital, he remained alive.[139] But three years earlier, another attempt at arresting stone-throwers saw 15-year-old Mahmoud Rafat Badran shot

---

[136] CivC 8206/06, ¶ 5 of justice Sohlberg's opinion.
[137] CivC 8206/06, ¶ 150 of justice Sohlberg's opinion.
[138] CivA 751/10, ¶ 4 of deputy chief justice Rivlin's opinion and ¶ 33 of justice Vogelman's opinion, respectively.
[139] T. Barnes, "Palestinian Teenager Shot by Israeli Army 'While Blindfolded and Handcuffed' in West Bank," *The Independent* (April 22, 2019), www.independent.co.uk/news/world/middle-east/palestine-israel-west-bank-teenager-shot-soldiers-army-handcuff-blindfold-a8881296.html.

dead and three other Palestinians injured, all of whom the military later admitted were uninvolved bystanders "mistakenly hit."[140]

3.4.2   Age-Based Food Restrictions

Following social theorist Michel Foucault, state power can be described, somewhat crudely, as operating in three mutually complementary forms. The first, sovereign power, involves the state's perceived right to kill or spare life. The second, disciplinary power, operates to modify individuals and their bodies, so as to make them more useful and docile, by means of punishment, training, education, separation, classification, and surveillance. The third form, biopower, regulates the population as a whole, focusing on its strength – its health, reproduction, and death – at the collective level.[141] All three forms of state power are evident, time and again, throughout this book. In this chapter, sovereign power can be associated with Israel's open-fire regulations, whereas disciplinary power can be said to be at work in Israel's age-related sentencing provisions.

As for biopower, one of its most conspicuous manifestations was, arguably, the restrictions on the entry of foodstuff imposed by Israel in the first three years of the Gaza closure (late 2007–2010). Unlike other aspects of the closure, its age-stratified logic has yet to receive scrutiny. Possibly the most definitive articulation of this logic is a 2008 military document titled *Food Consumption in the Gaza Strip – Red Lines*.[142] First revealed in a 2009 press report,[143] the military document was formally published in 2012, following freedom of information proceedings.[144] Two different versions of it were disclosed: one, dated 1 January 2008, had been presented by the military during the district court hearings, and the other, dated 27 January 2008, had been presented to the supreme

[140] D. Macintyre, "Israeli Troops 'Mistakenly' Kill Palestinian Teenager," *The Guardian* (June 21, 2016), www.theguardian.com/world/2016/jun/21/israeli-troops-mistakenly-kill-palestinian-teenager-stone-throwers.

[141] M. Foucault, "17 March 1976," in his *"Society Must Be Defended": Lectures at the Collège de France, 1975–76* (M. Bertani and A. Fontana eds., New York: Picador, 2003 [1976]), pp. 239–64.

[142] COGAT, *Food Consumption in the Gaza Strip – Red Lines* (January 1, 2008) [hereinafter: *Red Lines*]. For an unofficial English translation by Israeli NGO Gisha, see www.gisha .org/UserFiles/File/publications/redlines/red-lines-presentation-eng.pdf.

[143] U. Blau and Y. Feldman, "Gaza Bonanza," *Haaretz* (June 15, 2009), www.haaretz.com/1 .5063295.

[144] AdminC (Tel Aviv Dist.) 2744/09 *Gisha v. Ministry of Defense* (March 22, 2011); AdminA 3300/11 *State of Israel – Ministry of Defense v. Gisha* (September 5, 2012).

court. Though the military told the court these were mere drafts unused in decision-making, the figures in them matched the actual quotas imposed on Gaza in the relevant time period.[145]

The military document exhibits great interest in the age and gender composition of the Gaza Strip population, though different categorizations and details appear in each of the two versions. A table presenting a demographic breakdown thus appears in both versions, dividing Gaza residents into seven age cohorts – "0–1," "2–3," "4–7," "8–15," "16–24," "25–50," and "51+" years – each of which is further bifurcated into "male" and "female." In addition, each of the two documents refers to "children." The earlier version explains (underlining for emphasis in the original):

> The goal of the [present] analysis – [is] to identify the point of intervention for prevention of malnutrition in the Gaza Strip. ... The [Israeli] Ministry of Health is conducting work for calculating the minimal subsistence basket based on the Arab sector in Israel. The "minimum basket" allows nutrition that is sufficient for subsistence without the development of malnutrition. ... The portion of [food] consumption is measured by the Health Ministry in Israel and provides for 2,000–2,500 calories per adult and 1,550 calories per child.[146]

The later document contains a "Conclusion and Recommendations" section, which includes the following remarks:

> There is a need for ongoing food supply ... over time in order to avoid a situation of malnutrition – [while placing] emphasis on children. The Ministry of Health model appears correct and leaves a "safety margin". The model meets the caloric model formulated by the World Health Organization (2,100 calories per person per day).[147]

Also provided in this version is a short table that presents average daily food portions for three cohorts. The first, "children," defined as those aged "up to 10" years, are allotted 1,758 calories and 1,448 grams on average per day. The other two groups, "women" and "men," are both defined, unusually, as aged "11+" years. For "women," the average daily

[145] A. Gross and T. Feldman, "'We Didn't Want to Hear the Word "Calories"': Rethinking Food Security, Food Power, and Food Sovereignty – Lessons from the Gaza Closure" (2015) 33:2 *Berkeley Journal of International Law* 379, 395 [hereinafter: "We Didn't Want to Hear the Word Calories"].

[146] COGAT, *Red Lines.*

[147] Ibid.

allocation is 2,162 calories and 1,831 grams, whereas for "men" it is 2,784 calories and 2,181 grams.

In an attempt to micromanage Palestinian life in the Gaza Strip, both versions list in a table the minimum necessary daily food intakes, in calories and grams, of eight different food categories: flour, rice, vegetables, fruit, milk, meat, oil, and sugar. Figures are specified in an array combining age and gender. "Female" is divided into three age brackets – "11–24," "24–50," and "51+" year-olds – whereas "male" comprises five age brackets: "11–14," "15–18," "19–24," "24–50," and "51+" year-olds.[148] No explanation is given of the recurrence of 24-year-olds in different age ranges – perhaps evincing yet again what I have described as Israel's use of inconsistency and vagueness to exercise control. Indeed, one critic, attributing to the food restrictions "deliberately nonrational bureaucracy," has highlighted other seemingly arbitrary aspects, such as Israel's decision to allow the entry of raw chickpeas while banning chickpea paste (hummus).[149]

Three younger age groups – "2–3," "4–6," and "7–10" year-olds – are not divided by gender at all, perhaps suggesting a concept of early childhood as either preceding gender or, at the very least, as having no gender differences when it comes to food consumption. The table makes no mention of under-two-year-olds. However, elsewhere in the later document, it is stated: "The total amount of food takes into consideration 'sampling' by toddlers under the age of 2 (adds 34 tons per day to the general population)." Both documents also include several references to "baby food," "baby formula," and "powdered milk."

Another table, elaborating further the age-gender-food matrix, appears only in the earlier document. It specifies the minimum daily amounts, in tons, for each age group as a whole. While using the exact same age and gender divisions as in the previous table, a younger age bracket is added: "–12 months," presumably denoting those under the age of 12 months (and leaving one-year-olds unaccounted for). Examples of the food allocations are: 14.83 tons of vegetables for "males" aged "51+" years, no oil whatsoever for under-four-year-olds, 51 tons of meat for all 24–50-year-old "females" compared with 62.15 tons of meat for their "male" peers, and 6.33 tons of fruit for the "–12 months" age group.

---

[148] While quantities for each food category vary slightly between the two versions of the table, the overall daily allocations are the same.

[149] See S. Bashi, "Controlling Perimeters, Controlling Lives: Israel and Gaza" (2013) 7:2 *Law and Ethics of Human Rights* 248–49, 260–63.

These and other figures, the documents read, were "translated ... into truckloads" in an attempt to address "[t]he security situation in the Gaza Strip [on the one hand] and, on the other hand, the interest in preventing a humanitarian crisis." It was decided by the deputy defense minister that "106 trucks carrying basic humanitarian products ..., including 77 basic food [trucks]," would suffice "to prevent the development of malnutrition" among the territory's estimated 1.5 million residents. Nevertheless, although restrictions on the entry of food were lifted in 2010, a decade later, largely due to Israel's ongoing impediments to the movement of supplies and people, more than half of Gazans were still reportedly relying on humanitarian food aid.[150]

For Israel, age and gender enabled the micromanagement of life in the Gaza Strip. But their utility also emanated from them being part of the language of international law. As explained in the previous two chapters, Israel has a long record of harnessing legal knowhow and mechanisms, including international law, to hone and legitimate its control over Palestinians. Typifying this legalism, the state attorney's office justified the closure, in late 2007, as a form of economic warfare compatible with international law, referring specifically to age and gender (emphasis in bold in the original):

> Article 23 of the fourth Geneva Convention states: "... [parties to an armed conflict] shall ... permit the free passage of all consignments of essential foodstuffs ... intended for children under fifteen, expectant mothers and maternity cases. ..." ... Clearly, the premise of this proviso is the waging of "economic warfare" as part of the parties' armed conflict. Implicitly, this proviso recognizes unequivocally the legality of this practice and merely seeks to set a minimum threshold for it.[151]

For reasons explained in Chapters 4, 5, and 7, privileging those defined as children and women (as the Geneva Convention does) is highly problematic. Here, however, I wish to highlight another issue. Admittedly, the age and gender logic guiding Israel's food restrictions seems profoundly dissimilar to that of the Geneva Convention. And yet, it is perhaps no mere coincidence that this quotation would end up in the

---

[150] J. Rankin, "One Million Face Hunger in Gaza after US Cut to Palestine Aid," *The Guardian* (May 15, 2019), www.theguardian.com/world/2019/may/15/1-million-face-hunger-in-gaza-after-us-cut-to-palestine-aid; see also Gross and Feldman, "We Didn't Want to Hear the Word Calories," pp. 398–99.

[151] State's Preliminary Response to Petition HCJ 9132/07 *Al-Bassiouni* v. *Prime Minister* (November 7, 2007), ¶¶ 39, 41, 44.

service of Israel's attempts to legitimize its continued control over the Gaza Strip. International humanitarian law, of which the Geneva Conventions are widely considered cornerstones, seeks to regulate the conduct of armed conflict through such principles as proportionality and distinction. It has been the recourse not solely of those resisting military control but also, as several scholars have observed,[152] of belligerent countries. Amalgamating sovereign power and biopower, contemporary warfare thus speaks the language of humanitarianism while professing a commitment to the sanctity of human life.[153] Indeed, the Israeli military's 2008 documents, in a show of what some may call "military humanitarianism,"[154] not only employ a humanitarian reasoning of sorts but also explicitly use the term "humanitarianism" no fewer than ten times.

For Israeli authorities, age and gender can thus be of great use, in at least two distinct ways. The first, as I have noted, is as means of garnering international and domestic legitimacy. In the next chapter, I demonstrate in detail how Israel has increasingly incorporated a legal language of children's rights in its efforts to legitimize its handling of incarcerated Palestinians. Similarly, regarding the Gaza closure, in citing age- and gender-focused international humanitarian law principles, and arguing that Israel was waging economic warfare according to these principles, the state attorney was in effect portraying the closure as a "humane war" (though without using these precise words). This attempt to derive legitimacy from humanitarianism becomes especially apparent when considering whom Israel appointed as its "coordinator of humanitarian aid" to Gaza at the time: a government minister also tasked with "explaining [to the world] Israel's reasons and legal position regarding the [closure's] inflicted damage."[155]

Second, humanitarian thinking about age and gender has proven useful to Israel as a tool of governing. The military's avowed preoccupation, according to its 2008 documents, with "preventing a humanitarian crisis" in the enclosed territory laid the ground for continued intervention by the Israeli security apparatus. That humanitarianism can be seen

---

[152] D. Kennedy, *Of War and Law* (Princeton: Princeton University Press, 2006); C. Douzinas, "The Many Faces of Humanitarianism" (2007) 2 *Parrhesia* 1; E. Weizman, "Legislative Attack" (2010) 27:6 *Theory, Culture & Society* 11.

[153] M. Dillon and J. Reid, *The Liberal Way of War: Killing to Make Life* (New York: Routledge, 2009).

[154] On the language of "military humanitarianism" and "humane war," see Douzinas, "The Many Faces of Humanitarianism," pp. 5–10.

[155] Weizman, "Legislative Attack," p. 15.

as a security matter was explicitly voiced, more recently, by the former commander of the Israeli military's Southern Command (overseeing Gaza-related issues). "Gaza is a pressure cooker," he told the Israeli media in 2019. "On one hand, we need to fight terrorism harder, but on the other, we need to reduce tension among civilians through projects and humanitarian aid that will make things a tiny bit better there."[156]

In committing to making things just "a tiny bit better," humanitarianism is thus framed as a mode of security governance based on maintaining a minimum threshold. This is precisely the sort of humanitarianism evident in the military's focus, a decade earlier, on "prevent[ing] the development of malnutrition," as well as in the state attorney's portrayal of international humanitarian law as authorizing economic warfare by "merely seek[ing] to set a minimum threshold for it." Over time, Israel's closure of the Gaza Strip has gradually turned what were initially minimum thresholds into maximum ones. Rather than being granted no less than the declared minimum, Gazans have been denied even that threshold, let alone anything exceeding it.[157]

3.4.3   Age as a Risk Management Tool in Israel's Movement Restrictions

Another age-based way for Israel to control Palestinians' lives is through the movement restriction apparatus outlined in Chapter 1. One in four Palestinians prosecuted in Israel's military courts are charged with violating these restrictions by illegally entering Israel's pre-1967 territory.[158] In the next chapter, I demonstrate how this apparatus potentially fragments Palestinian society and confines political thinking. My focus here is on its deployment of age as a risk management category: its classification of certain age groups as a security risk in need of heavy physical

---

[156] Y. Limor, "'Israel Has No Policy on Gaza'," *Israel Hayom* (March 29, 2019), www .israelhayom.com/2019/03/29/israel-has-no-policy-on-gaza/.

[157] E. Weizman, *The Least of All Possible Evils: Humanitarian Violence from Arendt to Gaza* (London: Verso, 2011), pp. 81–86.

[158] MAG, *Annual Activity Report – 2017* (2018), p. 46 [Hebrew], www.idf.il/media/34839/% D7%93%D7%95%D7%97-%D7%94%D7%A9%D7%A0%D7%AA%D7%99-%D7%A9% D7%9C-%D7%94%D7%A4%D7%A8%D7%A7%D7%9C%D7%99%D7%98%D7%95% D7%AA.pdf.

confinement. Bearing the major brunt have been Palestinians ranging from teenagers to those in their 30s. At different points in time, severe constraints have been placed on Palestinians aged 16–25 years wishing to travel overseas, as well as on 16–35-year-old East Jerusalemites traveling specifically to Jordan. In a similar vein, 15–35-year-old residents of the city of Nablus, especially male residents, were for several years forbidden to exit their city.[159]

Epitomizing Palestinians' geographical confinement is the nearly 500-kilometer-long West Bank barrier, which comprises walls, fences, patrol roads, and military posts constructed since the turn of the century. Rather than running along Israel's pre-1967 border, the barrier seals off more than 8 percent of the West Bank, which is referred to by Israel as the "Seam Zone."[160] In keeping with Israel's legalism, the supreme court has approved the barrier in its current route as well as its associated regime of movement restrictions.[161] Combining age and ethnicity distinctions, the barrier confines Palestinians in at least two key ways. First, inside the West Bank, it has cut off many Palestinians from their families, communities, and farms in the Seam Zone. Palestinian permit requests must be submitted in advance, and are frequently denied; moreover, the permits that are granted are time-limited.[162] Permits to attend weekly prayers in Al-Aqsa Mosque, a religious site of especial importance in East Jerusalem, are denied to all Muslim Palestinian men under the age of

[159] These restrictions were imposed in the 1970s, 1980s, and early 2000s respectively. See N. Yeshuvi and Y. Ginbar, *Trials of Soldiers, Restrictions on Overseas Travel* (Jerusalem: B'Tselem, November 1989), p. 10 [Hebrew], www.btselem.org/sites/default/files/publica tions/update_november_1989_heb.pdf; petition in HCJ 7577/06 *ACRI* v. *Military Commander in the Judea and Samaria Region* (September 18, 2006) [Hebrew], https:// law.acri.org.il/pdf/petitions/hit7577.pdf.

[160] B'Tselem, "The Separation Barrier" (November 11, 2017), www.btselem.org/separation_ barrier; E. Hareuveni. *Arrested Development: The Long Term Impact of Israel's Separation Barrier in the West Bank* (Jerusalem: B'Tselem, October 2012), pp. 25–41, www.btselem.org/sites/default/files2/201210_arrested_development_eng.pdf.

[161] For analysis of these rulings, see A. M. Gross, "The *Construction of a Wall* between The Hague and Jerusalem: The Enforcement and Limits of Humanitarian Law and the Structure of Occupation" (2006) 19 *Leiden Journal of International Law* 393–440; M. Sfard, "Proportionality," in Ben-Naftali, Sfard, and Viterbo, *The ABC of the OPT*, pp. 327–42.

[162] See Hamoked, "Military Data Obtained by HaMoked Reveals: Dramatic Rise in the Denial of Access of Palestinian Farmers to Their West Bank Farmlands Lying Beyond the Separation Wall. Security Is Rarely the Reason for Denying Access" (January 3, 2019), www.hamoked.org/Document.aspx?dID=Updates2051.

55 and all women under the age of 45 from the other side of the barrier. Age restrictions are also placed on work in Jewish settlements, with minimum ages of 26 for settlements within the Seam Zone and 18 for those elsewhere in the West Bank.[163]

Second, entry to Israel is forbidden, for most purposes, to men under 55 and women under 50 – constituting approximately 90 percent of West Bank's Palestinian population. In addition, as a prerequisite for traveling overseas via Israel, West Bank Palestinians aged 18–60 must undergo special security checks. Work within Israel is subject to quotas and limited to specific sectors based on Israel's economic and security priorities. West Bank Palestinians under certain ages, ranging from 21 to 25 depending on the sector, cannot be employed. Israeli high-tech employers can also request that West Bank employees be permitted to attend training in Israel, but this is limited to married Palestinians aged 22 and older with children.[164]

Far harsher is the confinement of Gazans, especially under the ongoing lockdown since 2007. Having allowed hundreds of thousands of Palestinians to work in Israel until the early 1990s,[165] Israel now limits their number to a few thousand. Those under a certain age – in recent year, variously from 30 to 25 years – are ineligible even to apply, thus excluding nearly 70 percent of Gaza's relatively young population.[166]

---

[163] COGAT, Unclassified Status of Permissions for Palestinians to Enter Israel, Their Movement between the Judea and Samaria Area and the Gaza Strip, and Their Exit Overseas (February 28, 2016), pp. 6, 36 [Hebrew], http://media.wix.com/ugd/36db95_90b52ca0423c425c8f995f8a7309509f.pdf [hereinafter: Unclassified Status of Permissions – 2016 version].

[164] Ibid., pp. 10, 31–35, 40, 43. The figure regarding the age structure of the West Bank Palestinian population, referring to 2018, is based on Central Intelligence Agency, *The World Factbook – Middle East: The West Bank* (n.d., last accessed on August 11, 2019), www.cia.gov/library/publications/the-world-factbook/geos/we.html.

[165] A. Paz-Fuchs and Y. Ronen, "Occupational Hazards" (2012) 30:2 *Berkeley Journal of International Law* 580, 580–81.

[166] COGAT, Unclassified Status of Permissions for Palestinians to Enter Israel, Their Movement between the Judea and Samaria Area and the Gaza Strip, and Their Exit Overseas (August 27, 2019), pp. 49–51 [Hebrew], www.gisha.org/UserFiles/File/LegalDocuments/procedures/general/50.pdf [hereinafter: Unclassified Status of Permissions – 2019 version]. The figure regarding the age composition of the Gazan population, referring to 2018, is based on Central Intelligence Agency, *The World Factbook – Middle East: The Gaza Strip* (n.d., last accessed on August 11, 2019), www.cia.gov/library/publications/resources/the-world-factbook/geos/gz.html [hereinafter: CIA, *Gaza Factbook*].

Permits to attend weekly prayers in the Al-Aqsa Mosque are limited to a few hundred Gazans over the age of 50, who can be accompanied by their grandchildren under the age of 16, all subject to security clearance.[167]

By curtailing their access to work, resources, their families, and their communities, Israel impoverishes and limits Palestinians' life chances. The impact of this not only on the life they can lead but also on whether they remain alive is evident, most conspicuously though not exclusively, in restrictions on travel for medical care. Each year, hundreds of thousands reportedly apply to Israel for permits to travel within or outside their territories for medical purposes. This is due to necessary medical care often being out of reach of Palestinians, especially those residing in the poverty-stricken Gaza Strip. Nearly half of Gazans' applications have been refused in recent years, however, while many others have not received a timely response.[168] Hence, eligibility to apply for a permit – my focus in this section – is a far different matter from actually receiving a permit.

Immediate family members may apply for permits to visit a gravely ill relative hospitalized elsewhere in the Palestinian territories or in Israel. This provision, like others concerning family contact, is age-based: patients' children over the age of 15 are forbidden to apply. Similarly, children over the age of 15 residing in Israel are barred from applying for permission to enter Gaza to visit their gravely ill parents. For relatives from Gaza, the military's regulations designate the patient's age as an additional consideration.[169]

Among those affected by the permit regime, according to a 2019 report, was a 24-year-old Gazan whom Israel had permitted to travel to a Palestinian hospital in East Jerusalem, where she gave birth to seriously ill triplets. Shortly afterwards, her permit expired, forcing her to leave her hospitalized children behind. Nine days after giving birth, she was notified by phone of the death of one of her babies. Two weeks later,

---

[167] COGAT, Unclassified Status of Permissions – 2016 version, pp. 15, 48.

[168] G. Mattar, *Denied 2: Harassment of Palestinian Patients Applying for Exit Permits* (Tel Aviv: Physicians for Human Rights, August 2016), p. 5, www.phr.org.il/wp-content/uploads/2016/09/Denied-2.pdf [hereinafter: *Denied 2*]; Physicians for Human Rights – Israel, "Israel: Record-Low in Gaza Medical Permits" (February 12, 2018), www.phr.org.il/en/israel-record-low-gaza-medical-permits/?pr=99.

[169] COGAT, Unclassified Status of Permissions – 2019 version, pp. 5, 13, 15, 17, 20–21, 23–24, 48–49.

she was informed of the death of another.[170] According to the Israeli branch of Physicians for Human Rights, Israel has, as a prerequisite for considering their applications, summoned Gazan patients to interrogations and pressured them to become informants, potentially deterring other future applicants. Also summoned to such interrogations, reportedly, have been relatives below the age of 55 applying to escort a patient. They were then barred from exiting Gaza and instructed to find an older relative as a substitute, leaving Gazan residents under 55 (comprising 95 percent of Gaza's population) ineligible to apply, including most parents of under-18-year-olds.[171]

3.5   Resistance through Age Manipulation

For Israeli authorities, age is an indispensable governance tool. It informs, albeit inconsistently, the treatment and punishment of Palestinians in conflict with Israeli law. It demarcates, formally if not in practice, which Palestinians should not be shot. It lends itself to the biopolitical Israeli warfare of food quotas. And, by labeling certain Palestinian groups as inherently a security risk, it limits their movement and thus denies them access to to work, medical treatment, resources, their families, and their communities. As laid bare in the next chapter, it is also on an age basis, among others, that Israeli authorities have sought to fragment Palestinian society. To maintain this elaborate age-based apparatus, Israeli authorities must be able to ascertain both the ages of individual Palestinians and the age composition of Palestinian society as a whole.

But if, as I have demonstrated, age is partly a matter of physical appearance, then the power to deploy and determine age lies not exclusively in Israeli hands, but also, potentially, with Palestinians. As shown throughout this book, Palestinians resort to a wealth of acts to resist or frustrate Israeli rule. Faced with Israel's age-based control mechanisms, a particularly defiant form of resistance emerges from my analysis of military judgments: the manipulation of perceived age. Since Palestinians require a movement permit that states their age, one way to circumvent the age-based movement restrictions is to carry false or

---

[170] O. Holmes, "A Jerusalem Hospital Where Palestinian Babies Die Alone," *The Guardian* (June 20, 2019), www.theguardian.com/world/2019/jun/20/a-jerusalem-hospital-where-palestinian-babies-die-alone.

[171] Mattar, *Denied 2*, pp. 6, 16, 18–21; CIA, Gaza Factbook.

fake documentation that misrepresents their actual age. Alternatively, if caught without a permit, Palestinians can attempt to lie about their age in the hope of receiving a lighter sentence (although such attempts, if they do not succeed, are likely to result in a harsher sentence).

This is precisely what 18-year-old Gaza resident Yussuf Nasser did in 2000, when arrested for attempting to enter Israel without a permit. In his interrogation and throughout the legal process that ensued, he impersonated his 17-year-old relative Yaqub. The first-instance court, not realizing the impersonation, sentenced him to three months' imprisonment and a suspended sentence, noting what the court believed to be his young age. But shortly thereafter, the impersonated relative, Yaqub, contacted the Israeli authorities to inquire why he had been mistakenly listed as a convicted criminal. As a result, while still imprisoned, Yussuf was additionally charged and convicted of impersonation, and had his prison and suspended sentences each increased by a month.[172]

Following an appeal by the military prosecution, the military court of appeals increased his sentence further to 20 months, ten in prison and ten suspended. In addition, the court of appeals imposed a fine that, if not paid on time, would have been substituted by two additional months behind bars. Although their birth dates are absent from the military judgment, the court's reference to the impersonated Yaqub as "a minor" and to his impersonator Yussuf as "not a minor," combined with the court's mention of their years of birth, suggest their respective ages of 17 and 18 years.

Also noted in the judgment, disapprovingly, is Yussuf's argument that his acts stemmed from his family's financial plight. The judgment adds:

[I]t is unclear to me why the lower court saw fit to treat the appellee so leniently. Initially, when the court still believed the offense involved a minor illegally exiting the Area [i.e., the Gaza Strip], a prison sentence of only 3 months could be acceptable. However, once the truth came to light, the [new] overall [prison] sentence of only 4 months was insufficient ... Public trust in the legal system is based on the assumption that the court would ascertain the truth ... I do not believe one additional month in prison reflects the gravity of the [appellee's impersonation] ... and the severity of the harm he has caused to the legal system.[173]

---

[172] MilC (Erez) 290/00 *Military Prosecutor* v. *Nasser* (2000); MilC (Erez) 329/00 *Military Prosecutor* v. *Nasser* (August 21, 2000).
[173] MilA 41/00 *Military Prosecutor* v. *Nasser* (September 27, 2000).

The following year, another Palestinian was arrested for illegally exiting the Gaza Strip. At that point, for reasons not clarified in the judgment in his matter, Israeli forces believed him to be a 15-year-old named Umar Abu Snima. Upon sentencing him to a month on probation, military judge Sigal Mishal noted her consideration of his young age.[174] A year later, when arrested again for illegally entering Israel, he presented himself to the Israeli interrogators by a different name – Muhammad Abu Snima – which the military court would later pronounce to be his real identity. Once his fingerprints were taken, he was discovered to be five years older (again illustrating the use of the body as evidence of age) – "about 20 years old," as the court would later put it.[175] Charged this time not only with illegally exiting Gaza but also with perjury, he was eventually given a much harsher sentence of two and a half months in prison and 45 days on probation.[176] As in the previous case, an appeal by the military prosecution led to an increased sentence of ten months in prison and nine months on probation. In its decision, the military court of appeals emphasized the gravity of age manipulation: "the offenses of which the appellee has been convicted are very grave, and apart from the severity of exiting the Area without permission is his false self-identification. The appellee ... even managed to deceive the court and receive a short sentence by presenting himself as a minor."[177]

These cases illustrate four interconnected elements: Israel's need to know Palestinians' "true" age, the performative dimension of age, Palestinian attempts to misrepresent their chronological age, and, finally, the harsh Israeli response to those caught doing so. It is as if these legal subjects temporarily turned back law's time, reverted to legal childhood, and thereby bent childhood's boundaries. Between the lines of the judgments also emerges the potential success of such resistance: if only events had unfolded slightly differently, the deception might have remained unknown to Israeli authorities.

By the time each of these two Gazans was arrested, the Israel–Gaza barrier had already been in place for several years. In contrast, construction of the previously mentioned West Bank barrier only began afterwards, potentially

---

[174] MilC (Erez) 164/01 *Military Advocate General* v. *Abu Snima* (2001).
[175] MilA 12/02 *Military Advocate General* v. *Abu Snima* (February 25, 2002). The military court of appeals speculated that Abu Snima used his "real" (first) name when arrested for the second time to evade the enforcement of his suspended sentence from 2001.
[176] MilC (Erez) 5/02 *Military Advocate General* v. *Abu Snima* (2002).
[177] MilA 12/02.

giving West Bank Palestinians greater chances of successfully manipulating their identity. Indeed, in an article based on fieldwork in a West Bank village around that time, anthropologist Tobias Kelly touches on a different, although partly related, form of identity manipulation. Unlike the cases I have traced, it did not consist of pretending to be under the age of majority. Rather, in an attempt to avoid having their legal status checked at the Israeli checkpoint, young male villagers altered their physical appearance in ways unavailable to their older counterparts. Whereas the latter "often wore clothes and facial hair that seemed to signal them as . . . Palestinians," these youth "dressed, cut their hair, and talked Hebrew in ways that made them largely indistinguishable from many Israeli teenagers. . . . Thus, . . . [they] could manipulate the social and economic assumptions held by the Israeli soldiers." With time, however, "the increase in checkpoints and permits caused great difficulty" for those attempting resistance through manipulation in the West Bank as well.[178]

As highlighted in the previous chapter and the next two, the liberal human rights community shares quite a few of the Israeli legal system's perceptions, including those concerning law and childhood. The desire to know Palestinians' age, and the agitation whenever this desire is not satisfied, are among them, though for different reasons when human rights organizations are concerned. Israeli NGO Yesh Din, for example, conducted observations of military court hearings and reported, worryingly:

> In 52 . . . cases the observers found it difficult to ascertain whether the detainee or defendant was a minor or an adult. The fact that the MCU [Military Court Unit] denied Yesh Din access to the records of the proceedings until near the end of the observations made it difficult to determine precisely whether the person was a minor or a legal adult.[179]

According to Yesh Din, the military courts, by obfuscating age, are the problem, but they also hold the solution, by potentially clarifying age.

For Israel and its human rights critics alike, then, age is crucial. Not knowing this cornerstone of the law and politics of childhood frustrates their efforts to shape discourses and practices surrounding young Palestinians. In the next chapter, I turn to examine how, and to what effect, Israeli and human rights actors envisage, demarcate, and utilize age distinctions in tandem with the spatial separation of Palestinians in Israeli custody.

---

[178] T. Kelly, "Documented Lives: Fear and the Uncertainties of Law during the Second Palestinian Intifada" (2006) 12:1 *Journal of the Royal Anthropological Institute* 89, 97–98.

[179] Yavne, *Backyard Proceedings*, p. 158.

Boundary Governance: Amending Childhood and Separating Palestinians

4.1 Introduction

While the previous chapter focused on age-related issues, this one links age to space. As discussed in the book's opening chapter, age and space jointly provide the primary basis for the social and legal demarcation of childhood. Supposedly age-appropriate practices thus require age-suitable spaces; conversely, social spaces have their own age fabric.[1] Space, according to jurist Andreas Philippopoulos-Mihalopoulos, can be broadly understood as the sphere of possibilities in which occurs the violence of drawing, dividing, and partitioning boundaries.[2] As jurist Sarah Blandy and geographer David Sibley note, a main concern of law is boundaries of various sorts, which represent something to be desired as well as feared.[3]

This chapter examines the interrelations of childhood spaces, legal and human rights forces, and territorial barriers. Whereas in the previous chapter I focused on childhood's fluidity, here I will turn the spotlight on law's claim to consolidate the supposedly normal boundaries – spatial, temporal, and other – of childhood. My case study will be a series of Israeli reforms, following sustained pressure from the human rights community, made during the first two decades of the century: the establishment of the world's only "military youth court"; segregation of incarcerated Palestinians on an age basis; assessment of young

---

[1] See, respectively, K. E. McHugh, "The 'Ageless Self'?: Emplacement of Identities in Sun Belt Retirement Communities" (2000) 14:1 *Journal of Aging Studies* 103, 106; R. Pain, "Age, Generation and Life Course," in R. Pain et al. (eds.), *Introducing Social Geographies* (New York and Oxford: Oxford University Press, 2001), pp. 141, 156–57.

[2] A. Philippopoulos-Mihalopoulos, "Law's Spatial Turn: Geography, Justice and a Certain Fear of Space" (2011) 7:2 *Law, Culture, and the Humanities* 187, 189–96.

[3] S. Blandy and D. Sibley, "Law, Boundaries and the Production of Space" (2010) 19:3 *Social & Legal Studies* 275, 277–78.

Palestinians' rehabilitation chances; raising the age of majority under military law; and other provisions concerning Palestinian youth.

Section 4.2 will start by illuminating parallels between these reforms, past colonial laws, and contemporary counterinsurgency. I will then explore the great lengths to which Israeli authorities have gone to portray the reforms in question as protecting the rights and best interests of young Palestinians. Many of Israel's human rights critics have taken these claims at face value, as have some foreign countries. However, through a painstaking analysis of the statutory structure and actual effects of these reforms, I will lay bare three ways in which Israel has made its reforms mostly tokenistic: (a) introducing symbolic amendments that do not affect its handling of Palestinians; (b) inconsistently applying, and even breaching, some of its new provisions; and (c) incorporating broad and frequently used statutory exceptions that render void Palestinians' formal rights.

From there, Section 4.3 will proceed to discuss, specifically, the segregation of young Palestinians in Israeli custody from their elders, as well as the Israeli judiciary's persistent calls to "rehabilitate" the now-segregated youth. By analyzing, among other sources, military and supreme court judgments, I will reveal that the Israeli legal system's growing support for these measures stemmed from its desire to prevent intergenerational knowledge transfer among Palestinians – and to undo such knowledge as already exists. Contrary to Israel's claims, I will contend that age-based separation and "rehabilitation" are, in several respects, harmful to incarcerated Palestinians of all ages. This will lead me to cast a critical light on human rights critics, both NGOs and scholars, many of whom have been blinded by their essentialism and legalism to the ills of age-based segregation and "rehabilitation," an issue aggravated by some organizations' depiction of intergenerational Palestinian interactions as a national security threat.

In order to better understand these issues, Section 4.4 will investigate Israel's reforms in relation to four broader contexts. First, I will argue that these reforms, rather than being an exception to child law, exemplify its long-standing complicity in the oppression of disempowered populations. Second, I will point to the multiple forms of separation Israel imposes on Palestinians in and outside prison, which, like their age-based segregation behind bars, operate to fragment Palestinian society. Third, I will place Israel's stymying of intergenerational knowledge transfer among incarcerated Palestinians within its wider endeavor of confining Palestinian minds. In the process of examining these last two contexts – the fragmentation of Palestinians and the confinement of their minds – I will highlight Palestinian acts of resistance: running study groups in prison, smuggling sperm of imprisoned men, and conducting readings and discussions in public protests. Finally, I will show that the reforms are symptomatic of a growing convergence between military and non-military Israeli law, which in turn is a symptom of the steady annexation of the West Bank.

4.2 Hyperlegality, Tokenism, and the Rule of Exception

Over the first decade-and-a-half of the century, the Israeli military introduced several reforms to the law as it applies to young noncitizen Palestinians in the West Bank. Two reforms garnered most attention, both locally and globally: the establishment of the world's only[4] "military youth court" in 2009, and the raising of the age of criminal majority for Palestinians from 16 to 18 years in 2011.[5] Taken together, these reforms were perceived as rectifying the spatial and temporal boundaries of childhood in line with international legal and human rights standards.

These reforms, along with others dissected in this chapter shortly, evince hyperlegality. This term, first used by legal scholar Nasser Hussain, refers to state practices that have two key features: the increased legal classification of people into subcategories, and the use of special tribunals. In Israel/Palestine, the sprouting age-based distinctions manifest the former feature, while the child-specific military court embodies the latter. As Hussain showed, hyperlegality has characterized both past colonialism and contemporary counterinsurgency.[6] This continuity is evident in Israel/Palestine: it was from British Mandate law that the Israeli military borrowed some of its statutory age distinctions (as detailed in the previous chapter), and it was also the British Mandate's

---

[4] UNICEF, *Children in Israeli Military Detention: Observations and Recommendations* (February 2013), www.unicef.org/oPt/UNICEF_oPt_Children_in_Israeli_Military_Detention_Observa tions_and_Recommendations_-_6_March_2013.pdf [hereinafter UNICEF 2013].

[5] See, respectively, Article 1 of the Order Concerning Security Provisions (Temporary Order) (Amendment No. 109) (Judea and Samaria) (No. 1644), 2009 [hereinafter: Order 1644] (introducing Articles 46a–46n into Order Concerning Security Provisions (Judea and Samaria) (No. 378), 1970); Article 3 of the Order Concerning Security Provisions (Amendment No. 10) (Judea and Samaria) (No. 1676), 2011 [hereinafter: Order 1676] (amending Article 139 of the Order Concerning Security Provisions (Integrated Version) (Judea and Samaria), (No. 1651), 2009 [hereinafter: Order 1651]).

[6] N. Hussain, "Hyperlegality" (2007) 4 *New Criminal Law Review* 514.

emergency regulations that first authorized military courts in the territory to act as youth courts.[7]

Time and again, the military has placed these hyperlegal reforms at the forefront of its legalistic rhetoric. In a leaflet in English given to foreign delegations since 2013, the military asserts:

> Within the efforts to protect the rights of all defendants and particularly minors, in 2009, a juvenile military court was established for minors under the age of 16 ..., [which] guarantees adequate and professional care for [Palestinian] juveniles and recognizes their welfare and best interests as a factor in the proceedings. Among other provisions, the [amended military law] ... provides for a separation between minor and adult detainees, as well as a wide range of additional provisions. In 2011, an amendment [to the military law] ... raised the age of majority from 16 to 18 years.[8]

The military's spokesperson likewise portrayed increasing the age of criminal majority as

> another significant step in protecting minors in the Judea and Samaria area [i.e., the West Bank], following earlier important steps, first and foremost of which is the establishment of the [military] youth court. ... [This] is of great importance, given the special procedures in place for minors. Their trials are heard by specially authorized judges, separately from adults' proceedings.[9]

Similar self-praise has appeared in the military's other statements, in both English and Hebrew. According to the military, these and other reforms concerning young Palestinians reflect a "legal approach seeking to enshrine in legislation the minor's rights as defendant, while taking into account the principle of the best interests of the minor." The reforms, characterized as "significant[ly] ... strengthening the protection of the rights of minors" through "practical and important provisions," purportedly have "great significance" and "substantial implications."[10]

---

[7] Article 33a of the Defense (Emergency) Regulations, 1945 (article enacted in 1947, in Amendment No. 15).

[8] Military Courts Unit, "The Military Courts Unit (Judea and Samaria)" (April, 2013), p. 3, www.militarycourtwatch.org/files/server/IDF%20Military%20Court%20Briefing%20Paper.pdf.

[9] IDF Spokesperson, "Amendment to the Military Law: The Age of Minority in Judea and Samaria Raised from 16 to 18" (October 4, 2011) [Hebrew], https://web.archive.org/web/20111006101350/http://www.idf.il/1133-13409-he/Dover.aspx.

[10] Office of the Legal Advisor to the IDF, "The Establishment of a Military Juvenile Court in Judea and Samaria" (August 26, 2009), ¶ 2 [Hebrew]; IDF Spokesperson's Office,

Some audiences seem to have been convinced by the military's claims. For example, a spokesperson for the British Foreign Office, when asked about the matter in 2018, cited "some improvements/progress by Israel" and specifically mentioned the establishment of "separate [military] juvenile courts."[11]

However, contrary to Israel's assertions, I will now show these to have mostly been token reforms, with little to no meaningful impact. Through a close inspection of their statutory architecture and effects, I will bring to light three mutually complementary reasons for this state of affairs: (a) Israel's recurrent prioritizing of symbolic amendments that it portrays as mending childhood's boundaries, but which do not change its handling of young Palestinians; (b) the inconsistent application, and even outright breach, of some provisions; and (c) the incorporation into the amended statutes of broad and frequently used qualification or exemption clauses.

The first issue – symbolic amendments that have no effect on the actual issues facing young Palestinians in conflict with Israeli law – characterizes both the military youth court and the increased age of criminal majority. The former resembles Israel's other military courts, except that it is legally obligated to hold its proceedings separately ("as much as possible")[12] from those involving older defendants. Though its judges are required by law to undergo "appropriate training," the precise nature of this training is not publicly known.[13] Similarly, increasing the age of criminal majority was no more than a semantic step that reclassified 16- and 17-year-olds as minors rather than adults. It has not been accompanied by any changes to the provisions regarding either the adjudication, sentencing, or incarceration of these newly classified

---

"Amendment to the Military Law: The Age of Minority in Judea and Samaria Raised from 16 to 18" (October 10, 2011) [Hebrew]; MAG Corps, "Security Legislation Amended to Define 'Minors' Under 18" (October 6, 2011), https://web.archive.org/web/20120313115118/http://www.mag.idf.il/163-4736-en/patzar.aspx; Office of the Legal Advisor to the IDF in Judea and Samaria, "Statutory Amendment: The Age of Minority in the Judea and Samaria Region Raised to 18" (October 5, 2011) [Hebrew].

[11] B. White, "UK Silence on Israel's Detention of Palestinian Children," *Al Jazeera* (May 9, 2018), www.aljazeera.com/news/2018/05/uk-silence-israel-detention-palestinian-children-180509141939606.html.

[12] Article 1 of Order 1644 (amending Articles 136–143 of Order 1651).

[13] DCIP, "Israeli Juvenile Military Court – Four Months On" (February 16, 2010), http://right2edu.birzeit.edu/israeli-juvenile-military-court-four-months/.

minors. Nor have the sentencing guidelines relating to them, or the actual sentences imposed on them, changed.[14]

It might be supposed that increasing the age of majority in 2011 at least changed where 16–17-year-olds were tried: youth-specific military courts instead of other military courts. This impression, expressed by some human rights actors, assumed that those aged 16 and over had previously been taken to non-youth military courts. The military advocate general reinforced this impression when announcing, upon launching the military youth courts in 2009, that they would hear only "cases of minors under the age of 16."[15] Yet, this statement was erroneous, as was human rights criticism based on it. In reality, from their very beginning, the military youth courts assumed jurisdiction over Palestinians up to the age of 18, albeit initially with no statutory basis for this jurisdiction. Less than a month after their establishment, the president of the military court of appeals noted in a ruling that these "courts have voluntarily adopted the age of minority in Israel [i.e., 18 years] as regards separating minors' proceedings from those of adults."[16] Other military judgments I have traced from that period support his remark. Aside from the tokenism of raising the age of majority, this highlights three issues identified in previous chapters: the incorrectness of some formal Israeli statements; the gap between judicial practice and statutory Israeli law; and human rights critics' misrepresentation of the legal state of affairs due to their insufficient awareness of these issues.

A series of other amendments, introduced in 2012 and 2013 in response to supreme court petitions on the matter,[17] also attracted considerable public attention. Though these amendments were described

---

[14] On the sentences imposed by the military youth courts, see N. Baumgarten-Sharon, *No Minor Matter: Violation of the Rights of Palestinian Minors Arrested by Israel on Suspicion of Stone-Throwing* (Jerusalem: B'Tselem, July 2011), www.btselem.org/down load/201107_no_minor_matter_eng.pdf. Additionally, as noted in the previous chapter (Section 3.2.1, "Youth as an Aggravating Factor"), the legal requirement to consider the defendant's young age is formally inapplicable to Palestinians aged over 16.

[15] See, respectively, Concord Research Center for Integration of International Law in Israel, *Letter to the Military Advocate General* (July 5, 2010) [Hebrew] (on file with the author); MAG, *Annual Activity Report – 2009* (2010), p. 91 [Hebrew], www.idf.il/media/32442/% D7%93%D7%95%D7%97-2009.pdf.

[16] MilA 2912/09 *Military Prosecutor* v. *Abu Rahma* (August 31,2009).

[17] Petition in HCJ 4057/10 *ACRI* v. *IDF Commander in the Judea and Samaria Region* (May 25, 2010), www.acri.org.il/pdf/petitions/hit4057.pdf; Petition in HCJ 3368/10 *Palestinian Ministry of Prisoners' Affairs and others* v. *Minister of Defense* (May 3, 2010) (on file with the author). Due to the overlap between these two petitions, the supreme court considered them together.

by the military as "shortening, very substantially, the [maximum] detention periods for [Palestinian] minors,"[18] what they have actually done is to keep detention potentially unlimited. This was done by explicitly preserving the authority of the military court of appeals to extend detention with no set limit, both at the pretrial stage and during the trial.[19]

These were by no means the only symbolic, and hence tokenistic, reforms. Two others, both in 2009, required military judges to assist unrepresented young Palestinians in examining witnesses, and entitled parents to examine witnesses.[20] Neither amendment, however, made much difference, due to the rarity of witness examination in Israeli military courts, as detailed in Chapter 2. Moreover, military judges have been reported as not informing Palestinian parents of their right to question witnesses,[21] and the military court of appeals has also authorized denying parents access to their children's hearings on "security grounds."[22]

Another amendment, from 2011, requires Israeli authorities to inform young Palestinians, prior to interrogation, of their right to legal counsel. However, the law places the onus of having an attorney's details not on the authorities, but on the young arrested Palestinians. And, even in the improbable event that the suspect under arrest does have this information, the interrogation can commence without awaiting the attorney's arrival.[23] Consequently, according to hundreds of testimonies of young Palestinian ex-detainees, rarely do arrested Palestinians receive legal counsel prior to their interrogation, and rarely are they interrogated in the presence of a parent.[24] The absence of these older Palestinians may

---

[18] Updated statement by the State in HCJ 3368/10 and HCJ 4057/10 (December 12, 2016), www.acri.org.il/he/wp-content/uploads/2012/12/hit4057idkun1212.pdf.

[19] Articles 38, 44 of Order 1651 (amended by Articles 5–6 of the Order Concerning Security Provisions (Amendment No. 16) (Judea and Samaria) (No. 1685), 2012; Article 2 of the Order Concerning Security Provisions (Amendment No. 25) (Judea and Samaria) (No. 1711), 2012; and Articles 1–2 of the Order Concerning Security Provisions (Amendment No. 34) (Judea and Samaria) (No. 1726), 2013).

[20] Articles 146(c), 147(b) of Order 1651.

[21] S. Ben-Natan, *All Guilty! Observations in the Military Juvenile Court* (No Legal Frontiers, July 2011), p. 34, http://nolegalfrontiers.org/images/stories/report_2011/report_en.pdf.

[22] See, e.g., MilA 1236/15 *Military Prosecution v. John Doe* (April 1, 2015).

[23] Article 136c of Order 1651.

[24] Military Court Watch, *Monitoring the Treatment of Children Held in Israeli Military Detention – Annual Report 2018/19*, pp. 10–11, www.militarycourtwatch.org/files/server/MCW%20ANNUAL%20REPORT%20(2019).pdf; UNICEF, *Children in Israeli Military Detention: Observations and Recommendations – Bulletin No. 2* (February,

assist Israeli authorities in their alleged attempts to use or recruit Palestinian youth as informants during and in between interrogations.[25]

Whereas all these reforms have left unchanged the conditions of Palestinian youth, several others have been rendered void by statutory exceptions incorporated into them. These exemption and qualification clauses are broad, heavily invoked by Israeli authorities, and, consequently, swallow the formal rules. Three examples are: a 2011 amendment, which obligates informing Palestinian parents or adult relatives of their child's arrest; another 2011 amendment, which sets a one-year statute of limitations for under-18s; and a 2014 amendment, which requires audio-visually recording interrogations of under-18s. All three provisions contain exception clauses that preclude their application to "security offenses"[26] – a term encompassing all common charges against young noncitizen Palestinians, as explained in Chapter 2. Thus, supposedly beneficial amendments were crafted so as almost never to apply.

In fact, the 2011 amendments – the requirement to inform a child's family of their arrest and the one-year statute of limitations – have been further eroded by two additional exception clauses. One exempts Israeli authorities from informing the family of the arrest when to do so might jeopardize "national security," "the success of the interrogation," or "the child's wellbeing" – open-ended terms enabling virtually unrestricted discretion. Maintaining such on-the-spot discretion is a key feature of the Israeli control regime, as explained in the previous chapter. The other exception clause likewise authorizes the military, at its discretion, to prosecute young Palestinians even after the one-year statute of limitations has expired.[27] These statutory exceptions thus became the effective rules, while the formal rules became the exceptions. Complementing these myriad exceptions are two additional factors, which reduce

2015), www.unicef.org/oPt/Children_in_Israeli_Military_Detention_-_Observations_and_Recommendations_-_Bulletin_No._2_-_February_2015.pdf [hereinafter: UNICEF 2015].

[25] On these attempts, see Addameer, "Imprisonment of Children" (December 2017), www.addameer.org/the_prisoners/children; Military Court Watch, "Monitoring the Treatment of Children Held in Israeli Military Detention – Annual Report 2018/19" (June 24, 2019), pp. 11–12, www.militarycourtwatch.org/files/server/MCW%20ANNUAL%20REPORT%20(2019).pdf.

[26] Articles 4, 5, 7 of Order 1676; Article 1 of the Order Concerning Security Provisions (Amendment No. 43) (Temporary Order) (Judea and Samaria) (No. 1745), 2014. Children suspected of "security offenses" are subject to a longer (two-year) statute of limitations.

[27] See, respectively, Article 4 of Order 1676 (amending Article 136b of Order 1651); Article 144 of Order 1651.

whatever is left of Palestinians' formal right to be informed of their child's arrest: one factor, reportedly, is the non-enforcement of this right even where none of the aforementioned exceptions applies; the other factor, acknowledged by a military judge, is Israel's frequent prevention, through various "security restrictions," of Palestinian parents from reaching the police station.[28]

It is against this backdrop that one should assess Israel's self-congratulatory claims, such as that reported in 2017 by the United States Department of State:

> The [Israeli] government rejected claims that interrogations of [Palestinian] minors breached [international law] ..., claiming that reforms implemented since 2008 improved the treatment of Palestinian minors, including the establishment of a Juvenile Military Court, raising the age of majority to 18 years old, introducing a special statute of limitation for minors, improving notification to a minor's family and the minors themselves regarding their rights, and reducing detention periods.[29]

Israel's use of all-embracing statutory exceptions is not new; nor is it confined to the military law. In 1967, shortly after taking over the West Bank and Gaza Strip, the military issued an order limiting to a year the maximum prison sentence for Palestinians aged 14–15. Initially, an exception clause excluded only a handful of offenses relating to political expression. But within less than three years, it was expanded considerably to include all offenses with maximum penalties of at least five years[30] – making the maximum sentence limitation inapplicable to all common charges against young Palestinians.

Beyond the military law, and contrary to Israeli claims,[31] reports suggest that young Palestinians in East Jerusalem are likewise frequently

---

[28] See, respectively, DCIP, *Bound, Blindfolded and Convicted: Children Held in Military Detention* (April 2012), p. 19, http://arabic.dci-palestine.org/sites/arabic.dci-palestine .org/files/report_0.pdf; C. Levinson, "Military Court: The Police Fails in Relation to Palestinian Minors," *Haaretz* (July 17, 2013; no longer available online) [Hebrew].

[29] United States Department of State, *Country Report for 2016: Israel and the Occupied Territories* (March 3, 2017), p. 4, www.state.gov/wp-content/uploads/2017/03/Israel-and-The-Occupied-Territories-The-Occupied-Territories.pdf.

[30] Article 5 of the Order Concerning the Adjudication of Young Offenders (West Bank Area) (No. 132), 1967 [hereinafter: Order 132], as amended by Order Concerning the Adjudication of Young Offenders (West Bank Area) (Amendment No. 3) (No. 371), 1970.

[31] See, e.g., "Response Letter from the Israeli Military Regarding Military Arrests of Palestinian Children in the West Bank," *Human Rights Watch* (July 13, 2015), www

denied their formal protections under the non-military law, due to the local police using statutory exceptions and even contravening the law. Two statutory provisions relating to interrogations exemplify this. The first entitles under-18s to have a parent or relative present at their interrogation, as well as to consult with this parent or relative, preferably prior to the interrogation. The second requires refraining from interrogating under-18s "at night" (defined as 20:00–07:00 for under-14s and 22:00–07:00 for those aged 14–17). Both provisions contain expansive and widely used exemption clauses. One clause exempts the police – an exemption reportedly used in three out of four cases – from providing family presence and contact during or before interrogation, on such grounds as safeguarding the interrogation or protecting national security. Invoking a similar exception clause, the Jerusalem police have also reportedly detained many young Palestinians at night.[32]

4.3   Generational Segregation and Its Pitfalls

While some reforms have been tokenistic, another has had an adverse effect on Palestinians. This was the increased separation of noncitizen Palestinians under the age of majority in Israeli custody, of which the military youth court was only one element. Palestinians can be incarcerated in either military or IPS facilities. In the past, they were held mostly in military custody, with very limited separation between Palestinians under and over 18. Military law did not separate Palestinians by age in prison. In detention, there was a requirement to separate those under

---

.hrw.org/news/2015/07/13/response-letter-israeli-military-regarding-military-arrests-pal estinian-children ("The Israeli Youth Law is applied equally to any and all suspects arrested in Israel.") [hereinafter: "Response Letter from the Israeli Military"].

[32] The above provisions and exceptions appear in Articles 9h and 9j of the Youth Law (Adjudication, Punishment and Methods of Treatment), 1971 [hereinafter: Youth Law]; Article 3(c)(2)(a) of Police Ordinance No. 14.01.05 Concerning the Police Handling of Minors, 2004. The violations are reported in N. Alyan, *Violations of the "Youth Law (Adjudication, Punishment and Methods of Treatment) – 1971" by the Israeli Police in East Jerusalem* (Tel Aviv: ACRI, March 2011), pp. 9–14, http://reliefweb.int/sites/ reliefweb.int/files/resources/Full_Report_1007.pdf; N. Baumgarten-Sharon, *Caution: Children Ahead – The Illegal Behavior of the Police toward Minors in Silwan Suspected of Stone Throwing* (Jerusalem: B'Tselem, December 2010), pp. 18–19, www.btselem.org/ download/201012_caution_children_ahead_eng.pdf; DCIP, *Voices from East Jerusalem: The Situation Facing Palestinian Children* (August 2011), pp. 42–44, https:// d3n8a8pro7vhmx.cloudfront.net/dcipalestine/pages/1297/attachments/original/1433986 700/DCIP_east_jerusalem_final.pdf?1433986700.

16,[33] but it was relevant to only a small minority of under-18s, as the majority were detained at the age of 16 and 17 (as Chapter 2 notes). Even for younger Palestinians in detention, such separation was not always enforced.[34]

There were periods of greater separation in specific facilities. In the 1980s, Israel designated a detention center in the West Bank for Palestinians aged up to 23 awaiting summary trial, who were reportedly subjected to torture and harsh conditions.[35] The 1990s saw one prison reportedly separating Palestinians under the age of 18 at night, while allowing them contact with five older inmates to assist them during the day. This arrangement was terminated, however, with the release of these older Palestinians.[36]

The first decade of the century ushered in a significant change: a shift toward systematic separation. Responsibility for all facilities in which Palestinians were detained and imprisoned gradually transferred from the military to the IPS.[37] The latter, pursuant to Israel's non-military law, generally separates all inmates under the age of 18.[38] Later, the military amended its law to extend separation to military facilities as well,[39] where noncitizen Palestinians can still be detained. As a result, both military and non-military Israeli law now require that Palestinian youth are placed either in separate facilities or in separate wings inaccessible to their older counterparts, with non-separation allowed only in certain exceptional circumstances.[40]

---

[33] Article 3 of Order 132.

[34] C. Cook, A. Hanieh, and A. Kay (in association with DCIP), *Stolen Youth: The Politics of Israel's Detention of Palestinian Children* (London: Pluto Press, 2004); DCIP and Save the Children - Sweden, *Child Rights - Situation Analysis: Right to Protection in the Occupied Palestinian Territory - 2008* (2009), http://resourcecentre.savethechildren.se/sites/default/files/documents/3321.pdf; MilA 67/96 *Jasser* v. *Chief Military Prosecutor* (1996); MilA 1307/10 *Barakan* v. *Military Prosecutor* (2010).

[35] GA, Thirty-Ninth Session - Agenda Item 71, UN Doc A/39/591 (July 17, 1985), http://unispal.un.org/UNISPAL.NSF/0/B7A72309FFEA6F1485256A68004F0024.

[36] Baumgarten-Sharon, *No Minor Matter*, p. 60.

[37] As reported, e.g., in HCJ 2690/09 *Yesh Din* v. *IDF Commander in the West Bank* (March 28, 2010).

[38] Articles 13(a), 34b(a) of the Youth Law; Article 21g of IPS Commission Ordinance 03.02.00: Guidelines Regarding Security Prisoners (March 15, 2002); Articles 8a, 8e of IPS Commission Ordinance 04.08.00 Concerning the Detention/Imprisonment of Minors (December 27, 2009).

[39] Article 46n of Order 1644.

[40] Articles 13(b1), 34b of the Youth Law; Articles 8–9 of IPS Commission Ordinance 04.08.00; Article 149(a1) of Order 1651; Article 46n of Order 1644.

The next subsection will critically analyze the Israeli legal system's support for such generational segregation, as well as judicial calls to rehabilitate young Palestinians in prison. Then, I will bring to light the harm that generational segregation and "rehabilitation" inflict on Palestinian youth in the name of child rights: depriving them of valuable support; exposing them to greater abuse; not leading to more moderate sentences; and all of this against Palestinians' own preferences. From there, I will turn to the human rights community, shedding light on its essentialism and legalism, its blindness to the ills of these reforms, and its occasional portrayal of Palestinians over the age of majority as a national security threat. I will argue that these reforms have facilitated the revocation and narrowing down of the rights of incarcerated Palestinians aged 18 and over, with near silence from human rights actors. In this sense, older Palestinians, no less than their juniors, were the target of these reforms.

4.3.1   The Battle over the Palestinian Child's "Soul"

Before and during this gradual shift, military judgments advocated separation as a means to achieve two complementary objectives: first, preventing unwanted intergenerational knowledge transfer among the incarcerated Palestinians; and, second, undoing the existing impact of these intergenerational influences through "rehabilitation." Military court of appeals judge Shaul Gordon suggested in 2003, unusually, that this be done by transferring a 12-year-old Palestinian convict to a Palestinian rehabilitation facility, as requested by the defense:

> [T]he appellant is incarcerated with other prisoners, older than him, who were convicted of security offenses ... If ... there is an alternative framework that may distance the appellant from those adults ..., then surely this framework must be preferred over prison ... [T]he appellant may indeed be distanced, for a while, from those adults who wished to capture his soul, and may even receive rehabilitative treatment that will help him oppose those adults ... in the future. Furthermore, ... there is inherent risk in imprisonment in the company of security prisoners, as the exposure to these prisoners' ideologies and the social pressure may also have their influence.[41]

The young Palestinian's "soul," judge Gordon suggests, is an object of a legal–political battle. This battle is fought over space – over the proximity

---

[41] MilA 358/03 *El-Nasirat* v. *Military Prosecutor* (December 18, 2003).

of older Palestinians to their juniors – as well as over time – over Israel's ability to promptly intervene before these youth are irreversibly inaugurated into an allegedly nationalistic adulthood.

In one key respect, Gordon's decision was highly unusual: unlike other inmates,[42] Palestinian "security offenders," including under-18s, are not normally referred to rehabilitation services in prison.[43] And, as Gordon himself acknowledged, Israeli authorities rarely consider Palestinian rehabilitation facilities an acceptable alternative.[44] But while his decision was unconventional, Gordon's rhetoric closely resembled that of other military judgments. This includes his own decision, the following year, to reject the military prosecution's appeal to increase the sentence of "a young [Palestinian] youth about 18 years old." Reiterating his earlier rationale, Gordon ruled: "if [he] has not yet adopted the ideology popular among many of the prisoners, then in fact a prolonged imprisonment might lead him to adopt it."[45]

Other military judges have voiced similar concerns. In 2009, judge Amir Dahan of the Judea military court warned that a 16-year-old's detention with older Palestinians "hinders ... his rehabilitation: it is not difficult to predict the consequences of a tender youth's long, continuous and daily stay with such adults in an institutional doctrinal [possibly meant to say 'indoctrinating'] framework."[46] That same year, Judea military court judge Sharon Rivlin-Ahai similarly noted that under the military law in effect at the time, "a 16-year-old defendant can be incarcerated with adults who committed grave security offenses ... Protracted incarceration in such conditions is likely to severely harm both his rehabilitation chances and the public interest."[47] Reproducing a

---

[42] Articles 11c–11d of Prisons Ordinance [New Version] (1972).

[43] Article 1b of IPS Commission Ordinance 04.54.02: Rehabilitation Frameworks for Prisoners (October 20, 2004; last amended August 8, 2010); Article 4b of IPS Commission Ordinance 03.02.00; AppR 4612/16 *John Doe* v. *Parole Board* (July 25, 2016); National Public Defense Office, Detention and Incarceration Conditions in Israeli Prison Service Facilities in the Years 2017–2018 (May 2019), pp. 37–41 [Hebrew], www.justice.gov.il/Units/SanegoriaZiborit/ DohotRishmi/Documents/PrisonConditionsReport2017-2018.pdf.

[44] See also MilC (Judea) 1261/09 *Military Prosecution* v. *El-Farukh* (February 23, 2009); Baumgarten-Sharon, *No Minor Matter*.

[45] MilA 372/03 *Military Prosecutor* v. *Sha'alan* (January 15, 2004).

[46] MilC (Judea) 4779/08 *Military Prosecutor* v. *Makhlouf* (February 1, 2009).

[47] MilC (Judea) 1261/09.

prevalent albeit debatable concept of the young as uniquely impression-
able and tractable, these judgments portray Palestinian youth as suggest-
ible, on the one hand, to the allegedly negative influence of older
Palestinians, and, on the other hand, to Israeli intervention. It is this
presumed plasticity that led the military judiciary to espouse preventative
generational segregation and corrective rehabilitation.

Taking this rationale further, the supreme court has repeatedly called
for young Palestinians in Israeli prison to be rehabilitated systematically
rather than on a case-by-case basis. No longer is generational segregation
considered sufficient for harnessing these youth's assumed plasticity to its
fullest. Instead of merely foiling Palestinian ideological influences, a new
frontier emerged in the battle over these youth: systematic Israeli
counter-influences. Most supreme court rulings on the matter have been
unanimous, with justice Elyakim Rubinstein writing the leading opinion.
In a 2007 decision to reject the appeals of two Palestinians, aged 14 and
15 at the time of their offenses, Rubinstein remarked:

> The lack of social treatment and educational arrangements [for young
> security prisoners] ... requires rethinking ... [N]obody wishes for minors
> (or others who are very young) ... [convicted of] terrorist offenses to be
> upgraded in criminality, and [for] prison to become their university for
> terrorist science ... in the absence of ... treatment [and] ... education.
> This is not only in the minors' interest ... It is in the public interest, in
> order to exhaust the possibility ... of bringing them to function in
> accordance with norms and productively.[48]

Over the following decade, Rubinstein reiterated these concerns in other
judgments,[49] as well as in his academic writing,[50] and his remarks on the
matter were later quoted by other Israeli judges.[51] Among other things,
Rubinstein maintained that Palestinian "minors or very young adults"
have "better rehabilitation chances" than those of their older counterparts.[52] Without rehabilitation, he warned, prison would be a "university

---

[48] CrimA 10118/06 *John Doe* v. *State of Israel* (April 30, 2007).
[49] See the cases cited below, as well as CrimA 4102/08 *Dirbas* v. *State of Israel* (December 1, 2009); CrimA 3572/16 *John Doe* v. *State of Israel* (January 3, 2017).
[50] E. Rubinstein, "The Minor in Law" (2010) 3–4 *The Family in Law* 35, 62 [Hebrew].
[51] CrimA 5559/16 *State of Israel* v. *John Doe* (August 4, 2016); AdminC (Beer-Sheva Dist.) 41696-08-16 *Al-Nadi* v. *IPS* (June 25, 2017).
[52] CrimA 7515/08 *State of Israel* v. *Gurin* (January 5, 2009).

for terror,"[53] "an academy for terrorism," and "a school for many future terrorist experts."[54]

The image of prison as a "school for terrorism" or a "school for crime" is hardly unique to Israel/Palestine.[55] But the version recurrent in the Israeli judgments seems to have originated from imprisoned Palestinians themselves. It is they who have long spoken of Israeli prison as "an academy of political activism," "a university," "a lecture hall," and "a school" for acquiring valuable political knowledge and consciousness. Having taken hold in Palestinian society at large, this imagery refers, among other things, to Palestinians' studies in prison. This includes both academic and informal studies. The former, mostly sponsored by the Palestinian Authority, were carried out through the Israeli Open University. The latter, usually conducted in groups segregated according to political affiliations, have covered, among other subjects, Palestinian and Zionist histories, Palestinian culture, Islam, security outside the prison, Arabic literacy, and Hebrew or English as a second language.[56]

Israeli authorities are well aware of Palestinians' original portrayal of prison as a political university. An article in the IPS journal, which discusses the perceptions of "security prisoners," characterizes Israeli prison as a "Palestinian academy for national leadership" – a phrase the article places in parentheses, presumably to attribute this quote to Palestinians. The article adds:

> For [such] prisoners . . ., [Israeli] prison is a stage in . . . national development, personally and collectively . . . [T]hese prisoners . . . have delved

---

[53] This phrase appears in CrimA 6257/10 *John Doe* v. *State of Israel* (May 29, 2011); CrimA 3673/15 *John Doe* v. *State of Israel* (March 14, 2016).

[54] The latter two phrases appear, respectively, in CrimA 7515/08; CrimA 1456/07 *John Doe* v. *State of Israel* (July 10, 2007).

[55] See, e.g., C. R. Jones, "Are Prisons Really Schools for Terrorism? Challenging the Rhetoric on Prison Radicalization" (2014) 16:1 *Punishment & Society* 74; B. Fine, "Struggles against Discipline: The Theory and Politics of Michel Foucault" (1979) 3:3 *Capital & Class* 75, 90.

[56] M. Rosenfeld, *Confronting the Occupation: Work, Education, and Political Activism of Palestinian Families in a Refugee Camp* (Stanford: Stanford University Press, 2004); J. Collins, *Occupied by Memory: The Intifada Generation and the Palestinian State of Emergency* (New York: New York University Press, 2004); J. Peteet, "Male Gender and Rituals of Resistance in the Palestinian Intifada – A Cultural Politics of Violence," in M. Ghoussoub and E. Sinclair-Webb (eds.), *Imagined Masculinities: Male Identity and Culture in the Middle East* (London: Saqi Books, 2000), pp. 103–26; L. Taraki, "The Development of Political Consciousness among Palestinians in the Occupied Territories, 1967–1987," in J. R. Nassar and R. Heacock (eds.), *Intifada: Palestine at the Crossroads* (New York: Praeger, 1990), pp. 53–71.

into Israeli issues, mainly by reading books, ... [and] have translated ... [writings by prominent Zionist leaders and thinkers]. They have had ideological debates on the ways and means of acquiring Palestinian political independence ... [and] the future character of the Palestinian state. Over the years, Open University studies were also made available in prison. Security prisoners completed Bachelor's and Master's degrees within the prison walls, and a few successfully pursued doctoral studies ... Not for nothing has prison been called "the national Palestinian academy."[57]

It is through incarcerated Palestinians' own conceptual framework, then, that the Israeli judiciary has come to criticize their intergenerational interactions. In an attempted reconfiguration of prison, this conceptual framework, along with the intergenerational politicization to which it alludes, was transformed. From markers of collective Palestinian empowerment, they were reconstructed into grounds for deploying Israeli divide-and-rule methods, including age-segregated incarceration.

Three later judgments, all from 2014, illustrate the supreme court's continued concern over the lack of rehabilitation services in prison for Palestinian youth. "This Court has repeatedly raised the issue of the treatment of security prisoners who are minors or young adults ... Yet unfortunately ... we see no actual change," justice Rubinstein remarked in one judgment.[58] In another, justice Uri Shoham wrote for a three-judge panel:

> We believe, regardless of our rejection of the [Palestinian minor's] appeal, that ... defining minors as security offenders and the [resultant] lack of a rehabilitative program [for them] ... is often a self-fulfilling prophecy ... [Admitting such] minors to a therapeutic-rehabilitative process tailored to their needs may bear positive outcomes and prevent [their] future return to activity of a security-ideological nature.[59]

The supreme court's calls to rehabilitate incarcerated young Palestinians have been reported in the Israeli press,[60] in addition to

---

[57] R. Shaked, "Security Prisoners in Israeli Prisons" (2008) 23 *Seeing Shabas – IPS Journal* 26–29, 27 [Hebrew]; see also ibid., pp. 28–29.

[58] CrimA 8639/13 *Taritari v. State of Israel* (March 17, 2014).

[59] CrimA 3702/14 *John Doe v. State of Israel* (September 28, 2014), ¶ 12 of justice Shoham's opinion. The third case is CrimA 3528/14 *Bakhirat v. State of Israel* (September 22, 2014).

[60] R. Hovel, "Supreme Court Repeats Call for Rehabilitation of Security Prisoners," *Haaretz* (April 22, 2014) [Hebrew], www.haaretz.co.il/news/law/1.2301528; C. Levinson, "Military Advocate General Denies Detained Palestinian Minors Access to Rehabilitation," *Haaretz* (May 23, 2014) [Hebrew], www.haaretz.co.il/news/politics/.premium-1.2329559.

either being cited approvingly by, or receiving support from, the military courts, members of parliament, the public defense, and the Youth Probation Service in the Ministry of Social Affairs and Social Services.[61] The IPS, in contrast, has been reluctant to adopt the court's rehabilitation vision. In a position paper submitted to the court, the IPS asserted that "security prisoners ... consider themselves neither offenders nor in need of social treatment. [They] ... are generally not interested in any contact with social workers whom they consider part of the Israeli establishment." However, justice Rubinstein insisted: "With due respect, I doubt that all the imprisoned minors share the view described by the IPS ... Even if this is the majority view, ... there is no room for giving up."[62]

The Israeli judiciary, along with human rights organizations, has thus pressed for two changes. One, the age segregation of Palestinians, became a reality. The other, Israeli "rehabilitation" of imprisoned Palestinian youth, was resisted by the prison authorities and, perhaps for this reason among others, remains mostly a rhetorical plea. In principle, the IPS is legally instructed to provide all under-18s in prison and pretrial detention with educational and vocational services.[63] In practice, and largely in line with the IPS's own regulations,[64] many detained Palestinian youth are either denied or inadequately provided with these services.[65]

4.3.2 Harming Young Palestinians in the Name of Child Rights

As they did with the other reforms I have analyzed, Israeli authorities made sure to portray generational segregation and "rehabilitation" as implementing international law and serving children's rights. "Regarding ... [Palestinian] minors' rights," Israel's deputy state attorney told the UN Committee Against Torture in 2009, "under international law ... [and IPS] rules, minors [are] ... held in separate facilities from

---

[61] See, respectively, MilC (Judea) 1261/09 *Military Prosecutor* v. *El-Farukh* (February 23, 2009); Special Committee for Public Petitions, 19th Knesset – Transcript 35 (December 31, 2013) [Hebrew], http://fs.knesset.gov.il/19/Committees/19_ptv_268301.doc; CrimA 1456/07; CrimA 10118/06.

[62] CrimA 1456/07, ¶¶ b(3), b(5) of justice Rubinstein's opinion.

[63] Articles 6–10 of Youth Regulations (Adjudication, Punishment, and Modes of Treatment) (Detention or Imprisonment Conditions for Minors), 2012.

[64] Article 27h of IPS Commission Ordinance 04.08.00.

[65] N. Alyan and M. Russo, *Arrested Childhood: The Ramifications of Israel's New Strict Policy toward Minors Suspected of Involvement in Stone Throwing, Security Offenses, and Disturbances* (Tel Aviv: ACRI, February 2016); DCIP, *No Way to Treat a Child*; Military Court Watch, "Monitoring the Treatment."

adults." The previously mentioned leaflet for foreign delegations similarly notes that the military now "provides for a separation between [Palestinian] minor and adult detainees."[66] Rehabilitation behind bars would, according to the supreme court, likewise serve young Palestinians' interest.

Contrary to this rhetoric, both separation and so-called rehabilitation for young Palestinians in Israeli custody are potentially detrimental to Palestinians, in several respects. The common rationale for age-based separation in criminal custody – the belief that it protects the young from older, and hence dangerous, criminals – does not apply to the Palestinians whom Israel classifies as security prisoners. They are neither criminals in the regular sense of the word nor usually incarcerated together with those classified as criminal prisoners. Further, the increased generational segregation might have robbed incarcerated Palestinian youth of valuable support. Reports suggest that, prior to the shift toward age-segregated incarceration, they received psychological, educational, and material care from their older counterparts, who also helped them peacefully resolve their violent conflicts and represented their concerns to the prison authorities.[67] Indeed, as detailed in the next chapter, testimonies by young ex-detainees cast joint incarceration with older Palestinians in an unequivocally positive light.

Such support is particularly crucial for most young Palestinians, who, like their older counterparts, are transferred to facilities within Israel's pre-1967 borders and thus denied contact with their families.[68] This

---

[66] See, respectively, UNCAT, Summary Record of the 881st Meeting – Consideration of Reports Submitted by States Parties Under Article 19 of the Convention, UN Doc CAT/C/SR.881 (November 25, 2009), ¶¶ 17–18, http://docstore.ohchr.org/SelfServices/FilesHandler.ashx?enc=6QkG1d%2FPPRiCAqhKb7yhsmoIqL9rS46HZROnmdQS5bPun cRLibGp0bpglCm2TkrosMxGBjjA1jzZ9yGrlRADP12cR0Krjv%2FwlqAVZOBbQeV97vh 2qRMCFayMT9zrJAO3; Military Courts Unit, "The Military Courts Unit (Judea and Samaria)," p. 3.

[67] P. Veerman and A. Waldman, "When Can Children and Adolescents Be Detained Separately from Adults?: The Case of Palestinian Children Deprived of Their Liberty in Israeli Military Jails and Prisons" (1996) 4:2 *International Journal of Children's Rights* 147; Cook, Hanieh, and Kay, *Stolen Youth*; Baumgarten-Sharon, *No Minor Matter*.

[68] Baumgarten-Sharon, *No Minor Matter*; DCIP, *In Their Own Words: A Report on the Situation Facing Palestinian Children Detained in the Israeli Military Court System* (January 29, 2011), http://resourcecentre.savethechildren.se/sites/default/files/docu ments/4705.pdf; DCIP, *No Way to Treat a Child: Palestinian Children in the Israeli Military Detention System* (April 2016), https://d3n8a8pro7vhmx.cloudfront.net/dcipales tine/pages/1527/attachments/original/1460665378/DCIP_NWTTAC_Report_Final_April_

practice, upheld twice by the supreme court,[69] is exacerbated by a number of impediments to family visits: the length and complexity of obtaining visitor permits; the frequent refusal of visits on alleged security grounds; the constantly changing prison visitation regulations; the low frequency of permitted visits; and the barring of family phone calls. Against this backdrop, older Palestinians in prison could offer the closest available substitute for parental care.

For the hundreds of Gazans in Israeli prisons, family visits were initially banned as part of the Gaza closure, again with the supreme court's blessing.[70] Visits were reinstated in 2012 following a hunger strike by prisoners, but at the time of writing no more than 50 weekly visits are allowed. This excludes the many prisoners affiliated with Hamas (Gaza's governing body), whom Israel has sweepingly denied visits since 2017[71] – yet another measure approved by the supreme court.[72] Like other travel restrictions, investigated in the previous chapter and later in this chapter, those concerning prison visits employ age as an exclusionary device. Prisoners from the West Bank are currently entitled to visits from any relative, but siblings and children aged 16–35 are only given permits that are valid for 60 days and allow for two entries.[73] Gazans, in contrast, were precluded from visiting their incarcerated parents in the first few years of the closure. In 2013, those under the age of eight began receiving permits, and over time the age maximum was raised to 16.[74]

The pitfalls of age-segregated incarceration do not end here. Some incarcerated youth might experience separation by age as extra punishment because in poor families, from which most of them come, young

---

2016.pdf; Military Court Watch, Newsletter – December 2015 (January, 2016), www .militarycourtwatch.org/page.php?id5I2MKZUiCJBa715152AvCMzjdt1H2.

[69] HCJ 253/88 *Sajdiyeh v. Minister of Defense* (1988) 42(3) PD 801; HCJ 2690/09.

[70] HCJ 5268/08 *Anbar v. IDF Southern Command Chief* (December 9, 2009).

[71] COGAT, Unclassified Status of Permissions for Palestinians to Enter Israel, Their Movement Between the Judea and Samaria Area and the Gaza Strip, and Their Exit Overseas (December 15, 2019 version), pp. 9, 15, 42, 52 [Hebrew], www.gisha.org/ UserFiles/File/LegalDocuments/procedures/general/50.pdf [hereinafter: Unclassified Status of Permissions].

[72] HCJ 6314/17 *Namnam v. Government of Israel* (June 4, 2019).

[73] COGAT, Unclassified Status of Permissions, p. 42.

[74] B'Tselem, "Distant Relatives: Severe Restrictions Imposed on Prison Visits by Immediate Family to Gazans Held in Israel" (January 22, 2018), www.btselem.org/gaza_strip/ 20180122_restrictions_on_gazans_prison_visits; B'Tselem, "Israel Prohibits Gazan Children from Visiting Imprisoned Fathers" (May 22, 2018), www.btselem.org/video/ 20130322_israel_prohibits_gazan_children_from_visiting_imprisoned_fathers#full.

and old often sleep in the same room.[75] Moreover, being separated from older Palestinians may well have made these young people more vulnerable to abuse by the Israeli prison and security forces, whose commonly reported abuse includes physical violence, threats, protracted handcuffing, and binding in stress positions (practices further examined in Chapter 6).[76] In addition, Israel has reportedly sometimes held young Palestinians in solitary confinement during their interrogation, for periods ranging from days to weeks, to secure confessions or gather information by cutting them off from the outside world.[77] Prolonged solitary confinement can be deeply damaging to the mental and, in some circumstances, physical health of the detained person.[78] When criticized by defense attorneys for this practice, the military authorities have cited the legal obligation to separate incarcerated youth and argued that, absent other youth in the facility, solitary confinement is inescapable.[79]

As for the supreme court's push for Israeli authorities to rehabilitate young Palestinian "security prisoners," many Palestinians roundly reject this proposition. For them, youth throwing stones at Israeli soldiers, for example (the most common charge against them, as discussed in Chapter 2), are not juvenile delinquents in need of such rehabilitation.[80] Further, even in circumstances where Palestinians regard imprisoned youth as requiring rehabilitation, it is highly questionable whether such rehabilitation should be carried out by Israeli authorities, whose primary commitment is not to Palestinian interests. Throwing the latter issue into sharp relief is Israel's history of seeking to reshape Palestinian consciousness. Recent examples vary. Alongside the desire to "rehabilitate" imprisoned Palestinian youth, there have also been calls by top Israeli

---

[75] Veerman and Waldman, "When Can Children and Adolescents Be Detained Separately from Adults?". On the socioeconomic profile of incarcerated Palestinian youth, see Alyan and Russo, *Arrested Childhood*; DCIP, *No Way to Treat a Child*.

[76] See, e.g., UNICEF 2015; Addameer, "Imprisonment of Children"; DCIP, *No Way to Treat a Child*; Military Court Watch, Newsletter – December 2015.

[77] See, e.g., L. Caspi, *Childhood in Chains: The Detention and Interrogation of Palestinian Teenagers in the West Bank* (Jerusalem: Hamoked, April 2018), pp. 6–7, www.hamoked.org/files/2018/1162860_eng.pdf; DCIP, "Increasing Numbers of Palestinian Children Held in Solitary Confinement" (July 26, 2016), www.dci-palestine.org/increasing_numbers_of_palestinian_children_held_in_solitary_confinement.

[78] See, generally, J. Lobel, "Prolonged Solitary Confinement and the Constitution" (2008) 11:1 *Journal of Constitutional Law* 115.

[79] MilA 20/02 *Ganam* v. *Military Prosecutor* (February 20, 2002); MilA 154/03 *A-Najjar* v. *Military Prosecutor* (February 12, 2003).

[80] Baumgarten-Sharon, *No Minor Matter*.

officials to "sear Palestinian consciousness" through military attacks on the Gaza Strip,[81] as well as, according to former Israeli soldiers, regular attempts at "sowing fear" and "displaying presence" through brutality toward West Bank Palestinians.[82] In the past, the Israeli military also closely monitored and censored Palestinian university and school curricula, textbooks, and extracurricular activities.[83] At present, and as described shortly, Israel limits Palestinians' access to information, their higher education options, and their studies behind the prison walls.

Moreover, the rehabilitation envisioned by the supreme court is neither a substitute for incarceration nor a mitigating sentencing factor. The idea is to "rehabilitate" young Palestinians in prison rather than outside it. Most of the previously cited supreme court judgments championing such rehabilitation neither avoided nor reduced, and sometimes actually increased, young Palestinians' prison sentences.

At the same time, to be considered for early release, Palestinians classified as "security prisoners" must convince the Israeli parole board that they have undergone ideological transformation, and they stand no chance of doing so without participating in the prison's rehabilitation programs.[84] For this reason, a few imprisoned Palestinians have petitioned the supreme court – unsuccessfully – against IPS decisions to exclude them from these programs.[85] The court also ruled, in 2016 and again in 2019, that unrehabilitated "security prisoners," including young ones, should not be paroled, even though the prison authorities were those barring them from rehabilitation.[86] Although a 2017 ruling entitled "security prisoners" who renounce association with any political association to a social worker's reassessment of their suitability for rehabilitation in prison, this provision was reserved exclusively for citizens and residents of Israel, whom the supreme court accurately described as a tiny

[81] A. Shavit, "Top PM Aide: Gaza Plan Aims to Freeze the Peace Process" *Haaretz* (October 6, 2004), www.haaretz.com/print-edition/news/top-pm-aide-gaza-plan-aims-to-freeze-the-peaceprocess-1.136686.

[82] M. Zagor, "'I Am the Law'! – Perspectives of Legality and Illegality in the Israeli Army" (2010) 43:3 *Israel Law Review* 551, 573.

[83] C. Bruhn, "Higher Education as Empowerment: The Case of Palestinian Universities" (2006) 49:8 *American Behavioral Scientist* 1125; I. Zelkovitz, "Education, Revolution and Evolution: The Palestinian Universities as Initiators of National Struggle 1972–1995" (2014) 43:3 *History of Education* 387.

[84] A. Baker, "Palestinian Prisoners: The Community and the Individual – An Inside Look" (2016) 8 *Law & Social Change* 95 [Hebrew].

[85] See, e.g., AppR 3770/14 *Kharuve v. IPS* (August 3, 2014).

[86] AppR 4612/16; AppR 119/19 *John Doe v. Parole Board* (April 14, 2019).

minority of Palestinian "security prisoners."[87] The following year, the state attorney declared a new policy giving greater weight to rehabilitation, but excluded from it all "security prisoners."[88] Absent access to the prison's rehabilitation programs, imprisoned Palestinians turned at one point to private mental health professionals to prepare rehabilitation plans for the parole board, and to confirm, when the prisoners were applying for temporary home leave, their non-dangerousness. But the IPS then prohibited contact with private mental health professionals as well, a policy upheld by the supreme court with the qualification that it would need to be enforced on a case-by-case basis.[89] Palestinians classified as security prisoners are thus placed in an impossible position: regardless of their willingness to cooperate with the problematic option of "rehabilitation" in Israeli prison, they are highly unlikely to be granted early release.

Whereas the Israeli judiciary's calls to "rehabilitate" Palestinian youth in prison have yet to become a reality, the military did make two other reforms, couched in a language of rehabilitation, which are likewise problematic. The first, in 2009, was to legally authorize military courts, at their discretion, to order pre-sentence reports on young convicts' circumstances, including an evaluation of their rehabilitation chances.[90] Such reports, and the rehabilitation evaluations they contain, are carried out by an Israeli body whose commitment to Palestinians is questionable: the Civil Administration, which oversees non-military affairs in the West Bank, such as the land registry, movement permits, and work permits.[91] The deputy minister responsible for this agency was quoted, in 2013, as calling Palestinians "beasts" and "non-human."[92] Moreover, the added time needed for evaluations between conviction and sentencing,

---

[87] Appeal 5754/15 *Khatib* v. *IPS* (July 2, 2017).

[88] R. Hovel, "State Attorney Changes Its Penal Policy: Prison for Fewer Offenders – Rehabilitation for More," *Haaretz* (January 16, 2018) [Hebrew], www.haaretz.co.il/news/law/.premium-1.5728918.

[89] AppR 4644/15 *Ra'ee* v. *Prison Service*, ¶ 10, 32 of justice Vogelman's opinion (June 15, 2016).

[90] Article 148 of Order 1651.

[91] N. Gordon, *Israel's Occupation* (Berkeley: University of California Press, 2008); I. Zertal and A. Eldar, *Lords of the Land: The War over Israel's Settlements in the Occupied Territories, 1967–2007* (New York: Nation Books, 2007).

[92] J. Brown, "Next Head of 'Civil Administration' Said Palestinians Are Sub-Human," *+972 Magazine* (May 8, 2015), http://972mag.com/next-head-of-civil-administration-said-palestinians-are-sub-human/106533.

reportedly exacerbated by the Civil Administration's delays, can ultimately prolong young Palestinians' detention.[93]

The second reform, in 2019, was an amendment granting the military court the option of ordering similar reports prior to remanding young Palestinians, to assist its assessment of their dangerousness and its consideration of alternatives to remand.[94] This reform, like most others concerning young Palestinians, was jointly pushed by the Israeli legal system – military judges and the state attorney general – and some of its human rights critics, with the latter even petitioning the supreme court on the matter in 2017.[95] Only after the fact did it occur to the petitioners that the new measure, like others they had previously supported, might be employed to Palestinians' detriment. The Civil Administration, the petitioners' attorney came to suggest, uses its unrecorded evaluation meetings with detained Palestinian youth as another opportunity to coerce them into confessing, without explaining to them the possible consequences of a guilty plea.[96]

4.3.3   The Blind Spots of the Human Rights Community

Israel's reforms reflected an agenda long campaigned for by the human rights community. Prior to the reforms, human rights critics characteristically combined precisely the sort of essentialism, developmentality, and legalism described (and defined) in this book's first two chapters. Their essentialist and developmentalist rhetoric depicted youth as an age group with inherently unique characteristics, needs, and interests. "The requirement to separate minors and adults is based on the simple concern that … an account should always be taken of the needs particular to

---

[93] For a report on such delay, see A. Hass, "Due to Noncompliance with a Judicial Order – A Sick Palestinian Minor Remains in Detention for a Month," *Haaretz* (February 12, 2019) [Hebrew], www.haaretz.co.il/news/politics/.premium-1.6931553. For earlier predictions this might happen, see DCIP, "Israeli Juvenile Military Court – Four Months On."

[94] Order Concerning Security Provisions (Amendment No. 64) (Detention Reviews for Minors) (Judea and Samaria) (No. 1818), 2019.

[95] For military judgments calling for such an amendment, see, e.g., MilA 2616/11 *Military Prosecution* v. *Kdareh* (July 18, 2012); MilA 1387/13 *John Doe* v. *Military Prosecution* (May 8, 2013). The petition was removed by the supreme court after the military announced it would amend its legislation accordingly. See HCJ 1845/17 *John Doe* v. *Military Commander in the West Bank* (March 7, 2018).

[96] Advocate Gaby Lasky's letter to the Civil Administration (February 12, 2019) (on file with author).

their stage of development," the United Against Torture Coalition of 14 organizations wrote in an open letter to the Israeli government.[97] "Child and adult prisoners are being held together without any attention to children's special needs," DCIP likewise complained.[98] Exhibiting similar essentialism, a legal clinic in one of the country's higher education institutions, in an open letter to the military advocate general in 2010, described the different ages of criminal majority applicable to Palestinians and Israelis as "bifurcating the concept of childhood."[99]

Marrying essentialism with legalism, human rights reports prior to the reforms repeatedly cited the essentialist norms of international child rights law, especially those formulated in the Convention on the Rights of the Child (CRC). "International law," Israeli NGO Yesh Din observed, "awards special protection to minors standing trial. However, the [military] ... has refrained from erecting a special juvenile court."[100] Similarly, three former DCIP staff, in a book published with the NGO, wrote: "Contrary to international guidelines, there are no [military] juvenile courts ... There is no distinction made between [Palestinian] adult and child prisoners ... [C]hildren are treated the same as adults."[101] Save the Children – Sweden exhibited similar legalism by condemning Israel for setting the age of criminal majority for Palestinians at 16. "The CRC definition of a child ... [as] any person under eighteen years of age," it concluded, "is only applied to children who are citizens of Israel."[102]

Despite their detrimental effects, Israel's reforms have not led the human rights organizations involved to reconsider their unwavering legalism. In 2011, for example, Palestinian NGO Addameer condemned

---

[97] UAT – The United Against Torture Coalition, "Joint Letter: The United Against Torture Coalition (UAT) Calls upon the Israeli Government, Military and Legal Authorities to Immediately Release Salwa Salah (Aged 17) and Sara Siureh (Aged 16)" (November 13, 2008), www.mezan.org/en/uploads/files/2550.pdf.

[98] DCIP, *Children of the Second Intifada: An Analysis of Human Rights Violations Against Palestinian Children in 2003* (2003), p. 32.

[99] Concord Research Center, *Letter to the Military Advocate General*, pp. 2–3, 9.

[100] L. Yavne, *Backyard Proceedings: The Implementation of Due Process Rights in the Military Courts in the Occupied Territories* (Tel Aviv: Yesh Din, December 2007), p. 156, www.hamoked.org/files/2012/8521_eng.pdf. See also ibid., pp. 22–23, 158, 162.

[101] Cook, Hanieh, and Kay, *Stolen Youth*, pp. 6, 83, 86.

[102] Save the Children – Sweden, *Briefing Papers on the Situation and Rights of Palestinian Children in the Occupied Palestinian Territories UN Commission on Human Rights* (2005). This common "straight 18" interpretation ignores the fluidity made possible by the CRC's caveat mentioned in the previous chapter (Section 3.3.2, "Elusive Childhood"): "unless, under the law applicable to the child, majority is attained earlier."

continued incidents of non-separation in detention for violating "both international and Israeli law."[103] Four years later, Israeli NGOs B'Tselem and Hamoked complained that such incidents were "in breach of the military order requiring that minors be held separately."[104] A handful of NGOs did question the desirability of separation – contrary to other statements they sometimes made – but this was mostly late into the shift toward generational segregation, or even after the fact.[105]

Human rights organizations have similarly adhered to their essentialism and developmentality. In 2017, B'Tselem and Hamoked jointly denounced Israel's treatment of the young Palestinians it detains in the following essentialist terms: "It stands to reason that the law enforcement system would treat these teenagers in an age-appropriate manner that takes their physical and mental maturity into account ... But that is not the case. Instead, Israel's law enforcement system treats them as members of a hostile population [indiscriminately] ..., minors and adults alike."[106] The Public Committee Against Torture in Israel likewise criticized the military in 2014 for "clearly not [being] punctilious in treating minors – those of the more sensitive soul upon whom any sign of roughness is liable to leave the indelible mark of trauma."[107] The latter image, in addition to its essentialist undertones, partly resembles the military judiciary's previously quoted preoccupation with the young Palestinian's "soul" – yet another parallel between the Israeli legal system and its human rights critics. Like the non-separation and non-distinction of young Palestinians, their non-rehabilitation in Israeli prison also

---

[103] Addameer, *Violation against Palestinian Prisoners and Detainees in Israeli Prisons and Detention Centers* (2011), p. 38, www.addameer.org/files/Reports/EN%20Addameer% 202010%20Violations%20Report.pdf.

[104] N. Kadman, *Backed by the System: Abuse and Torture at the Shikma Interrogation Facility* (Jerusalem: B'Tselem and HaMoked, December 2015), pp. 37–38, www .btselem.org/sites/default/files2/201512_backed_by_the_system_eng.pdf.

[105] See, respectively, DCI, *From Legislation to Action?: Trends in Juvenile Justice Systems Across 15 Countries* (2007), 42, www.defenceforchildren.org/wp-content/uploads/2010/ 04/DCI-JJ-Report-2007-FINAL-VERSION-with-cover.pdf; Baumgarten-Sharon, *No Minor Matter*, pp. 59–60.

[106] Y. Stein, *Unprotected: Detention of Palestinian Teenagers in East Jerusalem* (Jerusalem: B'Tselem and Hamoked, October 2017), p. 5, www.btselem.org/download/201710_ unprotected_eng.pdf.

[107] A. Linder, *Irresolute Criminal Investigations Divisions: Systemic Failures in Investigating Soldiers' Violence against Detainees* (June 2014) [Hebrew], pp. 22, http://stoptorture.org .il/wp-content/uploads/2015/09/%D7%91%D7%9E%D7%A6%D7%97-%D7%9C%D7% 90-%D7%A0%D7%97%D7%95%D7%A9%D7%94-%D7%99%D7%95%D7%A0%D7% 99-2014.pdf.

continues to attract knee-jerk condemnations from human rights critics, both locally and internationally.[108]

Legal scholarship, too, exhibits such essentialist and legalist insistence on generational segregation, regardless of its harms. In her 2019 book on young Palestinians' lives under Israeli rule, Nadera Shalhoub-Kevorkian accuses Israel of having "put the Palestinians in one category only, not even accounting for childhood as a status that would have demanded a different treatment." Although her focus, sources, and theoretical approach all differ markedly from mine, Shalhoub-Kevorkian mentions the military youth court in passing, to illustrate her claim that Israel violates "international juvenile justice law":

> [T]he military introduced a juvenile court, … [but] in practice …, juvenile [Palestinian] defendants are often brought into courts alongside adult defendants to be tried by the same presiding judge. The failure to distinguish between Palestinian children and adults demonstrates a lack of sensitivity to the needs of children, the association of children with adult capacity for intentional decision-making, and the presumption of children's criminal responsibility.

Elsewhere, she claims that "the children's rights discourse disappears [as a consequence of] … Israel's brutality against … [Palestinian] children."[109] The country's increased engagement with the child rights discourse is thus misrepresented, while the complicity of this discourse in the harm done to Palestinians goes unnoticed.

Israel's growing reliance on the legalistic and essentialist language of children's rights has created an affinity of sorts with its human rights critics. Occasionally, the affinity goes even further. Some in the Israeli human rights community have shared the supreme court's rationale, highlighted earlier, that exposure to the influences of older Palestinians in prison is a security threat. The previously mentioned academic legal clinic, in its open letter to the military advocate general, wrote:

> [T]he obligation to consider child defendants' wellbeing … is also supported by instrumentalist considerations. The possibility of rehabilitating [Palestinian] children is, ultimately, … a security interest as well. Would it be preferable to treat a sixteen-year-old child as an adult … and

---

[108] See, e.g., UNCRC, Concluding Observations on the Second to Fourth Periodic Reports of Israel, CRC/C/ISR/CO/2-4 (July 4, 2013), www2.ohchr.org/english/bodies/crc/docs/co/ CRC-C-ISR-CO-2-4.pdf; DCIP, *No Way to Treat a Child.*

[109] N. Shalhoub-Kevorkian, *Incarcerated Childhood and the Politics of Unchilding* (Cambridge and New York: Cambridge University Press, 2019), pp. 39–40, 88, 111–12.

incarcerate him with adults who committed security offenses, thus exposing him to their influence? Indeed, the need to consider rehabilitation ...
seems particularly essential in the [security] context with which the
military courts normally deal.[110]

Such convergence between the Israeli legal system and its human
rights critics is hardly an isolated event, as this book constantly highlights. In 2016, a representative of the NGO B'Tselem criticized Israel's
hyperincarceration of young Palestinians with rhetoric closely resembling that of the legal clinic's letter: "There is no attempt to provide
alternatives to imprisonment. The question is what a 14- or 16-year-old
who spends a year in prison with security prisoners learns about life, the
world and the Israeli–Palestinian conflict. It only sends them back to the
cycle of violence."[111]

B'Tselem and other human rights actors may justify such security
language as purely tactical – an excuse also potentially applicable to their
essentialism and legalism. Indeed, one of the pitfalls of fighting human
rights campaigns on the abuser's playing field is the apparent temptation
to convince the abuser through its own narratives and concepts.[112] The
findings of this chapter and the next indicate, however, that such tactics –
if they are indeed that – end up working to the detriment of Palestinians.
And, as I will now explain, it is Palestinians of all ages who have borne
the brunt.

4.3.4   Harming Older Palestinians

In the previous chapter, I demonstrated some of the ways in which
ostensibly child-focused measures impact and target people over the
age of majority. Generational segregation and rehabilitation in Israeli
prisons are no exception. The increased generational segregation – as
carried out by reserving courts, incarceration facilities, and wings for
Palestinian youth – refashioned the regular facilities and courts as adult
specific. More than merely a symbolic change, this meant that issues
pertaining to incarcerated Palestinians over the age of majority no longer

---

[110] Concord Research Center, *Letter to the Military Advocate General*, p. 11.
[111] S. Pulwer, "Sharp Rise in the Number of Palestinian Children in Prison," *Haaretz* (April
24, 2016), www.haaretz.com/israel-news/.premium-1.716006.
[112] On this pitfall, see M. Sfard, "The Price of Internal Legal Opposition to Human Rights
Abuses" (2009) 1:1 *Journal of Human Rights Practice* 37, 46.

affected their younger counterparts as much as before. Consequently, human rights organizations ceased pressuring Israel to ensure that its courts, detention facilities, and prisons met children's rights standards. The adult-specific legal sites created through generational segregation – which hold around 95–97 percent of Palestinian "security prisoners"[113] – received no such scrutiny, as a number of human rights organizations have directed their attention elsewhere. Equally importantly, the emotionally potent image of the child has been rendered unavailable to campaigns on behalf of incarcerated Palestinians aged 18 and over, whose gender and religion – the overwhelming majority are Muslim men, as noted in Chapter 2 – further erodes public empathy toward them in Israel and much of the Global North, due to a combination of Islamophobia and sexism.

Indeed, the human rights community has, for instance, paid far greater attention to violations of parents' right to be informed of their child's arrest than to the military's legally enshrined authority to keep the arrest of Palestinians aged 18 and over entirely secret for up to 12 days.[114] Similarly, whereas young Palestinians are now formally entitled to be informed of their right to legal counsel, there has been no noticeable outcry over the absence of such a provision for "security detainees" over the age of majority, who can be refused legal counsel for up to a month.[115] Thus, generational segregation has resulted in the division of incarcerated Palestinians into two groups: those defined as children – a small minority – for whom human rights organizations reserve abundant compassion and concern; and Palestinians (especially men) aged 18 and over – the overwhelming majority – whose conditions attracted much less interest. In the next chapter, I further show how the child rights discourse legitimizes harshness and apathy toward disempowered and ill-treated people who are legally classified as adults – Palestinian and other.

---

[113] B'Tselem, "Statistics on Palestinian Minors in the Custody of the Israeli Security Forces" (n.d.), www.btselem.org/statistics/minors_in_custody; B'Tselem, "Statistics on Palestinians in the Custody of the Israeli Security Forces" (n.d.), www.btselem.org/statistics/detainees_and_prisoners.

[114] Article 55 of Order 1651.

[115] Articles 58–59a of Order 1651; Article 17.22.(2) IPS Commission Ordinance 03.02.00. On these restrictions, see M. Rosenfeld, *When the Exception Becomes the Rule: Incommunicado Detention of Palestinian Security Detainees* (Jerusalem: PCATI and Palestinian Prisoner Society, November 2010), http://stoptorture.org.il/wp-content/uploads/2015/10/When-the-Exception-Becomes-the-Rule-2010.pdf.

As human rights discourses surrounding the now-separated Palestinian inmates transformed, so did Israel's modes of governance and punishment. For the most part, Palestinians of all ages continued to be denied rights, but this denial has adopted more sophisticated legal methods. On the one hand, those under the age of majority were formally being granted greater rights or special treatment, yet often with little, or even a detrimental, effect, as I have shown. On the other hand, Palestinians aged 18 and over witnessed the revocation or narrowing down of rights they once enjoyed, with near silence from the human rights community.

Thus, prior to the shift toward age-segregated incarceration, the primary IPS regulations concerning "security prisoners" made no specific reference either to "adults" or to precharge detention. A 2014 amendment, however, now categorically denies visits to "adults" in precharge detention suspected of "security offenses." Further, as detailed earlier, the restrictions on family visits to imprisoned Gazans have become even stricter than those imposed on their West Bank brethren. Given that, unlike their West Bank counterparts, no more than a handful of Gazans in Israeli prisons are under the age of majority,[116] the brunt has been borne almost entirely by those defined as adults.

In addition, the presumed incorrigibility of those Palestinians classified by Israel as adult security prisoners furnished justification for retracting another benefit in 2011: enrollment in Israeli Open University courses, which were previously taken by an average of 250 imprisoned Palestinians each year.[117] Although not explicitly named, Palestinians over the age of majority were those affected by this ban on tertiary education as well. In their petition to overturn it, imprisoned Palestinians argued at length that the Open University studies facilitated their rehabilitation, an argument reiterated by their lecturers who joined the case as amicus curiae. The IPS, in response, described such prisoners

---

[116] B'Tselem, "Statistics on Palestinians from the Gaza Strip in the Custody of the Israeli Security Forces" (n.d., last accessed on March 25, 2020), www.btselem.org/statistics/gaza_detainees_and_prisoners.

[117] Petition in HCJ 204/13 *Sallah* v. *IPS* (April 14, 2015); R. Shaked, "100 Palestinian Prisoners Complete Academic Studies in Jail," *Ynet News* (April 8, 2009), www.ynetnews.com/articles/0,7340,L-3756751,00.html. The revocation of both entitlements is evident when comparing the December 26, 2011 version of IPS Commission Ordinance 03.02.00: Guidelines Regarding Security Prisoners (March 15, 2002) with the July 10, 2014 amendment to it.

as incapable of meaningful rehabilitation, and both a district court and the supreme court denied the petitions.[118]

The Israeli government, when announcing the ban in 2011, presented it as a means to pressure Hamas into releasing Israeli soldier Gilad Shalit from captivity in Gaza. The truth is quite different: around 30 courses had already been banned four years prior to Shalit's capture, and, furthermore, despite his release in exchange for imprisoned Palestinians in 2011, the ban remains in place.[119] Regardless, using Shalit as an excuse seems to have been an effective choice largely because, in Israeli society, he was widely viewed as "the child of us all" (an infantilizing discourse analyzed in Chapter 7). Thus, the figure of the child – in this instance, an infantilized Israeli soldier – was yet again deployed to withdraw the entitlements of older Palestinians.

The sociolegal category "child" thus operates as a template for governing Palestinians of all ages. Also reflecting this, to a degree, is the previously described preoccupation of the Israeli judiciary with Palestinians over the age of majority: those behind bars, whose allegedly nationalistic influences Israel has sought to block, as well as the future "adults" into which, absent age segregation, young Palestinians could turn.

4.4   The Bigger Picture: Contextualizing Palestinians' Age-Segregated Incarceration

A critical analysis of Israel's reforms regarding young Palestinians can yield important insights into at least four broader contexts: (a) the pitfalls of child law; (b) related forms of separation of Palestinians, in and beyond prison; (c) the attempted confinement of Palestinian minds beyond prison; and (d) the growing convergence between military and non-military Israeli law. By thus contextualizing Israel's reforms, it is possible to better understand their meaning and implications. I now turn to inspect each of these four contexts.

---

[118] See, respectively, AdminC (Nazareth Dist.) 16207-09-11 *Sultany* v. IPS (March 7, 2012); HCJ 204/13.

[119] Access to these courses was resumed only following imprisoned Palestinians' petition on the matter: AdminC (Nazareth Dist.) 761/02 *Jadrat* v. IPS (2002). A later ruling allowed the IPS to bar Palestinian prisoners from taking certain courses on a case-by-cases basis: AdminC (Tel Aviv Dist.) 1882/03 *Hussein* v. IPS (June 26, 2003).

4.4.1   The Pitfalls of Child Law

As shown in this book's opening two chapters, human rights critics, by attributing to Israel disregard of the law, fail to recognize law's complicity in state control and violence. As seen in this chapter, this is equally applicable to child law, which the Israeli authorities handling young Palestinians have increasingly invoked. Rather than being an isolated instance of child law gone astray, the reforms analyzed in this chapter – above all, those concerning generational segregation – are symptomatic of some broader pitfalls of child law.

Indeed, modern child law developed, in part, as a means to remove those defined as children from allegedly depraved or unfit parents, and then to reform them, often in the name of national interests. Among those thus segregated were hundreds of thousands of Indigenous children in North America and Australia, who were placed in special boarding schools or put up for adoption. Notwithstanding undeniable differences from the Palestinian case, Indigenous child removal was also couched in a language of benevolence and legalism. Its exponents presented it as "rescuing ... [Indigenous] children and youth" from the "deleterious" and "prejudicial influences" of their "degraded parents." Further, the previously quoted claim of the Israeli judiciary about young Palestinians' "better rehabilitation chances" has parallels with the view of proponents of Indigenous child removal, who placed their "main hope ... with the youthful generations who are still measurably plastic."[120]

There are other noteworthy parallels with the Israeli–Palestinian case, including links between generational segregation, incarceration, and counterinsurgency. The first government-supported off-reservation boarding school for Native American children was established at an unused military base by a prominent military officer, who came up with the idea while experimenting in "rehabilitating" Indigenous war prisoners. Initially, there were dozens of children among the prisoners, but most of them were eventually removed to boarding schools, despite the authorities knowing that such "separation ... is what [these prisoners] ... constantly dread." Due to their military-like drills and order, many children likened these schools to prisons, while Australian

---

[120] H. Viterbo, "Ties of Separation: Analogy and Generational Segregation in North America, Australia, and Israel/Palestine" (2017) 42:2 *Brooklyn Journal of International Law* 686, 703–05, 721–22.

Indigenous children used similar comparisons when describing the institutions in which they had been placed. State officials in North America also saw generational segregation as a counterinsurgency measure: "It is unlikely," one argued, "that any Tribe ... would give trouble of a serious nature ... whose members had children completely under Government control."[121] Though Israel's reforms seem different in that their stated objective is not to separate children from their parents, the reality, as I have previously discussed, is that most incarcerated Palestinian youth are indeed denied parental contact.

The global history of child law and policy brims with comparable instances of generational segregation, including that of the Yenish (often described as "gypsies") in 1970s Switzerland, the Inuit in Danish-ruled Greenland in the 1950s, non-European Jewish immigrants in 1950s Israel, impoverished immigrants in nineteenth- and twentieth-century United States, "mixed-race" families in French colonial Morocco and Dutch colonial Indonesia, Andamanese tribes in British colonial India, and Christians in the Ottoman-ruled Balkans. At the time of writing, China is reportedly segregating Muslims (Uyghurs and others) on a generational basis: hundreds of thousands (and possibly more) over the age of majority have been extrajudicially incarcerated in "reeducation" internment camps. Many of their children, who the government alleges have been incited by their parents, have been removed to securitized schools. Other examples of generational segregation in modern times include certain forms of child emigration and transnational child adoption programs.[122]

Also identifiable beyond Israel/Palestine are the harms of age-segregated incarceration, including some of those I have highlighted in this chapter. For example, like their Palestinian peers, countless incarcerated children across the globe have found themselves in solitary confinement, often for long periods, due to the prison staff abiding by the law's age segregation requirement. Solitary confinement, in addition to its grave psychological effects, also cuts inmates off from crucial sources of support and information, as well as potentially facilitating unchecked abuse at the hands of staff. Another example concerns peer violence:

[121] Ibid., pp. 700–03, 706–08.
[122] H. Viterbo, "The Pitfalls of Separating Youth in Prison: A Critique of Age-Segregated Incarceration," in A. Cox and L. S. Abrams (eds.), *The Palgrave International Handbook of Youth Imprisonment* (Palgrave Macmillan, 2021); Viterbo, "Ties of Separation," pp. 723–28.

inmate-on-inmate violence and aggression are rife in youth prisons throughout the world, sometimes at higher levels than in adult prisons – precisely the issue older Palestinians in Israeli custody helped resolve before they were separated from their juniors. Moreover, a potential harm of age segregation is its unwitting contribution to making incarceration more immune to criticism, by helping it present itself as a humane and hence acceptable solution to social transgressions.[123]

This last point applies more broadly to the focus – on the part not only of Israel but also of human rights organizations – on reforming rather than abolishing Israel's military rule over Palestinians.[124] For example, in Chapter 2, I discussed a high-profile delegation of British lawyers that visited Israel/Palestine to assess the treatment of young Palestinians in Israeli military custody. The delegation's report, in 2012, described the following as one of its "guiding principles": "Without embarking on its legality or desirability, we treat as a given fact the use of military courts to try Palestinian civilians, in particular children." Rather than challenging Israel's prosecution of Palestinians in such courts, the delegation limited its remit to assessing whether "Israeli military law and practice [meet] ... the standards of international law and international children's rights."[125]

International law's complicity, unwitting or not, in harms such as those I have identified stems from its tendency to enshrine child–adult separation. The widely ratified International Covenant on Civil and Political Rights is categorical in its requirement to separate "juvenile offenders,"[126] while the CRC, the main reference point in international child law, restates the separation norm with a vague exception: "Every child deprived of liberty shall be ... separated from adults unless it is considered in the child's best interest not to do so."[127] In principle, the CRC's "best interest" exception is open to competing interpretations; the

---

[123] Viterbo, "The Pitfalls of Separating Youth in Prison."

[124] For a brief overview of the difference between reform and abolition, see, e.g., A. Y. Davis and D. Rodriguez, "The Challenge of Prison Abolition: A Conversation" (2000) 27:3 *Social Justice* 212, 216.

[125] S. Sedley et al., *Children in Military Custody: A Report Written by a Delegation of British Lawyers on the Treatment of Palestinian Children under Israeli Military Law* (Foreign and Commonwealth Office, June 2012), pp. 2, 6, www.childreninmilitarycustody.org.uk/wp-content/uploads/2012/03/Children_in_Military_Custody_Full_Report.pdf.

[126] Article 10(2)(b) and (3) of the International Covenant on Civil and Political Rights (ICCPR), adopted December 16, 1966, GA Res. 2200A (XXI), 21 UN GAOR Supp. (No. 16) at 52, UN Doc A/6316 (1966), 999 UNTS 171, entered into force March 23, 1976.

[127] Article 37(c) of the CRC.

same can be said, as I argued in Chapter 1, about international treaty law more generally, whose inevitably indeterminate language lends itself to endless interpretive struggles. In reality, the human rights community's essentialist conception of childhood has led it to repeatedly oppose and even disregard the possibility of non-separation. In particular, the UN Committee on the Rights of the Child has emphasized that the CRC's "best interest" exception "should be interpreted narrowly" – a position reiterated by the UN Special Rapporteur on Torture.[128] Numerous children's rights reports, including those of UNICEF, Save the Children, Amnesty International, and Human Rights Watch, go so far as to erase this exception outright, by omitting it when quoting the CRC's separation requirement.[129] Additional blindspots and pitfalls of the child rights framework are unveiled in the next chapter.

4.4.2   Separation in and beyond Prison

The generational segregation of Palestinians in Israeli custody complements, parallels, and resonates with other forms of separation. Though neither uniform nor fully successful, this apparatus of separation operates to divide and rule Palestinians, to fragment them spatially, politically, and socially. In recent years, there has been a proliferation and refinement of this apparatus, both in and outside prison. It is from this wider sociopolitical context that Israel's reforms concerning young Palestinians derive their significance and effects.

Within prison, at roughly the same time as the shift toward generational segregation, Palestinians were also being increasingly segregated into wards and facilities based on their regions of residence.[130] This geographically based segregation, while not uniformly implemented across all IPS facilities, resonates with the general fragmentation of the Palestinian territories, which can be ascribed to what Israeli officials have

---

[128] See, respectively, UNCRC, General Comment No. 10: Children's Rights in Juvenile Justice (44th session, 2007), UN Doc CRC/C/GC/10 (April 25, 2007), ¶ 104; UN Special Rapporteur on Torture and Other Cruel, Inhuman or Degrading Treatment or Punishment, Juan E. Méndez, Report to the Human Rights Council, 28th Session, Agenda Item 3, UN Doc A/HRC/28/68, ¶ 76 (March 5, 2015).

[129] See reports cited in Viterbo, "The Pitfalls of Separating Youth in Prison."

[130] Addameer, *Violations against Palestinian Prisoners*; W. Daka, "Consciousness Molded or the Re-Identification of Torture," in A. Baker and A. Matar (eds.), *Threat: Palestinian Political Prisoners in Israel* (London: Pluto Press, 2011), pp. 234–54.

publicly termed Israel's "separation policy."[131] As described in the previous chapters, the Gaza Strip, under constant if changeable closure, has been cut off from the West Bank, while the latter, enclosed by the Separation Wall and subject to restrictions on Palestinian movement, has been splintered into enclaves that each experience Israel's control somewhat differently.

More closely resembling age-segregated incarceration, in terms of its hindrance to intergenerational Palestinian continuity, is Israel's ban on prisoners' conjugal visits. In yet another display of what the previous chapter described as Israel's biopolitical warfare, physical contact is strictly forbidden between incarcerated Palestinian men and their wives. As a result, those imprisoned for long periods are prevented from having children, while their wives grow old and become infertile. Petitions on the matter by noncitizen Palestinians classified as security prisoners have been dismissed.[132] In contrast, Jewish prisoners who are thus classified, including the assailant of Israeli prime minister Yitzhak Rabin, are granted conjugal rights and are even allowed to have their sperm samples used to artificially inseminate their wives.[133]

Nonetheless, like other measures examined in this book, the ban on conjugal visits has been neither unopposed nor fully successful. Since at least 2012, sperm of incarcerated Palestinian men has been smuggled from prison, reportedly resulting in the birth of more than 70 babies through in vitro fertilization in Palestinian clinics.[134] Some of those able to have children in this manner regard sperm smuggling as a form of political resistance. According to one Palestinian prisoner's wife, "this is our way of breaking Israel's siege on us ... We are challenging [Israel's] occupation and getting something beautiful in return." To symbolize their success in defeating the ban on conjugal visits, the couple named their daughter "Hurriyah" – Arabic for "freedom."[135]

---

[131] Gisha, *The Separation Policy: List of References Prepared by Gisha* (July 2014), http://gisha.org/UserFiles/File/publications/separation_policy_2014.pdf.

[132] AdminC (Nazareth Dist.) 609/08 *Daka v. State of Israel* (September 21, 2009); AdminC (Nazareth Dist.) 54950-11-11 *Daka v. Israeli Police* (February 16, 2012).

[133] AppR 4714/04 *Amir v. IPS* (2005) 59(6) PD 145; HCJ 2245/06 *Dobrin v. IPS* (June 13, 2006).

[134] F. AbdulKarim, B. Ehrenreich, and T. Habjouqa, "The Palestinian Sperm Smugglers," 23 *Topic* (May 2019), www.topic.com/the-palestinian-sperm-smugglers.

[135] R. Eglash and S. Taha, "Palestinian Prisoners Are Smuggling Sperm out of Israeli Jails So Wives Can Have Babies," *The Washington Post* (May 2, 2014), www.washingtonpost.com/world/middle_east/palestinian-prisoners-are-smuggling-sperm-out-of-israeli-jails-

Beyond prison, some forms of separation parallel Israel's separation of incarcerated Palestinians from their family members by denying them family visits. Among the measures fragmenting families outside prison is the prohibition of nonresident Palestinian spouses of Israelis (usually non-Jews) from living in Israel. It was made into law in 2003, following a recommendation of a team appointed by the minister of the interior to "reduce the naturalization of non-Jews,"[136] and has since then been upheld twice by the supreme court.[137] As a consequence, nearly 10,000 affected Palestinians live in Israel with neither residency nor citizenship status, about 250 of whom are under the age of 18 (according to data obtained from Israeli authorities, referring to 2016).[138]

Akin to Palestinians' generational segregation, as well as to movement restrictions examined in the previous chapter, the statutory prohibition on family unifications contains an age-based exception. It grants the minister of the interior the discretionary power to allow residence in Israel for Palestinian spouses above certain ages – 35 for men and 25 for women – as well as for their children aged up to 14.[139] In this age-based statutory exception lies yet another testament to what, in the previous chapter, I described as governing through uncertainty. While it refers to Palestinian "minors up to the age of 14 years," the military's regulations on "family unifications" create uncertainty by using a different age range: Palestinian "minors up to the age of 12 (and in special cases up to the age of 18)." Amplifying the uncertainty is these regulations' elastic definition of "minor" as anyone "aged up to 12 and in exceptional cases up to 18."[140]

so-wives-can-have-babies/2014/05/02/f2b7f29e-cc8a-11e3-95f7-7ecdde72d2ea_story.html.

[136] O. Ben-Naftali, "Kinship," in O. Ben-Naftali, M. Sfard, and H. Viterbo, *The ABC of the OPT: A Legal Lexicon of the Israeli Control over the Occupied Palestinian Territory* (Cambridge and New York: Cambridge University Press, 2018), pp. 228–29.

[137] HCJ 7052/03 *Adalah Legal Centre for Arab Minority Rights in Israel v. Minister of Interior* (2006) 61(2) PD 202; HCJ 466/07 *MK Galon v. Attorney General* (2012) 65(2) PD 44.

[138] N. Hasson, "About 250 Minors Without Status in Israel Due to the Ban on Family Unifications," *Haaretz* (June 16, 2016) [Hebrew], www.haaretz.co.il/news/politics/.premium-1.2977513.

[139] Articles 2–3a of the Citizenship and Entry into Israel Law (Temporary Order), 2003.

[140] Articles 1–2 of COGAT Directive Concerning Family Unification in Israel for Palestinian Residents – Procedure for Granting Entry Permits (July 2015) [Hebrew], http://gisha.org/UserFiles/File/LegalDocuments/procedures/movement_between_israel_and_the_west_bank/167.pdf.

Far from emerging in a vacuum, these obstacles to family contact reflect Israel's deep investment, since its establishment as a state, in cultivating as large a Jewish majority as possible.[141] Accordingly, Israeli law entitles all Jews living anywhere in the world to migrate to Israel and acquire Israeli citizenship, a right also extended to their children, grand-children, spouses, their children's spouses, and their grandchildren's spouses.[142] This, for example, is what enabled Alex Stein – one of the country's current (Jewish) supreme court justices, previously a lawyer for the Israeli military, and at one point an exponent of disproportionate attacks on Gaza – to migrate to Israel from Russia at the age of 16.[143] In contrast, noncitizen Palestinians, whose progenitors were born in Palestine/Israel, are denied this right to citizenship.

Another way in which Israeli authorities fragment Palestinian families is by forbidding Gazans from reuniting with their families in the West Bank, save in "exceptional circumstances." Exemplifying some of the potential consequences of this policy is Kawthar Hemo's case. In 2017, 15 years after separating from her husband in the West Bank and relocating to Gaza with her children, Hemo was reportedly unemployed and suffering from depression, and hence applied to return to the West Bank to reunite with her parents and siblings. The Israeli military granted her and most of her children permission, but not her three-year-old son, whose registered birthplace (unlike that of his siblings) was the Gaza Strip. It took an NGO's petition to the supreme court, and a process that lasted nearly three years, for the child to be given permission. At that point, however, the state attorney's office required a reassessment of Hemo and her two eldest children. At the time of writing, their case remains unresolved.[144]

---

[141] See, e.g., I. S. Lustick, "Israel's Migration Balance: Demography, Politics, and Ideology" (2011) 26:1 *Israel Studies Review* 33; R. A. Kanaaneh, "Babies and Boundaries," in her *Birthing the Nation: Strategies of Palestinian Women in Israel* (Berkeley and Los Angeles: University of California Press, 2002), pp. 23–80.

[142] Articles 1–2, 4a of the Law of Return, 1950.

[143] A. Greenzweig, "The Anti-Revolution Warrior," *Channel 7* (March 1, 2018) [Hebrew], www.inn.co.il/News/News.aspx/367447; H. Ma'anit, "Conservative in the Supreme Court: Will Prof. Stein Meet the Justice Minister's Expectations?," *Globes* (August 9, 2018) [Hebrew], www.globes.co.il/news/article.aspx?did=1001249398.

[144] A. Hass, "Why Is a Six-Year-Old Child Barred from Traveling with His Mother to Her Family's Home? Because the State Decided So," *Haaretz* (June 28, 2019) [Hebrew], www.haaretz.co.il/news/politics/.premium-1.7418538; A. Hass, "After Two Years of Denying His Exit from Gaza, the State Allowed a 6-Year-Old to Move with His Mother to the

As apparent across these examples, much of the separation of Palestinians rests on Israel's deployment of age as a risk management tool – an issue illustrated in the previous chapter and further explored in the next subsection. Certain age groups, or so the logic goes, are innately more dangerous and hence require separation from others, be it in or outside prison. In this context, the convergence between the approaches of liberal human rights organizations and those of Israeli authorities is once again encountered. Such convergence was particularly evident in a 2019 supreme court petition by Israeli NGO Hamoked and two Palestinians, regarding the previously mentioned restrictions on nonresident Palestinian spouses of Israelis. The petition asked that all Palestinian spouses above a certain age – 55 years for men and 50 for women – be granted permanent residency permits, as this "older population ... no longer poses any security threat." In support of this argument, the NGO cited the military regulations on Palestinians' entry from the West Bank to Israel, which "unequivocally [exempt] ... women aged 50 and older and men aged 55 and older [from the obligation] ... to obtain entry permits ... The security bodies' position, then, is that ... this sector of the population ... poses no security risk."[145] Thus, rather than challenging the military's characterization of all younger Palestinians as a threat, this human rights organization adopted it with a show of reverence. This complements the previously examined allegation, made by Israeli judges and NGOs supportive of age-segregated incarceration, that Palestinians over the age of majority are a security threat.

A similar example is a 2016 decision of the Red Cross to reduce the frequency of family visits that it coordinates for male Palestinians aged 18 and over in Israeli prisons, while leaving unchanged the frequency of visits for incarcerated Palestinians identified as children and women. This discriminatory decision was strongly condemned by the families of incarcerated men, who make up the overwhelming majority of prisoners.[146] Thus, Hamoked and the Red Cross either emulated or

---

West Bank," *Haaretz* (July 16, 2019) [Hebrew], www.haaretz.co.il/news/politics/.premium-1.7529935.

[145] Petition in HCJ 1018/19 *Ashour* v. *Knesset* (February 10, 2019) [Hebrew], ¶¶ 2, 5–6, 47, www.hamoked.org.il/Document.aspx?dID=Documents4028 (case currently pending).

[146] J. Khouri, "Anger among Palestinian Prisoners' Families about the Red Cross Decision to Reduce Visits," *Haaretz* (May 31, 2016) [Hebrew], www.haaretz.co.il/news/politics/.premium-1.2961744; Middle East Monitor, "Rights Group Criticises Red Cross Decision

even endorsed Israel's logic of using age as a tool for managing Palestinians' lives. Equally importantly, both organizations prioritized a small minority of Palestinians, be it spouses in their fifties and older or imprisoned children and women, while abandoning most others. I delve further into the pitfalls of such differentiation between age groups in Chapters 5 and 7.

4.4.3 Confining Palestinian Minds

Incarceration, by definition, is a form of separation. In Israeli hands, it separates political activists,[147] including physically nonviolent ones,[148] from the Palestinian populace and territory. Further, as I observed in Chapter 2, the mass incarceration of Palestinians mirrors the transformation of their territory into a fragmented network of prisons of sorts. The confinement of Palestinians is not a new feature of the Israeli control regime. The first two decades of statehood, as I mentioned in Chapter 1, saw Israel placing Palestinian citizens under military rule, restricting their movement, and trying in military courts those who failed to carry proper permits. Israel's conquest of the West Bank and Gaza Strip ushered in the age-based movement restriction apparatus of subsequent decades, as analyzed in the previous chapter.

At the same time, by creating material and legal barriers, Israel does not merely confine Palestinians' bodies; also stymied is the movement of their ideas, knowledge, and communication across time and space. Barriers are thus erected not only between and within geographical territories, but also between the producers and potential consumers of resistant knowledge, as well as between imagined subjects and sites. At both the individual and collective levels, therefore, the actual Israeli prison – and to some extent the broader prison that is the West Bank and Gaza Strip – operate to confine Palestinian minds as well as Palestinian bodies.

---

to Cancel 50% of Prison Visits" (May 28, 2016), www.middleeastmonitor.com/20160528-rights-group-criticises-red-cross-decision-to-cancel-50-of-prison-visits/.

[147] R. James, "Savage Restraint: Israel, Palestine and the Dialectics of Legal Repression" (2001) 47:4 *Social Problems* 445; E. Nashif, *Palestinian Political Prisoners: Identity and Community* (London: Routledge, 2008).

[148] J. Peteet, "Cosmopolitanism and the Subversive Space of Protests" (2009) 37 *Jerusalem Quarterly* 86; R. Jaraisy and T. Feldman, "Protesting for Human Rights in the Occupied Palestinian Territory: Assessing the Challenges and Revisiting the Human Rights Defender Framework" (2013) 5:3 *Journal of Human Rights Practice* 421.

Within prison, as I have described, Palestinians engaged in both academic and informal studies. However, Israel, in addition to its previously mentioned ban on the enrollment of imprisoned Palestinians in academic courses, has clamped down on their self-run study groups. A 2011 amendment to the prison regulations prohibits those in one cell from attending study groups in other cells. The same amendment also revoked a provision that previously allowed "security prisoners" to teach others in their ward.[149] In 2018, reports emerged that the prison authorities were confiscating many of these Palestinians' study books, as well as barring their families from bringing them new ones.[150] These and other measures have, reportedly, led to a decline in the activity of such study groups.[151] In her 2018 media appearances, a Palestinian girl, whose high-profile detention by Israel I mentioned in previous chapters, touched on young Palestinians' involvement in the struggle over education behind bars:

> Along with the other girls, I tried to make study groups, but the prison administration did not encourage this and broke up the class ... They would shut down our classes when we were trying to learn. During our international law or human rights courses, they would sound the alarm to send us back to our cells. They tried in every way to stop us from turning the prison into a school, but we were able to turn the prison into a school.[152]

Although the emancipatory power of education should not be idealized, incarcerated Palestinians' studies represent what anthropologist Esmail Nashif once described as their "revolutionary pedagogy": their

---

[149] See, respectively, Articles 21a(1), 21b of the IPS Commission Ordinance 03.02.00 (26 December, 2011 version).

[150] Addameer, "Deterioration in Detention Conditions: Suffocating Prisoners" (October 29, 2018), www.addameer.org/publications/deterioration-detention-conditions-suffocating-prisoners; R. Younis, "Before Approval of Recommendations, IDF Worsens Palestinian Prisoners' Conditions," *Local Talk* (November 12, 2018) [Hebrew], https://mekomit.co.il/%d7%aa%d7%a0%d7%90%d7%99-%d7%94%d7%90%d7%a1%d7%99%d7%a8%d7%99%d7%9d-%d7%94%d7%a4%d7%9c%d7%a1%d7%98%d7%99%d7%a0%d7%99%d7%9d-%d7%9e%d7%95%d7%a8%d7%a2%d7%99%d7%9d.

[151] Daka, "Consciousness Molded"; M. Rosenfed, "The Movement of Palestinian Political Prisoners and the Struggle against the Israeli Occupation: A Historical Perspective" (paper presented at the Middle East Studies Association Annual Meeting, Washington DC, 25 November 2014).

[152] A. Tamimi, "Occupied Childhood: Ahed Tamimi Pens a Heartfelt Letter about Life in and after Prison," *Vogue* (October 4, 2018), https://en.vogue.me/fashion/perspectives/ahed-tamimi-palestine-open-letter; D. Takruri, "Ahed Tamimi Freed from Israeli Prison," *Al Jazeera* (October 9, 2018), www.youtube.com/watch?v=lJqH7_xYKi4.

use of reading and writing as a form of "resistance . . . not just in and by itself but, more importantly, as part of the community-building process . . ., as a space between captives that transcended the space of the prisons."[153] Such resistant community building has long been a source of concern for Israeli authorities. As early as 1980, supreme court justice Yehuda Cohen warned that "security prisoners are an organized body acting as a uniform ideological body . . . The unique organizational nature of security prisoners justifies [imposing on them] . . . harsher security measures . . . than those applied to criminal prisoners." In 2007, the IPS likewise cautioned about Palestinian attempts to "turn prison into a place of training, instruction, forming an ideology . . . [and operating] committees for organizing [education and] . . . instructing prisoners."[154] More recently, in 2018 and 2019, the following remarks by IPS officials were quoted in the Israeli media: "our role is to deepen the rifts [between Palestinian prisoners], not to let them unite," and "any rift between the prisoners should be exploited and deepened."[155]

The much dreaded ideological and study activities of imprisoned Palestinians had two distinct features. The first was intergenerational knowledge transfer. Prior to their generational segregation, Palestinians' study groups transferred from one incarcerated generation to another what they considered valuable knowledge. For this reason, among others, Palestinians came to see detention and imprisonment as a kind of rite of passage – a transition from childhood to adulthood, and especially from boyhood to manhood.[156] "Like you have a military," one imprisoned Palestinian told an Israeli reporter in 2019, "we have prison – it is like a

---

[153] Nashif, *Palestinian Political Prisoners*, pp. 73–74.

[154] See, respectively, HCJ 221/80 *Darwish* v. *IPS* (1980) 35(1) PD 536, ¶ 5 of justice Y. Cohen's opinion; A. Virtzer, *Security Prisoners Incarcerated in the Israel Prison Service* (IPS Spokesperson, 2007), pp. 8, 10 [Hebrew] https://web.archive.org/web/20160303230525/http://ips.gov.il/Items/05637/bitchonim_heb_2007.pdf.

[155] See, respectively, J. Breiner and A. Harel, "Opposition Within Security System to Worsening of Security Prisoners' Conditions for Fear of Unrest," *Haaretz* (November 6, 2018) [Hebrew], www.haaretz.co.il/news/politics/.premium-1.6631166; J. Breiner, "Disparaging the Death Penalty and Talking Politics: A Glance into the Political Prisoners' Life," *Haaretz* (January 25, 2019) [Hebrew], www.haaretz.co.il/news/politics/.premium-MAGAZINE-1.6872259.

[156] Peteet, "Male Gender and Rituals of Resistance"; Nashif, *Palestinian Political Prisoners*; S. Quota, R.-L. Punamäki, and E. El Sarraj, "Prison Experience and Coping Styles Among Palestinian Men" (1997) 3:1 *Peace and Conflict: Journal of Peace Psychology* 19. Prison's function as a rite of initiation is not unique to Israel/Palestine. See, e.g., A. Van Zyl, *The Custody of Indigenous and Young Men: A Rite of Passage? – Northern Territory (Australia), Western Canada and Alaska (USA)* (Winnellie: Winston Churchill

rite of initiation into adulthood."[157] Intergenerational knowledge trans-fer, while practiced in a particular form in prison, has occurred in wider Palestinian society as well, with one generation passing on to another stories and memories of dispossession and expropriation[158] (a theme explored in the next chapter).

The second feature was comparative thinking, with a focus on issues in faraway places that were analogous to those affecting Palestinians, including generational segregation, colonization, and national struggle. Thus, of the academic courses Israel has banned, the one most popular among the imprisoned Palestinians deals with, among other subjects, Indigenous child removal in Australia and the United States. The course also encourages students to draw lessons from such events, and it characterizes as "colonial" not only Australia and the United States but also Israel's treatment of Palestinians.[159] Similarly, Palestinians' informal study groups reportedly placed emphasis on studying the experiences of liberation movements elsewhere, as well as examining parallels and differences between military and colonial regimes.[160]

Given these two features, the crackdown by Israeli authorities on Palestinians' studies in prison, combined with the shift to generational segregation, threatened to confine Palestinian minds in two complemen-tary ways. First, these measures obstructed the continuity and movement of political knowledge from one imprisoned Palestinian generation to another. And, second, they hindered Palestinians' endeavor to ideation-ally traverse the Israeli prison's confines through, for instance, critical and comparative reflection on generational segregation. Israeli

---

Memorial Trust of Australia, 2001), www.churchilltrust.com.au/media/fellows/Allan_Van_Zyl_2001.pdf.

[157] J. Breiner, "Disparaging the Death Penalty and Talking Politics: A Glance into the Political Prisoners' Life," *Haaretz* (January 25, 2019) [Hebrew], www.haaretz.co.il/news/politics/.premium-MAGAZINE-1.6872259. The military's role as a rite of initi-ation for Jewish Israelis is discussed in Chapter 7, Section 7.3.2 ("Israeli Settler Children as Soldiers in the Making").

[158] See L. Abu Lughod and A. Sa'di, "Introduction: The Claims of Memory," in A. Sa'di and L. Abu-Lughod (eds.), *Nakba: Palestine, 1948, and the Claims of Memory* (New York: Columbia University Press, 2007), pp. 1–24.

[159] A. Gutfeld, *Genocide in the "Land of the Free": The Indians of North America 1776–1890* (Raanana: Open University of Israel Press, 2006), pp. 9, 17–19, 21, 24, 29, 59, 88, 145–47, 186–87 [Hebrew]; A. Jamal, "Racialized Time and the Foundations of Colonial Rule in the Israeli-Palestinian Context," in Y. Auron and I. Lubelsky (eds.), *Genocide: Between Racism and Genocide in the Modern Era* (Raanana: Open University of Israel Press, 2011), p. 185 [Hebrew].

[160] Rosenfeld, *Confronting the Occupation*; Collins, *Occupied by Memory*.

authorities have thus operated – albeit, not necessarily successfully or wittingly – to confine the minds of those they have already physically incarcerated.

Further curtailing avenues for thought and communication, the IPS regulations have increasingly cut imprisoned Palestinians off from outside information and contact that are available to most Israelis in prison: books, visits from members of parliament, and (non-Israeli) media.[161] Palestinians deemed especially troublesome, such as hunger strikers, are even more radically isolated from fellow inmates and the outside world.[162] As a result, in 2017, more than a thousand Palestinians in Israeli prisons went on hunger strike and demanded – unsuccessfully – the "re-allowing [of] education through the Hebrew Open University," the "introduction of books [and] newspapers," and the addition of non-Israeli "satellite channels suitable for the needs of [Palestinian] prisoners."[163]

Palestinians' attempts at education behind bars parallel their practices outside prison. In 2018, for instance, Palestinian anti-Israeli demonstrations in Gaza reportedly included reading and discussion activities on issues such as colonialism and imperialism.[164] Similarly, Israel's attempted confinement of Palestinian minds inside prison is paralleled by its endeavors to do so in wider society. In the past, students from the Gaza Strip could attend Palestinian universities in the West Bank (enrollment in 1998, for instance, was around 1,000 students). They did so for various reasons, including the broader range of academic programs and the much larger number of lecturers in the West Bank. At the turn of the century, the Israeli military started denying all applications to travel to the West Bank for such purposes. In 2007, as part of the newly imposed

---

[161] Articles 21a, 21c, 21e of IPS Commission Ordinance 03.02.00; Temporary IPS Order – Acquisition of Newspapers and Magazines for Criminal/Security Prisoners (December 31, 2013); Addameer, "Deterioration in Detention Conditions"; J. Khoury, "Prison Service Limiting MP Visits to Security Prisoners," *Haaretz* (August 4, 2016) [Hebrew], www.haaretz.co.il/.premium-1.3028664. The denial of MPs' visits was upheld by the supreme court in HCJ 4252/17 *Jabareen v. Knesset* (July 14, 2020).

[162] Article 6a and Appendix A of the IPS Commission Ordinance 04.16.00: Prisoners' Hunger Strike (May 1, 2001), www.gov.il/BlobFolder/policy/041600/he/041600.pdf. On the actual use of solitary confinement, see S. Francis and K. Gibson, "Isolation and Solitary Confinement of Palestinian Prisoners and Detainees in Israeli Facilities," in Baker and Matar (eds.), *Threat: Palestinian Political Prisoners in Israel*, p. 212.

[163] Addameer, "On Seventh Day: Mass Hunger Strike Continues Despite Escalation" (April 23, 2017), www.addameer.org/news/seventh-day-mass-hunger-strike-continues-despite-escalation.

[164] F. O. Al-Naji, "The Gaza Border Is a Theater of Cultural Resistance," *Mondoweiss* (April 27, 2018), http://mondoweiss.net/2018/04/theater-cultural-resistance/.

closure, the military made this a blanket ban,[165] classifying all Gaza residents aged 16–35 years, and students in particular, as a "high-risk group" prone to terrorist activity.[166] The same year, the supreme court dismissed a petition asking the military to at least assess travel applications of ten occupational health students on a case-by-case basis. The court, whose deference to Israel's policies regarding noncitizen Palestinians is illustrated throughout this book, authorized the profiling of 16–35-year-olds and rejected the petitioners' claim that the travel ban "demonizes all Palestinian students."[167]

At the same time as confining Palestinian minds within the Gaza Strip, Israel has also limited their access to outside information. For a few years until 2010, Israeli authorities banned the entry of certain Palestinian newspapers from the West Bank. When the ban was lifted, it was Hamas (the ruling party in Gaza) that continued the bar on entry due to these newspapers' support of the rival Fatah movement.[168] Electronic sources of information in Gaza – internet and cell phones – are badly affected by the ever-present electricity shortage[169] (an issue touched on in Chapter 1). In 2016, the Israeli press also reported that the delivery of about 300,000 science and math textbooks from the West Bank to the Gaza Strip was being delayed in order for Israel to inspect and approve them.[170]

4.4.4   The Growing Convergence between Military and Non-military Israeli Law

The reforms analyzed in this chapter formally brought Israel's military law into closer alignment with its non-military law (even if, in practice,

---

[165] Gisha, "The Impact of the Separation between the Gaza Strip and the West Bank on Higher Education" (May 2010), pp. 1–2, www.gisha.org/UserFiles/File/safepassage/InfoSheets/English/students.pdf.

[166] HCJ 11120/05 *Hamdan v. Commander of the Southern Command* (August 7, 2007), ¶¶ A, H, P of justice Rubinstein's opinion (an unofficial English translation by Israeli NGO Gisha, which represented the petitioners, is available at https://gisha.org/UserFiles/File/publications/10_years_10_judgments/Hamdan%201.pdf).

[167] Ibid., ¶¶ J, M, P of justice Rubinstein's opinion.

[168] Human Rights Watch, "Gaza: Lift Restrictions on Books, Newspapers" (March 7, 2011), www.hrw.org/news/2011/03/07/gaza-lift-restrictions-books-newspapers.

[169] M. Niezna, *Hand on the Switch: Who's Responsible for Gaza's Infrastructure Crisis?* (Tel Aviv: Gisha, January 2017), http://gisha.org/UserFiles/File/publications/infrastructure/Hand_on_the_Switch-EN.pdf.

[170] J. Khoury, "Israel Delaying Delivery of 300,000 Textbooks to Gaza Schools, Palestinians Claim," *Haaretz* (August 28, 2016), www.haaretz.com/israel-news/.premium-1.738962.

Palestinians are not treated better). The military highlighted this growing resemblance between the two legal systems in its statements about the reforms. The military youth courts, it asserted in 2009, brought about "resemblance to the statutory situation in Israel." Among those attending the military youth court launch was the president of Israel's non-military youth courts, who also gave a lecture to the new court's judges.[171] Two years later, the increase of the age of criminal majority from 16 to 18 years was likewise presented by the military as "matching the age of majority in Israel."[172] The military's response, in 2015, to an inquiry from Human Rights Watch about its handling of young noncitizen Palestinians was similar: "The [non-military] law applicable in Israel [i.e., within the pre-1967 borders] is also applied, de facto, to law enforcement in Judea and Samaria [i.e., the West Bank]."[173]

Around the same time, there occurred a converse process of modeling amendments to Israel's non-military youth justice law after the military law. Two of these amendments, from 2014 and 2015, were detailed in the previous chapter and will hence be described here briefly. The first resembled a 1988 military order that authorized imposing a financial sanction on Palestinian parents based on mere suspicion of their child's wrongdoing. Publicly acknowledging the past use of this measure under the military law, the Israeli state prosecutor's office reportedly started fining Palestinian parents of children in East Jerusalem who were suspected (not convicted) of stone throwing.[174] The second amendment, somewhat redolent of the current military law, denies state benefits to parents of convicted child "security prisoners."[175] Two other amendments, enacted in 2015, were mentioned in Chapter 2: the minimum age for custodial sentences was reduced from 14 to 12 years, and stone throwing was specifically criminalized, with a maximum prison sentence

---

[171] T. Yaniv and D. Yom-Tov, "A Military Youth Court Has Been Established," *IDF Spokesperson's Announcements* (November 2, 2009) [Hebrew].

[172] See, respectively, Office of the Legal Advisor to the IDF, "The Establishment of a Military Juvenile Court in Judea and Samaria"; Military Courts Unit, "The Military Courts Unit (Judea and Samaria)."

[173] "Response Letter from the Israeli Military."

[174] N. Hasson, "Prosecution Imposes Fines on Rioters' Parents," *Haaretz* (October 31, 2014) [Hebrew], www.haaretz.co.il/news/politics/.premium-1.2472769.

[175] Article 3 of Penal Code (Amendment No. 120 and Temporary Order), 2015. At the time of writing, a petition against this amendment is pending before the supreme court: petition in HCJ 3390/16 *Adalah* v. *Knesset* (April 21, 2016) [Hebrew], www.adalah.org/uploads/Children_Allowances_Sawsan_April_2016.pdf.

of 20 years. As I have shown, these amendments, though formally applicable to all children in Israel, were also presented by the Israeli government as specifically targeted at young Palestinians in East Jerusalem.

Two contrasting processes thus took place. On the one hand, non-military youth justice elements were being incorporated into the military law. On the other hand, youth justice provisions resembling the military law were being introduced into the non-military law. Combined, these processes are a symptom of a growing confluence between the two legal systems. Exemplifying the adoption of non-military law elements into the military law is the application, since 1992, of the evidentiary rules of non-military criminal proceedings to military courts, which were previously subject to courts-martial rules of evidence.[176] A more recent example is the incorporation of some key non-military criminal law concepts in the central military order regarding "security offenses" in 2015.[177] Yet another amendment, in 2017, rendered military judgments admissible evidence in non-military courts.[178]

In addition, following decades of Palestinians being placed in "administrative detention," the non-military law has come to authorize incarcerating African asylum seekers without trial for up to a year. Some of the facilities in which the asylum seekers have been detained previously housed Palestinian "security prisoners," and the warden of one facility also once supervised a prison for Palestinians in the West Bank.[179] The incarceration of asylum seekers from Africa is carried out under an amended version of a 1954 statute originally enacted to criminalize reentry into Israel of Palestinian refugees. The statutory term denoting these Palestinians – "infiltrators" – is retained in the amended law targeting African asylum seekers. Though Egypt, the asylum seekers' gateway, is not considered an enemy state, it is the military rather than the border police that handles unauthorized entrants from the Egyptian border. Military lawyers, in particular, have continuously advised the

---

[176] N. Benichou, "Criminal Law in the Judea, Samaria, and Gaza Regions" (2004) 18 *Law & Military* 293, 300–01 [Hebrew]. This provision currently appears as Article 86 of Order 1651.

[177] Order Concerning Security Provisions (Amendment No. 45) (Criminal Responsibility Rules) (Judea and Samaria) (No. 1754), 2015.

[178] Law Amending the Evidence Ordinance (No. 18), 2017.

[179] Addameer, "Negev Desert (Ketziot) Prison" (n.d., last accessed on December 25, 2019), www.addameer.org/content/ketziot-prison.

Israeli government on handling African asylum seekers.[180]

Earlier, I showed how the military's child-related reforms turned what are formally statutory exceptions into the de facto norm. The growing convergence between the military and non-military Israeli law manifests a partly comparable, albeit much more fundamental, process regarding the West Bank. As detailed in this book's opening chapter, many in Israel envision this territory as a temporary exception, inhabited by Palestinian foreigners, external to and separate from normal Israeli space. At the same time, Israel has increasingly annexed the West Bank, effectively if not yet formally, thereby politically and legally merging exception and norm.[181] The increased convergence between the two Israeli legal systems demonstrates how, in tandem with the annexation of this territory, there has been a blurring of the lines between the supposedly exceptional military law and the country's non-military law and policy. Given that the latter target noncitizen residents (Palestinians and others, as I have shown), what they have borrowed from the military law is not only specific provisions but also its broader function.

---

[180] H. Viterbo, "Outside/Inside," in Ben-Naftali, Sfard, and Viterbo, *The ABC of the OPT*, pp. 319–24.

[181] See Chapter 1, Sections 1.3.2 ("The West Bank, Excluding East Jerusalem") and 1.4 ("Methodology and Sources").

5

Stolen Childhood: Voice, Loss, and Trauma in Human Rights Reports

5.1 Introduction

A common thread running through the previous chapters is the growing prominence of law and human rights – especially child law and children's rights – in Israel's conduct and rhetoric toward Palestinians. In this regard, Chapters 2–4 also cast a critical light on the role of the liberal human rights community: its legalistic and essentialist support for detrimental state practices, its misunderstanding and misrepresentation of the legal state of affairs, and its portrayal of certain Palestinians as a national security threat.

The present chapter continues this inquiry by homing in on the ways human rights organizations represent young Palestinians' encounter with Israel and its legal system. The objects of this analysis are four inter-related interpretive frameworks recurrent in human rights reports: (a) a mental health discourse of childhood trauma and loss; (b) a depiction of Palestinian childhood itself as lost or stolen; (c) talk of a "right to childhood"; and (d) a claim to represent young Palestinians' voices.

Starting with the first theme, the next section will analyze the diverse uses of the mental health language of trauma and loss in human rights reporting. After shedding light on the expertise and approaches privileged by this language, I will identify three pitfalls in it, which partly overlap with those brought to light earlier in the book. First, it individualizes, and thereby potentially decontextualizes, the issues in question. Second, it pathologizes the young Palestinians affected by these issues. Lastly, it positions these Palestinians, yet again, as a prospective security threat.

Section 5.3 will focus on the image of childhood as lost or stolen. I will explain how this image operates to cement what are considered the normal boundaries of childhood, while at the same time casting doubt on the universality of these boundaries and lending itself to competing political ideologies. In addition, the stolen-childhood narrative neglects the opposite trend revealed in the previous chapter, whereby Israel, rather than eroding childhood, has been legally entrenching the "child"/"adult" divide. Further, in an apparent attempt to translate local issues to global audiences, this narrative portrays Palestinians as both an exception to normal childhood and an epitome of the worldwide demise of childhood, without sensitivity to the actual sociopolitical context. Finally, I will look at how human rights texts tie the loss of childhood to another loss – that of the Palestinian homeland – and how this linkage depicts Palestinians' collective past, present, and future.

In Section 5.4, I will turn to the somewhat related suggestion, as made by some in the human rights community, that Palestinians classified as children have a "right to childhood." This notion, it will be argued, is symptomatic of two deleterious tendencies of children's rights and child law: first, the disempowerment and social exclusion of young people; and, second, the legitimation of apathy and harshness toward older people. Each of these will be discussed in turn.

The final interpretive framework to be examined is the claim of many of Israel's human rights critics to represent young Palestinians' voices. Contrary to this claim, I will suggest in Section 5.5 that human rights organizations might obscure these voices, as well as the broader complexity of "voice," in six respects: (a) by disregarding young Palestinians' accounts, including those appearing in human rights publications; (b) by prioritizing older people's voices, such as those lamenting the loss of Palestinian childhood; (c) by excluding youth from the writing and editing of human rights reports; (d) by omitting crucial information relating to the testimonies they quote; (e) by failing to report witnesses' nonverbal expressions; and (f) by ignoring the inseparability of human voice from the messy social fabric.

Having considered each of these discursive frameworks separately, the chapter will conclude by revisiting them as a whole. This will be done, in Section 5.6, through the prism of three dualities that bind them together: one surrounding the broader sociopolitical context, another concerning the status of young Palestinians as sources of evidence, and another relating to the boundaries of childhood.

5.2 The Mental Health Discourse and Its Pitfalls

5.2.1 Interpretive Frameworks and Expertise

The mental health disciplines have profoundly impacted a multitude of social areas. Among them are child protection policies,[1] so-called

---

[1] S. White, "Interdiscursivity and Child Welfare: The Ascent and Durability of Psycho-Legalism" (1998) 46:2 *Sociological Review* 264 [hereinafter: "Interdiscursivity and Child Welfare"].

national security discourses,[2] conceptions of childhood (legal and other),[3] debates on the effects of armed conflict in Israel/Palestine,[4] and humanitarian projects for Palestinians aged under 18.[5]

Prominent in the mental health discourse of human rights reports on young Palestinians are the terms "trauma" and "loss." Palestinian NGO Addameer has thus argued that "Israel ... traumatizes the children it arrests," described their "detention [as] a traumatic experience," and listed a number of specific "post-traumatic stress disorder (PTSD) symptoms."[6] Similarly, according to Israeli NGO Hamoked, arrests are a "traumatic ... experience" with a potentially "long-term impact" on young Palestinians.[7] Psychological literature on the prevalence of PTSD among young Palestinians is expansive and ever-growing,[8] and some of these studies also end up being cited in human rights reports.[9]

---

[2] S. J. Baele, "Are Terrorists 'Insane'? A Critical Analysis of Mental Health Categories in Lone Terrorists' Trials" (2014) 7:2 *Critical Studies on Terrorism* 257.

[3] In relation to legal conceptions, see M. King and C. Piper, *How the Law Thinks About Children*, 2nd ed. (Aldershot: Ashgate, 1995), pp. 68–72. In relation to social conceptions generally, see D. Kennedy, *The Well of Being: Childhood, Subjectivity, and Education* (Albany: State University of New York Press, 2006), pp. 4–5, 7–9, 15, 63–66, 69, 76–78, 98–99.

[4] D. Fassin, "The Humanitarian Politics of Testimony: Subjectification through Trauma in the Israeli-Palestinian Conflict" (2008) 23:3 *Cultural Anthropology* 531, 554; E. Lomsky-Feder and E. Ben-Ari, "Trauma, Therapy and Responsibility: Psychology and War in Contemporary Israel," in A. Rao et al. (eds.), *The Practice of War: Production, Reproduction and Communication of Armed Violence* (New York and Oxford: Berghahn Books, 2007), pp. 111–12, 117–19, 122–23.

[5] J. Hart and C. Lo Forte, "Mandated to Fail? Humanitarian Agencies and the Protection of Palestinian Children" (2013) 37:4 *Disasters* 627, 632–40; D. J. Marshall, "'All the Beautiful Things': Trauma, Aesthetics and the Politics of Palestinian Childhood" (2013) 17:1 *Space & Polity* 53, 54, 60.

[6] See, respectively, Addameer, *In the Shadow of the 2014 Gaza War: Imprisonment of Jerusalem's Children* (2016), p. 57, www.addameer.org/sites/default/files/publications/imprisonment_of_jerusalems_children_2016.pdf; Addameer, "Education within the Israeli Prisons: A Deliberate Policy to De-educate" (June 9, 2019), www.addameer.org/publications/education-within-israeli-prisons-deliberate-policy-de-educate; Addameer, *The Right of Child Prisoners to Education* (2010), pp. 90–91, www.addameer.org/sites/default/files/publications/addameer-report-the-right-of-child-prisoners-to-education-october-2010-en.pdf.

[7] L. Caspi, *Childhood in Chains: The Detention and Interrogation of Palestinian Teenagers in the West Bank* (Jerusalem: Hamoked, April 2018), www.hamoked.org/files/2018/1162860_eng.pdf.

[8] For a literature review, see A. Sagi-Schwartz, "The Well-Being of Children Living in Chronic War Zones: The Palestinian-Israel Case" (2008) 32:4 *International Journal of Behavioral Development* 322.

[9] See, e.g., Addameer, *The Right of Child Prisoners to Education*, p. 89; C. Cook, A. Hanieh, and A. Kay (in association with DCIP), *Stolen Youth: The Politics of Israel's Detention of*

Studies of such issues often take as their point of departure psychological definitions of trauma and loss. Trauma has thus been characterized as an emotional injury that leads to lasting damage in the psyche, and which is caused by the experience of, or prolonged exposure to, terrifying (and usually violent) events.[10] Loss, in comparison, has been defined as the reduction of resources in which one is emotionally invested, ranging from relatively insignificant possessions to one's close family members, home, body parts, or personal identity. Thus conceptualized, the two terms partly overlap yet differ: whereas trauma involves a major loss, not all losses amount to trauma.[11] However, contrary to what such rigid definitions suggest, trauma and loss are not mere facts. Instead, they are interpretive frameworks[12] in the hands of human rights actors and others, and as such will be shown to operate in a much messier fashion.

For diagnosis of and solutions to trauma and loss, human rights organizations repeatedly appeal to mental health professionals – psychologists, psychiatrists, and social workers – whom they portray as uniquely able to access the scarred psyche. Thus, the mental health discourse prioritizes not only particular languages for conceptualizing wrongs, but also particular forms of expertise. For example, a 2016 report by Defence for Children International – Palestine (DCIP), while repeatedly speaking of trauma, also invokes psychological expertise and calls for prompt psychological intervention:

> Night arrests traumatize children . . . [and these] potentially traumatizing military arrests . . . [are followed by interrogations. In addition, detention] can be a stressful time for children who have recently undergone the trauma of military arrest . . . Palestinian child prisoners – many of whom undergo traumatic experiences during military arrest – have few therapeutic outlets. . . . [A] critical long-term risk for former Palestinian child

---

Palestinian Children (London: Pluto Press, 2004), pp. 130–31; Palestinian Human Rights Monitoring Group, "Children in Conflict and in the Media" (2003).

[10] S. Felman, The Juridical Unconscious: Trials and Traumas in the Twentieth Century (Cambridge, MA and London: Harvard University Press, 2002), p. 171.

[11] B. L. Green, "Traumatic Loss: Conceptual and Empirical Links between Trauma and Bereavement" (2000) 5:1 Journal of Loss and Trauma 1, 2–4; J. H. Harvey, Perspectives on Loss and Trauma: Assaults on the Self (Thousand Oaks and London: Sage, 2002), pp. 5–6; J. H. Harvey and E. D. Miller, "Preface," in J. H. Harvey and E. D. Miller (eds.), Loss and Trauma: General and Close Relationship Perspectives (New York and Abingdon: Routledge, 2000), p. xiii.

[12] K. Farrell, Post-Traumatic Culture: Injury and Interpretation in the Nineties (Baltimore and London: Johns Hopkins University Press, 1998), p. 7.

detainees is untreated trauma symptoms following military arrest. Murad Amro, clinical psychologist at the Palestine Counseling Center, told DCIP that when trauma is treated within [a] few days, [its] impact ... could be significantly reduced. ... Without psychological supports, detained Palestinian children who underwent traumatizing experiences ... may repress their memories. The repressed memory can surface later and cause disruptive psychological symptoms.[13]

Some of the NGO's other publications,[14] including one jointly published with Defence for Children International – Israel,[15] offer a similar mental health framing. The same framing is used by other human rights organizations. Among them is the Association for Civil Rights in Israel, which has cited "an expert psychological evaluation" that describes a young Palestinian as exhibiting "behavioural signs of trauma" following his detention.[16]

5.2.2   Essentialism and Developmentality

Often, the truth-claims put forward by mental health professionals brim with essentialism and developmentality. Since Chapters 1 and 4 critically analyzed these worldviews in depth, and with further criticism provided later in this chapter, a few brief examples will suffice here. One is a position paper on the issue of young Palestinians' coerced false confessions, published jointly by three Israeli and Palestinian NGOs, and presented as underpinned by an Israeli psychiatrist's detailed opinion.[17]

---

[13] Defence for Children International – Palestine (DCIP), *No Way to Treat a Child: Palestinian Children in the Israeli Military Detention System* (April 2016), pp. 25, 37, 55, 61, 67, https://d3n8a8pro7vhmx.cloudfront.net/dcipalestine/pages/1527/attachments/original/1460665378/DCIP_NWTTAC_Report_Final_April_2016.pdf.

[14] See, e.g., DCIP, *Palestinian Child Prisoners: The Systematic and Institutionalised Ill-treatment and Torture of Palestinian Children by Israeli Authorities* (June 2009), p. 6, https://d3n8a8pro7vhmx.cloudfront.net/dcipalestine/pages/1298/attachments/original/1433987832/DCIP_childprisoner_report.pdf?1433987832; DCIP, *Bound, Blindfolded and Convicted: Children Held in Military Detention* (April 2012), p. 54, http://arabic.dci-palestine.org/sites/arabic.dci-palestine.org/files/report_0.pdf.

[15] Defence for Children International – Israel and DCIP, *Alternative Report for Consideration Regarding Israel's Initial OPAC Periodic Report to the Child's Rights Committee* (July 17, 2009), pp. 24–25, https://reliefweb.int/sites/reliefweb.int/files/resources/72FF6238DD307E8A852576110057D764-Full_Report.pdf.

[16] N. Alyan, *Violations of the "Youth Law (Adjudication, Punishment and Methods of Treatment) – 1971" by the Israeli Police in East Jerusalem* (Tel Aviv: ACRI, March 2011), p. 8, http://reliefweb.int/sites/reliefweb.int/files/resources/Full_Report_1007.pdf.

[17] A. Dayif and F. El-'Ajou, *False Confessions by Palestinian Children and Adolescents Under Coercion* (Physicians for Human Rights – Israel, Adalah, and Al Mezan Center for Human Rights, November 2011), www.mezan.org/en/uploads/files/12994.pdf.

This opinion specifies a number of "developmental factors," biological and psychological, which purportedly make young people more susceptible to coercive interrogation techniques and more likely to subsequently suffer from PTSD.[18]

Similarly, in 2020, Israeli NGO Parents Against Child Detention applied to file an amicus curiae brief in a supreme court case concerning a detained Palestinian youth. The application weaves together essentialism, developmentality, and trauma:

> As medical health professionals specializing in child and youth development, we warn that ... the categorical classification of Palestinian children and youths as "security" [detainees], a category that does not distinguish between adults and minors, blinds the court to the fact that they are children, who have yet to acquire the cognitive and emotional skills to cope on their own with traumatic experiences such as arrest and interrogation.[19]

Other reports quote essentialist and developmentalist assertions by mental health experts, who insist, among other things, that young Palestinians are traumatized children even when their appearance and behavior suggests otherwise. Thus, DCIP quotes one of its social workers as emphatically contrasting "children" with "adults":

> Adolescents are especially vulnerable to torture ... – their specific stage in development places them at especially high risk. ... Every arrested child is traumatised because he is a child, is immature and not an adult, even if he has an adult's physique. The [Palestinian] community doesn't allow child prisoners to be dealt with as children as they are considered heroes and political prisoners.[20]

Another Palestinian NGO, Addameer, has accused Israeli detention of leaving young Palestinians with "emotional scars and traumas." In an attempt to substantiate this claim, the head of the psychosocial department at the Madaa Creative Center in East Jerusalem is quoted throughout its report. "They are still children," she is reported as saying. "Believe me, from my experience you see a 16 or 17 year old acting like a hero or a man, but inside he is still a child. It is not an easy experience he has faced,

---

[18] G. Carmon, "Coerced False Confessions: The Case of Palestinian Children – Psychiatric Expert Opinion" (Tel Aviv: Physicians for Human Rights – Israel, May 2011), pp. 87–91.

[19] Parents Against Child Detention, Facebook post (August 19, 2020) [Hebrew], www.facebook.com/ChildDetention/posts/651144205754758.

[20] Cook, Hanieh, and Kay, *Stolen Youth*, pp. 129, 135.

and he will be totally affected by it."[21] Beneath an adult appearance or behavior, then, young Palestinians are thought to remain traumatized children. The conclusion, readers are told, is that medical health experts alone, by seeing through this adult exterior, can bring to light both the childhood and the trauma supposedly buried out of sight in these Palestinians' psyche.

5.2.3   Individualization and Pathologization

Human rights discourses and practices, as I observed in Chapter 1, often criticize rights violations in isolation from their structural causes. By endorsing the mental health discourse – whose target, traditionally, is the individual and her or his disorders – human rights publications risk further decontextualizing the issues they seek to address, as well as potentially pathologizing young Palestinians.[22] Two representative examples of this pathologizing aspect, outside human rights reports, are the claim, in an academic study from 2017, that "rates of psychopathology in children exposed to political violence are high,"[23] and a 2014 piece in *The Washington Post* describing Palestinians as a "PTSD nation."[24]

At the same time, not unlike law and human rights, the mental health discourse does not speak in a single voice. It can thus be utilized, among other things, to diagnose Palestinians' collective plight rather than simply their individual disorders. The Palestinian Centre for Human Rights, for instance, has spoken of the "collective trauma" of all young Palestinians

---

[21] Addameer, *In the Shadow of the 2014 Gaza War*, p. 52.

[22] On these pitfalls of mental health approaches to young Palestinians, see D. J. Marshall and C. Sousa, "Decolonizing Trauma: Liberation Psychology and Childhood Trauma in Palestine," in C. Harker, K. Hörschelman, and T. Skelton (eds.), *Conflict, Violence and Peace* (Singapore: Springer, 2017), pp. 287, 289–90, 292, 296–98 [hereinafter: "Decolonizing Trauma"]; B. K. Barber et al., "Whither the 'Children of the Stones'? An Entire Life under Occupation" (2016) 45:2 *Journal of Palestine Studies* 77, 80–81 [hereinafter: "Whither the Children of the Stones"].

[23] L. E. Miller-Graff and E. M. Cummings, "The Israeli-Palestinian Conflict: Effects on Youth Adjustment, Available Interventions, and Future Research Directions" (2017) 43 *Development Review* 1.

[24] J. S. Gordon, "Gaza Isn't Just a Physical Wreck. The Psychological Damage Is Even Worse," *The Washington Post* (November 3, 2014), www.washingtonpost.com/posteverything/wp/2014/11/03/gaza-isnt-just-a-physical-wreck-the-psychological-damage-is-even-worse/?hpid=z3.

in Gaza,[25] adding that "Palestinian children are the most tragic victims of the Israeli occupation policy ... as they are subjected to traumatic incidents."[26] Other publications have been more explicit in placing trauma and loss within their broader political-legal contexts. One, titled *Stolen Youth*, does so through its subtitle: *The Politics of Israel's Detention of Palestinian Children*. Published in association with DCIP, it reads: "imprisonment is not the sole trauma that Palestinian children will sustain during their childhoods. The very poor child rights situation in the [Palestinian territories] ... is a function of a political situation that results in simultaneous violations of children's rights on a daily basis."[27] Another report, jointly authored by DCIP and Al Mezan Center for Human Rights, is likewise dedicated to Palestinians "living with memories of trauma and loss and hoping that the perpetrators will someday be held accountable for their actions."[28] Nonetheless, while these quotes illustrate the ability of mental health rhetoric to transcend the individual, they also exemplify its complicity in two problematic narratives examined later in this chapter: the association of young people with vulnerability and victimhood, and the image of Palestinian childhood as lost or stolen.

5.2.4 Securitization

When discussing trauma, some human rights organizations focus on its potential impact on young Palestinians' future behavior. A report by Palestinian NGO Addameer thus warns that, according to Palestinian psychologists working with torture victims, the "trauma" of "arrest, interrogation or abuse" could "increase the probability of suffering psychological and behavioral disorders in adulthood."[29] According to geographer David Marshall, it is through such framing that

---

[25] Palestinian Centre for Human Rights, *Blood on Their Hands: Child Killings by the Israeli Occupation Forces (IOF) in the Gaza Strip, June 2007 – June 2008* (2008), pp. 36–38, www.pchrgaza.org/files/Reports/English/pdf_spec/Blood%20on%20their%20hands.pdf.

[26] Palestinian Centre for Human Rights, *Violations of Children's Rights* (2007), www.pchrgaza.org/portal/en/index.php?option=com_content&view=article&id=3024:violations-of-childrens-rights-&catid=52:theme-packages.

[27] Cook, Hanieh, and Kay, *Stolen Youth*, p. ix.

[28] DCIP and Al Mezan Center for Human Rights, *Bearing the Brunt Again: Child Rights Violations during Operation Cast Lead* (September 2009), p. 3, https://d3n8a8pro7vhmx.cloudfront.net/dcipalestine/pages/1284/attachments/original/1433971286/Bearing_the_Brunt_Again_September_2009.pdf?1433971286.

[29] Addameer, *I've Been There: A Study of Torture and Inhumane Treatment in Al-Moscobiyeh Interrogation Center* (2018), pp. 35–36, www.addameer.org/sites/default/

> trauma discourse positions Palestinian youths as security risks ... Implicit
> in trauma relief projects is the threat that children's untreated psycho-
> logical troubles and pent up emotional energy will be violently released in
> the future ... As such, Palestinian children are depicted as both at risk
> and risky. The question thus arises as to whether the purpose of trauma
> relief is to protect Palestinian children or to protect against them.[30]

This criticism can be developed in at least three respects. First,
Marshall describes as "implicit" the notion that young Palestinians pose
a security threat. However, this notion has been articulated fairly explicitly in the Child Rights Committee of the Israeli parliament. In
Chapter 8, I analyze parliamentary committee debates on Israel's pullout
from Gaza, specifically debates over the trauma and loss young Israeli
settlers were said to have suffered as a result. Compared with its intense
preoccupation with young settlers, the parliamentary Child Rights
Committee has dedicated fewer meetings to issues concerning young
Palestinians and far less attention to their alleged trauma and loss.[31]
An exception, however, was a 2004 meeting on what the committee chair
described as the "charged subject" of Israeli settlers harassing young
Palestinians in the West Bank. One of the participants, a Palestinian
psychiatrist, briefly spoke about interviews he had conducted, in collaboration with Physicians for Human Rights – Israel, with young harassed
Palestinians. Framing trauma in a seemingly neutral manner, he
remarked that "[a]s a psychiatrist, I know there are traumatized children
on both sides, Israelis and Palestinians," adding:

> After examining these [harassed Palestinian] children for an hour, letting
> them ... draw,[32] we found that they suffered trauma ... [Wherever] we
> work [in the West Bank], we find the same issues with [Palestinian]
> children. They suffer, and ... grow up with hatred ...[33]

---

files/publications/al_moscabiyeh_report_0.pdf?fbclid=IwAR0Lo_XUzxcmcbF-EqA6E-
2JpXwMxNvb6tIdVHTni2u18sN2MyLk1iVuNCo.

[30] D. J. Marshall, "Save (Us from) the Children: Trauma, Palestinian Childhood, and the
Production of Governable Subjects" (2014) 12:3 *Children's Geographies* 281, 282–83
[hereinafter: "Save Us from the Children"]. See also ibid., pp. 285, 288–89.

[31] The committee dedicated eight meetings to young Israeli settlers between 2005 and 2012,
as compared with three meetings dedicated to young Palestinians between 2004 and 2012.

[32] In Chapter 8 (Section 8.4, "Between Mental Health and Visual Representation"), I analyze
an Israeli psychologist's interpretation, at the parliamentary Child Rights Committee, of
young Israeli settlers' drawings as evidence of their trauma and loss.

[33] Special Committee for the Rights of the Child, 16th Knesset – Transcript 88 (November
2, 2004) [Hebrew], http://fs.knesset.gov.il//16/Committees/16_ptv_388456.docx.

From an Israeli standpoint, to suggest that young traumatized Palestinians grow up hating Israelis may very likely be a way to position them as a potential security risk. As I similarly demonstrated in the previous chapter, some Israeli human rights actors have described contact between Palestinians under and over the age of majority in Israeli custody as a security threat, and Israel's rehabilitation of Palestinian youth as "a security interest." The rights and trauma of young Palestinians are thus repeatedly framed, explicitly or not, in security terms.

Second, the dual image of young people as simultaneously a risk and at risk is far from unique to Israel/Palestine. Modern child law and policy – specifically the introduction of specialist youth justice and child protection legislation – was informed at least as much by a desire to protect society from the menacing young as it was by the intention to protect young people at risk from overly harsh legal treatment.[34] In some contexts, this image has served to fuel and fund political campaigns.[35] More broadly, across the neoliberal Global North, risk and its management have occupied a growing space in child-related debates and policies,[36] leading one scholar to maintain that "no age group is more associated with risk in public imagination than that of 'youth'."[37]

Third, the depiction of young Palestinians as both threatened and a threat can be understood as connected, in part, to a central theme of the previous chapters: the oscillation of childhood's boundaries between fluidity and fixity. According to education scholar David Buckingham, the boundaries between adults and children

> have ... become blurred [in recent years]; yet in several respects, they have also been reinforced and extended. Thus, on the one hand, children have increasingly gained access to aspects of 'adult' life, and ... [on] the other hand – and particularly in response to this – children have been

---

[34] K. Hanson, "Separate Childhood Laws and the Future of Society" (2016) 12:2 *Law, Culture and the Humanities* 195, 199–200.

[35] See M. L. Kenny, "Orators and Outcasts. Wanderers and Workers: Street Children in Brazil," in D. T. Cook (ed.), *Symbolic Childhood* (New York and Oxford: Peter Lang, 2002), p. 37 [hereinafter: "Orators and Outcasts"].

[36] See, e.g., N. Parton, "Risk, Advanced Liberalism and Child Welfare: The Need to Rediscover Uncertainty and Ambiguity" (1998) 28:1 *British Journal of Social Work* 5; S. Brown et al., "Risk, Resistance and the Neoliberal Agenda: Young People, Health and Well-Being in the UK, Canada and Australia" (2013) 15:4 *Health, Risk & Society* 333; P. Kelly, "Growing Up as Risky Business? Risks, Surveillance and the Institutionalized Mistrust of Youth" (2003) 6:2 *Journal of Youth Studies* 165.

[37] K. Thompson, *Moral Panics* (London and New York: Routledge, 1998), p. 43.

increasingly segregated and excluded. ... One fairly obvious way of interpreting these developments is through notions of risk and security ... Thus, it could be argued that children are increasingly under threat from dangers of various kinds ... The boundaries, in other words, have to be perpetually drawn and redrawn; and they are subject to a constant process of negotiation.[38]

The blurring and reinforcement of childhood's boundaries are, indeed, interrelated with risk and security. However, although Buckingham describes such blurring as a consequence of risks, boundaries are not simply blurred by preexisting risks; rather, they largely inform what would be considered a risk to begin with. Often, what renders a certain phenomenon a perceived risk to the young is the initial assumption that it blurs the conventional boundaries – moral, spatiotemporal, or other – of childhood. As explained in the previous chapter, this is illustrated by human rights organizations' concern over the non-separation of young Palestinians in Israeli custody: their claim that non-separation poses a risk to these youth seems to be rooted in, and reinforcing of, the notion that joint incarceration violates the normal spatiotemporal boundaries of childhood.

5.3   Childhood Lost and Stolen

5.3.1   Lost Childhood

As seen so far, some human rights publications feature the term "loss" along with "trauma." Unlike the latter term, "loss" does not necessarily connote mental health. However, by placing it within a narrative of trauma and suffering, numerous human rights publications ensure that its psychological dimensions remain to the fore. Lamented by many of these publications is a specific loss: the alleged loss of Palestinian childhood, in and beyond Israeli custody.

Exemplifying the loss-of-childhood narrative, the Special Rapporteur of the UN Commission on Human Rights has warned: "It is impossible to assess the long-term psychological harm caused to [Palestinian]

---

[38] D. Buckingham, *After the Death of Childhood: Growing Up in the Age of Electronic Media* (Cambridge: Polity, 2000), pp. 74–77. See also ibid., pp. 5–6; H. Strandell, "New Childhood Space and the Question of Difference," in H. Zeiher et al. (eds.), *Flexible Childhood? Exploring Children's Welfare in Time and Space* (Odense: University Press of Southern Denmark, 2007), pp. 49–51, 54.

children ... Many have simply lost their childhood."[39] A joint report by the UK and Swedish sections of Save the Children paints a similar picture: "Palestinian children are losing their childhood in circumstances widely known to the authorities that have the primary responsibility to protect their rights ... Witnessing lost childhoods ... [Palestinian children] are losing their childhood. As one parent put it: '... our children behave like grown-ups'."[40] Similarly, in a meeting of the parliamentary Child Rights Committee, Ran Cohen, an Israeli lawmaker from the left-wing Meretz party, complained that young Palestinians from the West Bank compelled to enter Israel to earn a living are "revoked of their very childhoods."[41] Such rhetoric, like the trauma discourse, is not confined to human rights and parliamentary circles, as evidenced by critical media commentary with headlines such as "Stolen Childhood: A Palestinian Story" and "Lost Childhood: Palestinian Children in Israeli Prisons."[42]

Some human rights organizations formulate this purported issue in criminal law terms, characterizing the denial of childhood as a property offense – a theft or robbery. A publication by Save the Children – Sweden thus quotes a Palestinian mother's complaint that "her oldest daughter has been robbed of her childhood."[43] Expressing a similar concern, the Palestinian NGO Miftah maintains that "the helplessness Palestinian parents are feeling towards protecting their children is just a part of the

---

[39] Commission on Human Rights, *Question of the Violation of Human Rights in the Occupied Arab Territories, Including Palestine*, Report of the Special Rapporteur of the Commission on Human Rights on the Situation of Human Rights in the Palestinian Territories Occupied by Israel Since 1967, John Dugard, E/CN.4/2002/32 (March 6, 2002), https://reliefweb.int/report/israel/report-special-rapporteur-commission-human-rights-situation-human-rights-palestinian.

[40] Save the Children – Sweden and Save the Children – UK, *Growing Up Under Curfew: Safeguarding the Basic Rights of Palestinian Children* (March 2003), pp. 3, 9, https://resourcecentre.savethechildren.net/sites/default/files/documents/1579.pdf.

[41] Quoted in O. Grinberg, "Radical Indeterminacies: Affirmations and Subversions of the Separation Wall – The Case of the Palestinian Children of the Junction" (2016) 31:3 *Journal of Borderlands Studies* 319, 329 [hereinafter: "Radical Indeterminacies"].

[42] H. Bazian, "Stolen Childhood: A Palestinian Story," *Al Jazeera* (August 2, 2015), www.aljazeera.com/indepth/opinion/2015/07/stolen-childhood-palestinian-story-150726082359649.html; R. Abd Ulhamid, "Lost Childhood: Palestinian Children in Israeli Prisons," *Informed Consent* (January 16, 2019), www.juancole.com/2019/01/childhood-palestinian-children.html.

[43] M. Gröndahl, *One Day in Prison – Feels Like a Year: Palestinian Children Tell Their Own Stories* (Stockholm: Save the Children – Sweden, 2003), p. 15, www.palestinasolidariteit.be/sites/default/files/One%20day%20in%20Prison%20-%20English.pdf.

mounting pressure these stolen childhoods are under."[44] The Palestinian Centre for Human Rights has argued that young Palestinians' "collective childhood is stolen,"[45] while another Palestinian NGO, Addameer, has included in two of its reports on imprisoned Palestinian youth sections titled "Early Adulthood, Stolen Childhood" and "Systematic Destruction of Childhood."[46] In a similar vein, a former DCIP employee has cautioned that the conditions of life under Israeli rule "prematurely force children into adult roles and rob them of their childhood."[47] The aptly titled book *Stolen Youth: The Politics of Israel's Detention of Palestinian Children* (published in association with DCIP) further elaborates some of these sentiments, while tying them to the trauma discourse. Brimming with developmentalist talk of "trauma" and "PTSD,"[48] it especially warns that the young "age, level of emotional maturity, physical stature, and other factors [of Palestinian children] leave them ... less prepared [than adults] for the trauma of prison." The book adds: "The experience may constitute the end of childhood and the beginning of their lives as adults."[49]

In warning that Israeli authorities "prematurely force children into adult roles and rob them of their childhood," or that Palestinians experience "early adulthood" and "stolen childhood,"[50] human rights organizations assume a violation of what they and many others hold to be the normal boundaries between childhood and adulthood. By depicting childhood as stolen, in combination with a mental health framing, they endeavor to rectify and buttress these ostensibly violated boundaries, in the process reinforcing an essentialist and developmentalist model of childhood and human development. It is not the loss of childhood per se that these human rights critics deplore so much as its ostensibly premature timing, as well as its location (be it Israeli custody or, more

---

[44] Miftah, "Accusation Follows Occupation for Palestinian Children" (June 14, 2004), www.miftah.org/Display.cfm?DocId=3999&CategoryId=3.

[45] Palestinian Centre for Human Rights, *Violations of Children's Rights*.

[46] See, respectively, Addameer, *Palestinian Children Political Prisoners* (2004); Addameer, "Imprisonment of Children" (February 2016), www.addameer.org/the_prisoners/children.

[47] C. Cook, "Palestinian Children and the Second Intifada," *Miftah* (April 5, 2004), www.miftah.org/display.cfm?DocId=3451&CategoryId=5.

[48] Cook, Hanieh, and Kay, *Stolen Youth*, pp. ix, xvi, 7, 27, 54, 66, 83, 102, 112, 124–31, 133, 135, 137, 139, 141.

[49] Ibid., p. 83.

[50] See, respectively, Cook, "Palestinian Children and the Second Intifada"; Addameer, *Palestinian Children Political Prisoners*; Addameer, "Imprisonment of Children."

broadly, the Israeli-controlled territories) and circumstances (life under Israeli law and domination). As a UN study put it as early as 1981, "the political upheavals in the area constitute an element which is not part of the experience of most children elsewhere."[51] Were Palestinians to "lose" their childhood at an age and in a manner considered normal by the essentialist and developmentalist standards of the human rights community, such anxieties, formulated as a loss of childhood, would probably not have been so pervasive. Indeed, despite a common belief within psychology and some other social arenas that childhood latently persists throughout human life,[52] law and human rights tend to envision people as leaving their childhood behind upon becoming fully functioning adults. This is among the reasons why, as soon as people reach legal adulthood, they are usually deemed no longer to be eligible for child rights, such as the rights to play and to free education (both of which are enshrined in the Convention on the Rights of the Child (CRC)).[53]

Not only is the accusation that Israel "prematurely force[s] children into adult roles and rob[s] them of their childhood" essentialist and developmentalist, it also overlooks the opposite trend detailed in the previous chapter. As I demonstrated, rather than simply eroding childhood, Israeli authorities have in fact been increasingly imposing legal distinctions and divisions between Palestinian "children" and "adults." This trend amounts not so much to robbing young Palestinians of their childhood but to confining them to a legal childhood harmful to Palestinians of all ages, purportedly in the name of international child law and children's rights.

At the same time, by suggesting that young Palestinians have lost their childhood and are hence, in a sense, non-children, human rights organizations undermine the essentialist premise of child rights – namely, that those defined as children are universally different from their older counterparts. If "early adulthood" is possible – if one can be turned into an adult "prematurely" – then no longer can such differences be viewed as inherent to childhood. The stolen-childhood narrative thus casts doubt on the boundaries it seeks to fix between childhood and adulthood, even

---

[51] UN, *Palestinian Children in the Occupied Territories* (October 1981), p. 22.
[52] Kennedy, *The Well of Being*, pp. 12, 95; C. Steedman, *Strange Dislocations: Childhood and the Idea of Human Interiority, 1780–1930* (Cambridge, MA: Harvard University Press, 1994).
[53] See, respectively, Articles 31, 28 of the CRC.

if this hardly resembles the erosion of those boundaries that is attributed to Israel's actions.

An exchange in the Israeli parliament in 2015 exposed this duality as well as the amenability of the stolen-childhood image to divergent political ideologies and interests. Yifat Shasha-Biton, the chair of the Child Rights Committee and a member of the right-wing coalition, described young noncitizen Palestinians in Israeli custody as "children who ... take adults' place by engaging in terrorism." Shortly thereafter, she added that "a child who ends up stabbing has no normal childhood," thus, in a sense, depicting young Palestinians who come into conflict with Israeli authorities as non-children. Shasha-Biton's remarks echo two social conceptions. The first is the view of young Palestinian "security offenders" as occupying a category traditionally reserved for those defined as adults: active, ideologically motivated, political actors. Seen in this light, the Palestinians in question pose a challenge to the adult/ child divide, to Israel's rule, and also to power relations in Palestinian society.[54] The second is the belief that young people in conflict with the law, in general, challenge the traditional dichotomy between "children," whose hallmarks are innocence, dependence, and helplessness, and "adults," who are associated with corruption (or knowledge), independence, and agency.[55] Palestinian member of parliament Haneen Zoabi was quick to point out that her colleague's views go against the essentialism of child's rights: "So [you are suggesting that] if they are terrorists they are no longer children. They are either terrorists or children. ... You are undermining the entire rationale behind children's rights."[56] Narratives about young Palestinians having no childhood

---

[54] On some of the ways in which young Palestinians, in actively opposing Israeli authorities, challenge Israeli and Palestinian social orders, see D. Rosen, *Armies of the Young: Child Soldiers in War and Terrorism* (New Brunswick and London: Rutgers University Press, 2005), pp. 112–13, 116, 118–21; D. Tuastad, "The Violent Rise of Palestine's Lost Generation" (2017) 26:2 *Middle East Critique* 159; J. Collins, *Occupied by Memory: The Intifada Generation and the Palestinian State of Emergency* (New York and London: New York University Press, 2004), p. 113; Grinberg, "Radical Indeterminacies," pp. 328, 330–31; G. Yair and N. Khatab, "Changing the Guards: Teacher-Student Interaction in the Intifada" (1995) 68:2 *Sociology of Education* 99.

[55] On this image of young offenders (beyond Israel/Palestine), see M. Flegel, *Conceptualizing Cruelty to Children in Nineteenth-Century England* (Farnham and Burlington: Ashgate, 2009), pp. 147–48; C. Jenks, *Childhood*, 2nd ed. (New York: Routledge, 2005), pp. 128–31.

[56] Special Committee for the Rights of the Child, 20th Knesset – Transcript 34 (December 21, 2015), pp. 43, 46 [Hebrew], http://fs.knesset.gov.il//20/Committees/20_ptv_322051 .doc.

thus serve competing political ideologies, while also exposing the tensions innate to children's rights.

5.3.2 Lost Context

The lost-childhood narrative is among the discursive tools employed by Israel's human rights critics to "translate" to their audiences and donors the situation of young noncitizen Palestinians. However, translation inevitably omits or excludes. Among the excluded elements here is the specific context. Like the related notion of a "right to childhood" (to which I will turn shortly), the image of Palestinian childhood as stolen rests on the idea that childhood is universal. It is this ostensibly universal childhood that provides a standard for assessing Palestinians' plight. And it is the alleged failure to live up to this standard that apparently leads human rights organizations and scholars to speak of Palestinians as being deprived of their childhood. As also noted in previous chapters, the universal model of childhood to which Israel's human rights critics commit themselves is enshrined in international legal norms, chiefly those articulated in the CRC. "Our highest value is the pursuit of each child's best interests," proclaims DCIP's website, for example, adding: "To this end, we are guided by the United Nation's Convention on the Rights of the Child."[57] However, the supposedly universal model of the CRC and other international legal documents advances a very particular social script. It reinforces certain assumptions about who really constitutes a child and what normal childhood looks like, while repressing alternative forms of life and thought.[58]

For human rights organizations, part of the appeal of the taken-for-granted universality of childhood may be the ease by which it "internationalizes" their concerns – in other words, its ability to render these concerns both intelligible and compelling to as many audiences (and donors) as possible the world over. If childhood has a universal meaning – transcending political, cultural, economic, and legal circumstances – then the image of stolen

---

[57] DCIP, "Who We Are" (n.d., last accessed on March 4, 2019), www.dci-palestine.org/who_we_are.

[58] I. Dussel, "Childhood and the Politics of Memory in Argentina," in K. Heltqvist and G. Dahlberg (eds.), *Governing the Child in the New Millennium* (New York and London: Routledge, 2001), p. 193 and the sources mentioned there; A. James, C. Jenks, and A. Prout, *Theorizing Childhood* (Cambridge: Polity Press, 1998), pp. 140–41 and the sources mentioned there.

childhood possesses a unique emotive power: it easily triggers outcry, regardless of how familiar its audiences actually are with the specificities concerning young Palestinians.

This may account for the prevalence of this image in countless other contexts. Among those from around the globe described as having their childhood stolen or robbed from them have been: street children;[59] young soldiers;[60] young people in wartime generally;[61] "Third World" young people;[62] young ethnic minority[63] and Indigenous[64] people; young abuse victims;[65] young people in trouble with the law;[66] poor or working-class youth;[67] "underachieving" pupils;[68] young unaccompanied migrants;[69]

[59] See, e.g., in relation to Brazil, Kenny, "Orators and Outcasts," pp. 54, 57.

[60] See, e.g., J. Briggs, *Innocents Lost: When Child Soldiers Go to War* (New York: Basic Books, 2005); T. Humphrey, "Child Soldiers: Rescuing the Lost Childhood" (2007) 13:1 *Australian Journal of Human Rights* 113; C. Mayr, "Little Girls Lost: Can the International Community Protect Child Soldiers?" (2008) 29 *University of La Verne Law Review* 219.

[61] L. Królikowski, *Stolen Childhood: A Saga of Polish War Children*, K. J. Rozniatowski (trans.) (San Jose and New York: Authors Choice Press, 2000); J. Hart, "Introduction," in J. Hart (ed.), *Years of Conflict: Adolescence, Political Violence and Displacement* (New York and Oxford: Berghahn Books, 2008), pp. 1, 11–12; N. Tyrer, *Stolen Childhoods: The Untold Story of the Children Interned by the Japanese in the Second World War* (London: Weidenfeld & Nicolson, 2011).

[62] E. Burman, "Innocents Abroad: Western Fantasies of Childhood and the Iconography of Emergencies" (1994) 18:3 *Disasters* 238, 242; L. Tousignant, "Millions of Kids Are Being Robbed of Their Childhood," *New York Post* (September 21, 2017), http://nypost.com/2017/09/21/millions-of-kids-are-being-robbed-of-their-childhood.

[63] S. Patton, "In America, Black Children Don't Get to Be Children," *The Washington Post* (November 26, 2014), www.washingtonpost.com/opinions/in-america-black-children-dont-get-to-be-children/2014/11/26/a9e24756-74ee-11e4-a755-e32227229e7b_story.html.

[64] H. Viterbo, "Ties of Separation: Analogy and Generational Segregation in North America, Australia, and Israel/Palestine" (2017) 42:2 *Brooklyn Journal of International Law* 695.

[65] M. Poretti et al., "The Rise and Fall of Icons of 'Stolen Childhood' since the Adoption of the UN Convention on the Rights of the Child" (2013) 21:1 *Childhood* 22.

[66] K. Ellis, "Contested Vulnerability: A Case Study of Girls in Secure Care" (2018) 88 *Children and Youth Services Review* 156, 159–60.

[67] J. Dillabough and J. Kennelly, *Lost Youth in the Global City: Class, Culture and the Urban Imaginary* (New York and Abingdon: Routledge, 2010); M. Shriver, "Missing Out on Childhood in Rural America," *U.S. News* (June 1, 2018), www.usnews.com/news/healthiest-communities/articles/2018-06-01/missing-out-on-childhood-in-rural-america.

[68] C. Griffin, "Discourses of Crisis and Loss: Analysing the 'Boys' Underachievement' Debate" (2000) 3:2 *Journal of Youth Studies* 167.

[69] S. Horton, "Consuming Childhood: 'Lost' and 'Ideal' Childhoods as a Motivation for Migration" (2008) 81:4 *Anthropological Quarterly* 925.

the young targeted by the nineteenth-century child rescue movement;[70] and, in the same era, slave youth.[71] The list could go on.

These examples might give the impression that those said to be deprived of their childhood only come from socially disempowered groups or face exceptional adversities. This, indeed, is the conclusion reached by some scholars.[72] However, laments of the loss of childhood are, in fact, far more ubiquitous. Well-situated young people in the Global North, too, have been subjected to this discourse, even if in partly different ways.[73] As the earlier discussion of risk and security intimated, contemporary thinking about childhood at large is governed by anxieties over perceived changes in social attitudes toward the young, changes in their behavior, and changing power relations between them and older people. Critics invoke all sorts of supposed evidence of the loss of childhood: an alleged rise in sexual activity, drug consumption, and crime among the young; the eroticization of young people in commercials and popular culture; young people's increased access to sights and information said to have been previously reserved for older people; the purported homogenization of young and adult language, eating habits, and leisure pursuits; parents' exaggerated concern, allegedly, with preparing their children for life rather than protecting them from it; and so forth.[74] To a large extent, therefore, just as those described as having lost their childhood are judged against an ostensibly universal standard, so too the alleged loss of childhood is perceived as a universal problem.

The portrayal of Palestinians as robbed of their childhood thus evinces two sentiments at once. On the one hand, it positions them as deviating from the supposedly universal norm. This alleged deviation may be seen as a pathology of sorts, especially considering the frequent mental health

---

[70] S. Mintz, *Huck's Raft: A History of American Childhood* (Cambridge, MA and London: Harvard University Press, 2004), pp. 154–84; S. Swain, "Sweet Childhood Lost: Idealized Images of Childhood in the British Child Rescue Literature" (2009) 2:2 *Journal of the History of Childhood and Youth* 200.

[71] W. King, *Stolen Childhood: Slave Youth in Nineteenth-Century America*, 2nd ed. (Bloomington: Indiana University Press, 2011).

[72] Burman, "Innocents Abroad," pp. 241–42, 248.

[73] See, e.g., S. C. Aitken, "Global Crises of Childhood: Rights, Justice and the Unchildlike Child" (2001) 33:2 *Area* 119; H. Davis and M. Bourhill, "'Crisis': The Demonization of Children and Young People," in Phil Scraton (ed.), *"Childhood" in "Crisis"?* (London and Bristol, PA: University College London Press, 1997), p. 28.

[74] See, e.g., N. Postman, *The Disappearance of Childhood* (New York: Vintage Books, 1982); M. Winn, *Children without Childhood* (Harmondsworth and New York: Penguin Books, 1984); Buckingham, *After the Death of Childhood*, pp. 21, 25–32, 35.

framing. On the other hand, the claim that Palestinians are deprived of their childhood places them alongside most other young people globally, whose childhood is also considered to be dissolving, lacking, or absent. These concurrent sentiments – that Palestinians are both an exception to and the epitome of childhood – are jointly context-insensitive. Rather than shedding light on Palestinians' specific circumstances, they indicate instead a decontextualized and essentialist anxiety over the tainting of childhood.[75]

5.3.3   Stolen Land

For several decades, the loss of childhood has been tied in Palestinian discourses to another loss: that of the Palestinian homeland. "The State of Israel," the author Anton Shammas wrote in 1988, "hasn't only confis-cated the land from under the feet of the Palestinians in the occupied territories; it has also taken away their childhood."[76] Three decades later, the legal scholar Nadera Shalhoub-Kevorkian similarly argued: "[The] local history of displacement . . . reveals . . . [how] colonised [Palestinian] children are denied childhood and their childhoods are distorted." Comparing childhood to a homeland, she criticized "[t]he eviction of Palestinian children from childhood," adding:

> [W]hen children are dispossessed of their childhood, when they are unchilded, the dispossession of the land is one and the same. Palestinian children come into a world where their firm foothold has already been stolen. . . . The newborn unchilded child and the dispossessed land are one and the same. . . . The purpose of settler colonialism is to remove children from their land as much as they are removed from their childhood. . . . The unchilded are a daily reminder that the land . . . is stolen.[77]

A linchpin of Palestinian national narratives, the loss of the homeland concerns the mass displacement and dispossession in the so-called Nakba

---

[75] For similar criticism, see E. Burman, "Local, Global or Globalized? Child Development and International Child Rights Legislation" (1996) 3:1 *Childhood* 46, 61.

[76] A. Shammas, "A Stone's Throw," *New York Review of Books* (March 31, 1988), www .nybooks.com/articles/4482.

[77] N. Shalhoub-Kevorkian, "The Biopolitics of Israeli Settler Colonialism: Palestinian Bedouin Children Theorise the Present" (2016) 15:1 *Journal of Holy Land and Palestine Studies* 7, 10, 24; N. Shalhoub-Kevorkian, *Incarcerated Childhood and the Politics of Unchilding* (Cambridge and New York: Cambridge University Press, 2019), pp. 18–19, 130, 133 [hereinafter: *Incarcerated Childhood*]. For two additional examples of linkages between these two losses, see J. Peteet, "Words as Interventions: Naming in the Palestine-Israel Conflict" (2005) 26:1 *Third World Quarterly* 153, 166 [hereinafter: "Words as Interventions"].

of 1948 and Naksa of 1967 (Arabic for "catastrophe" and "setback," respectively).[78] At least three human rights publications link this loss to the purported loss of childhood. Two of them – a 2001 report by the British cross-party, not-for-profit organization the Council for Arab-British Understanding[79] and a 2008 report by DCIP[80] – do so at length.[81] The former paints a fairly bleak picture:

> Children represent the dreams of the Palestinian community, their aspirations and their hopes for the future. But ... Palestinians ... have been unable to prevent the steady erosion of childhood. ... The nakba ... had a devastating effect on all Palestinians, including children. ... Palestinian children's dreams reveal ... the desperate desire to liberate their people and regain their homeland. But their day-to-day reality fails to live up to the world of fantasy.[82]

The DCIP report goes further in referring not only to the loss of lands in the Nakba but also to Israel's ongoing land grab. While echoing some of the former publication's sentiments, it envisages a more hopeful horizon. The text contains excerpts from interviews with three Palestinians, "representing three generations" of a family living in a refugee camp in the West Bank: 16-year-old Sh'aban, his father, and his grandmother. Among other things, Sh'aban's father is said to blame Israel "for robbing him of his childhood," and Sh'aban himself is quoted as saying: "Palestinian children do not lead normal lives. We are forced to grow up while we are still children."[83] The report adds:

> Because of the ever-increasing restrictions on movement within the ... [West Bank] and the construction of the Wall, many ... children have never set foot on what was once their family's land. ... [T]he interviews clearly revealed ... common themes such as stolen childhood, innocence lost, a longing to return home, and an undying hope for a better

---

[78] See, e.g., A. H. Sa'di and L. Abu-Lughod (eds.), *Nakba: Palestine, 1948, and the Claims of Memory* (New York: Columbia University Press, 2007); L. Farsakh (ed.), *Commemorating the Naksa, Evoking the Nakba* – Vol. 8 of the *MIT Electronic Journal of Middle East Studies* (Boston: MIT, 2008).

[79] M. Holt, *The Right of the Child Denied: Palestinian Children under Occupation* (London: CAABU – The Council for Arab-British Understanding, 2001), p. 1, http://citeseerx.ist .psu.edu/viewdoc/download?doi=10.1.1.729.4613&rep=rep1&type=pdf (emphasis added).

[80] DCIP, *60 Years after the Nakba: Three Generations of Palestinians Reflect on Their Past and Future* (2008).

[81] The third publication is DCIP, *Twenty Years of Building a Palestinian Community Fit for Children – 1991–2011* (2011), p. 46.

[82] Holt, *The Right of the Child Denied*, pp. 1–2, 17.

[83] DCIP, *60 Years after the Nakba*, pp. 2, 7, 9–10.

> future. ... Palestinian boys hope to ... live life free from the arbitrary
> arrest and detention that cruelly steals the youth of thousands of
> Palestinians. Having lost their own childhood to forced
> displacement ..., the *Nakba* generation has witnessed the innocence of
> their children's youth lost to the occupation and the first *Intifada* [popular
> Palestinian uprising], and that of their grandchildren to the second
> *Intifada*. ... After decades of waiting for their *right to return* to come to
> fruition, the *Nakba* generation now hopes that their grandchildren will
> return and bury their remains on what was once their land.[84]

The loss of childhood and the loss of the homeland – which the last
excerpt links, in part, to arrest and detention by Israel – are thus
characterized as intergenerational experiences shared by many
Palestinians. They are objects of nostalgia, a painful longing for a lost
home (indeed, the term "nostalgia" is a compound of "nostos" and
"algos," Greek for "home" and "pain" respectively).[85] These collective
losses are seen as almost causally interconnected, and as long as the
homeland remains out of reach so too will childhood. The Palestinian
right of return – a cornerstone of the Palestinian political-legal
struggle[86] – is thus presented as a right to return not only to the
homeland but also to childhood. In this sense, the child and the homeland become metonymic: national displacement leads to the demise of
childhood, while children embody the homeland through their potential
return to it. Childhood and the homeland alike, therefore, evoke dreams –
and nightmares – about the collective past and future.

As previously explained, the stolen childhood image offers human
rights actors a tool for globalizing the issues faced by young noncitizen
Palestinians. Indeed, the reports by DCIP and the Council for Arab-
British Understanding, as well as the other publications quoted in this
section, are all in English and thus primarily targeted at international
audiences. At the same time, though this globalizing image can have a
decontextualizing effect, its linkage to the Nakba allows it to resonate
with a local idiom.[87]

---

[84] Ibid., pp. 1, 10 (emphases in the original).
[85] A. Huyssen, "Nostalgia for Ruins" (2006) 23 *Grey Room* 6, 6.
[86] On Palestinian refugees and the "right of return," see, e.g., R. I. Khalidi, "Observations on
the Right of Return" (1992) 21:2 *Journal of Palestine Studies* 29. On the place of the "right
of return" in Zionist and Palestinian discourses, see Peteet, "Words as Interventions,"
pp. 162, 165–67.
[87] While some may describe this as an instance of "glocalization," this widely used concept
risks implying an oversimplistic global/local dichotomy. Human rights, despite their
universal posture, are always time- and place-specific in their articulations and

The dual loss – that of childhood and that of the homeland – reverberates with themes and issues explored elsewhere in this book. Like the increased separation of incarcerated Palestinian youth (investigated in the previous chapter), this dual loss largely revolves around issues of generational (dis)continuity and (dis)placement. In the next chapter, I revisit these themes, as embodied in the cartoon figure of Palestinian boy Handala, which appears in some NGO (and other) publications. Further, like the intersection of generational and national boundaries (another issue discussed in the previous chapter), the dual loss illustrates childhood's relationship with national space. More broadly, the discourse around this dual loss throws into sharp relief the intertwining of two key themes of previous chapters: spatiality (national territory, restrictions on movement) and temporality (the personal and national past and future, young age, and premature adulthood).

Also drawing this link between the two losses is a 2016 photoreport by War on Want (a UK-based charity working on issues of injustice and inequality), titled "They Have Stolen His Childhood." Dealing with Israel's land grab more extensively than the two previous reports do, the photoreport ties it almost causally (albeit indirectly) to what Akram, a Palestinian from the West Bank, describes as the loss of his son's childhood:

> Akram and [his 16-year-old son] Aziz live in Biddu, a village [that] . . . has lost much of its land to the [surrounding Israeli] settlements and the Wall. . . . Biddu residents hold frequent demonstrations against the Apartheid Wall and the settlements. The Israeli authorities often target children in arrest raids after demonstrations. . . . Aziz was arrested in one such raid . . . Akram worries about the psychological effect of Aziz's arrest and detention. . . . [and] about how Aziz has changed since his release from prison. He says: ". . . The Israeli soldiers come in to the village every night and you can see the stress and fear it causes. They have stolen his childhood."[88]

Israeli human rights organizations are not among those found to link the alleged loss of Palestinian childhood to the loss of the Palestinian homeland or lands. Given the long-standing contention over the history of

---

applications. See I. Balfour and E. Cadava, "The Claims of Human Rights: An Introduction" (2004) 103:2–3 *South Atlantic Quarterly* 277, 282; D. Kennedy, "The International Human Rights Movement: Part of the Problem?" (2002) 15 *Harvard Human Rights Journal* 101, 102–03 [hereinafter: "Part of the Problem?"].

[88] War on Want, "'They Have Stolen His Childhood'" (n.d.), http://waronwant.org/stories/they-have-stolen-his-childhood.

Israel/Palestine, their shying away from the latter loss is unlikely to be coincidental. Indeed, a study conducted between 2002 and 2013 found that Israeli human rights reports, including those focused on noncitizen Palestinians, very rarely mentioned the 1948 Nakba and the Palestinian right of return.[89]

5.4   The Right to Childhood

If, as human rights publications repeatedly suggest, depriving Palestinians of their childhood amounts to a form of theft or robbery – a property offense – then childhood is a property of sorts. Implicit in this analogy is the idea that, just as the right to property is protected by law, those classified as children deserve a socially and perhaps legally recognized right to childhood. While some human rights and mental health texts promote this notion implicitly, a few invoke "the right to childhood" explicitly. Thus, at the time of writing, reports on DCIP's website are divided into six themes, one of which is the "Right to Childhood."[90] The claim that "every child has the right to be a child" also appears in a lengthy opinion by an Israeli psychiatrist on false confessions of detained Palestinian youth, which, as previously mentioned, furnished the basis for a joint report by several Israeli and Palestinian NGOs.[91] More emphatically still, a press release by the Public Committee Against Torture in Israel proclaims: "Childhood is not a Privilege but a Right! . . . Torture Destroys Childhood . . . [T]he threshold in which an act of abuse would be considered torture in the situation of an adult must be lowered when it comes to children."[92]

Similar language can be found in some of the academic literature on young Palestinians. One legal scholar thus criticized Israel in 2019 for having "stripped . . . [Palestinian] children of their right to childhood." She explicated: "locations that are typically reserved as 'safe spaces' for children – such as schools, [homes,] . . . and playgrounds – are targets of . . . violence. . . . [T]hese children have no right to a play-filled

[89]   Z. Orr and D. Golan, "Human Rights NGOs in Israel: Collective Memory and Denial" (2014) 18:1 *International Journal of Human Rights* 68, 71–72.

[90]   DCIP, "News and Resources" (n.d., last accessed on January 30, 2018), www.dci-palestine .org/news.

[91]   Carmon, "Coerced False Confessions," p. 6.

[92]   PCATI, "Childhood Is Not a Privilege but a Right!" (posted December 31, 2013; amended January 8, 2014), https://web.archive.org/web/20151214033154/www.stoptorture.org.il/ en/node/1951.

childhood. ... [Thus, Israel subjects Palestinian children to] systematic evictions from the normal experiences of childhood."[93]

But what exactly does this so-called right to childhood entail? An invention of the Romantic era, it enshrines a particular conception of childhood as a sacred space, the happiest time of life, whose innocence must be protected.[94] Rather than a right to take a fully active part in society, the supposed right to childhood tends to be narrowly understood as a right to be protected.[95] This relates to a much broader, irreconcilable tension between what are often described, somewhat crudely, as the three constitutive elements of children's rights, also known as the "three Ps": protection (from exploitation and abuse), provision (of support and services), and participation (in relevant decisions).[96] Despite a growing emphasis in recent decades on participation rights in the language of child law and policy,[97] the desire to "protect" the young from the "adult" world still tends to prevail.[98] Even when those under the legal age of majority do get to participate, they are usually allowed to do so only "as children" (to use the words of the previously quoted DCIP social worker),[99] and only on older people's terms.[100]

---

[93] Shalhoub-Kevorkian, *Incarcerated Childhood*, pp. 44, 47, 113, 126, 129. For similar language, see ibid., pp. 26, 52, 54.

[94] H. Cunningham, *The Children of the Poor: Representations of Childhood since the Seventeenth Century* (Oxford: Blackwell, 1991); A. Richardson, "Romanticism and the End of Childhood" (1999) 21:2 *Nineteenth-Century Contexts* 169.

[95] D. Jefferess, "Neither Seen Nor Heard: The Idea of the 'Child' as Impediment to the Rights of Children" (2006) 7 *Topia: Canadian Journal of Cultural Studies* 75, 81–82, 90–91; D. Hartas, *The Right to Childhoods: Critical Perspectives on Rights, Difference and Knowledge in a Transient World* (London and New York: Continuum, 2008), pp. vii–viii.

[96] See, e.g., A. Quennerstedt, "Children, but Not Really Humans? Critical Reflections on the Hampering Effect of the '3 P's'" (2010) 18:4 *International Journal of Children's Rights* 619; J. Qvortrup, "Monitoring Childhood: Its Social, Economic and Political Features," in E. Verhellen (ed.), *Monitoring Children's Rights* (The Hague: Martin Nijhoff, 1996), pp. 36, 44.

[97] See, e.g., T. Buck et al., *International Child Law*, 2nd ed. (Abingdon and New York: Routledge, 2011), pp. 129–30; A. Lewis, "Silence in the Context of 'Child Voice'" (2010) 24:1 *Children & Society* 14, 14 [hereinafter: "Silence"].

[98] J. Roche, "Children: Rights, Participation and Citizenship" (1999) 6:4 *Childhood* 475; A. Meyer, "The Moral Rhetoric of Childhood" (2007) 14:1 *Childhood* 85.

[99] Cook, Hanieh, and Kay, *Stolen Youth*, p. 135.

[100] A. Daly, "No Weight for 'Due Weight'? A Children's Autonomy Principle in Best Interest Proceedings" (2018) 26:1 *International Journal of Children's Rights* 61; J. Ennew, "Children as 'Citizens' of the United Nations (UN)," in A. Invernizzi and J. Williams (eds.), *Children and Citizenship* (London and Thousand Oaks: Sage, 2008), p. 66; W. Stainton Rogers, "Promoting Better Childhoods: Constructions of Child

The exclusion of young people in the name of their so-called right to childhood is therefore not an instance of children's rights going astray. Quite the opposite. Premised on essentialist and developmentalist ideas, children's rights, and child law in general, serve to keep those who are legally classified as children as a distinct, separate, and thus, ultimately, excluded group. To a large extent, therefore, child-related laws and policies operate as means of discipline and domination, restricting and reducing, rather than expanding, the freedoms and potential of young people.[101] This can diminish and curtail young people's skills and capabilities, and thus provide evidence, supposedly, of the initial presumption that they are innately less capable and more vulnerable than their elders.

Further, as illustrated throughout this book, child law targets and affects people over the age of majority. An example analyzed in the previous chapter is the age-based incarceration of Palestinians, which, as I have shown, enabled Israel, with relative disregard from the human rights community, to revoke or narrow the rights of Palestinians aged 18 and over. Similarly, the supposed right to childhood reserves special protection and happiness to those defined as children, and thereby, unwittingly or not, legitimizes apathy and harshness toward older people.[102] As a case in point, a 2016 publication by DCIP, tellingly titled *No Way to Treat a Child*, states: "In no circumstance should children face detention and prosecution under the jurisdiction of military courts. . . . Children must not be subjected to physical or psychological violence."[103] If, as the title of the report posits, the problem is that this is "no way to treat a child" (rather than no way to treat anyone), and if, as the quote suggests, it is "children" (rather than all Palestinians) who require protection, then the implication might be that, by singling out the young and sparing them these practices, the problem would be solved. The report by DCIP was part of an identically titled advocacy campaign in collaboration with the US-based Quaker organization the American Friends Service Committee. The latter's director described the campaign as

---

Concern," in M. J. Kehily (ed.), *An Introduction to Childhood Studies*, 2nd ed. (Maidenhead and New York: Open University Press, 2009), p. 141.

[101] See, e.g., R. Farson, *Birthrights* (New York: Macmillan, 1974), pp. 2–4.

[102] See, e.g., Addameer, *I've Been There*, pp. 34–35 (quoting the 1959 Declaration of the Rights of the Child: "The child shall enjoy special protection," and complaining that Israeli "interrogators do not distinguish between [Palestinian] minors and adults in the interrogation process").

[103] DCIP, *No Way to Treat a Child*, pp. 2, 75.

"calling on the US Congress to pressure Israeli authorities to end the detention and ill treatment of Palestinian children by Israeli forces." She further emphasized: "no child belongs in military detention. . . . Military detention is no way to treat a child."[104]

In pursuit of these objectives, the No Way to Treat a Child campaign organized a congressional briefing in the United States in 2015. During the briefing, members of Congress were exhorted to sign a letter initiated by a Democratic lawmaker that urged the secretary of state to "elevate the human rights of Palestinian children to a priority status in our bilateral relationship with the Government of Israel."[105] Two years later, and then again in 2019, the same lawmaker introduced bills "requir[ing] that United States funds do not support military detention, interrogation, abuse, or ill-treatment of Palestinian children."[106] The US lawmaker publicly thanked DCIP for their advocacy efforts, and specifically cited their *No Way to Treat a Child* report.[107] Throughout this campaign, older Palestinians – who make up the vast majority of those detained, interrogated, abused, and ill-treated by Israel – were sidelined. Even from a purely tactical perspective (if there is such a thing), there was no apparent gain to be had. As the bills themselves acknowledged, existing federal law already forbids the US government from funding foreign security forces involved in gross human rights violations. With such a prohibition already in place, these initiatives might give the impression

---

[104] J. Bing, "Military Detention Is No Way to Treat a Child: Abuses in Palestine," *Truth Out* (September 16, 2016), https://truthout.org/articles/military-detention-is-no-way-to-treat-a-child-abuses-in-palestine/. The campaign webpage is https://nwttac.dci-palestine.org.

[105] On the briefing, see DCIP, "DCIP Participates in Congressional Briefing on Child Detention" (June 10, 2015), www.dci-palestine.org/dcip_participates_in_congressional_briefing_on_child_detention. The letter, sent a few days later, is available at www.afsc.org/sites/default/files/documents/Palestinian%20Children-Human-Rights-letter-to-house_0_0.pdf.

[106] Promoting Human Rights by Ending Israeli Military Detention of Palestinian Children Act, H.R. 4391, 115th Cong. (2017), www.congress.gov/115/bills/hr4391/BILLS-115hr4391ih.pdf; Promoting Human Rights for Palestinian Children Living under Israeli Military Occupation Act, H.R. 2407, 116th Cong. (2019), https://nwttac.dci-palestine.org/hr2407_full_text.

[107] See, respectively, Remarks by Congresswoman Betty McCollum, US Campaign for Palestinian Rights National Conference (September 29, 2018), https://mccollum.house.gov/sites/mccollum.house.gov/files/documents/18.0929McCollum-remarks_USCPR.pdf; "Resources on H.R. 2407, Promoting Human Rights for Palestinian Children Living under Israeli Military Occupation Act" (n.d.), https://mccollum.house.gov/palestinianchildrensrights.

that violations not directly affecting young people are somehow less reprehensible.

In 2020, amid the coronavirus (COVID-19) pandemic, DCIP strengthened this impression further. It launched a petition, as part of the same campaign, demanding that "Israeli authorities take immediate action to release all Palestinian child detainees ... There is no way Israeli prison authorities can ensure the health and well-being of Palestinian child detainees as long as they continue to be in a custodial detention setting." Three weeks later, a group of more than 60 Israeli and Palestinian lawyers penned an open letter to the military and the IPS, similarly demanding the immediate release of all incarcerated Palestinians below the age of 18. Subsequently, the US activist organization Jewish Voice for Peace teamed up with DCIP to launch yet another petition, calling for the "immediate release of all Palestinian child detainees."[108] Publicly available data, however, was indicating clearly that those classified as children were, in fact, the least vulnerable to the virus.[109] Accordingly, some countries were responding to the pandemic by releasing people from prison regardless of their age.[110] Others were releasing only elderly inmates, who were deemed the most vulnerable.[111] And yet,

---

[108] See, respectively, DCIP, "Israel Must Release All Palestinian Child Detainees amid COVID-19 Pandemic" (n.d., last accessed on April 1, 2020), https://nwttac.dci-palestine .org/petition_israel_must_release_all_palestinian_child_detainees_amid_covid_19_pan demic; Lawyers on behalf of Parents Against Child Detention, "The Immediate Release of All Minors Detained and Imprisoned for Security Offenses in Israeli Custody Due to the Corona Pandemic – Ahead of the Ramadan Holiday," *Facebook* (April 21, 2020) [Hebrew], www.facebook.com/ChildDetention/photos/pcb.571356357066877/ 571355707066942; Jewish Voice for Peace, "Free Palestinian Children Detainees NOW" (n.d., last accessed on April 30, 2020), https://secure.everyaction.com/ 1Nu35eEmZUmZQMpwH3Hk2A2.

[109] See, e.g., W. Wan and J. Achenbach, "Coronavirus Is Mysteriously Sparing Kids and Killing the Elderly. Understanding Why May Help Defeat the Virus," *The Washington Post* (March 10, 2020), www.washingtonpost.com/health/2020/03/10/coronavirus-is-mysteriously-sparing-kids-killing-elderly-understanding-why-may-help-defeat-virus; S. Pappas, "Why Are Children 'Missing' from Coronavirus Outbreak Cases?," *Live Science* (February 10, 2020), www.livescience.com/why-kids-missing-coronavirus-cases .html.

[110] See, e.g., J. O'Neill, "100 Prisoners to Be Released by Monday," *BBC News* (April 3, 2020), www.bbc.co.uk/news/uk-northern-ireland-52157100; R. Mostaghim, M. Tawfeeq, and A. Dewan, "Iran to Temporarily Free 54,000 Prisoners as Coronavirus Spreads," *CNN* (March 4, 2020), https://edition.cnn.com/2020/03/04/middleeast/iran-corona virus-response-intl/index.html.

[111] See, e.g., J. Naftulin, "Mayor Bill de Blasio: New York City Will Release Select Inmates Who Are over 70 and Have Certain Pre-Existing Conditions," *Business Insider* (March

DCIP's petitions and the lawyers' open letter reserved their empathy exclusively to those under the age of majority.[112]

Similar was a 2017 petition initiated by the NGO Avaaz "to pressure the Israeli authorities to release all child prisoners in Israeli jails." Every single issue mentioned in the petition – including prosecution in military courts, the denial of rights during interrogations, harsh detention conditions, the denial of family visits, and abuse – concerns older Palestinians in prison as much as their younger counterparts. Yet, the NGO, whose remit is by no means limited to children's rights, excluded these older Palestinians from its petition.[113] The legal scholar who, as quoted earlier, blamed Israel for having "stripped … [Palestinian] children of their right to childhood," likewise wrote in 2019: "Israel's brutality against … all children in Gaza … reveals clearly how the unthinkable act of attacking children becomes … thinkable, acceptable, and justifiable"[114] – implying, even if unwittingly, that attacking older Gazans is somehow more tolerable.

Such constant singling out of the young – even when done for purportedly tactical reasons – may well paint the suffering and vulnerabilities of older people as somehow less deserving of empathy, care, or attention. Also evincing this sentiment is the abovementioned assertion by the Public Committee Against Torture in Israel: "the threshold in which an act of abuse would be considered torture in the situation of an adult must be lowered when it comes to children." One of the attorneys in the NGO's legal department similarly said, in a 2018 discussion in the Israeli parliament on young Palestinians in Israeli custody: "As an attorney, … I see [Palestinian] kids that have been [abused in detention] … A minor, *as opposed to men of legal age*, is considered a child, and they require our protection."[115] Inevitably if unintentionally, these claims legitimize a higher level of abuse of older Palestinians.[116]

24, 2020), www.businessinsider.com/nyc-mayor-de-blasio-releasing-inmates-over-70-coronavirus-19-2020-3?r=US&IR=T.

[112] A petition by other human rights organizations, calling for the release of imprisoned Palestinians over the age of 60 and those with chronic illnesses, was dismissed by the supreme court later that year. HCJ 3300/20 *Hamoked* v. *IPS* (June 24, 2020).

[113] Avaaz, "UN Secretary General: We Demand the Immediate Release of all Palestinian Child Prisoners in Israeli Jails" (June 21, 2017), https://secure.avaaz.org/en/petition/UN_Secretary_General_We_Demand_the_Immediate_Release_of_all_Child_Prisoner.

[114] Shalhoub-Kevorkian, *Incarcerated Childhood*, p. 112.

[115] PCATI, Facebook post (July 3, 2018), www.facebook.com/PCATI/posts/913826842145076 (emphasis added).

[116] For similar criticisms, see Collins, *Occupied by Memory*, p. 45; Marshall and Sousa, "Decolonizing Trauma," p. 290.

The Israeli–Palestinian case, as I argued in the previous chapter, is symptomatic of broader pitfalls of the child rights framework. Indeed, various legal and human rights discourses and practices relating to young people, far beyond Israel/Palestine, have legitimized apathy and harshness toward their older yet similarly disempowered and ill-treated counterparts. Exemplifying these are the calls, in a number of countries, to abolish youth imprisonment, or to ban solitary confinement only for youth. In reserving their compassion exclusively for the young, what they effectively do is condone the damaging incarceration of the overwhelming majority of the prison population: those over the age of majority.[117] Likewise, in international humanitarian legal discourse, the frequent use of "women and children" as a shorthand for civilians disregards men's unique vulnerabilities in armed conflict and has sometimes paved the way for their indiscriminate targeting by the belligerent parties[118] – an issue I revisit in Chapter 7. The privileging of the young in humanitarian aid campaigns disenfranchises older people by presenting them as less deserving of empathy and assistance.[119] The rhetoric of an endangered childhood innocence has repeatedly served to expand the policing and incarceration of purportedly dangerous individuals over the age of majority.[120] Some attempts at redesigning family courts in a "child-sensitive" fashion have also contrasted innocent children in need of protection with older people (parents or others) in conflict with the law, portraying the latter as culpable criminals deserving imprisonment.[121] Across these contexts, those over the age of majority bearing the major brunt, as in Israel/Palestine, have been from "othered" and disempowered groups.

5.5 Lost Voices

Earlier, when discussing the stolen-childhood narrative, I investigated not only how human rights publications portray loss, but also what is lost

---

[117] H. Viterbo, "The Pitfalls of Separating Youth in Prison: A Critique of Age-Segregated Incarceration," in A. Cox and L. S. Abrams (eds.), *The Palgrave International Handbook of Youth Imprisonment* (Palgrave Macmillan, 2021).

[118] R. C. Carpenter, *"Innocent Women and Children": Gender, Norms and the Protection of Civilians* (London and New York: Routledge, 2006).

[119] E. Burman, "Innocents Abroad."

[120] E. R. Meiners, *For the Children?: Protecting Innocence in a Carceral State* (Minneapolis: University of Minnesota Press, 2016).

[121] A. L. Ananth, "The Gracious Spaces of Children's Law: Innocence and Culpability in the Construction of a Children's Court" (2014) 63 *Studies in Law, Politics, and Society* 89.

as a result of their exclusions and blind spots. This leads to the final issue to be investigated in this chapter: the loss of young Palestinians' voices in the human rights discourse. Numerous human rights reports, including some employing the image of childhood as lost or stolen, profess to make young Palestinians heard. They do so in different ways and to varying degrees. Some provide excerpts from interviews with young Palestinians. Others, especially those published by Save the Children and DCIP, have titles or subtitles such as *Palestinian Children's Voices*,[122] *In Their Own Words*,[123] *Palestinian Children Speak Out*,[124] *Palestinian Children Tell Their Own Stories*,[125] and *Voices from East Jerusalem*.[126] As I have argued, in portraying young Palestinians as robbed of their childhood as well as their right to childhood, human rights organizations risk obscuring the relevant context. The claim of these organizations to represent these Palestinians' voices, as I will explain, might additionally obscure these very voices, as well as the complexity of voice more generally. At least seven issues arise in this regard, some pertaining specifically to the discourses of stolen childhood and the right to child-hood, others extending further.

5.5.1 Overlooking Young People's Accounts

In the previous chapter, I presented a detailed critique of a series of Israeli reforms. Among them was the separation of incarcerated Palestinian youth, which was shown to have worked to their detriment in a number of ways. One of my arguments was that this separation removes Palestinian youth from their older counterparts, who had previously

---

[122] M. Gröndahl, *I Miss My House and My Pink Dress: Palestinian Children's Voices* (Stockholm: Save the Children – Sweden, October 2004), https://resourcecentre .savethechildren.net/node/3913/pdf/3913.pdf.

[123] DCIP, *In Their Own Words: A Report on the Situation Facing Palestinian Children Detained in the Israeli Military Court System – Reporting Period: 1 July to 31 December 2010* (January 29, 2011); DCIP, *In Their Own Words: A Report on the Situation Facing Palestinian Children Detained in the Israeli Military Court System – Reporting Period: 1 July to 31 December 2011* (January 30, 2012).

[124] Save the Children – Sweden and Save the Children – UK, *Living Behind Barriers: Palestinian Children Speak Out* (March 2004), p. 10, https://resourcecentre .savethechildren.net/sites/default/files/documents/3323.pdf.

[125] Gröndahl, *One Day in Prison*.

[126] DCIP, *Voices from East Jerusalem: The Situation Facing Palestinian Children* (August 2011), https://d3n8a8pro7vhmx.cloudfront.net/dcipalestine/pages/1297/attachments/ori ginal/1433986700/DCIP_east_jerusalem_final.pdf?1433986700.

assisted, supported, protected, and politically empowered them. Once segregated, these young Palestinians are more vulnerable to abuse and manipulation by the Israeli authorities, as well as to peer violence. In facilities with no other youth, the legal requirement to separate them from older inmates has also been cited as justifying placement in solitary confinement.

However, NGOs fervently objected to joint incarceration with older Palestinians prior to this reform, and many persist in their objection. Rarely have they noticed that their own published interviews with young Palestinian ex-detainees offer a competing – and largely overlooked – story. Israeli NGO B'Tselem, for example, published a testimony in 2008, titled "12-year-old Beaten and Imprisoned with Adults." In view of the NGO's habit of using such titles to highlight what it regards as problems, one would expect to encounter a negative account of imprisonment with "adults." The testimony, however, provides the precise opposite:

> They [the Israeli soldiers] took [me and a fourteen-year-old friend] ... to Ofer Prison and put us in [a] ... section ... which had eighty-three detainees, of all ages ... The detainees treated us well. They gave us candy, chocolate and potato chips. I felt comfortable ... A detainee helped me ask for the doctor to treat my leg ... At first, I was afraid and cried sometimes, because my family was far away ... The adult detainees took care of me because I was the youngest detainee in the Department, and they decided to make me assistant to the [detainee acting as] sergeant of the Department.[127]

Equally positive views about non-separation can be extracted from a 2004 book published in association with DCIP. The authors – former staff and volunteers with the NGO – cite its social workers as pointing to a "range of factors that helped children survive their time in prison." They add:

> Some [children] specifically mentioned adult detainees who were role models, and a critical source of care and support in a very hostile environment: "The adult detainees helped me a lot. They developed my character and I benefited from their experience of culture and life. They made me feel comfortable. Without their support I would have been lost in prison"; "The children lived with adults who took a lot of care of us. Support was

---

[127] B'Tselem, "Testimony: 12-Year-Old Beaten and Imprisoned with Adults" (September 11, 2008), www.btselem.org/testimonies/20080911_muhammad_khawajah_age_12_detained_by_idf.

strong and detainees discussed their problems. I am still in touch with
friends I made in prison even though they are much older than me."

Despite these unreservedly positive accounts, the authors immediately
add their own caveat: "Being detained with adult prisoners could provide
an enormous support structure and encouragement to study, although it
could push a child to behave more like an adult."[128] Thus, these human
rights activists seem resolute to protect an abstract notion of normal
childhood at least as much as they do the actual young Palestinians for
whom they profess to speak.

Even more inattentive to young Palestinians' positive descriptions of
non-separation is a 2014 shadow report to the UN Human Rights
Committee, jointly submitted by DCIP, the Palestine branch of War
Child Holland, and the young Palestinians' welfare organizations
Madaa and YMCA. Among the "common complaints and areas of
concern" listed by the NGOs is being "detained with adults," an issue
they describe as occurring in about 3 percent of cases. However, no actual
evidence is provided to demonstrate why non-separation is either a
"complaint" or an "area of concern." On the contrary, a 15-year-old's
testimony toward the end of the report portrays incarceration with
Palestinians over the age of majority in an unequivocally positive light:
"I was in the minor's section of Ofer prison. There were adult inmates in
the prison that took care of us. They sorted out the food and gave us
chores to do during the day."[129] Given that "denial of adequate food and
water" is said to be an issue in nearly 80 percent of cases, the NGOs'
blindness to the testimony appearing in their own report is all the
more astounding.

Another report, published by DCIP in 2016, likewise lists being
"detained with adults" as a "type of ill-treatment" in nearly 6 percent of
recorded cases. According to the same report, however, imprisoned
Palestinians themselves have shown support for non-separation. They
did so by securing, in 2009, the right to have a few elected inmates over
the age of majority oversee their younger counterparts while still being

---

[128] Cook, Hanieh, and Kay, *Stolen Youth*, p. 134.
[129] DCIP, Madaa Silwan Creative Center, YMCA East Jerusalem, and War Child Holland,
*Israel's Compliance with the International Covenant on Civil and Political Rights –
Shadow Report to the Fourth Periodic Report of Israel, 112th Session of the Human
Rights Committee* (October 2014), http://tbinternet.ohchr.org/Treaties/CCPR/Shared%
20Documents/ISR/INT_CCPR_CSS_ISR_18219_E.docx, pp. 3–4, 26 [hereinafter:
Shadow Report to the Human Rights Committee].

held separately from them at night. This intergenerational contact is reported to have improved the youths' welfare in several respects, though Israel is said to have weaponized it against them. One of Israel's long-standing tactics for soliciting confessions from detained youth has been to place them either in the same cell as older Palestinian informants or in an adjacent cell with a small opening. Reportedly, these informants now pose as the elected older Palestinians who are allowed contact with youth.[130] The problem seems, therefore, to be the use of informants, not joint incarceration as such. Nonetheless, the NGO – committed to international child rights norms – framed joint incarceration as "ill-treatment," despite the express support for it from imprisoned Palestinians.

Among the possible reasons for this disregard of young people's accounts is the tendency, as suggested earlier, to associate childhood with vulnerability and innocence. Despite occasionally taking the empower-ment and political agency of young Palestinians into account,[131] the dominant human rights discourse almost invariably subordinates them to the perceived victimhood, innocence, and suffering of this popula-tion.[132] Numerous examples appear in this chapter and throughout this book. The stolen-childhood narrative, in particular, paints the allegedly premature adulthood of Palestinians in an unequivocally negative light. This supposedly untimely experience, the assumption goes, robs young Palestinians of the joy and precious innocence of childhood and exposes them to the harsh realities of adulthood. The situation is thus framed not as Palestinians gaining adulthood and maturity, but, solely, as the loss of their childhood.

However, young people's own accounts are often different and much more complex. This is evident beyond Israel/Palestine as well, such as with accounts of young carers,[133] young workers,[134] and, as further

---

[130] DCIP, *No Way to Treat a Child*, pp. 22, 54–61.

[131] Marshall and Sousa, "Decolonizing Trauma," pp. 300–01. For an example, see Addameer, *In the Shadow of the 2014 Gaza War*, p. 51.

[132] Collins, *Occupied by Memory*, pp. 44, 46; Marshall and Sousa, "Decolonizing Trauma," pp. 287, 289, 303.

[133] L. O'Dell et al., "Constructing 'Normal Childhoods': Young People Talk About Young Carers" (2010) 25:6 *Disability & Society* 643; Stainton Rogers, "Promoting Better Childhoods."

[134] See, e.g., A. Invernizzi and B. Milne, "Are Children Entitled to Contribute to International Policy Making?: A Critical View of Children's Participation in the International Campaign for the Elimination of Child Labour" (2002) 10 *International Journal of Children's Rights* 403; S. Okyere, "Are Working Children's Rights and Child

elaborated in Chapter 7, young soldiers.[135] Just as the previous chapter described Palestinians' perception of incarceration as a politically empowering experience, so the testimonies quoted here suggest that, for young Palestinians, incarceration with their older counterparts can serve a similarly empowering function. One Palestinian girl, whose high-profile incarceration by Israel was mentioned in previous chapters, took this argument further, telling the media in 2018: "The minors were really the strongest part of the prison [population]. They would even give the adults strength. The [adult prisoner] representative of the section wouldn't make decisions without consulting them. That's how well they understand our cause."[136]

Similarly, some Palestinians, when interviewed about the experience of growing up during the Intifada of 1987–93, said it had made them stronger, more self-reliant, politically and socially aware, and more responsible than they would have otherwise been.[137] In disregarding or downplaying these aspects of Palestinians' experiences, the discourses of trauma, stolen childhood, and human rights ultimately end up silencing the voices they profess to make heard. In framing and addressing young Palestinians' issues through mental health, they further foreclose certain Palestinian responses to the Israeli regime, such as political empowerment and resistance.[138]

5.5.2   Prioritizing Older People's Voices

In human rights reports, including those containing excerpts from interviews with Palestinians identified as children, it is rarely under-18s

Labour Abolition Complementary or Opposing Reals?" (2012) 56:1 *International Social Work* 80.

[135] See, e.g., D. M. Rosen, "Child Soldiers, International Humanitarian Law, and the Globalization of Childhood" (2007) 109:2 *American Anthropologist* 296; H. G. West, "Girls with Guns: Narrating the Experience of War of FRELIMO's 'Female Detachment'" (2000) 73:4 *Anthropological Quarterly* 180.

[136] D. Takruri, "Ahed Tamimi Freed from Israeli Prison," *Al Jazeera* (October 9, 2018), www.youtube.com/watch?v=lJqH7_xYKi4.

[137] M. Netland, "Exploring 'Lost Childhood': A Study of the Narrative of Palestinians Who Grew Up during the First Intifada" (2013) 20:1 *Childhood* 82, 88, 92–93 [hereinafter: "Exploring Lost Childhood"]. For further criticism of the relative scholarly neglect of young Palestinians' nontraumatic experiences during the 1987–93 Intifada, see B. K. Barber, "Political Violence, Social Integration, and Youth Functioning: Palestinian Youth from the Intifada" (2001) 29:3 *Journal of Community Psychology* 259, 260–61.

[138] For a slightly different articulation of the latter point, see Marshall, "Save Us from the Children."

themselves who describe their childhood as lost or stolen. Almost invariably, this imagery is used by older individuals, be they the authors or the interviewees. This also applies to some of the academic literature on Israel/Palestine. An article published in 1993, for instance, touches on "the traumatization of [Gaza's] ... youth" and alleges that "Gaza is a society devoid of childhood." However, despite mention of a "series of interviews with [Gazan] children ... [which] reveal ... the loss of their youth," none of the quotes in the article come from an under-18 actually using this trope.[139]

Two more recent studies, from 2013 and 2016, likewise report that some of their Palestinian participants described themselves as having had their childhood lost or stolen prematurely in the 1987–93 Intifada. At the time these studies were conducted, however, the participants were all adults in the legal sense of the word, and hence were retrospectively narrating their childhood. Aside from the participants' ages, in both studies – albeit in different ways and to varying degrees – it was the researchers, rather than the participants themselves, who put forward the image of childhood as lost. Thus, in the 2016 study, the researcher asked participants whether they agreed with the statements "I feel like I lost my childhood" and "I regret that I lost my childhood." The authors of the 2013 article inferred from statements – which contain no such phrases – the loss of childhood at the text's "latent level."[140]

The tendency to rely on older people's perceptions of childhood is significant not because those above and below the age of majority should be viewed or treated as inherently distinct groups, a notion I question throughout this book.[141] Rather, what is noteworthy is the way in which human rights and academic publications alike frequently undermine their own logic and claim of attending to young people's actual voices. Accordingly, even where the image of childhood as lost or stolen does

---

[139] S. M. Roy, "Gaza: New Dynamics of Civic Disintegration" (1993) 22:4 *Journal of Palestine Studies* 20, 28.

[140] Netland, "Exploring Lost Childhood"; Barber et al., "Whither the Children of the Stones," pp. 102–03.

[141] Cf. P. Alldred and E. Burman, "Analysing Children's Accounts Using Discourse Analysis," in S. Greene and D. Hogan (eds.), *Researching Children's Experience: Approaches and Methods* (London and Thousand Oaks: Sage, 2005), p. 193 [hereinafter: "Analysing Children's Accounts"] (questioning whether the presentation of young people's perspective as different and uniform actually serves their interests).

appear in young people's own testimonies,[142] it still deserves problematizing, for reasons I will explain shortly.

5.5.3 Ambivalence about Young People's Reliability

The human rights community displays ambivalence about young people's reliability as witnesses. On the one hand, as evident throughout this book, human rights reports repeatedly cite young Palestinians' testimonies, thereby treating them as a valuable source of information. On the other hand, human rights organizations sometimes cast doubt on the reliability of such testimonies.

A report by B'Tselem on the arrest and detention of young Palestinians in East Jerusalem, for example, issues the following caveat about the testimonies it quotes: "Since these are comments made by children, often with no other material to corroborate them, we relate to them cautiously. However, some of the parents reported that they saw bruises on the body of their children and some of the children were examined by a physician."[143] Interestingly, B'Tselem's claim brings to mind an issue laid bare in Chapter 3: Israeli military judges' prioritization of young Palestinians' bodies and the adult gaze as preferable sources of information. B'Tselem's attempt to compensate for the perceived evidentiary deficit of young people's verbal accounts, by citing what their parents and a physician saw, bears resemblance to this approach of the Israeli military judiciary. Here lies yet another convergence, alongside those identified earlier, between the Israeli legal system and its human rights critics.

The ambivalence of human rights organizations may emanate, in part, from a broader social and legal duality. On the one hand, young people are considered to be simpler and purer, and hence more honest and direct, than their older counterparts. On the other hand, they are deemed unable to fully distinguish fact from fantasy, or to accurately recollect and

---

[142] See, e.g., A. Goodman, "Meet Janna Jihad, the 13-Year-Old Palestinian Journalist Exposing the Israeli Occupation," *Democracy Now* (August 8, 2019), www.democracynow.org/2019/8/8/janna_jihad_palestinian_youth_journalist. Quotes of young people saying that Israel's West Bank wall "prevents us from . . . our childhood" and "force[s us] . . . to grow up while we are still children" also appear later in this chapter.

[143] N. Baumgarten-Sharon, *Caution: Children Ahead – The Illegal Behavior of the Police toward Minors in Silwan Suspected of Stone Throwing* (Jerusalem: B'Tselem, December 2010), p. 23, www.btselem.org/download/201012_caution_children_ahead_eng.pdf.

clearly communicate past events.[144] In addition, as touched on in Chapters 3 and 6, pro-Zionist audiences, in Israel and abroad, often mistrust young Palestinians not only due to their assumed immaturity but also because of their national identity. This is among the possible explanations for the impunity of, or leniency toward, soldiers who abuse Palestinians, an issue to be tackled in the next two chapters.

5.5.4   Marginalizing the Young

Human rights organizations deny young people a say on, involvement in, or at least input into the writing and editing of the reports claiming to voice their concerns. This participatory deficit occurs not only when young people are involved. Typically governed by a top-down, nondemocratic professionalism, human rights organizations tend to allow only a limited and regimented participation to non-experts and non-practitioners.[145] But whereas wronged and abused people over the age of majority normally have some degree of access to alternative avenues of political participation, younger people are either categorically excluded from the adult world or, at most, are allowed participation only on older people's terms. This wholesale marginalization of the young takes place, as I have noted, in the name of law, children's "best interests," and their protection. Thus, along with its broader enslavement to legalism (as examined in previous chapters), the human rights community all too often ends up reinforcing child law's exclusion and disempowerment of young people.

5.5.5   Shrouding Young People's Testimonies

It is difficult to assess how true human rights publications are to young Palestinians' voices. There are three key reasons for this. First, they often selectively use excerpts, without reporting what was said before and after the quoted text. Second, they tend to withhold from the reader the questions or comments made by the interviewer before and during the

---

[144] On these different views, see, e.g., King and Piper, *How the Law Thinks About Children*, pp. 66–72; N. Lee, "The Challenge of Childhood: Distributions of Childhood's Ambiguity in Adult Institutions" (1999) 6:4 *Childhood* 455, 462–65.

[145] C. A. Odinkalu, "Why More Africans Don't Use Human Rights Language" (2000) 2 *Human Rights Dialogue* 3–4; Kennedy,"Part of the Problem?," pp. 119–20; N. Perugini and N. Gordon, *The Human Right to Dominate* (New York: Oxford University Press, 2015), pp. 134–37.

interview. And, third, they provide insufficient information about the identity of the witness, or (if the aim is to maintain anonymity) the circumstances in which the testimony was obtained.

Evidencing all three limitations, to varying degrees, is a human rights publication that, exceptionally, attributes to a Palestinian under the age of 18 the claim of a lost childhood. The report, jointly published by the UK and Swedish branches of Save the Children, quotes the Palestinian as saying that Israel's West Bank wall "prevents us from the most beautiful thing we own which is our childhood." This statement, readers are told, was made in a drama workshop run by the organization for 192 Palestinians aged 10–12 years. But the exact context, and the instruction given to the interviewee – both of which are necessary for assessing this statement – remain unknown.[146] Regrettably, such lack of context is a feature of many publications that attribute quotes to "children."[147] Furthermore, even when organizations provide supposedly full testimonies, they usually do so in the form of an uninterrupted monologue, concealing the dialogic and relational nature of most human rights testimonies.

5.5.6   Reducing Voice to Speech

Human rights publications seem to equate "voice" exclusively to speech. Non-audible or nonverbal actions and elements, perceived perhaps as meaningless, are rarely reported or acknowledged. Contrary to this narrow conception, silence, nonverbal utterances, and bodily movements can all indicate a person's trepidations, uncertainties, deliberation, and therefore have evidentiary value.[148] In some cases, silence, nonverbal utterances (such as a sigh, laughter, a cry, or a scream), and physical

---

[146] Save the Children – Sweden and Save the Children – UK, *Living Behind Barriers*, p. 10.
[147] For example, on this issue in research with young people, see Alldred and Burman, "Analysing Children's Accounts."
[148] On the need to move beyond associating voice with spoken utterances, see L. A. Mazzei, "An Impossibly Full Voice," in A. Y. Jackson and L. A. Mazzei (eds.), *Voice in Qualitative Inquiry: Challenging Conventional, Interpretive, and Critical Conceptions in Qualitative Research* (Abingdon and New York: Routledge, 2009), pp. 45–62. On the need, in particular, to incorporate young people's silence into the concept and practice of "child voice," see Lewis, "Silence," pp. 16–17; S. Spyrou, "Researching Children's Silences: Exploring the Fullness of Voice in Childhood Research" (2016) 23:1 *Childhood* 7. On the importance of young people's screams and nonverbal gestures, see, respectively, R. Rosen, "'The Scream': Meanings and Excesses in Early Childhood Settings" (2015) 22:1 *Childhood* 39; S. Komulainen, "The Ambiguity of the Child's

movements (such as a hand gesture) may be deliberate. An example, to be examined in Chapter 8, is the refusal of arrested settler girls to speak to the Israeli authorities while in custody. On other occasions, silence, as well as certain utterances and bodily movements (particularly involuntary ones, such as coughs, sneezes, or spasms), may not be, or at least may not appear to be, fully thought out. While this may make them less unequivocal, it does not detract from their evidentiary importance.

To this should be added my reservation, as explained in Chapter 1, about the desirability, and even the possibility, of attributing intentions to actions. Moreover, silence relates not only to pauses but also to omissions and absences. As I argue in the next chapter, testimony derives part of its evidentiary value precisely from what appears to be missing from it. Hence, the absence or exclusion of certain details from a verbal testimony can be as revealing as their inclusion, especially if considered in relation to the broader context of the witness's circumstances.

5.5.7   Blindness to Power Relations

A partly related criticism – albeit one that receives little to no attention in mainstream child rights discourse – concerns the quest for young people's true, pure, and authentic voice. What this pursuit ignores is the impact of older people, especially of their perceptions and ideologies, on the ways in which voices attributed to "children" are shaped, framed, interpreted, and mediated.[149] When a young Palestinian interviewee uses the image of childhood as stolen, for instance, and where a human rights report quotes this remark, these actions echo and reinforce the dominant adult discourses within which they occur. In one of its publications, DCIP makes a point of noting that its "lawyers and field researchers [who] collect affidavits from [Palestinian] children . . . are trained to ask a series of non-leading questions."[150]

'Voice' in Social Research" (2007) 14:1 *Childhood* 11 [hereinafter: "The Ambiguity of the Child's Voice"].

[149] For further discussion, see A. James, "Giving Voice to Children's Voices: Practices and Problems, Pitfalls and Potentials" (2007) 109:2 *American Anthropologist* 261; N. Khoja, "Situating Children's Voices: Considering the Context When Conducting Research with Young Children" (2015) 30:4 *Children & Society* 314; Komulainen, "The Ambiguity of the Child's Voice"; S. Spyrou, "The Limits of Children's Voices: From Authenticity to Critical, Reflexive Representation" (2011) 18:2 *Childhood* 151.

[150] DCIP, *No Way to Treat a Child*, p. 4.

It may appear that this criticism, like the previous ones, can be addressed through greater self-reflection and changed practices. However, practices such as "non-leading questions" cannot undo the power dynamic between young Palestinians and their older interviewers, nor do they negate the social forces informing such testimonies.

More fundamentally, moving beyond dominant liberal conceptions of voice and subjectivity calls into question the very existence of an autonomous, unitary, rational, intentional, accessible, and authentic self. Human subjectivity, some scholars have suggested, is inseparable from its messy social fabric, its institutional context, and the multiple and contradictory power and knowledge relations surrounding it. Therefore, when Palestinians – of any age – are said to describe themselves as having been robbed of their childhood, it is not simply that their inner selves are being influenced by external social forces. Rather, there is no self apart from its social and historical context, a context that includes social conceptions of childhood. If there is indeed no unitary subject with an authentic voice speaking the truth about her inner self, or about her social surroundings, then there is no voice to find, retrieve, and liberate.[151]

Throughout this book, I throw light on Palestinian actions and claims, especially those posing a challenge to power relations and prevailing ideas. Yet, it is precisely for the reasons presented here that I make no claim to represent the "actual," "real," or "lived" experiences of Palestinians. Nor do I attribute intentions to the legal and human rights bodies under examination, for reasons explained in Chapter 1. My aim, in so doing, is to reject the simplistic notions of voice that dominate far too much of the children's rights discourse.

5.6   Overarching Dualities

Four discursive frameworks, as I have shown, recur in human rights publications on young Palestinians: one revolving around young people's mental health, particularly their purported trauma and loss; another alleging the loss or robbery of their childhood; another claiming they deserve special protection by virtue of their supposed "right to childhood"; and another professing to represent their voices. Having thus far

---

[151] For further discussion, see A. Y. Jackson and L. A. Mazzei (eds.), *Voice in Qualitative Inquiry: Challenging Conventional, Interpretive, and Critical Conceptions in Qualitative Research* (Abingdon and New York: Routledge, 2009).

investigated each of these discursive frameworks separately, I will now revisit them as a whole through the prism of three overarching dualities.

The first concerns the specific sociopolitical context. On the one hand, by focusing on symptoms and effects, the interpretive lens of mental health has the decontextualizing tendency to neglect structural political issues. The image of Palestinian childhood as lost or stolen is likewise context-insensitive, in two complementary ways: it positions young Palestinians as an exception to a supposedly universal norm, while using the globally ubiquitous image of a lost childhood, an image that is anything but exceptional or specific. In these and other respects, the two discursive frameworks – mental health and stolen childhood – share an essentialist and developmentalist conception of childhood, in which assumptions about normal childhood routinely overshadow social and political specificity. Further, the focus on young people's supposedly unique plight, and the desire to grant them special protections, minimize issues experienced by Palestinians of all ages, and might ultimately legitimize disregard for Palestinians above the age of majority. The risk, therefore, is that the human rights discourse might not only misrepresent but also inadvertently aggravate Palestinians' hardships – as the previous chapter indeed illustrated in relation to Israel's legal reforms regarding young Palestinians.

On the other hand, in some, albeit limited ways, these discursive frameworks highlight aspects of the broader context. On a number of occasions, human rights organizations have used "trauma" as a description of a collective Palestinian experience resulting from the current political situation. Some (non-Israeli) organizations have also contextualized the purported loss of childhood. They have done so by linking it to two focal points of Palestinian history and narratives – the loss of the Palestinian homeland and the right of return – as well as to Israel's land grabs and the restriction of Palestinian movement.

A second duality in the examined discourses concerns the status of young Palestinians as sources of evidence and, relatedly, as sociopolitical agents. On the one hand, the rhetoric of child law and policy has increasingly emphasized young people's right to participate and be heard. Accordingly, human rights reports – including those using the language of mental health and lost childhood – quote and sometimes base their claims on interviews with young Palestinians, repeatedly profess to represent their voices, and employ titles such as *Palestinian Children Tell Their Own Stories*.[152]

---

[152] Gröndahl, *One Day in Prison*.

On the other hand, the interpretive frameworks of mental health and lost childhood frequently ignore, or downplay, young Palestinians' accounts of their conflict with Israeli authorities as a politically and socially empowering experience. In so doing, they perpetuate the reductive portrayal of young Palestinians as vulnerable victims – a tendency of the dominant human rights discourse that was also explored in the previous chapter. Aggravating this state of affairs is the fact that young people get no say or involvement in the writing and editing of human rights reports that profess to represent their perspectives. Also potentially misrepresenting young Palestinians' voices is the overreliance of human rights publications on imagery, such as that of childhood as lost or stolen, which originates, by and large, not from these young people themselves but from others: human rights professionals, scholars, or older interviewees. All of this attests to a broader issue, far from confined to Israel/ Palestine: those classified as children are allowed to speak and participate only to a limited extent, and in a highly circumscribed manner, and thus have their potential and skills curtailed. This, in turn, reinforces the raison d'être of child law: the association of childhood with dependence, difference, incapacity, and vulnerability.

Further, even when reference is made to young Palestinians' testimonies, human rights organizations sometimes cast doubt on their reliability, preferring, instead, claims by older people. In addition, it is difficult to assess how true human rights reports are to the original testimonies: often, excerpts appear without the context of the preceding and subsequent interview; the interviewer's questions and comments are withheld; necessary information is missing; and, on the rare occasions that supposedly full testimonies are provided, they usually appear in the misleading form of an uninterrupted monologue. Moreover, like many others, the human rights community has an overly simplistic conception of voice, in three respects. First, it tends to equate voice with speech, thereby ignoring valuable nonverbal evidence such as silence, sighs, and bodily movements. Second, it fails to consider the role of adult ideologies, perceptions, and interpretations in framing and mediating young people's voices. And, third, it displays a widely held but questionable belief in the existence of an authentic, unitary self that is able to express an inner truth.

Finally, human rights publications evince a duality of sorts regarding the boundaries of childhood, one that is woven throughout much of this book as a common thread. On the one hand, in line with their essentialism, developmentality, global vision of childhood, and commitment to a "right to childhood," human rights organizations aim to mend and fortify what they and many others perceive as childhood's normal boundaries. On the other hand, by characterizing young Palestinians as adult-like – due either to the alleged loss of their childhood or to the menace they are said to pose – the discursive frameworks in use symbolically erode these much-cherished boundaries. The boundaries of childhood are thus constructed and conceptualized, time and again, as oscillating between firmness and instability.

6

Sights of Violence: Childhood in the
Visual Battlefield

6.1   Introduction

Each of the previous chapters shed new light on the law–rights–childhood triad through specific thematic lenses, foremost among which were age, space, mental health, and voice. In this chapter, I employ as my analytical framework the theme of in/visibility. My focus is on the legal and political forces determining how, to what degree, and by whom Israeli state violence against young Palestinians is seen, known, and experienced during, before, and after its infliction.

Visual imagery – one of my key objects of inquiry here – has played a major role in reflecting and shaping modern conceptions of childhood.[1] In addition, visual images of young people have served as emotionally evocative markers of the gravity of state violence. Iconic examples are the photographs of the three-year-old Syrian refugee lying lifeless on a beach in 2015, nine-year-old Kim Phuc (the so-called Napalm girl) from the Vietnam War, and the Jewish boy driven from the Warsaw Ghetto with his hands up during the Second World War.[2] An iconic image of a different kind is Handala – the figure, created by Palestinian cartoonist Naji al-Ali, of a ten-year-old Palestinian facing away from the viewer with his hands clasped behind his back. Having become a symbol of Palestinian resistance, this image now appears in, among other places,

---

[1] See, e.g., A. Higonnet, *Pictures of Innocence: The History and Crisis of Ideal Childhood* (London: Thames & Hudson, 1998); P. Holland, *Picturing Childhood: The Myth of the Child in Popular Imagery* (London: I.B. Tauris, 2004). Relatedly, the effect of young people's appearance on judicial decisions is brought to light in Chapter 3, Section 3.2.2 ("The Appearance of Age").

[2] On these photographs, see, respectively, P. Molnar, "The Boy on the Beach: The Fragility of Canada's Discourses on the Syrian Refugee 'Crisis'" (2016) 4:1–2 *Contention* 67; N. K. Miller, "The Girl in the Photograph: The Vietnam War and the Making of National Memory" (2004) 24:2 *JAC – A Journal of Composition Theory* 261; R. Raskin, *A Child at Gunpoint: A Case Study in the Life of a Photo* (Aarhus: Aarhus University Press, 2004).

the logo of the pro-Palestinian BDS (Boycott, Divestment, Sanctions) campaign.[3]

Media images, and media coverage generally, have substantially influenced Israeli and global perceptions of young Palestinians living under Israel's military control.[4] Videos featuring Palestinian youth, in particular, have not only ignited heated reactions of various sorts but also, in some cases, led to court litigation. A famous example is the French media's broadcast of footage of 12-year-old Palestinian Muhammad al-Durrah caught with his father in crossfire between Israeli and Palestinian forces in Gaza in 2000 and shot dead shortly after. The ensuing dispute over the facts of the incident led to defamation hearings in France between 2004 and 2013, ultimately reaching the country's supreme court.[5] Another videotaped incident – the shooting of 13-year-old Iman al-Hams by Israeli fire in Gaza in 2004 – was discussed in Chapter 3. More recently, in 2018, 16-year-old Palestinian Ahed Tamimi was filmed by her family slapping a soldier outside her home after the military had shot her 15-year-old cousin in the head at close range. Following considerable international attention, Israel detained and later sentenced Tamimi to eight months in prison.[6] Other cases caught on camera are analyzed later in this chapter and the next.

Recent decades have seen militaries and law enforcement authorities around the world, as well as liberal human rights actors, increasingly employing visual technologies.[7] Israel/Palestine, specifically, has become a visual battlefield of sorts, with countless cameras operating as, among

---

[3] On Handala, see T. Hamdi, "Bearing Witness in Palestinian Resistance Literature" (2011) 52:3 *Race & Class* 21. The BDS logo appears at www.bdsmovement.net.

[4] On the Israeli and foreign media's representation of young noncitizen Palestinians respectively, see, e.g., D. Birenbaum-Carmeli, "Health Journalism in the Service of Power: 'Moral Complacency' and the Hebrew Media in the Gaza-Israel Conflict" (2014) 36:4 *Sociology of Health & Illness* 613; R. Duschinsky, "Slaughtered Innocence: Child Victims in Political Discourse during the Second Intifada and Gaza Conflict" (2011) 21:1 *Social Semiotics* 33.

[5] On this case, see Duschinsky, "Slaughtered Innocence," pp. 38–39.

[6] Aspects of this case are touched on in Chapters 1 (Section 1.1, "Challenging Dominant Discourses") 2 (Section 2.4, "The Military Court System"), 4 (Section 4.4.3, "Confining Palestinian Minds"), and 5 (Section 5.5.1, "Overlooking Young People's Accounts").

[7] See, e.g., regarding military, law enforcement agencies, and the human rights community respectively, A. J. Bousquet, *The Eye of War: Military Perception from the Telescope to the Drone* (Minneapolis: University of Minnesota Press, 2018); L. P. Beutin, "Racialization as a Way of Seeing: The Limits of Counter-Surveillance and Police Reform" (2017) 15:1 *Surveillance & Society* 5; S. Ristovska and M. Price (eds.), *Visual Imagery and Human Rights Practice* (Cham: Palgrave Macmillan, 2018).

other things, "weapons" of state surveillance.[8] Israeli soldiers and autonomous weapons, such as drones, are equipped with cameras to identify and incriminate Palestinian protestors and insurgents.[9] Meanwhile, in Palestinian and other hands, cameras – including those installed on now-ubiquitous mobile phones – are counter-surveillance devices.[10] "I always say that my camera is my weapon of choice, because ... it's a ... way to resist this occupation," said 13-year-old Palestinian Janna Jihad, one of the world's youngest press-card-carrying journalists, in 2019.[11] Another Palestinian was 17 years old when recording, in 2008, an Israeli soldier shooting a handcuffed and blindfolded Palestinian.[12] Such Palestinian video activism, in turn, is regarded by Israel as grounds for continuously enhancing its visual infrastructure. "The Palestinians have realized that the camera is the best weapon ... while we remain with no adequate response," a former military officer told the Israeli media in 2015, after a soldier had been caught on camera clashing with Palestinians under the age of 18. "Soldiers," he concluded, "must be equipped with GoPro [head] cameras, ... so that our global image isn't as horrible as it is

---

[8] See, e.g., E. Zureik, D. Lyon, and Y. Abu-Laban (eds.), *Surveillance and Control in Israel/Palestine: Population, Territory, and Power* (London and New York: Routledge, 2011); Y. Zitun, "Counterterrorism: The IDF Already Deploys Hundreds of Cameras in Judea and Samaria," *Ynet News* (October 6, 2015) [Hebrew], www.ynet.co.il/articles/0,7340,L-4707531,00.html. On the camera's surveillance of imprisoned Palestinians, specifically, see, e.g., Addameer, "Deterioration in Detention Conditions: Suffocating Prisoners" (October 29, 2018), www.addameer.org/publications/deterioration-detention-conditions-suffocating-prisoners.

[9] See, e.g., H. Matar, "The IDF's New Tool for Tracking Palestinian Protesters: Drones," *+972 Magazine* (August 15, 2015), www.972mag.com/the-idf-has-a-new-way-of-tracking-palestinian-protesters-drones; S. Gal, "The War Diaries: The Iron Dome Battles as Seen from the Camera Lens," *Channel 2 News* (June 26, 2015) [Hebrew], www.mako.co.il/news-military/security-q2_2015/Article-e65c0d1a0213e41004.htm.

[10] See, e.g., R. Ginsburg, "Gendered Visual Activism: Documenting Human Rights Abuse from the Private Sphere" (2018) 66:1 *Current Sociology* 38.

[11] A. Goodman, "Meet Janna Jihad, the 13-Year-Old Palestinian Journalist Exposing the Israeli Occupation," *Democracy Now* (August 8, 2019), www.democracynow.org/2019/8/8/janna_jihad_palestinian_youth_journalist.

[12] This case is analyzed in Chapter 7, Section 7.2.2 ("Infantilized Soldiers on Trial"). The Palestinian cameraperson's age is mentioned in HCJ 7195/08 *Abu Rahma v. Military Advocate General* (2009) 63(2) PD 325, ¶ 4 of justice Melcer's opinion. The video is available at B'Tselem, "Prosecute Soldier Who Fired 'Rubber' Bullet at Palestinian Detainee, Investigate the Involvement of an Officer in the Event and Suspected Cover-Up" (July 20, 2008), www.btselem.org/press_releases/20080720.

now."[13] In this interplay of mutual documentation and reciprocal surveillance, cameras frequently come face to face, recording each other
recording.

While deploying cameras and images for surveillance, disciplining,
propaganda, or even entertainment purposes, the Israeli military also
goes to great lengths to prevent the recording and publishing of unflattering or incriminatory evidence. A former soldier critically recounted, for
example, how a Palestinian,

> around 17 years old, annoyed one of the company commander's staff. . . .
> He smiled or something, so immediately an order was given to arrest
> [him]. There was an Israeli press photographer who simply stood there.
> Wouldn't leave . . . so the soldiers grabbed him by force, threw his camera
> on the ground, made him lie down, shackled him. . . . While he was
> shackled, he said: "Just get my camera inside my bag." . . . It was returned
> to him without the film. He was . . . treated violently.[14]

Indeed, as I will demonstrate, the Israeli–Palestinian visual battleground
revolves around the concealment as it does around the production of
sights and knowledge, a dynamic informing state violence against young
Palestinians as well as the legal and human rights discourses that sur-
round this violence.

Against this backdrop, the next section will investigate how, and to
what effect, Israel subjects Palestinians to its gaze and seeks to make them
internalize it. Under examination will be three different contexts: (a)
Israel's use of posters with photographs of Palestinian youth or their
parents – a visual tool of deterrence and disciplining presented by Israel
as serving young Palestinians' best interests; (b) the photographing of
unsuspected Palestinian youth at home and on the street, who are
presumed potential rather than actual wrongdoers; and (c) Israeli soldiers
filming their violence against young Palestinians.

Complementing this inquiry, Section 6.3 will start by examining the
myriad methods used by Israel and its agents to conceal jeopardizing
evidence. Existing scholarship has paid little attention, if any, to judgments concerning Israeli soldiers. Filling this gap, this section will analyze various judgments concerning soldiers who abused or killed

[13] O. Heller, "Combatant Recorded in Nabi Salih Unlikely to Face Disciplinary Action,"
Channel 10 News (August 30, 2015) [Hebrew], https://13news.co.il/10news/mmnews/
132029.
[14] Breaking the Silence, "A Kind of Game" (2011), www.breakingthesilence.org.il/testi
monies/database/337778.

Palestinian under-18s, as well as relevant statutes, policies, and human rights publications. From these documents, I will extract six mutually complementary concealment practices: (a) destroying potentially incriminating evidence; (b) preventing state violence from being witnessed in real time; (c) forbidding the publication of certain information; (d) not recording, or only partly recording, interrogations of Palestinians; (e) torturing Palestinians without leaving marks on their bodies; and (f) legally sanctioned secrecy across a range of areas. From there, I will proceed to analyze the techniques Israeli soldiers and judges employ to deny, dismiss, and downplay complaints about violence against young Palestinians. Examples and figures will also be provided to reveal the de facto impunity of alleged perpetrators. I will then elaborate on the Israeli judiciary's tendency to frame acts of violence as isolated exceptions and the perpetrators as a few rotten apples.

Finally, Section 6.4 will shed new light on how to address state violence. To this end, I will offer a rethinking of the pitfalls and potential of critical evidence, visual and other. Drawing on cases and data relating to violence against young Palestinians, I will demonstrate a tendency among the legal system and its human rights critics to privilege two types of evidence: video footage and state agents' testimonies. Such evidence, I will argue, potentially plays into Israel's hands in two ways: first, it validates the dismissal of uncorroborated Palestinian allegations; and, second, it potentially serves the Israeli "rotten apples" narrative. In a reconceptualization of evidence, I will suggest that alternative images – pictures of absence, reenactment photographs, and sketches – possess the unique evidentiary potential to highlight the state's concealment apparatus.

6.2 The Visibility of State Violence

6.2.1 Arresting Images

Risk management and early intervention – themes explored from different angles in Chapters 3–5 – have come to dominate a range of social domains.[15] Among them are counterinsurgency and so-called

---

[15] See, e.g., B. Anderson, "Preemption, Precaution, Preparedness: Anticipatory Action and Future Geographies" (2010) 34:6 *Progress in Human Geography* 777.

counter-radicalization,[16] as well as modern child law.[17] The latter has evolved to deliver intervention at an early age, with the aim of preventing those labeled as high-risk individuals from becoming dangers or burdens to society.[18] Further, visual and other representations of young people often figure centrally in debates on how to manage what is considered an unpredictable and insecure social future.[19]

For Israel, averting undesirable eventualities has been a top priority even before it conquered the West Bank and Gaza Strip. The 1967 war that resulted in Israel's control over these territories was justified by its officials, questionably, as preemptive self-defense against future Arab aggression. A few decades later, state officials likewise described extra-judicial assassinations (also euphemistically known as "targeted killings") as a means to preempt terrorist attacks. Another state practice, "administrative detention" – imprisonment without trial based on classified and potentially speculative materials, as discussed in previous chapters – has as its stated goal the prevention of speculated risks rather than the punishment of actual offenses.[20] Similarly future-oriented, as I argued in Chapter 4, is generational segregation in Israeli custody, whose aim is to prevent young Palestinians from adopting unwanted ideologies.

A growing number of future-oriented measures seem to have found their way to the visual battlefield. Israeli military law now requires that all arrested Palestinians have their pictures taken upon arrival at a detention

---

[16] See, e.g., regarding risk prevention and early intervention respectively, L. Amoore, "Risk before Justice: When the Law Contests Its Own Suspension" (2008) 21:4 *Leiden Journal of International Law* 847; V. Coppock and M. McGovern, "'Dangerous Minds?' Deconstructing Counter-Terrorism Discourse, Radicalisation and the 'Psychological Vulnerability' of Muslim Children and Young People in Britain" (2014) 28:3 *Children and Society* 242.

[17] See, e.g., S. Case, "Young People 'At Risk' of What? Challenging Risk-focused Early Intervention as Crime Prevention" (2006) 6:3 *Youth Justice* 171; K. Clarke, "Childhood, Parenting, and Early Intervention: A Critical Examination of the Sure Start National Programme" (2006) 26:4 *Critical Social Policy* 699.

[18] See, e.g., K. Hanson, "Separate Childhood Laws and the Future of Society" (2016) 12:2 *Law, Culture and the Humanities* 195, 199–200.

[19] See, e.g., C. Katz, "Childhood as Spectacle: Relays of Anxiety and the Reconfiguration of the Child" (2008) 15:1 *Cultural Geographies* 5; R. Butler, "Images of the Child and Environmental Risk: Australian News Photography of Children and Natural Disasters, 2010–2011" (2013) 28:2 *Visual Studies* 148.

[20] For detailed discussion of these and similar measures, see H. Viterbo, "Future-Oriented Measures," in O. Ben-Naftali, M. Sfard, and H. Viterbo, *The ABC of the OPT: A Legal Lexicon of the Israeli Control over the Occupied Palestinian Territory* (Cambridge and New York: Cambridge University Press, 2018), pp. 118–40.

facility, while the prison service ordinances require these pictures to be attached to the detainees' files.[21] These visual records are retained for possible future use, aiding the monitoring of convicted Palestinians long after their release from prison. The military, as part of its growing dissemination of images on social media for publicity purposes,[22] also filmed its arrest of a 16-year-old Palestinian suspected of stabbing and killing an Israeli settler in 2016 and then posted the footage online.[23]

Also photographed are young Palestinians, such as protestors or those clashing with the military, whom Israel regards as lawbreakers or security threats. To be effective, the military must not only render these and other Palestinians visible, but also make them aware of its gaze and ensure they see it as a manifestation of state power.[24] Thus, in 2013, Israeli troops put up posters in a West Bank village, featuring four such photographs. Apparently taken by the military at an earlier protest, these pictures featured local Palestinians aged 14–17. Above each photograph was a heading in poor Arabic, warning that Israel, having already laid its eyes on those visually captured by its photographs, would also lay its hands on them: "We are the military. Watch out, we're going to *catch you if we see you*, or we'll come to your house."[25] The spokesperson of the local military division, in response to an NGO's query on the matter, emphasized the future-oriented dimension of the images: "[T]he activity was carried out for deterrence purposes, as part of a range of activities taken in view of the phenomenon of stone-throwing ... This action is intended

[21] See, respectively, Article 14(i) of the Order of the Major-General of the Center Region Command (Amendment No. 25) (Judea and Samaria) (2012) (an unofficial English translation by NGO Military Court Watch is available at www.militarycourtwatch.org/files/server/FOI%20-%20ARREST%20PROCEEDURES.pdf); Article 3c in Section B of IPS Commission Ordinance No. 04.30.00: Reception, Detention, and Release of Detainees (May 1, 2002; last amended January 25, 2016), www.hamoked.org.il/files/2018/1163123.pdf.

[22] See A. Kuntsman and R. L. Stein, *Digital Militarism: Israel's Occupation in the Social Media Age* (Stanford: Stanford University Press, 2015).

[23] IDF Spokesperson, "Last Night, the IDF and ISA Arrested the Terrorist Who Murdered Dafna Meir on January 17th," *Twitter* (January 19, 2016), https://twitter.com/IDFSpokesperson/status/689465048763277313.

[24] G. Z. Hochberg, *Visual Occupations: Violence and Visibility in a Conflict Zone* (Durham, NC and London: Duke University Press, 2015), p. 26.

[25] B'Tselem, "Kafr Qadum: Military Plasters Photos of Minors, Threatening Capture on Sight" (June 27, 2013), www.btselem.org/demonstrations/20130627_kafr_qadum_flyers (emphasis added).

to deter teenagers from taking part in popular terrorism, which may also endanger them personally."[26]

Other posters, plastered around East Jerusalem a few months later, appeared to have a different future-oriented goal. Rather than targeting young suspects, they displayed photographs of nine parents of already incarcerated youth. But here, the primary targets were not the nine specific parents, whose details were already known to the Israeli authorities, and who could thus have been confronted directly (their names appeared on the poster and, with their sons behind bars, their addresses were easy to ascertain). Rather, the poster addressed other parents, threatening to similarly display their pictures if their sons and daughters come into conflict with Israeli law:

> To the parents: We hereby inform you that your children are involved in terrorist activities against citizens of the State of Israel. . . . If you do not keep them from continuing to engage in these activities, you will be subjected to severe restrictions . . . [I]f you do not want your photos to appear in a notice like this one, . . . [t]ell your children to stop the acts of aggression for the sake of their safety and their future.[27]

In 2018, Palestinians in East Jerusalem woke up to see posters yet again, this time put up by the security service. The notices, containing text without visual images, similarly threatened to revoke work permits from parents of young stone-throwers:

> [I]t is senseless to stretch out our hand and provide you a place of work, while discovering that your son is throwing stones or Molotov cocktails . . . [I]t is your duty as a parent to keep an eye on your child . . . in order to ensure their education and your family's livelihood. You should know, should we revoke your work permit, that we are not to blame.[28]

Notwithstanding the differences between them, all three posters shared an important commonality. They depicted state deterrence as protecting

[26] H. Matar, "IDF Soldiers to West Bank Children: 'We Are the Army, Be Careful if We See You'," +972 Magazine (June 1, 2013), http://972mag.com/israeli-soldiers-post-leaflets-warning-children-from-attending-west-bank-demonstrations/72601.

[27] B'Tselem, "Al-'Arrub R.C.: Posters by Military Warn Residents of Retribution Should Their Sons Throw Stones and Molotov Cocktails" (January 26, 2014), www.btselem.org/demonstrations/20130122_al_arub_flyers.

[28] Y. Marom, "Shin Bet: Lose Your Job if Your Kid Throws Stones," +972 Magazine (January 4, 2018), https://972mag.com/shin-bet-threatens-to-revoke-permits-from-stone-throwers-families/132164/.

young Palestinians from acts that might "endanger them" and as serving their best interests: "their safety," "their future," and "their education." In Chapter 4, I showed how Israeli authorities have likewise presented their harmful reforms as protecting the rights and best interests of young Palestinians in Israeli custody. Thus, time and again, Israel has justified oppression and violence through a rhetoric of children's rights and child protection. In the next chapter, I analyze another version of this rhetoric: Israel's claim that, in order to "protect its children," it must militarily attack Palestinians.

6.2.2   *Visually Capturing the Potential Delinquent*

So far, the examples investigated in this section have related, in varying ways, to Palestinian youth whom Israeli authorities regard as lawbreakers. However, the Israeli military does not wait for actual wrongdoing to occur. In a stated attempt to deter and preemptively thwart offending, it has also photographed unsuspected under-18s while they were merely roaming the street or even asleep at home. In 2016, a military force gathered about 20 Palestinian males under the age of majority (18 years) on a street in the city of Hebron, apparently at random, seven of whom were reportedly under the age of criminal responsibility (12 years). After lining them up against a wall and questioning them about a stone-throwing incident in the area earlier that day, the soldiers, using mobile phones, photographed each of them. Later, one of these Palestinians would recount how a soldier "warned us that they have our pictures, in case we throw stones in [the] future."[29] Following this and another similar event, the military's spokesperson confirmed that such documentation is indeed future-oriented, aiming "to foil the throwing of stones" and to "prevent situations in which terrorists hurl rocks."[30]

Serving a similar function have been nightly incursions by Israeli armed forces into Palestinians' homes in the West Bank, known as

---

[29] B'Tselem, "Soldiers Gather Children in Hebron Neighborhood, Photograph Them and Release Them" (June 5, 2016), www.btselem.org/video/20160605/soldiers_photograph_minors_in_hebron#full.

[30] Quoted, respectively, in G. Cohen, "Israeli Soldiers Photographed 20 Palestinian Minors in Hebron," *Haaretz* (June 4, 2016), www.haaretz.com/israel-news/.premium-1.723121; P. Goldman, "On Video: Israeli Soldiers Raid Homes, Question Kids as Young as 9," *NBC News* (March 14, 2015), www.nbcnews.com/news/world/israeli-soldiers-raid-homes-question-kids-young-9-n322706.

"mappings." Occurring as frequently as every night,[31] "mappings" provide Israeli authorities with visual records and other information on the household. This practice combines invisibility and hypervisibility. On the one hand, it seeks to keep state violence invisible. Troops sometimes conceal their faces with masks[32] and, on one occasion, they also watched and then confiscated footage showing Israeli violence against Palestinians, which the residents had filmed for NGO B'Tselem.[33] On the other hand, such "mappings" render Palestinians, especially their young, hypervisible to Israel. In videos taken by Palestinians whose houses were raided in recent years, the soldiers and police are seen searching the house, waking up the "children," photographing them, writing down their names and ages, sometimes taking pictures of the parents as well as of their identity cards, and occasionally recording the layout of the house.[34]

According to former Israeli soldiers who were involved in such "mappings," every Palestinian was presumed "a potential future terrorist, and that's why we have to know everything about them all." The goal seems to be the proactive gathering of as much information as possible, in case it proves to be legally or operationally useful at some future point. For this reason, raids are "deliberately directed toward … [Palestinians] that are known to be innocent of any wrongdoing, known to have nothing to do with terrorists, and with the only objective of having information about everyone."[35] "We are looking for potential terrorists," a military

---

[31] O. Hemo, "Documentation: The Military's Activity in the Territories," *Channel 2 News* (March 8, 2015) [Hebrew], www.mako.co.il/news-channel2/Channel-2-Newscast-q1_2015/Article-add391aeabafb41004.htm.

[32] See, e.g., B'Tselem, "Masked Soldiers Enter Palestinian Homes in Dead of Night, Order Residents to Wake Their Children, and Photograph the Children" (March 29, 2015), www.btselem.org/hebron/20150324_night_search_in_hebron; N. Hasson, "Police Raid East Jerusalem Houses Every Night," *Haaretz* (February 3, 2017) [Hebrew], www.haaretz.co.il/news/local/.premium-1.3626076.

[33] B'Tselem, "Soldiers Enter Home of B'Tselem Volunteers in Hebron, Awake Children, Photograph Them, and Confiscate Footage Filmed by the Volunteers" (April 19, 2015), www.btselem.org/hebron/20150419_night_search_and_confiscation#full.

[34] B'Tselem, "B'Tselem Volunteers Film Soldiers Waking Children in Nabi Saleh to Take Their Photographs" (February 14, 2011), www.btselem.org/video/2011/08/soldiers-wake-children-nabi-saleh; B'Tselem, "Soldiers Enter Home of B'Tselem Volunteers in Hebron"; L. Yehuda, "Letter to the IDF Legal Advisor in the Judea and Samaria Region Regarding Searches in Residents' Homes ('Mappings') – An Illegal Pattern in the Territories" (Tel Aviv: ACRI, February 25, 2008) [Hebrew], www.acri.org.il/he/?p=1759.

[35] Breaking the Silence, "Mappings" (n.d.), www.breakingthesilence.org.il/testimonies/videos/27830.

commander said in 2015, while two years later an officer boasted of the military's ability to preemptively "get to their house" while "the [Palestinian] kid doesn't [even] know that he is a terrorist yet."[36]

At the same time, some ex-soldiers believe that obtaining information on potential offenders might not have been the primary objective. According to a veteran whose military service included taking pictures during "mappings," he "had the pictures for around a month" but "no commander asked about them, no intelligence officer took them. ... At one point I deleted the pictures, I realized it was all a joke."[37] Another former soldier similarly recalled: "I don't think any mapping information ever went any higher [i.e., to the intelligence agencies]. I don't remember ever sending any photographs from the camera."[38]

Such military indifference to the information it gathers suggests that "mappings" may perform another function: "to make the Palestinians feel that we were there all the time," as one veteran put it.[39] Indeed, a staple of Israel's military rule over the West Bank is the display of omnipresence, as well as the sowing of fear.[40] In assaults on the Gaza Strip, the military has publicly endeavored to "create a sense of persecution" among Gazans and to "sear the Palestinian consciousness"[41] by using "disproportionate force," thereby turning them against their own

[36] Quoted, respectively, in R. Ben Yishai, "Door Pounding, Ski Mask: Report from a Palestinian House – This Is How the IDF Is Trying to Stop the Next Terrorist," *Ynet* (December 7, 2015) [Hebrew], www.ynet.co.il/articles/0,7340,L-4734559,00.html; O. Hirschauge and H. Shezaf, "Revealed // How Israel Jails Palestinians Because They Fit the 'Terrorist Profile'," *Haaretz* (May 31, 2017), www.haaretz.com/israel-news/.premium-1.792206.

[37] Breaking the Silence, "Pictures at 3 AM" (n.d.), www.breakingthesilence.org.il/testimonies/videos/70540.

[38] Breaking the Silence, "'An Element of Overachievement'" (May 6, 2011), www.breakingthesilence.org.il/testimonies/videos/14959.

[39] Breaking the Silence, "Pictures at 3 AM."

[40] See Breaking the Silence, *Occupation of the Territories: Israeli Soldier Testimonies 2000–2010* (2011), pp. 29, 36–38, www.breakingthesilence.org.il/wp-content/uploads/2011/02/Occupation_of_the_Territories_Eng.pdf; M. Zagor, "'I Am the Law'! – Perspectives of Legality and Illegality in the Israeli Army" (2010) 43:3 *Israel Law Review* 551, 573–74.

[41] See, respectively, Y. Kubovich, "'Success Is Measured by the Number of New Targets Created': How the IDF Creates Its Target Bank in Gaza," *Haaretz* (December 14, 2019) [Hebrew], www.haaretz.co.il/news/politics/.premium-1.8266167; A. Shavit, "Has the Disengagement Been Successful?," *Haaretz* (July 5, 2006) [Hebrew], www.haaretz.co.il/misc/1.1118413.

government.[42] Thus, certain forms of state violence are meant for Palestinian eyes and hence require hypervisible spectacles. In this and other respects, acts presented as deterrence, prevention, and preemption are not merely preclusive but also productive. In the process of ostensibly thwarting undesirable eventualities, they produce new and often greater threats and harms,[43] deliberately or not, including heightened Palestinian fear or animosity toward Israel, mass suffering, and sometimes the loss of civilian lives.

6.2.3   The Complicit Camera

Violence and abuse by Israeli state agents have been caught on camera on numerous occasions. Sometimes, the filming has been done by the targeted Palestinians, by witnesses, or by the media, with examples of such cases appearing later in this chapter and the next. But, time and again, it is also the perpetrators themselves who have recorded their actions. The camera, when put to use in this way, potentially prompts, augments, orchestrates, and visually preserves, becoming, as a result, an accomplice to violence.[44]

Veterans' testimonies, as well as other Israeli sources, indicate a recurring pattern of soldiers filming their violence against Palestinians.[45] One former soldier, for example, described how "a [military] driver showed me pictures of two kids they had caught, shackled, and kicked … He showed me the video he took on his cell phone. Sitting shackled, and some soldier walks by and – pow – kicks them in the back or something."[46] Whereas this particular video has not become publicly available,

[42] See H. Marouf, *Israel's Military Operations in Gaza: Telegenic Lawfare and Warfare* (London and New York: Routledge, 2016), pp. 42–61; D. Liel, "Eizenkot: 'IDF Using Disproportionate Force in Gaza to Prevent Firing'," *Channel 2 News* (March 22, 2017) [Hebrew], www.mako.co.il/news-military/security-q1_2017/Article-7c77ef89bf4fa51004.htm.

[43] On the productive nature of such future-oriented measures, see B. Massumi, "Potential Politics and the Primacy of Preemption" (2007) 10:2 *Theory & Event*; S. Crook, "Ordering Risks," in D. Lupton (ed.), *Risk and Sociocultural Theory: New Directions and Perspectives* (Cambridge and New York: Cambridge University Press, 1999), pp. 160, 171.

[44] J. Butler, *Frames of War: When Is Life Grievable?* (London: Verso, 2009), pp. 83–84.

[45] See, e.g., Breaking the Silence, *Children and Youth – Soldiers' Testimonies 2005–2011* (2012), pp. 66–67, www.breakingthesilence.org.il/wp-content/uploads/2012/08/Children_and_Youth_Soldiers_Testimonies_2005_2011_Eng.pdf; Breaking the Silence, "It's a Game" (n.d.) (testimony catalog number: 84695), www.breakingthesilence.org.il/testimonies/database/84695.

[46] Breaking the Silence, *Children and Youth – Soldiers' Testimonies 2005–2011*, pp. 9–10.

others like it, as well as photographs taken by soldiers to record their abuse of detained Palestinians, have come to light over the years (an issue elaborated in the next chapter).[47]

At the same time, state agents seek to keep their violence visible only on their own terms. As a case in point, in 2002, four border police soldiers abused and eventually killed a 17-year-old Palestinian in the West Bank by pushing him out of a moving military jeep. They video-taped their actions, but after the fact, upon realizing the incriminatory nature of the footage, they destroyed it. In addition, they disposed of the deceased Palestinian's coat, altered the journey records of the jeep, and coordinated their stories. During their eventual trial, the soldiers also harassed and threatened a comrade who had testified against them.[48] Thus, where visibility is deemed jeopardizing to the state, to its agents, or to both, concealment comes into play. The next section examines the practices used by Israel to this end.

6.3   State-Induced Invisibility

6.3.1   Concealment

Destruction and alteration of potentially incriminating evidence are among the concealment methods of Israeli soldiers and their comrades. In 2004, for instance, three border police soldiers severely assaulted and abused two Palestinians, aged 17 and 18 years. According to the judg-ment in their matter, they deliberately did not fill out any report or record of the event, and colluded to completely disavow their actions in the event of an inquiry.[49] In 2011, another border police soldier resorted to a different concealment tactic: standing guard outside a room in which his comrade was abusing a detained and hooded Palestinian youth, in order to prevent anyone from seeing the abuse.[50]

---

[47] For an example involving soldiers who videotaped their abuse of a blindfolded and cuffed Gazan they had arrested, see CMA 59/14 *Chief Military Prosecutor* v. *Rom* (August 3, 2014).

[48] CrimC (Jer. Dist.) 907/05 *State of Israel* v. *Wahaby* (September 14, 2005); CrimC (Jer. Dist.) 3172/07 *State of Israel* v. *Lalza* (April 28, 2008); CrimC (Jer. Dist.) 157/03 *State of Israel* v. *Butvika* (verdict September 2, 2008, sentencing April 27, 2009); CrimA 5136/08 *State of Israel* v. *Lalza* (March 31, 2009); CrimA 10594/05 *Wahaby* v. *State of Israel* (May 22, 2006).

[49] CrimC (Jer. Dist.) 390/04 *State of Israel* v. *Brier* (April 5, 2005).

[50] Amended indictment in CrimC (Jer. Dist.) 2420-05-11 *State of Israel* v. *Sevilia* (July 4, 2011).

As detailed later, the Israeli legal system readily downplays such cases by framing them as isolated transgressions by a few rotten apples. However, state authorities, including the legal system, hide and deny Israel's violence using similar tactics on a much larger scale. As mentioned in Chapter 2, former Israeli officials have admitted, for example, to systematically and deliberately concealing what they regard as politically sensitive state documents. In addition, Israeli authorities have obstructed media coverage of their conduct in the West Bank and Gaza Strip,[51] and have also issued gagging orders prohibiting the publication of information on, among other things, detained Palestinians.[52] Further, under Israeli law, publishing the names of prosecuted soldiers is forbidden if their alleged offenses were committed during "military operations,"[53] a term open to multiple interpretations.[54]

Especially elaborate is the concealment apparatus developed around interrogations of Palestinians. As explained in Chapter 2, Palestinians' "real" trial largely takes place in the interrogation room. It is there that their confession is extracted to provide the main, and sometimes only,[55] basis for their near-certain conviction. Young Palestinian ex-detainees have frequently reported having been abused at this and other pretrial stages. According to a report based on testimonies of 101 Palestinians aged under 18 who were detained in 2018, 69 percent complained they had been subjected to physical violence during their arrest, transfer to

---

[51] See, e.g., P. Beaumont, "Israeli Soldiers Attack Journalists on West Bank," *The Guardian* (September 25, 2015), www.theguardian.com/world/2015/sep/25/israeli-soldiers-attack-agence-france-presse-journalists-west-bank; G. Izikovich and AP, "Foreign Journalists Speak Out against Ban on Entry to Gaza," *Haaretz* (November 28, 2008), www.haaretz .com/foreign-journalists-speak-out-against-ban-on-entry-to-gaza-1.258420.

[52] See, e.g., Addameer, "The Israeli Occupation's Military Court Bans Addameer from Publishing any Information on Several Detainees Under Interrogation" (October 7, 2019), www.addameer.org/news/israeli-occupation%E2%80%99s-military-court-bans-addameer-publishing-any-information-several-detainees.

[53] Articles 325(f3), 539a(c) of Military Adjudication Law, 1955; Article 70(e3) of Courts Law (Integrated Version), 1984.

[54] For critical analysis of Israeli law's broad definition of the related term "combat action," in the context of Palestinians' tort claims, see G. J. Bachar, "Access Denied – Using Procedure to Restrict Tort Litigation: The Israeli–Palestinian Experience" (2017) 92:3 *Chicago-Kent Law Review* 841.

[55] An estimated 95 percent of convictions of Palestinians aged under 18 are based on their confessions: DCIP, *No Way to Treat a Child: Palestinian Children in the Israeli Military Detention System* (April 2016), pp. 49–50, https://d3n8a8pro7vhmx.cloudfront.net/dcipa lestine/pages/1527/attachments/original/1460665378/DCIP_NWTTAC_Report_Final_ April_2016.pdf.

detention, or interrogation, while 67 percent complained of having been verbally threatened, and 63 percent reported having been verbally abused.[56] Similar reports abound.[57] There are four key ways in which Israel and its legal system hide from the public this "real trial" and the abuse it entails.

First, as detailed in Chapter 4, Israeli law generally allows interrogators to exclude the attorney and relatives of the detained person – potential witnesses to interrogator misconduct – from the interrogation room. Frequently, those in detention themselves are also prevented from seeing their interrogators, due to the commonly reported practices of blindfolding and hooding.[58] These latter tactics, when employed prior to interrogation, serve the additional function of "softening up" detained Palestinians.[59]

Second, unlike interrogations of other suspects, those of suspected "security offenders" – a term covering all common charges against noncitizen Palestinians aged under 18 – are legally exempt from being audiovisually recorded.[60] A petition to have such interrogations recorded was dismissed in 2013 by the supreme court, whose deference to the country's security apparatus is documented throughout this book.[61] Although a 2014 amendment to the military law requires filming police interrogations of under-18s, it makes an exception for suspected "security offenders."[62] This once again illustrates the trend, highlighted in

---

[56] Military Court Watch, *Monitoring the Treatment of Children Held in Israeli Military Detention – Annual Report 2018/19* (June 24, 2019), pp. 8–13, www.militarycourtwatch .org/files/server/MCW%20ANNUAL%20REPORT%20(2019).pdf.

[57] See, e.g., B'Tselem, *Abuse and Torture in Interrogations of Dozens of Palestinian Minors in the Israel Police Etzion Facility* (August 21, 2013), www.btselem.org/download/ 201308_etzion_eng.pdf; DCIP, *In the Shadow of the 2014 Gaza War: Imprisonment of Jerusalem's Children* (2016), pp. 34–47, www.addameer.org/sites/default/files/publica tions/imprisonment_of_jerusalems_children_2016.pdf.

[58] See, e.g., Military Court Watch, *Monitoring the Treatment of Children*, pp. 7–8; B'Tselem and Hamoked, *Kept in the Dark: Treatment of Palestinian Detainees in the Petah Tikva Interrogation Facility of the Israeli Security Agency* (October 2010), pp. 14–16, 41, 49–51, 59, www.btselem.org/download/201010_kept_in_the_dark_eng.pdf.

[59] On the "softening up" of detained Palestinian youth through abuse and blindfolding, see, e.g., A. Hass, "60% of Youth Arrested in the Territories: We Suffered Violence," *Haaretz* (March 30, 2017) [Hebrew], www.haaretz.co.il/news/politics/.premium-1.3959111.

[60] Articles 4, 17 of Criminal Procedure Law (Interrogation of Suspects), 2002; Article 136d of the Order Concerning Security Provisions (Integrated Version) (Judea and Samaria) (No. 1651), 2009 (Article introduced in 2014).

[61] HCJ 9416/10 *Adalah v. Ministry of Public Security* (February 6, 2013).

[62] Article 1 of the Order Concerning Security Provisions (Amendment No. 1745) (Temporary Order) (Judea and Samaria) (No. 1745), 2014.

Chapter 4, of statutory exception clauses that render Israel's token reforms void. Consequently, most interrogations of noncitizen Palestinians under 18 are not filmed. This state of affairs has been acknowledged even by the Israeli military advocate general.[63] It is also described in affidavits of hundreds of young Palestinians, who also recounted how, even when recording devices were used in interrogations, the devices were switched off when the interrogators were threatening, assaulting, or trying to solicit the suspects to serve as informants.[64]

Third, young Palestinians have repeatedly claimed that they were interrogated several times, but with only one of the interrogations being recorded on camera. The unrecorded sessions reportedly involved abuse and, in some cases, attempts to recruit the detained youth as an informant.[65] Thus, undocumented abuse and coercion can invisibly influence those interrogations that are fully or partly filmed. In addition, as detailed in Chapter 4, since 2019 the military law has authorized assessing the dangerousness of detained Palestinians aged under 18 prior to their remand, but the unrecorded assessment meetings are reportedly used to coerce the Palestinians into confessing, without informing them of the possible ramifications.[66]

Fourth, since the 1990s there has been a reported change in Israel's torture tactics.[67] To avoid leaving visible physical marks – bruises or broken skin, bones, or muscles – Israeli interrogators have come to employ prolonged stress positions, sleep deprivation, painful shackling

[63] Cited in Military Court Watch, *Children in Military Custody: Progress Report – 2 Years On* (September 1, 2014), p. 12, www.militarycourtwatch.org/files/server/CHILDREN%20IN%20MILITARY%20CUSTODY%20-%202%20YEARS%20ON%20(1).pdf (asserting that two-thirds of noncitizen Palestinians aged under 18 who were detained in 2013 had no part of their interrogations filmed).

[64] Hamoked, *Childhood in Chains: The Detention and Interrogation of Palestinian Teenagers in the West Bank* (April 2018), pp. 5–6, www.hamoked.org/files/2018/1162860_eng.pdf; DCIP, *No Way to Treat a Child*, p. 49.

[65] Hamoked, *Childhood in Chains*, p. 4; Military Court Watch, *Children in Military Custody: Progress Report – 2 Years On*, pp. 12, 19.

[66] Order Concerning Security Provisions (Amendment No. 64) (Detention Reviews for Minors) (Judea and Samaria) (No. 1818), 2019; Advocate Gaby Lasky's letter to the Civil Administration (February 12, 2019) (on file with author).

[67] On this shift, see J. Ron, "Varying Methods of State Violence" (1997) 51:2 *International Organization* 275, 276, 285–86. See also G. E. Bisharat, "Courting Justice? Legitimation in Lawyering under Israeli Occupation" (1995) 20:2 *Law & Social Inquiry* 349, 379–80.

and binding, verbal abuse, and threats.[68] While these methods can be no less agonizing than those of the past, their utility for Israel lies in preventing Palestinians from utilizing their tortured bodies as corroborative evidence.

Secrecy is another legally sanctioned form of concealment. An example mentioned in Chapter 4 is the military's legal authority to keep Palestinians' arrests secret for up to 12 days. Another example, discussed in Chapter 2, is judicial review of so-called administrative detention, which is held in military courts behind closed doors using classified materials undisclosed to the defense. Military judges do not independently verify these materials as part of their review. Nor do they actually meet the Palestinian informants[69] – often the source of the alleged evidence – whose collaboration is usually the result of coercion and sometimes payment by Israel.[70] Some security agents have admitted to resorting to administrative detention in order to avoid disclosing the alleged (and under-scrutinized) evidence to incarcerated Palestinians.[71]

Also classified are the Israeli military's open-fire regulations (rules of engagement), an issue examined in Chapter 3. Accordingly, quotes from the regulations are redacted in the judgments I have traced that involve young Palestinians,[72] as well as in (unsuccessful) supreme court petitions against particular elements of the regulations.[73] Further, military investigation findings on suspected violations of the open-fire regulations are inadmissible in court,[74] and testimonies relating to the regulations

---

[68] See, e.g., PCATI, *Independent Report to the UN Committee Against Torture towards the Review of the Fifth Periodic Report on Israel* (March 1, 2016), http://stoptorture.org.il/wp-content/uploads/2016/06/INT_CAT_NGO_ISR_23475_E-Last.pdf.

[69] See, e.g., former judge Oded Pessenson's interview in the Israeli documentary *The Law in These Parts* (2013; director: Ra'anan Alexandrowicz).

[70] H. Cohen and R. Dudai, "Human Rights Dilemmas in Using Informers to Combat Terrorism: The Israeli–Palestinian Case" (2005) 17:1–2 *Terrorism and Political Violence* 229, 233–36.

[71] S. Krebs, "Lifting the Veil of Secrecy: Judicial Review of Administrative Detentions in the Israeli Supreme Court" (2012) 45:3 *Vanderbilt Journal Transnational Law* 639, 645, note 15.

[72] See, e.g., CMA 64/04 *Koretsky* v. *Chief Military Prosecutor* (November 15, 2004), ¶¶ 24, 37.

[73] HCJ 66/89 *League for Human and Civil Rights in Israel* v. *Minister of Defense* (1989) 44(2) PD 221; HCJ 873/89 *Hess* v. *Minister of Defense* (November 6, 1994).

[74] Article 539a of Military Adjudication Law. In the context of suspected violations of the open-fire regulations, an example of enforcing this statutory provision is CMC (South) 400/04 *Military Prosecutor* v. *Captain R* (November 15, 2005), Appendix: Decision on the Admissibility of Operational Investigation (May 10, 2005).

are heard behind closed doors.[75] Still, due to the country's mass conscription, an enormous number of Israelis are constantly exposed to the military's open-fire regulations during their military service, making these documents something of an open secret. Consequently, local human rights organizations, if they wish to avoid national security charges, must tread a fine line between disclosing and obscuring these documents. Israeli NGOs B'Tselem and Yesh Din have thus cited and even quoted specific regulations,[76] but they have not explicitly claimed to have copies of them. The military, in turn, utilizes this ambiguity to categorically deflect accusations: "Considering that B'tselem [sic] does not actually have in its possession a copy of those official rules and procedures, [its report] . . . is baseless."[77] Unlike the military, the police made its open-fire regulations public in 2016 following an NGO's supreme court petition on the matter. However, the published document is heavily redacted, and the non-redacted text contains no reference either to "children" or to age.[78]

6.3.2   Denial

Denial and self-justification are potent social forces in Israel[79] (and elsewhere[80]). Sometimes, the deniers are the alleged perpetrators, as well as their comrades. The four soldiers who, as described earlier, killed a

---

[75] See, e.g., CMC 400/04, ¶¶ d, f, j.

[76] See, e.g., B'Tselem, *Crowd Control: Israel's Use of Crowd Control Weapons in the West Bank* (January 2013), pp. 6–7, 29, www.btselem.org/download/201212_crowd_control_eng.pdf; B'Tselem, "Autopsy of Teenager Killed by Soldiers in al-Jalazun R.C. Calls Military's Account into Question" (February 11, 2014), www.btselem.org/firearms/20140211_killing_of_wajih_ramhi; Petition in HCJ 5817/08 *Arameen v. Attorney General* (petition filed on June 29, 2008, case decided on July 10, 2011), www.hamoked .org.il/files/2015/1159518.pdf.

[77] B'Tselem, *Crowd Control*, pp. 52–53.

[78] Operational Police Procedure 90.211.110.008: Open-Fire Procedure (December 16, 2015), www.adalah.org/uploads/uploads/new_police_regs.pdf. A related, two-page document, which mentions neither "children" nor age, is Police Command 06.02.14: Use of Firearms (September 3, 2007), https://web.archive.org/web/20191025182548/www .police.gov.il/Doc/pkodotDoc/sug_2/060214_2.pdf.

[79] D. Dor, *The Suppression of Guilt – The Israeli Media and the Reoccupation of the West Bank* (London and Ann Arbor, MI: Pluto Press, 2005); Z. Orr and D. Golan, "Human Rights NGOs in Israel: Collective Memory and Denial" (2014) 18:1 *International Journal of Human Rights* 68; N. Peled-Elhanan, "Legitimation of Massacres in Israeli School History Books" (2010) 21:4 *Discourse & Society* 377.

[80] S. Cohen, *States of Denial: Knowing About Atrocities and Suffering* (Cambridge and Malden, MA: Polity Press, 2001); S. Sontag, *Regarding the Pain of Others* (London and New York, NY: Penguin, 2004).

young Palestinian by pushing him out of a moving jeep initially denied all accusations when investigated about the matter.[81] In another case, two border police soldiers who witnessed their comrade assaulting three Palestinian youths during transfer to a detention facility initially denied the Palestinians' allegations to the investigators. The two soldiers confessed only after being informed of the existence of corroborating evidence (no charges were pressed against these two soldiers for their initial falsehoods). As for the abuser himself, he continued to deny most of the charges throughout his hearings and argued, in his defense, that "Arabs tend to exaggerate." The abused Palestinians also told the court that, throughout the incident, the soldier had self-identified by a false name, and that his two comrades had called him by that name in their presence. This, the defendant subsequently admitted, was accepted conduct within his military company that was designed to avoid prosecution in the event of a complaint.[82]

Israeli authorities and their allies also tend to distrust and deny Palestinian allegations.[83] Often, their mistrust and denial exhibit an unyielding logic. On the one hand, when Palestinians complain, they are readily dismissed as untrustworthy. In 2018, Israel's deputy state attorney reportedly attributed "the lack of criminal investigations" into torture to "the fact that ... [Israeli interrogators] are usually more credible than [the] complaining Palestinian prisoners."[84] In like manner, a former military judge was once asked whether he had ever doubted the reliability of the security agents who sought to place Palestinians in "administrative detention." "No." he replied. "As a rule, I didn't doubt what they said. . . . [In contrast, whenever a Palestinian] detainee tells me what they did to him, I'm pretty suspicious. Because he has his interests.

[81] CrimA 5136/08.

[82] CrimC (Jer. Dist.) 204/99 *State of Israel* v. *Nakash* (verdict January 25, 2000, sentencing February 8, 2000), ¶¶ 4, 30, 34, 36–37, 42, 47; CrimA 1752/00 *State of Israel* v. *Nakash* (2000) 54(2) PD 72.

[83] On mistrust toward Palestinians in Israel and the United States, see L. Allen, *The Rise and Fall of Human Rights: Cynicism and Politics in Occupied Palestine* (Stanford: Stanford University Press, 2013), p. 173; L. Hajjar, *Courting Conflict: The Israeli Military Court System in the West Bank and Gaza* (Berkeley, CA and London: University of California Press, 2005), pp. 67, 69.

[84] Y. J. Bob, "Video of Shin Bet Interrogations Leading to Disciplinary Measures," *Jerusalem Post* (November 29, 2018), www.jpost.com/Israel-News/Live-video-of-Shin-Bet-interroga tions-leading-to-disciplinary-measures-573172.

To begin with, I believe the agent of the [Israeli] authorities. Because his job is to protect me."[85]

When, on the other hand, Palestinians choose not to lodge a formal complaint – as, according to claims by the military, occurs in 97 percent of cases[86] – Israeli authorities cite this, too, as supposed evidence of their deceitfulness. This reasoning guided the military's response to a human rights report on its arrests of young noncitizen Palestinians:

> [W]hilst the minors and their parents spoke extensively with the press regarding the claims of alleged ill treatment . . ., no formal complaint was ever submitted. . . . [O]ne would assume that if the claims made by the minors were indeed factual, their defense counsel or their parents themselves would have raised these claims in court. . . . Furthermore, if the complaints were indeed genuine, one would assume that an official complaint would also have been submitted.[87]

This assertion, however, ignores the host of disincentives deterring Palestinians from complaining to Israeli authorities. Among them are: distrust in Israel's investigation mechanisms; fear of retaliation; fear of Israeli attempts to recruit young Palestinians as informants if they file a complaint; fear of Israeli pressure on these Palestinians to change their story; sometimes having to file the complaint at the same police station where the alleged abuse took place, or at a station in an Israeli settlement; and, due to the inaccessibility and opacity of Israel's complaints procedures, being forced to seek assistance from NGOs or private lawyers, whose services not all Palestinians can easily use. The rarity of complaints during the trial, specifically, can be attributed to another reason: fear of fruitlessly delaying their court process and thus unnecessarily prolonging the complainants' detention prior to their near-certain conviction.[88]

[85] Colonel (retired) Oded Pesensson (served as a military judge from 1988 to 2008), as interviewed in the documentary *The Law in These Parts*.
[86] This figure, referring to 2013, is cited in Military Court Watch, *Children in Military Custody: Progress Report – 2 Years On*, p. 24.
[87] Israel Defense Forces, "Response Letter Regarding Military Arrests of Palestinian Children in the West Bank," *Human Rights Watch* (July 13, 2015), www.hrw.org/news/2015/07/13/response-letter-israeli-military-regarding-military-arrests-palestinian-children.
[88] Military Court Watch, *Children in Military Custody: Progress Report – 2 Years On*, pp. 24–25; Yesh Din, *Law Enforcement against IDF Soldiers Suspected of Harming Palestinians – 2016 Summary* (March 2018), pp. 3–4, https://s3-eu-west-1.amazonaws.com/files.yesh-din.org/March+2018+MPCID+datasheet/YeshDin+-+Data+3.18+-+Eng.pdf.

At times, the object of denial and distrust is Palestinians' appearance, especially their apparent ages (an issue elaborated in Chapter 3). Thus, soldiers who in 2010 were convicted of using a nine-year-old Gazan as a human shield denied in court having realized that the victim was a "child."[89] Taking this logic a step further, one Israeli military prosecutor, when asked about the young composition of many Palestinian defendants, replied: "Don't let them fool you. They might look like children, but they are really adults. If they look fifteen, they are probably twenty-five. You can't trust Palestinians for anything, even their ages."[90] Somewhat similarly, in 2018, a Palestinian girl's confrontation with Israeli soldiers was filmed and published across the world. In response, an Israeli deputy minister (and formerly Israel's ambassador to the UN) announced that a "classified [parliamentary] subcommittee" had investigated "whether [the girl's family] ... was a real family ... [or just actors] specially put together for propaganda." The subcommittee, he reported, had inquired whether "members of the family were chosen for their appearance" – blond, blue-eyed, and light-skinned – and their "clothing ... [which was] American ..., not Palestinian," but "didn't reach unequivocal conclusions."[91] Human rights critics might find such statements outrageous; however, as shown in the previous chapter, they too, in their own way, repeatedly cast doubt on young Palestinians' reliability – an issue I will revisit later in this chapter.

6.3.3 Impunity

Data accumulated throughout Israel's decades-long rule over the West Bank and Gaza Strip suggests a culture of impunity. Complaints rarely lead to prosecution. Of all the complaints DCIP submitted between 2012 and 2015 about abuse or ill-treatment of detained Palestinians aged under 18, none led to an indictment; according to the NGO, it was often unclear whether an investigation had been initiated at all.[92] Some investigations, including those concerning abuse of Palestinian under-18s, are closed without even contacting the alleged Israeli abusers or examining

---

[89] CMC (South) 150/10 *Chief Military Prosecutor* v. *John Does* (October 3, 2010), p. 24.

[90] Hajjar, *Courting Conflict*, p. 117.

[91] Y. Berger and J. Lis, "Israel Secretly Debated Whether Family Members of Palestinian Teen Ahed Tamimi Are Non-Related 'Light Skinned' Actors," *Haaretz* (January 25, 2018), www.haaretz.com/israel-news/.premium-israel-investigated-whether-ahed-tamimi-s-family-was-real-1.5762887.

[92] DCIP, *No Way to Treat a Child*, p. 70.

relevant records.[93] A former soldier, describing this culture of impunity during his military service, recalled "a [Palestinian] detainee being brought in, a 16–17-year-old kid … He was shackled, blindfolded, and claimed he was beaten all the way there." Asked whether this information had been passed on, the soldier replied sarcastically: "Yeah, right … his hitters were put on trial … No, I'm kidding."[94] Deadly firing at young Palestinians, too, rarely results in indictments. In 2011, a petition to prosecute four border police who had shot dead a 10-year-old Palestinian girl was dismissed by the supreme court, which attributed the lack of sufficient incriminating evidence to the inadequate investigation.[95] Such judicial reasoning – the use of Israel's own investigative flaws as grounds to absolve its shooters – has been employed in similar court cases as well.[96] In 2020, the supreme court dismissed a petition to press charges against a colonel who had been caught on camera shooting to death a 17-year-old Palestinian in violation of Israel's open-fire regulations.[97]

Beyond incidents involving Palestinians under 18 specifically, the culture of impunity exists across the various Israeli authorities entrusted with powers of investigation. The military advocate general closed with no indictment nearly 97 percent of NGO B'Tselem's 739 complaints between 2000 and 2015.[98] Very similar was the fate of the 948 investigations conducted by the criminal investigation division of the military police from 2011 to 2016,[99] and also that of internal military investi-

---

[93] Yesh Din, *"We Were Unable to Locate the Perpetrator": The Failure of Israel's Law Enforcement System to Investigate and Prosecute Military and Police Personnel Who Committed Criminal Offenses against Palestinians in the West Bank* (December 2018), https://s3-eu-west-1.amazonaws.com/files.yesh-din.org/LoAla_2018/YeshDin+Lo+Ala+-+English.pdf.

[94] Breaking the Silence, *Children and Youth – Soldiers' Testimonies 2005–2011*, pp. 15–16.

[95] HCJ 5817/08.

[96] See, e.g., CMC 400/04 (resulting in acquittal); CMC (North) 497/03 *Military Prosecutor v. Stein* (September 7, 2005) (resulting in a relatively lenient three-month suspended sentence).

[97] HCJ 1782/19 *Kosba v. Attorney General* (September 3, 2020) (although the youth had earlier hurled a stone at a military vehicle, he was shot while fleeing the scene and posing no danger to the soldiers).

[98] B'Tselem, *The Occupation's Fig Leaf: Israel's Military Law Enforcement System as a Whitewash Mechanism* (May 2016), pp. 16, 40, www.btselem.org/sites/default/files/publications/201605_occupations_fig_leaf_eng.pdf.

[99] Yesh Din, *Law Enforcement against IDF Soldiers*, p. 7.

gations into 9,250 shootings at Palestinians in the period 2000–2017.[100] Not a single one of the approximately 1,300 complaints of torture and ill-treatment complaints to Israel's Inspector for Complaints against the Security Agency between 2001 and 2020 resulted in prosecution, and only one led to a criminal investigation (which closed without charges).[101]

On the rare occasions that soldiers are taken to court, the charges against them, even in high-profile cases, tend to be on the lenient side, and the chances of conviction are relatively low. Since the turn of the century, while Israel has killed more than 6,000 noncitizen Palestinians,[102] only a handful of soldiers have been prosecuted for these killings, and they were all charged not with murder but with lesser offenses, such as manslaughter and negligent killing.[103] Among them were the soldiers who, as described earlier, pushed a 17-year-old Palestinian to death from a moving jeep.[104] Most such cases ended without conviction.[105] Parenthetically, a large proportion of the cases I have traced involved border police soldiers, who, unlike most soldiers, are handled by the investigation, prosecution, and adjudication bodies dealing with civilian police officers.[106] As the police has higher investi-

[100] J. Brown, "Azaria's Defense Team Changes Strategy and Claims Selective Enforcement," *Haaretz* (April 5, 2017) [Hebrew], www.haaretz.co.il/blogs/johnbrown/BLOG-1.4002447.

[101] PCATI, "Torture in Israel 2020: Situation Report" (June 2020), http://stoptorture.org.il/wp-content/uploads/2020/06/%D7%90%D7%A0%D7%92%D7%9C%D7%99%D7%AA-%D7%9C%D7%90%D7%99%D7%A0%D7%98%D7%A8%D7%A0%D7%98.pdf.

[102] B'Tselem, *Fatalities Before Operation "Cast Lead"* (n.d.), www.btselem.org/statistics/fatalities/before-cast-lead/by-date-of-event (referring to September 29, 2000 – December 26, 2008); B'Tselem, *Fatalities Since Operation Cast Lead* (n.d., last accessed on January 9, 2020), www.btselem.org/statistics/fatalities/after-cast-lead/by-date-of-event (referring to January 19, 2009 – 26 December 2019).

[103] G. Cohen, "IDF Soldiers Have Been Tried for Manslaughter – But Most Were Not Convicted," *Haaretz* (August 28, 2016), www.haaretz.com/israel-news/.premium-soldiers-have-been-tried-for-manslaughter-before-azaria-1.5429989; J. Brown, "Exclusive: Prosecution Retrieves Charges against Artillery Soldiers Who Fatally Shot a Teen at his Back Neck," *Haaretz* (June 4, 2018) [Hebrew], www.haaretz.co.il/blogs/johnbrown/1.6140314.

[104] CrimC 157/03; CrimC 907/05; CrimC 3172/07; CrimA 10594/05; CrimA 5136/08.

[105] Brown, "Azaria's Defense Team Changes Strategy and Claims Selective Enforcement"; Cohen, "IDF Soldiers Have Been Tried for Manslaughter – But Most Were Not Convicted."

[106] Article 25 of Defense Service Law (Integrated Version), 1986.

gation, prosecution, and conviction rates than the military,[107] some of the prosecuted border police soldiers claimed that their indictment was discriminatory.[108]

For the few soldiers who were convicted, sentences tended to be light. Thus, in four different incidents between 2005 and 2019, soldiers convicted of shooting to death Palestinians aged 3, 8, 10, and 15 years, in violation of the military's open-fire regulations, were all spared imprisonment and given non-custodial sentences.[109] Two soldiers convicted of using a nine-year-old Palestinian as a human shield – a case and a practice investigated in the next chapter – were not sentenced to prison either.[110] Prison sentences, when imposed, have been relatively short. A soldier who shot and killed a 16-year-old Palestinian was sentenced to two months' imprisonment. An appeal to increase his sentence was dismissed; he remained in the military, and was later promoted to lieutenant commander.[111] Similarly, a soldier who, as described earlier, abused and threatened a detained and hooded Palestinian youth was imprisoned for three months.[112] In another previously examined case, concerning three soldiers who assaulted and abused two young

[107] Y. Kubovich, "One in Every Ten Policemen Investigated in the Police Investigation Department in 2013," *Haaretz* (April 6, 2014) [Hebrew], www.haaretz.co.il/news/law/.premium-1.2289162. More recently, however, the police's indictment rate decreased significantly. See J. Breiner, "Number of Indictments Filed by DIPI against Police Halved within Two Years," *Haaretz* (January 27, 2020) [Hebrew], www.haaretz.co.il/news/law/.premium-1.8446988.

[108] See, e.g., Verdict in CrimC 3172/07, ¶ 9.

[109] CMC (North) 186/04 *Military Prosecutor* v. *Vinik* (verdict April 14, 2005, sentencing May 3, 2005); CMA 59/05 *Vinik* v. *Chief Military Prosecutor* (July 25, 2005); CMC 497/03; CrimC (Ramla Mag.) 16723-06-10 *State of Israel* v. *Abu* (verdict October 30, 2012, sentencing July 3, 2013); Y. Kubovich and J. Khoury, "15-year-old Palestinian Was Shot to Death. Israeli Soldier Who Fired at Him Got One Month of Community Service," *Haaretz* (October 30, 2019), www.haaretz.com/israel-news/.premium-israeli-soldier-gets-month-s-community-service-after-death-of-palestinian-teenager-1.8057024.

[110] Channel 2 News staff, "Suspended Prison Sentence Imposed on Givati Soldiers Who Performed 'Child Procedure' in Operation Cast Lead," *Channel 2 News* (November 21, 2010) [Hebrew], www.mako.co.il/news-military/security/Article-4d44b89a05d6c21004.htm.

[111] See, respectively, CMC (GOC) 135/03 *Chief Military Prosecutor* v. *Koretsky*; CMA 64/04; Z. Koretsky, "Artillery – The Queen of Battle," *IDF Artillery Corps News* (August 11, 2014) [Hebrew], https://web.archive.org/web/20180202112025/www.beithatothan.org.il/node/1325.

[112] CrimC 2420-05-11.

Palestinians, one of the perpetrators was spared prison and the other two were given prison sentences of eight and ten months.[113]

All of this stands in stark contrast to Israel's handling of noncitizen Palestinians, as evident from the figures provided earlier in this book.[114] Whereas accusations against state agents rarely lead to a conviction or even an indictment, nearly all military court trials of Palestinians end in conviction. For the few convicted soldiers, including those found guilty of killing Palestinians under the age of 18, sentences are often far lighter than those imposed on Palestinian stone-throwers aged under 18, whose actions usually cause no harm either to persons or to property. Chapter 7 investigates how, and to what effect, this disparity intersects with the dissolving of the "combatant"/"child" distinction, while Chapter 8 elaborates on the institutionalized discrimination between Palestinians and Israelis aged under 18.

Given the rarity of indictments (let alone convictions), Palestinians can pursue an alternative legal avenue: compensation from Israel through civil litigation. However, Israel has repeatedly amended its law to limit its civil liability, in addition to placing procedural obstacles to potential lawsuits. Subsequently, the success rate of Palestinian plaintiffs has more than halved between 1992 and 2012, and it has continued to drop ever since.[115]

6.3.4 Framing Violence as an Isolated Exception

Despite the concealment, secrecy, denial, and impunity surrounding state violence, some Israeli perpetrators have been taken to court and either convicted (in criminal proceedings) or ordered to pay compensation (in civil lawsuits). Nevertheless, the judiciary has made a point of framing such cases as exceptions unrepresentative of the military's moral, legal, and disciplinary record.

Such was the judicial rhetoric in a case involving two military police soldiers who assaulted two blindfolded and handcuffed Palestinians, aged 15 and 17 years, on their way to detention. The court-martial's judgment describes the conduct of one of the perpetrators as "serious, especially given ... his obligation to different norms. ... It is all the graver given that the defendant and his comrade had been instructed ... to avoid

---

[113] CrimC 390/04.
[114] See Chapter 2, Section 2.5 ("The Real Trial").
[115] Bachar, "Access Denied," pp. 845–47.

violence toward the detainees, an instruction apparently given to the soldiers frequently."[116] Regarding his comrade, the judgment remarks: "The company commander ... noted that the company has excellent discipline and that the ... [defendant's offenses] characterize neither the company nor the defendant." This is despite the defendant's own admission to also having slapped detained Palestinians on previous occasions.[117] The court martial appeal court added: "The Israel Defense Forces are guided by basic principles of human morality and dignity. Deviation from them, even in isolated incidents, damages the entire camp."[118]

The supreme court employed a similar narrative in its 2006 judgment concerning the young Palestinian who, as mentioned earlier, was fatally shoved out of a military jeep in motion. Justice Edmond Levy characterized this as, in his opinion, "a serious and grave case like few others, ... [bringing] shame on a large group of armed forces who faithfully perform their draining duty in full respect of others' dignity, let alone their physical integrity."[119] As if Israel had not killed thousands of Palestinians around that time, many of them under-18s, justice Ayala Procaccia followed suit, describing as "exceptional and extraordinary" the "circumstances of this case." Procaccia's opinion is just as much an apotheosis of Israel, the military, and Judaism as it is a denouncement of so-called rotten apples:

> It is difficult to comprehend how anyone born and raised in Israel, ... who served as a combatant in the IDF, ... would be capable of such horrible acts..., [which violate] the law and ... basic human and Jewish morals... [The defendants'] wrongdoing ... [is] the antithesis of the values of enlightened humankind and the Jewish people throughout its history.... [It] casts considerable moral responsibility on the entire Israeli society, for allowing such rotten apples to exist within it. ... [These offenses are marked by] unusual exceptionality ... [I]t is hard to bear the thought that ... in Israel, which was established on foundations of equality and the sanctity of life ..., [such] killing of innocents due to their ethnic origin is possible, especially when committed by soldiers and police enforcing the law.[120]

[116] CMC (Center) 222/03 *Chief Military Prosecutor* v. *Lieberman* (July 8, 2003), p. 4.
[117] CMC (Center) 222a/03 *Chief Military Prosecutor* v. *Rozner* (July 28, 2003), p. 3.
[118] MilA 128/03 *Chief Military Prosecutor* v. *Lieberman* (August 21, 2003), ¶ 15. The court quoted this text from another judgment: CMA 27/02 *Chief Military Prosecutor* v. *Hazan* (February 27, 2002), p. 7.
[119] CrimA 10594/05, ¶ 3.
[120] CrimA 5136/08, ¶¶ 13, 21, 23 of justice Procaccia's opinion.

It is unsurprising, in light of the evidence presented here, that the perpetrators likely to face punishment tend to be low-ranking troops whom the Israeli legal system can characterize as having disobeyed orders, deviated from social norms, or acted on their own volition. Acts falling into this category include unauthorized (as opposed to legalized) abuse or killing, as I have shown, as well as looting[121] and vandalism.[122] The penalizing of such supposedly undisciplined soldiers fulfils two functions: first, as demonstrated so far, it is used to venerate and absolve Israel and its military; second, it is designed to tighten the state's control over its troops – to ensure their violence against Palestinians operates precisely as envisioned by policymakers.[123]

In the few successful Palestinian civil lawsuits for compensation, courts have often held not the state but the defendants alone liable. This, for example, was the outcome in a 2008 judgment concerning three border police soldiers who had physically assaulted three Palestinian siblings, aged 10, 13, and 14 years. The plaintiffs argued, among other things, that Israel was liable for failing to protect Palestinians, properly guide and supervise its security personnel, and root out the border police's culture of violence. However, the court rejected these accusations, and ordered the individual soldiers alone to pay compensation. The judgment adds: "the fact that ... [the soldier who arrested the 10-year-old boy] did not know the age of criminal responsibility [i.e., 12 years] does not support the claim that [these soldiers] ... did not receive proper training"[124] – a telling assertion about the relationship between legality, age, and accountability.

Following sociologist Stanley Cohen's widely cited typology of state denial, this judicial framing can be said to represent a shift from "factual" to "interpretive" denial. The former – the state's blatant denial of either an alleged fact (in this case, a violent incident) or knowledge of this fact –

---

[121] See, e.g., CMA 35/16 *Chief Military Prosecutor* v. *John Doe* (July 6, 2017); CMC (Center) 650/14 *Military Prosecutor* v. *Krimov* (verdict January 12, 2015, sentencing February 24, 2015).

[122] See, e.g., CMC (South) 445/16 *Military Prosecutor* v. *Corporals John Does* (verdict September 19, 2016, sentencing November 10, 2016); B'Tselem, "Officer Indicted for Vandalizing Palestinian Vehicles" (June 21, 2011), www.btselem.org/accountability/ 20110621_officer_indicted_vandalizing_palestinian_vehicles.

[123] On how states resort to law in order to simultaneously legitimate their violence and improve their control over their armed forces, see D. Kennedy, "Lawfare and Warfare," in J. Crawford and M. Koskenniemi (eds.), *The Cambridge Companion to International Law* (Cambridge: Cambridge University Press, 2012).

[124] CivC 6545/04 (Jer. Mag.) *Ja'abari* v. *Albilia* (November 3, 2008), ¶¶ 22–25, 57, 61.

is evident throughout this chapter, as well as in Chapters 3 and 7. In the latter form of denial, as exemplified by these last judgments, the state, rather than denying the alleged incidents, disputes the meaning attributed to them.[125] Such judgments, while acknowledging a few violent incidents, reject two allegations: first, that these incidents are in any way representative of the country's moral and legal record; and, second, that the state too, rather than only individual soldiers, is imputable.

For Israel, the greater than usual attention given to high-profile cases makes the protection of its self-image as law-abiding all the more imperative. This, indeed, is unmistakable across many of the cases mentioned so far. For example, the court martial appeal court remarked in 2002 that the physical assault of a young Palestinian "stain[ed] the IDF's moral image [and] severely damaged its reputation."[126] The following year, the court described another physical assault on Palestinian youths as having caused:

> a reputational damage in the "battle over consciousness." The defendant's wrongdoings play into our enemies' hands. ... Current fighting [in the West Bank and Gaza Strip] comprises two elements: a real-physical element and a consciousness one. ... [The latter] concerns fighting over consciousness, ... domestically and abroad, ... and through the various Israeli and global media.[127]

Similar judicial rhetoric appeared in several other cases discussed earlier,[128] as well as in additional high-profile abuse cases.[129] One previously cited judgment, for example, held:

> Assault and abuse by law enforcement officials ..., especially of minors, ... have ramifications beyond the [harm caused to the victims]. ... [T]hey undermine the public image of the security forces ... [as well as] the image in the international arena of the State

[125] Cohen, *States of Denial*, pp. 7–9.
[126] CMC (Center) 272/02 *Chief Military Prosecutor* v. *Cohen* (2002), p. 3.
[127] CMA 128/03, ¶¶ 19–20. The quoted case is CMA 62/03 *Chief Military Prosecutor* v. *Eilin* (May 27, 2003) (remarking that the soldier's actions "damage the reputation of all uniformed personnel").
[128] For similar rhetoric, see CrimC 907/05, ¶¶ 6, 11; verdict in CrimC 3172/07, ¶ 8 (quoting the defense); CrimA 9507/11 *Sevilia* v. *State of Israel* (April 4, 2012), ¶ 13 of justice Danziger's leading opinion (quoting the prosecution).
[129] CMA 44/88 *Nessimi* v. *Chief Military Prosecutor* (1988) 1988 MPD 449; CMA 52/88 *Harpaz* v. *Chief Military Prosecutor* (1988) 1988 MPD 417.

of Israel, whose soldiers are presented in the various media as unscrupulous and immoral combatants.[130]

When indications surface that violence against Palestinians might be commonplace, and that there might be an entrenched culture of impunity and concealment, the judiciary often brushes them off. For instance, the judgment for the soldier who, as described earlier, assaulted young Palestinians on their way to detention, states: "Some of the witnesses attempted to depict the violent conduct toward the suspects ... as well as not reporting such actions – as a norm in the IDF or the border police. The testimonies indicate that ... this claim [is] ... based on rumors rather than actually witnessing such events." The judgment prefers an alternative framing, one that associates violence exclusively with specific companies while contrasting it with the alleged standards of the border police: "In any event, if such a 'norm' exists in one company or another, commanders should clarify to their subordinates that such a norm is wrong and must be avoided, as it is not only illegal but also might damage the morality and reputation of the IDF and the border police."[131]

The border police itself has made use of a similar framing on other occasions. In 2004, when three of its soldiers were charged with assaulting and abusing noncitizen Palestinian youth, and nine others were being investigated for abusing and robbing Palestinian citizens of Israel, the border police pronounced that "it considers as very serious such exceptional cases of lone policemen abusing their power illegally and in violation of procedures and instructions."[132] In deploying this language, the border police conveniently ignored reports in the mainstream Israeli media, according to which most of the perpetrators' company had also previously abused Palestinians on a regular basis.[133] A later case, in 2011, saw the border police likewise publicly denouncing one of its soldiers,

---

[130] CrimC 390/04, ¶ 18.
[131] CrimC 204/99, ¶¶ 131–32. For similar rhetoric from the prosecution in a later case, see CrimA 9507/11, ¶ 13.
[132] E. Weisz and S. Rofeh-Ophir, "Following the Abuse Case: BP Ceases Training," *Ynet* (June 2, 2004) [Hebrew], www.ynet.co.il/articles/0,7340,L-2925837,00.html.
[133] Walla! News staff, "MP Kara: Release the 4 Border Policemen Suspected of Killing a Palestinian," *Walla! News* (May 19, 2003) [Hebrew], https://news.walla.co.il/item/389382.

who had been convicted of abusing and threatening a hooded Palestinian youth, as having violated its values.[134]

A different rhetorical strategy appeared in a court case concerning a soldier who concealed his abuse and killing of a young Palestinian. Here, the judgment absolved Israeli society by portraying the defendant as an immigrant informed by foreign mores:

> [One of the defendants] confirmed that he did not report their actions to anyone, because "I don't report. I wasn't raised to immediately run and tell anything I see." ... The defendant's attorney ... noted that the defendant and his family were immigrants from the former Soviet Union, where it was not accepted to snitch to the authorities on a comrade's misconduct.[135]

As most Israeli Jews are either first, second, or third generation immigrants – many of them from the former Soviet Union[136] – such a problematic excuse is available to countless other soldiers.

Investment in the troops' reputation not only entails condemnations after the fact, but can also prevent incidents from coming to light in the first place. In the interest of protecting this reputation, soldiers may decide to conceal wrongdoings, as indeed occurred in the case of the border police soldier who assaulted young Palestinians on their way to detention. During the soldier's trial in 2000, his comrade was asked why, despite having witnessed the assault, he had not reported it. His reply attests to his preoccupation with the military's reputation, alongside other disincentives to reporting misconduct:

> I knew they [the detained Palestinians] wouldn't complain. Such things always happen in patrols. ... The system wouldn't have backed me up even if I did report. Even today I wouldn't report again ... [I]n the company, camaraderie overrides morals. If such a thing gets revealed, everyone corroborates [each other's accounts]. ... [T]here's peer pressure.

---

[134] G. Alkabetz, "Soldier Who Abused Arab Teen Heading to Jail," *Mynet Jerusalem* (November 21, 2011; no longer available online) [Hebrew].

[135] Verdict in CrimC 157/03, ¶¶ 9, 11.

[136] In the first six decades of Israel's existence, 3.2 million Jews immigrated to the state. About 1.2 million Israeli residents are immigrants from the former Soviet Union. See, respectively, Central Bureau of Statistics, *Israel's 2018 Annual Statistical Report* (December 2018), p. 19 [Hebrew], https://old.cbs.gov.il/shnaton69/shnaton69.pdf; M. Sheps, "Select Figures on Persons from the Former Soviet Union, in Commemoration of the Twenty Fifth Anniversary of the Aliyah Wave" (2016) 105 *Hed Ha'Ulpan Ha'hadash* 62 [Hebrew], http://meyda.education.gov.il/files/AdultEducation/hed_haulpan/hed_105_marina_sheps.pdf.

Another reason for not reporting is wanting to avoid what happened afterward – a trial, ... excommunication from the company, and damage to the reputation of the company and its commander.[137]

While targeting such purported rotten apples, the legal system grants categorical immunity to those involved in state-sponsored violence,[138] whose actions, as I have mentioned, cost far more Palestinian lives. Regarding extrajudicial killing, the supreme court held that, in principle, "if [the targeted Palestinian] can be arrested, interrogated, and tried, those are the means which should be employed ... Trial is preferable to use of [lethal] force."[139] But in reality, when leaked documents in 2008 suggested that Palestinians who could have been arrested had been assassinated, the attorney general refused to investigate the matter. The only ones prosecuted, and later convicted, were the former soldier who leaked this information and the Israeli journalist who published it.[140] Similarly, as touched on earlier, the supreme court has paved the way for continued torture in interrogations.[141]

6.4 Incriminatory Evidence Reenvisaged: How Visibility Conceals and What Invisibility Can Highlight

6.4.1 "Strong" Evidence and Its Pitfalls

In the face of state concealment, secrecy, denial, and impunity, what sort of evidence nonetheless results in convictions of Israeli perpetrators? Palestinian testimonies – the evidence at the heart of most complaints – are highly unlikely to achieve this outcome without corroboration by the sort of evidence that Israeli authorities find difficult to discount. Two

---

[137] CrimC 204/99, ¶¶ 43, 111.
[138] A. Cohen, "Administering the Territories: An Inquiry into the Application of International Humanitarian Law by the IDF in the Occupied Territories" (2005) 38:3 *Israel Law Review* 24, 71–72.
[139] HCJ 769/02 *PCATI* v. *Government of Israel* (2006) 62(1) PD 507, ¶ 40 of justice Barak's opinion.
[140] Viterbo, "Future-Oriented Measures," pp. 124–26.
[141] Hundreds of sworn affidavits of Palestinian ex-detainees indicate the persistence of interrogational torture. See B. Shoughry-Badarne, "A Decade after the High Court of Justice 'Torture' Ruling, What's Changed?," in A. Baker and A. Matar (eds.), *Threat: Palestinian Political Prisoners in Israel* (London: Pluto Press, 2011), pp. 114, 116.

types of corroborating evidence appear to be considered relatively strong: video footage and state agents' testimonies.[142]

A case in point is the Israeli legal system's handling of homicide allegations. As touched on earlier, only a handful of soldiers have been convicted of the manslaughter of noncitizen Palestinians since the turn of the century. The evidence that secured their convictions is telling. One of these soldiers had his own commander testifying against him.[143] Another, as detailed in the next chapter, was caught on camera by B'Tselem as he shot dead a Palestinian who was lying on the ground disarmed and injured.[144] A soldier who was convicted for shooting to death a 17-year-old Palestinian had been filmed by a CNN News crew, as well as by security cameras (his charges, however, were eventually reduced from manslaughter to negligent killing and grievous bodily harm). As further corroboration, the autopsy found three live bullets, refuting the initial claims of the military and the soldier that he had used only rubber-coated bullets.[145] Another manslaughter conviction may be attributed to a different factor: the atypical national and ethnic affiliations of the parties. Thus, the deceased was a British citizen killed in Gaza, whose life might be accorded greater weight than those of Palestinians. And the soldier who fired the fatal shot was a Palestinian Bedouin citizen of Israel, to whom the Zionist state might be less committed than to its Jewish citizens.[146]

A similar trend characterizes the sort of evidence that leads to convictions for abuse and physical violence.[147] For example, it was a squad

[142] On Israeli society's credence in its armed forces, see J. Eastwood, *Ethics as a Weapon of War: Militarism and Morality in Israel* (Cambridge and New York: Cambridge University Press, 2017), p. 197.

[143] Brown, "Exclusive: Prosecution Retrieves Charges against Artillery Soldiers Who Fatally Shot a Teen at His Back Neck."

[144] B'Tselem, "Video: Soldier Executes Palestinian Lying Injured on Ground after the Latter Stabbed a Soldier in Hebron" (March 24, 2016), www.btselem.org/video/20160324_soldier_executes_palestinian_attacker_in_hebron#full.

[145] The judgments are CrimC (Jer. Dist.) 47607-11-14 *State of Israel v. Deri* (sentencing April 25, 2018); CrimA 4497/18 *State of Israel v. Deri* (August 19, 2018). For further information on the case, see Y. Berger, "Border Policeman Who Killed Unarmed Palestinian Teen Released from Prison after Less Than Year," *Haaretz* (January 3, 2019), www.haaretz.com/israel-news/.premium-border-policeman-who-killed-unarmed-palestinian-teen-released-early-from-prison-1.6806775.

[146] CMC (South) 10/04 *Military Prosecutor v. Teisir* (verdict June 27, 2005, sentencing August 11, 2005).

[147] While my focus here is on Palestinian victims aged under 18, cases involving older Palestinians also evince this trend. See, e.g., CMA 28/04 *First Sgt John Doe v. Chief*

commander's soldiers who witnessed and later reported his physical assault of a mentally disabled 16-year-old Palestinian in 2002.[148] And it was also soldiers who, the following year, reported the physical assault of two arrested Palestinian youths by two military police soldiers.[149] Slightly more complex was the chain of events in the previously analyzed case of the border police soldier who abused and assaulted young Palestinians en route to a detention facility. Initially, two soldiers who had witnessed his actions denied the Palestinians' complaint. They confessed only after another soldier, in whom they had confided about the incident, threatened to report it. This led the defendant, who up to that point had denied the allegations, also to admit his guilt. In addition, once additional Palestinians came forward to report having been assaulted and abused by the defendant on previously unreported occasions, two border police soldiers, one of whom was Druze, corroborated the allegations in their investigation.[150]

The Israeli border police who, as discussed earlier, abused and threatened a detained Palestinian youth in 2011 likewise confessed to the crimes.[151] And so did, four months after the fact, the Druze soldier who drove the military jeep from which his three comrades, as I have described, pushed out a 17-year-old Palestinian to his death.[152] In the latter case, another soldier, the roommate of two of the defendants, also testified that he had heard them talking about the killing.[153] Another previously mentioned conviction, of the soldiers who used a young Palestinian as a human shield, was based not only on the Palestinian's testimony, which the court deemed to "warrant caution," but also on another soldier's testimony.[154]

As for photographic or video evidence, in one of the previously examined cases, a local photographer took pictures of the young Palestinian's bruises, which were later published in the Israeli press.[155]

Military Prosecutor (July 14, 2004), in which the soldier, convicted of abusing and assaulting Palestinians, similarly had his actions videotaped.

[148] MilC 272/02, p. 5.
[149] MilC 222/03, p. 2.
[150] CrimC 204/99, ¶¶ 23, 42–43, 85, 109–12.
[151] CrimC 2420-05-11.
[152] CrimC 157/03, ¶ 12.
[153] CrimC 157/03, ¶ 18.
[154] MilC 150/10, p. 25.
[155] Y. Lis, "BP Policemen Admit to Abusing Palestinian Minors Near Jerusalem," *Haaretz* (June 2, 2004) [Hebrew], www.haaretz.co.il/misc/1.970948.

Despite the invisibility imposed by Israeli authorities, similar evidence sometimes emerges from Israeli authorities themselves. An example mentioned earlier is Israeli security camera records (on the occasions that they are retained and made publicly available). Another example is Israel's filming of its interrogations. Although it is unsystematic and partial, it has resulted in a few interrogation videos of Palestinians aged under 18 becoming public in recent years. Possibly due to its rarity, this footage attracted considerable public attention locally[156] and globally,[157] which focused on the visible misconduct: verbal abuse; failure to inform the young interrogees of their right to remain silent; disregard of detainees' requests to have a lawyer present; discrepancies between the interrogees' words and the interrogators' notes; and, in one instance, a soldier, despite being a key witness against the Palestinian, attending the questioning and even aiming a gun at him.

In court, defense attorneys harnessed this footage to argue that the rights of their clients had been violated and, therefore, that any confessions were inadmissible. This argument sometimes bore fruit: two judges, after being shown the interrogation videos, ordered that the defendant be released on bail;[158] another judge ordered, extraordinarily, that the young Palestinian's testimony be excluded; and in another case, the charges were withdrawn.[159] At the same time, one judge, despite acknowledging "serious defects in the interrogation," insisted that they "did not result in

---

[156] See, e.g., C. Levinson, "Key Witness Aimed Gun at Palestinian Teen during Police Interview," *Haaretz* (March 13, 2014), www.haaretz.com/news/diplomacy-defense/.premium-1.579534; ACRI, "'Minor A.' from Nabi Saleh: The Rights of Minors in Criminal Proceedings in the West Bank" (2012), www.acri.org.il/en/wp-content/uploads/2012/02/Minors.pdf.

[157] See, e.g., I. Kershner, "Palestinian's Trial Shines Light on Military Justice," *The New York Times* (February 18, 2012), www.nytimes.com/2012/02/19/world/middleeast/palestinians-trial-shines-light-on-justice-system.html; H. Sherwood, "The Palestinian Children – Alone and Bewildered – in Israel's Al Jalame Jail," *The Guardian* (January 22, 2012), www.guardian.co.uk/world/2012/jan/22/palestinian-children-detained-jail-israel.

[158] MilA 2683/11 *Military Prosecution v. Amouri* (December 13, 2011); MilA 2175/12 *Military Prosecution v. Kawazbe* (July 30, 2012).

[159] See, respectively, A. Hass, "In First, Israeli Military Court Throws out Palestinian Boy's Interrogation," *Haaretz* (February 28, 2017), www.haaretz.com/israel-news/.premium-1.774274; C. Levinson, "Israeli Military Drops Charges against Palestinian Youths," *Haaretz* (December 10, 2014), www.haaretz.com/news/diplomacy-defense/.premium-1.630869.

a greater than necessary violation of ... [the defendant's] right to criminal due process."[160]

The preferential treatment of these types of evidence has also informed local human rights work, such as that of Israeli NGOs B'Tselem and Breaking the Silence (whose evidence is cited throughout this chapter), as well as that of the Palestinian organization Youth Against Settlements. B'Tselem describes its project, which is aptly called in Hebrew "armed with cameras," in reference to the privileging of video evidence:

> The impact and power of the written word are greatly amplified when coupled with visual documentation. Images provide a direct experience that cannot be ignored, compelling the viewer to face reality... In 2005, B'Tselem created a video department [and] ... two years later, we ... [began providing] video cameras and training to Palestinians..., helping them become citizen journalists. ... [F]ootage shot by the project's volunteers ... has helped bring to public attention ... incidents that would not have gotten any coverage whatsoever if it were not for the presence of cameras.[161]

Youth Against Settlements has similarly been filming Israeli soldiers' violence in and around the West Bank city of Hebron since 2006. In a video published by the organization in 2014, for example, an Israeli soldier is seen cocking his weapon to intimidate young Palestinians. Another video from the same year shows one of the organization's founders protesting to an Israeli soldier that the organization's "cameras do what you don't do [i.e., protect Palestinians]," to which the soldier replies: "We protect Jews, not you, shitface. ... Mother fucker, the first chance I get I'll shoot you."[162] Breaking the Silence, an organization consisting of former soldiers, publishes their testimonies – the other type of preferred evidence – with the aim of ending Israel's control over the

---

[160] MilC (Judea) 1367/11 *Military Prosecution v. Ayyoub* (January 9, 2012).

[161] B'Tselem, "About B'Tselem Video" (November 19, 2017), www.btselem.org/video/cdp_background. On the NGO's camera project as a form of counter-surveillance, see S. Bachmann and P. P. Miretski, "The Panopticon of International Law: B'Tselem's Camera Project and the Enforcement of International Law in a Transnational Society" (2014) 52 *Osgoode Hall Law Journal* 235.

[162] A. Hass, "'We Are Protecting Jews, Not You, Shitface. When I Get the Chance I Will Shoot You'," *Haaretz* (May 9, 2014), www.haaretz.co.il/news/politics/.premium-1.2316540. On this organization's work, see also Desai, "*Shooting Back* in the Occupied Territories," pp. 120–21. On Palestinian youth movements and their use of technology, see A. Dwonch, *Palestinian Youth Activism in the Internet Age: Online and Offline Social Networks after the Arab Spring* (London and New York: I.B. Tauris, 2019).

West Bank and Gaza Strip. Alluding to the elevated status of this evidence, the NGO describes itself as having "acquired a special standing in the eyes of the Israeli public and in the media because of its unique role in giving voice to the experience of soldiers."[163] The privileged status of the evidence produced by both Breaking the Silence and B'Tselem may explain the considerable attention they have attracted in Israel and overseas, as well as the hostility they have faced from the Israeli government.[164]

At the same time, despite their elevated status, neither corroborative footage nor soldiers' testimonies are guaranteed to lead to prosecution. There are ample examples to the contrary, some of which were touched on earlier.[165] Among the tactics used by Israeli officials to dismiss such evidence is to portray incriminating videos as unclear, incomplete, fabricated, or manipulatively edited, and to accuse critical veterans of lying.[166] Such Israeli dismissals benefit from a broader social and legal ambivalence toward visual evidence: the common belief that visual images are the closest available substitute for seeing the "real" thing,

---

[163] Breaking the Silence, "About Us" (n.d., last accessed on February 25, 2020), www.breakingthesilence.org.il/about/organization. For analysis of this NGO's work, see S. Helman, "Challenging the Israeli Occupation through Testimony and Confession: The Case of Anti-Denial SMOs Machsom Watch and Breaking the Silence" (2015) 28:4 International Journal of Politics, Culture, and Society 377; T. Katriel and N. Shavit, "Speaking Out: Testimonial Rhetoric in Israeli Soldiers' Dissent" (2013) 116 Versus 79.

[164] See, e.g., J. Lis, "Israel Passes Law Meant to Keep Breaking the Silence Out of Schools," Haaretz (July 17, 2018), www.haaretz.com/israel-news/.premium-israel-passes-law-targeting-groups-that-support-soldiers-indictment-1.6284735; Times of Israel staff and R. Ahren, "Netanyahu Denounces B'Tselem Chief's UN Speech as 'Full of Lies'," Times of Israel (October 18, 2018), www.timesofisrael.com/netanyahu-denounces-btselem-chiefs-un-speech-as-full-of-lies.

[165] See, e.g., R. Hovel, "Anti-occupation NGO Spokesman Didn't Lie About Beating a Palestinian, Prosecution Admits," Haaretz (June 24, 2019), www.haaretz.com/israel-news/anti-occupation-ngo-spokesman-didn-t-lie-about-beating-a-palestinian-prosecution-ad-1.7405083; B'Tselem, The Occupation's Fig Leaf, pp. 61, 82; B'Tselem, Whitewash Protocol: The So-Called Investigation of Operation Protective Edge (September 2016), p. 19, www.btselem.org/download/201609_whitewash_protocol_eng.pdf.

[166] See, respectively, N. Sheizaf, "Beitunia Killings and the Media's Incredibly High Bar for Palestinian Stories," +972 Magazine (May 21, 2014), http://972mag.com/beitunia-killings-and-the-medias-incredibly-high-bar-for-palestinian-stories/91166/; J. Maltz, "How Israel Is Trying to Break Breaking the Silence – And How It Could Backfire," Haaretz (November 21, 2017), www.haaretz.com/israel-news/.premium-how-israel-is-trying-to-break-breaking-the-silence-1.5467507.

coupled with the frequent concern about their potential manipulation and deceptiveness.[167]

At the individual level, these types of evidence support Palestinian allegations, potentially increase Palestinians' public visibility, and in some limited instances produce more favorable outcomes for Palestinians. But at the broader level, notwithstanding its considerable value, such corroborating evidence plays into Israel's systematic effort to conceal its violence and discredit alternative types of evidence. It does so in two ways.

First, the privileging of such evidence, by legal as well as human rights actors, ultimately validates Israel's distrust and dismissal of uncorroborated Palestinian allegations. The preference for real-time videos and photographs, in particular, might make more likely, in their absence, the dismissal of other sources of information, including retrospective, first-hand oral testimonies or sketches by the victims. Human rights video activism, while responding to this trend, risks becoming complicit in it. This, as intimated earlier, is made abundantly clear by the language B'Tselem uses about its camera project (capitalization for emphasis in the original):

> "AN IMAGE IS WORTH A THOUSAND WORDS" ... [B'Tselem's footage provides] evidence in cases where the Israeli courts, police and the army chose to underestimate the spoken testimony of [Palestinian plaintiffs or defendants] ... This [sort of evidence makes it] ... impossible to ignore the situation in the occupied territories. ... Photography can change agendas, conduct, and ... influenc[e] public opinion.[168]

If, as this problematic quote suggests, "an image is worth a thousand words," then a Palestinian's word is worth a mere thousandth of what is being characterized as convincing evidence. B'Tselem might thus end up reinforcing what it describes as Israel's tendency to "underestimate ... [Palestinians'] spoken testimony." Consequently, it is not merely that Palestinians' oral and written testimonies continue to be treated by Israel as less reliable, less accurate, and hence inferior. The peril, albeit one difficult to prove, is that each resort to videos and photographs might

---

[167] On this ambivalence, see, e.g., J. L. Mnookin, "The Image of Truth: Photographic Evidence and the Power of Analogy" (1998) 10:1 *Yale Journal of Law & the Humanities* 1, 1–3, 14–43.

[168] B'Tselem, "About B'Tselem Video" (n.d., last accessed on January 23, 2020), www .btselem.org/video/about.

raise the minimum evidentiary threshold expected to be met by future complainants.

Also manifesting this pitfall, albeit differently, are attitudes toward the Israeli state's evidence, be it verbal (perpetrators' confessions and comrades' testimonies) or audiovisual (such as interrogation and security camera videos). The legal system's relative faith in such evidence contrasts sharply with its habitual distrust of Palestinian evidence. Whenever corroborative Israeli evidence is considered as making Palestinian claims more believable than they would otherwise be, this helps Israel brush aside other, uncorroborated Palestinian allegations.

A second pitfall is that such privileged evidence can end up aiding the previously discussed Israeli depiction of violent soldiers as merely a "few rotten apples" unrepresentative of "the world's most moral military."[169] Exemplifying this is the case analyzed earlier concerning the assault of a young and mentally disabled Palestinian. "It is our impression," the judges maintained, "that the case before us does not reflect a norm but, rather, an individual's deviation from the values accepted in the IDF. We have reached this conclusion, among other things, given ... the complaint that was ultimately filed [by a soldier]."[170] Thus, the Israeli judiciary has implied that soldiers' confessions attest to the military's morality and hence substantiate the rarity of violence against Palestinians.

Similarly serving Israel's "rotten apples" narrative is the social and legal tendency to focus on the specific events depicted in photographic and video evidence, by directing attention away from what remains outside the frame: the institutional forces and state agents that enable, cover up, and legitimize such violence. In this regard, valuable lessons can be learned from videos and photographs of torture by US and UK forces: their publication left high-ranking officials unaccountable, as only the perpetrators visible in the images were punished (with relatively lenient sentences).[171]

---

[169] On this Israeli depiction of its military, see, e.g., E. Halperin et al., "Socio-Psychological Implications for an Occupying Society: The Case of Israel" (2010) 47:1 *Journal of Peace Research* 59, 66.

[170] MilC 272/02, p. 5.

[171] For detailed discussion of these pitfalls, see H. Viterbo, "Seeing Torture Anew: A Transnational Reconceptualization of State Torture and Visual Evidence" (2014) 50:2 *Stanford Journal of International Law* 281; H. Viterbo, "Torture's In/visibility," in S. Molloy and L. W. Olson (eds.), *Interdisciplinary Perspectives on Torture* (Leiden and Boston, MA: Brill, 2019), pp. 23–43.

These pitfalls, however, are not inherent to the evidence which tends to be treated as strong. Rather, they reflect and are a product of the specific evidentiary paradigm dominating the social and legal imagination. Alternative approaches to evidence, therefore, may open up possibilities for engaging differently with state violence and childhood. In the next subsection, I explore this potential with visual examples from human rights reports on Israeli state violence against young Palestinians.

6.4.2 Alternative Visual Evidence: Metapictures of Invisibility and Absence

Under the prevailing evidentiary paradigm, visual images tend to qualify as strong evidence only insofar as they offer their viewer a sense of directly witnessing reality. To satisfy this expectation, images must suppress all traces of the mediation and representation at work.[172] Departing from this common conception, I argue that images that fail to meet these standards can be interpreted as possessing a unique evidentiary potential. My focus will be on what visual scholar W. J. T. Mitchell has termed "metapictures" – images of image making, representations of the representation process itself.[173] Rather than suppressing the work of representation, images of this sort bring it center stage. Numerous visual studies have considered the potential of images to invite certain kinds of seeing.[174] Along these lines, I will point to several ways in which visual representations can testify to the invisibility shrouding both state violence and young witnesses.

A Human Rights Watch report from 2009 features such a metapicture on its front and back cover. It is a photograph, as readers are told, of the hands of a Gazan holding "the photos of his daughter Shadar and niece Isra, both killed by an Israeli drone-launched missile."[175] Instead of

---

[172] J. Tagg, *The Burden of Representation: Essays on Photographs and Histories* (Basingstoke: Macmillan Education, 1988), pp. 99–100.

[173] W. J. T. Mitchell, "Metapictures," in his *Picture Theory: Essays on Verbal and Visual Representations* (Chicago and London: University of Chicago Press, 1994), pp. 35–82.

[174] On such studies, see generally G. Rose, *Visual Methodologies: An Introduction to the Interpretation of Visual Materials*, 2nd ed. (Los Angeles and London: Sage, 2007), pp. 11–12.

[175] M. Garlasco et al., *Precisely Wrong: Gaza Civilians Killed by Israeli Drone-Launched Missiles* (New York: Human Rights Watch, June 2009), www.hrw.org/sites/default/files/reports/iopt0609webwcover_0.pdf.

simply using photographs of the two dead girls, the report resorts to this metapicture: a photograph of their photographs in a bereaved Palestinian's hands. This provides a visual testimony centered on the loss and subsequent absence of these young lives. Also accompanying the report is a photographic feature, which includes, along with this picture, another one displaying the same Palestinian man's hands, this time holding remnants of his dead daughter's jeans.[176] The repeated high-lighting of those who outlived or outlasted her – the father, the photo-graph, and the clothes – renders her absence all the more conspicuous, thereby offering a unique visual testimony of the consequences of state violence.[177] Another report, by DCIP, conveys a different and temporary kind of absence: the seven-month-long "administrative detention" of 16-year-old "Salwa S." To emphasize Salwa's absence from home, the report likewise employs a metapicture: a photograph of her grandmother hold-ing the photograph of her incarcerated granddaughter.[178]

Also containing such a metapicture is a 2008 report by the Palestinian Centre for Human Rights. The report describes, among other things, the killing of a 12-year-old Gazan by an Israeli drone missile. Accompanying this textual account is a photograph, which features the bereaved family with a photograph, hanging on a wall behind them, of the deceased.[179] Again, the absence of the young Palestinian is underscored by juxtaposing his past image with the present family members. Two years earlier, the NGO described, in another report, the killing of a nine-year-old Palestinian by Israeli armed forces. This time, those shown in the photograph were her classmates, sat in the classroom in which she had reportedly been killed by Israeli gunfire. Also displayed in the picture are other markers of her death and

[176] Garlasco et al., *Precisely Wrong*, p. 9.
[177] Cf. H. Belting, "Image, Medium, Body: A New Approach to Iconography" (2005) 31:2 *Critical Inquiry* 302, 312 (arguing that images of the dead maintain the body's absence and turn it into "visible absence").
[178] DCIP, *Palestinian Child Prisoners: The Systematic and Institutionalised Ill-treatment and Torture of Palestinian Children by Israeli Authorities* (June 15, 2009), p. 85, https://d3n8a8pro7vhmx.cloudfront.net/dcipalestine/pages/1298/attachments/original/1433987832/DCIP_childprisoner_report.pdf?1433987832 [hereinafter: "*Palestinian Child Prisoners 2009*"].
[179] Palestinian Centre for Human Rights, *Blood on Their Hands: Child Killings by the Israeli Occupation Forces (IOF) in the Gaza Strip, June 2007 – June 2008* (2008), p. 47, www.pchrgaza.org/files/Reports/English/pdf_spec/Blood%20on%20their%20hands.pdf.

absence: a wreath placed on what used to be her desk, as well as her dress spread over the adjacent bench and desk.[180]

Reenactment photographs are metapictures of a different kind. Sometimes, as in three DCIP reports from 2009, the reenactors are the young Palestinians claiming to have been abused at the Israeli military's hands. One photograph shows a ten-year-old reenacting the stress position to which he alleged he had been subjected: standing on one foot and lifting his hands in the air for about half an hour.[181] Two other photographs feature two Palestinians, aged 15 and 16, who are seen jointly reenacting how soldiers detained and used them as human shields (a practice discussed in the next chapter). Two more photographs present four Palestinians, 12–13-year-olds, reenacting their detention, handcuffing, and blindfolding by the army.[182] Treating reenactment images as nothing but a simulation of real events misses their capacity to call attention to the absence of real-time photographs or videos that would more likely be considered strong corroborating evidence. Perhaps, as social theorist Didier Fassin suggests, testimony derives its value fundamentally from what is absent from it – an absence that bears witness to what cannot be witnessed.[183] Maybe, as social theorist Judith Butler has argued, although visual images can fail to capture their referents, they also have the potential to display this very failure.[184] Seen in this light, such images can bring to mind the reason for having to resort to

[180] Palestinian Centre for Human Rights, *Confirm the Kill: IOF Killings of Children during the al-Aqsa Intifada* (May 29, 2006), p. 32, www.pchrgaza.org/files/S&r/English/pdf/confirm_study_38.pdf.

[181] DCIP, *Palestinian Child Prisoners 2009*, pp. 88–90.

[182] These four photographs appear in DCIP, *Bearing the Brunt Again: Child Rights Violations during Operation Cast Lead* (September 2009), pp. 53–54, 101, 105, https://d3n8a8pro7vhmx.cloudfront.net/dcipalestine/pages/1284/attachments/original/1433971286/Bearing_the_Brunt_Again_September_2009.pdf?1433971286. The latter two photographs also appear in DCIP and Defence for Children – Israel, *Alternative Report for Consideration Regarding Israel's Initial OPAC Periodic Report to the Committee on the Rights of the Child* (July 17, 2009), pp. 47, 49, 51, https://reliefweb.int/sites/reliefweb.int/files/resources/72FF6238DD307E8A852576110057D764-Full_Report.pdf.

[183] D. Fassin, "The Humanitarian Politics of Testimony: Subjectification through Trauma in the Israeli–Palestinian Conflict" (2008) 23:3 *Cultural Anthropology* 531, 535–36. Fassin's argument draws on G. Agamben, *Remnants of Auschwitz: The Witness and the Archive* (New York: Zone Books, 1999). On the importance of analyzing seemingly absent or invisible elements of images, see Rose, *Visual Methodologies*, p. 165.

[184] J. Butler, *Precarious Life: The Powers of Mourning and Violence* (London and New York: Verso, 2004), p. 146. See also ibid., p. 144.

reenactment in the first place: the state's concerted efforts to hide its violence from unwanted audiences. This makes concealment part of the story and thus possibly opens it up for critical scrutiny.[185]

A similar evidentiary potential, albeit by different means, can be attached to a photograph in a 2003 publication by the Swedish section of Save the Children. Presented in the photograph are three elements of a representation process: first, the witness, a 16-year-old Palestinian; second, the platform for her visual testimony, a sketchbook she is holding; and, third, her visual testimony, drawings illustrating the torture positions and violence she claims to have suffered in an Israeli prison. By presenting all three elements together, this photograph can do more than authenticate her visual testimony; it also juxtaposes her "real" self with her "unrealistic," amateurish, and retroactive sketches, characterized by a childlike simplicity. This juxtaposition may offer a reminder of the absence of seemingly more realistic, and hence supposedly stronger, visual evidence, which required her to draw her experiences from memory. As if reiterating this reminder, one of her sketches reappears elsewhere in the report.[186] These images, like reenactment photographs, potentially furnish evidence not only of the violence and abuse they seek to capture, but also of the state apparatus that conceals and prevents audiovisual records. This provides a visual framework for scrutinizing the role of representation and invisibility with regard to state violence.

Sketches portraying detained Palestinian youth in torture positions are also found in two publications by DCIP.[187] Created by a professional illustrator, these drawings appear more realistic than those by the 16-year-old Palestinian, but they are also condemned to a lesser evidentiary status than that of first-hand sketches by victims or witnesses. The drawings are, therefore, likely to be seen not as evidence per se, but, at best, as merely illustrating the evidence on which they are based: the

---

[185] On the potential of images to expose mechanisms of restriction, regulation, and censorship, see Butler, *Precarious Life*, pp. 71–73.

[186] M. Gröndahl, *One Day in Prison – Feels Like a Year: Palestinian Children Tell Their Own Stories* (Stockholm: Save the Children – Sweden, 2003), pp. 18–19, 21, www .palestinasolidariteit.be/sites/default/files/One%20day%20in%20Prison%20-%20English .pdf.

[187] C. Cook, A. Hanieh, and A. Kay (in association with DCIP), *Stolen Youth: The Politics of Israel's Detention of Palestinian Children* (London: Pluto Press, 2004), p. 79; DCIP, *Palestinian Child Prisoners* (2007), pp. 3–4, 7, 13, 43, https://archive.crin.org/en/docs/ PCPReport.pdf.

verbal testimonies of young former detainees. However, the illustrator's drawings enable their viewers to look invisibility in the face, so to speak: like images in other reports,[188] they all present detained Palestinians as blindfolded or hooded. In so doing, these images cast light on the decisive impact of invisibility on how detained Palestinians, their Israeli captors, and the viewer all experience or perceive state violence.[189] This potentially creates some affinity between the viewer and the depicted detainee, both of whom are forced to be visually impaired, albeit in radically different ways, by state concealment.

Moreover, the concealment of eyes and faces in these images can be interpreted as allegorical of two issues tackled in this and previous chapters. The first is law's all-too-frequent failure to prevent, disavow, and bring to light state violence. The resemblance of the depicted figures to the blindfolded Lady Justice – the personification of the law – provides an opportunity to critically reflect on this contribution of the law to state violence. Although Lady Justice's blindfold has come to symbolize the supposed impartiality of law, it once signified something quite different: law's inability to deliver justice.[190] As my findings so far suggest, this critical interpretation of the iconic blindfold deserves reviving.

The second issue concerns the doubts facing young complainants and witnesses. Far from exclusive to state authorities, such doubts are also, as shown in the previous chapter, expressed by the human rights organizations that claim to represent these young people's interests. The Palestinian eyes and faces covered in DCIP's report are specifically those of under-18s – exactly the age group subject to this suspicion. This might prevent these illustrations from prompting the sort of emotional reaction typically expected to be elicited by photographs of suffering or crying

---

[188] See, e.g., Y. Lein, *Absolute Prohibition: The Torture and Ill-treatment of Palestinian Detainees* (Jerusalem: B'Tselem and Hamoked, May 2007), pp. 50, 52, 70, 72, 73, www.btselem.org/download/200705_utterly_forbidden_eng.pdf; DCIP, *Bearing the Brunt Again*, p. 101; DCIP, *Palestinian Child Prisoners 2009*, p. 88.

[189] For a similar analysis in a different context, see W. J. T. Mitchell, *Cloning Terror: The War of Images, 9/11 to the Present* (Chicago and London: University of Chicago Press, 2011), p. 62.

[190] E. Panofsky, *Studies in Iconology: Humanistic Themes in the Art of the Renaissance* (New York: Harper & Row, 1972), pp. 109–10; M. Jay, "Must Justice Be Blind?: The Challenge of Images to the Law," in C. Douzinas and L. Nead (eds.), *Law and the Image: The Authority of Art and the Aesthetics of Law* (Chicago and London: University of Chicago Press, 1999), pp. 19–35.

young faces[191] (such as those appearing elsewhere in human rights reports).[192] But allegorically, this concealment of young people's mouths and eyes parallels the distrust of their testimonies, thereby rendering conspicuous their invisibility as witnesses.

None of these visual effects are necessarily those intended by the authors of the reports. Nevertheless, visual representations have a life of their own and as such lend themselves to multiple interpretations, apart from any intentions those who produced them may have had. Further, for reasons explained in the methodology section of Chapter 1, intentions are problematic as an explanatory concept.[193] Equally, while there is no assurance that the suggested engagement with metapictures is probable or intuitive, evidentiary potential is not a matter of if and how some viewers can or will react. If certain responses are currently considered improbable or counterintuitive, then visual intuition ought to be reinvented by challenging the dominant social assumptions surrounding such images. This would enable engaging with visual representations not only as objects obstructed by state-induced invisibility, but also as means to render conspicuous the relationship between in/visibility and state violence.

This, however, does not simply mean that supposedly weak visual evidence is actually strong, or vice versa. The objective of the proposed critical aesthetic is not simply to have visual images expose the invisibility surrounding state violence and childhood, but rather to investigate how, and to what effect, visual representations, like the violence and childhood they aim to portray, oscillate between invisibility and visibility, absence and presence. Moreover, the task at hand is not to "resolve" the in/visibility of state violence by proclaiming the invisible to be visible or vice versa, as if such a thing is even possible. Instead, alternative ways of looking and thinking may call for the visible/invisible binary to be deconstructed.

[191] On the emotionally evocative power of young faces crying or suffering, see, e.g., Holland, *Picturing Childhood*, pp. 143–77; K. Wells, *Childhood in a Global Perspective* (Cambridge and Malden, MA: Polity Press, 2009), pp. 30–43.
[192] See, e.g., Palestinian Centre for Human Rights, *Confirm the Kill*, pp. 10–11, 22–23, 27–29; DCIP, *Bearing the Brunt Again*, p. 46.
[193] See specifically Chapter 1, Section 1.4 ("Methodology and Sources").

7

Infantilization and Militarism: Soldiers as Children, Children as Soldiers

7.1   Introduction: The Child/Soldier Dyad

From a human rights perspective, childhood belongs outside the military realm. The child and the soldier, in this view, are and should remain diametric opposites, in order to prevent the contamination of childhood and of its associated innocence, purity, and vulnerability.[1] However, the blind spots and perils of such essentialist, developmentalist, and legalistic views are made abundantly clear throughout this book. Take, for example, the position that those classified as children (as well as those classified as women) should be presumed noncombatants and hence spared harm. This position has ended up rendering men above the age of majority, absent exonerating evidence, killable by belligerent parties. Also overlooked by those taking this position are the unique vulnerabilities of draft-age men in armed conflict, such as their higher risk of being summarily killed, arbitrarily detained, and forcefully recruited. Humanitarian agencies, wishing to appear neutral, find it less controversial to assist affected people defined as children than those defined as older men.[2] This brings to mind the 2016 Red Cross decision, criticized

---

[1] On romantic anxieties about the contamination of childhood specifically, see, e.g., A. Taylor, "Reconceptualizing the 'Nature' of Childhood" (2011) 18:4 *Childhood* 420, 422, 429. This sentiment may have informed some of the criticism of Israel's "military youth court," the legal invention analyzed in Chapter 4 (Section 4.2, "Hyperlegality, Tokenism, and the Rule of Exception"), which professes to marry what otherwise tend to be considered two complete strangers: youth justice and military law. See, e.g., S. Ben-Natan, "Abolish the Israeli Juvenile Military Court," *Social Justice* (January 31, 2018), www.socialjusticejournal.org/abolish-the-israeli-juvenile-military-court ("Israel should completely renounce the prosecution of children and teenagers in military courts, abolishing the Juvenile Military Court altogether").

[2] R. C. Carpenter, *'Innocent Women and Children': Gender, Norms and the Protection of Civilians* (London and New York: Routledge, 2006). For a related example involving US drone attacks on older men in Afghanistan, see C. Wilke, "Seeing and Unmaking Civilians in Afghanistan: Visual Technologies and Contested Professional Visions" (2017) 42:6 *Science, Technology & Human Values* 1031, 1045.

in Chapter 4, to reduce family visits for imprisoned Palestinian men while leaving unchanged visits for their younger and/or female counterparts.

Similarly, the widely held image of "child soldiers" as victims[3] misrepresents reality, as does their portrayal as deviant products of adult abuse. In the overwhelming majority of cases, the young people in question, rather than being forcefully recruited or abducted, join armed forces voluntarily, and many of them later describe their participation in combat as liberating and empowering. To deem their actions and views as irrational not only oversimplifies their sociopolitical circumstances and disregards their reasons for enlisting, but it also idealizes the autonomy and independence of older people. Moreover, whereas former young soldiers have been granted access to postwar development funds, their victims have often been neglected.[4]

For these and other reasons, and in line with the anti-essentialism guiding me since Chapter 1, I refrain from joining the many scholars and human rights activists who uncritically call to enforce the existing child/soldier distinction. Instead, my aim in this chapter is to cast new light on the subject by tackling the following questions: How do the categories "child" and "soldier" inform, and how are they shaped by, legal and human rights discourses? What role do militarism and childhood – two major forces in Israeli society – play in this regard? And, crucially, what are the political consequences for each of the populations concerned: Palestinians and Israelis?

Section 7.2 addresses these questions by analyzing court cases concerning either soldiers' violence against Palestinians, particularly those below the age of 18, or military hazing. As I will demonstrate, both Israeli law and the local human rights discourse, while formally labeling soldiers as adults, also infantilize – characterize as children – those charged with abuse and violence. I will pay special attention to the conjuring up, in judgments involving violence against Palestinians aged under 18, of two potentially conflicting childhoods: that of the young Palestinian and that of the accused soldier.

---

[3] See, e.g., UNCRC, General Comment No. 6: Treatment of Unaccompanied and Separated Children Outside Their Country of Origin, 39th session, UN Doc CRG/GC/2005/6 (May–June 2005) ("Child soldiers should be considered primarily as victims of armed conflict").

[4] See, e.g., D. M. Rosen, "Child Soldiers, International Humanitarian Law, and the Globalization of Childhood" (2007) 109:2 *American Anthropologist* 296; H. G. West, "Girls with Guns: Narrating the Experience of War of FRELIMO's 'Female Detachment'" (2000) 73:4 *Anthropological Quarterly* 180.

Offering a complementary perspective, Section 7.3 will turn to the militarization of the young – that is, their characterization or treatment in military terms. Regarding young Palestinians, I will discuss their use (alleged or actual) as human shields, as well as Israeli contentions that they are trained for combat from an early age. Regarding young Israelis, specifically those evacuated from settlements in the Gaza Strip, I will examine their portrayal as soldiers in the making. Across these contexts, I will inspect how state actors (lawyers and others), as well as human rights critics, invoke, shape, and challenge two versions of the child/ soldier dichotomy: first, international law's categorization of people below certain ages as protected civilians (as opposed to non-protected combatants), and, second, the international legal ban on recruiting underage soldiers.

7.2 Soldiers as Children

Childhood is a category of personhood imposed on individuals of all ages.[5] Accordingly, conceptions and representations of childhood evince anxieties, hopes, and attempts to gain control not only over those legally classified as children, but also over the child in every adult.[6] Infantilization – the characterization or treatment of formally adult individuals as children – brings some of this dynamic to the surface.

Infantilization operates in diverse and, at times, conflicting ways. Over the course of human history, various groups have been infantilized, among whom are women, non-White groups,[7] the elderly,[8] the Global

---

[5] D. Archard, *Children: Rights and Childhood* (New York: Routledge, 1993), pp. 36–37; D. Kennedy, *The Well of Being: Childhood, Subjectivity, and Education* (Albany: State University of New York Press, 2006), p. 144.

[6] D. Buckingham, *After the Death of Childhood: Growing Up in the Age of Electronic Media* (Cambridge: Polity, 2000), p. 10; P. Holland, *Picturing Childhood: The Myth of the Child in Popular Imagery* (London and New York: I.B. Tauris, 2004), pp. 15–16.

[7] Regarding both women and non-White groups, see, e.g., C. T. Field, *The Struggle for Equal Adulthood: Gender, Race, Age, and the Fight for Citizenship in Antebellum America* (Chapel Hill: University of North Carolina Press, 2014).

[8] See, e.g., M. Salari and M. Rich, "Social and Environmental Infantilization of Aged Persons: Observations in Two Adult Day Care Centers" (2001) 52:2 *International Journal of Aging and Human Development* 115.

South,[9] mental asylum inmates,[10] and criminals.[11] While each has been treated differently, there is a common thread: their infantilization has reinforced their perceived status as deficient, other, incapable of exercising certain rights, and, accordingly, in need of special supervision, control, and even outright subjugation.[12] Similar has been the infantilization of Palestinian society in Israeli state rhetoric. "Palestinians," Israeli prime minister Benjamin Netanyahu asserted in 2018, "are like a spoiled child ... They are not interested in dialogue and they are refusing to make peace."[13]

A country's own armed forces, however, are an entirely different matter. As the nation's sons and daughters – the children of the motherland or fatherland – their infantilization typically signals the need for a familial-like love. This sort of love involves varied and sometimes competing attitudes: mercy (including leniency and even impunity for lawbreaking soldiers, as elaborated in the previous chapter), tough love (strict disciplining), guidance, or support. Thus, as early as the fifth century BCE, Chinese military strategist Sun Tzu advised rulers: "Regard your soldiers as your children, and they will follow you into the deepest valleys; look upon them as your own beloved sons, and they will stand by you even unto death."[14] Since then, military personnel have cited his advice[15] and voiced similar views. A US Army Lieutenant Colonel's 1921 article, for instance, instructed officers: "Soldiers are much like children. You must see that they have shelter, food and

---

[9] See, e.g., E. Burman, "Innocents Abroad: Western Fantasies of Childhood and the Iconography of Emergencies" (1994) 18:3 *Disasters* 238.

[10] M. Foucault, *Madness and Civilization* (Abingdon: Routledge, 1989), p. 239 ("Madness is childhood. Everything in the Retreat is organized so that the insane are transformed into minors. They are regarded as 'children who have an overabundance of strength and make use of it'.").

[11] J. Muncie, *Youth and Crime*, 3rd ed. (Los Angeles and London: Sage, 2009), p. 67 (quoting the influential psychologist Granville Stanley Hall: "criminals are like overgrown children").

[12] At the same time, some members of colonized groups sought to be legally classified as minors in order to gain greater leverage with the colonial authorities. See B. Premo, "Meticulous Imprecision: Calculating Age in Colonial Spanish American Law" (2020) 125:2 *American Historical Review* 396.

[13] "PM Netanyahu's Remarks at the Start of the Weekly Cabinet Meeting," *Israel Ministry of Foreign Affairs* (March 20, 2018), https://mfa.gov.il/MFA/PressRoom/2018/Pages/PM-Netanyahu's-remarks-at-the-start-of-the-weekly-Cabinet-meeting–20-March-2018.aspx.

[14] Sun Tzu, *The Art of War*, L. Giles (trans.) (Leicester: Allandale, 2015), p. 44.

[15] See, e.g., E. C. O'Dowd and R. F. Schopp, "International Human Rights, Morality in War, and the Structure of Rights" (1993) 2:1 *Pacific Rim Law & Policy Journal* 37, 43.

clothing, the best that your utmost efforts can provide. You must be far more solicitous of their comfort than of your own. ... And by doing all these things you are ... creating a soul in the organization that will make the mass respond to you as though it were one."[16] Countries involved in the First and Second World Wars, too, infantilized their armed forces.[17]

In this section, I will investigate how, and to what effect, soldiers are infantilized in Israeli law and society. Following an overview of the dual image of soldiers as adults and children, I will home in on cases involving soldiers' violence against Palestinians, especially those aged under 18, as well as their violence against other soldiers as part of hazing rituals. As noted in Chapter 1, child law scholarship focuses on issues concerning those statutorily defined as children; in contrast, the analysis that follows offers a broader framework for thinking about law's relationship with childhood and state violence.

7.2.1 Between Adulthood and Childhood

The invention of childhood as a separate and distinct category, an issue discussed in Chapter 1, was equally the invention of adulthood in its modern form.[18] Israeli society regards its soldiers as simultaneously occupying both categories – child and adult[19] – a duality reflected in law. On the one hand, the statutory age of conscription, 18 years,[20] is the same as the statutory age of adulthood.[21] "Clearly," the supreme court

[16] C. A. Bach, "When an Officer Leads His Men" (1921) 13:68 *The Military Engineer* 178, 180.

[17] See, respectively, D. Jiménez Torres, "Journalists at the Front: Ramiro de Maeztu, Inglaterra en armas and Spanish Intellectuals during the First World War" (2013) 90:8 *Bulleting of Spanish Studies* 1291, 1292, 1302–03; M. K. Winchell, "'To Make the Boys Feel at Home': USO Senior Hostesses and Gendered Citizenship" (2004) 25:1 *Frontiers* 190.

[18] Kennedy, *The Well of Being*, pp. 5, 63, 76–78.

[19] On changes over time in social perceptions of soldiers as adults or children, see E. Lomsky-Feder and E. Ben-Ari, "Trauma, Therapy and Responsibility: Psychology and War in Contemporary Israel," in A. Rao, M. Bollig, and M. Böck (eds.), *The Practice of War: Production, Reproduction and Communication of Armed Violence* (New York and Oxford: Berghahn Books, 2007), pp. 120, 123; Z. Israeli and E. Rosman-Stollman, "Men and Boys: Representations of Israeli Combat Soldiers in the Media" (2015) 30:1 *Israel Studies Review* 66.

[20] Article 13 of Defense Service Law (Integrated Version), 1986 [hereinafter: Defense Service Law].

[21] Article 1 of the Youth Law (Adjudication, Punishment, and Modes of Treatment), 1971; Article 3 of the Law of Legal Competence and Guardianship, 1962.

observed in 2016, "a young person does not become a prudent and responsible adult 'overnight' on his 18th birthday, yet the legislature has deemed this age a transition point, in which one legally becomes an adult, is eligible to vote, to enlist in relevant circumstances and so forth."[22] Added to these confluent statutory age thresholds is an enduring perception of the male warrior as an epitome of ultimate (adult) manhood.[23] Moreover, contrary to most other countries with compulsory military service,[24] Israel conscripts women as well as men, thereby extending this marker of adulthood regardless of gender (while exempting from conscription on the basis of ethnicity and religion instead, including exemptions for Palestinian citizens and ultra-Orthodox Jews).[25]

Soldiers, then, are supposed to be adults, both culturally and legally. Their status as such has been reiterated by courts-martial in a wide variety of cases. One judgment, concerning a soldier who had killed his unit members, justified his conviction as follows: "a minor's criminal responsibility is reduced [by law] ... A soldier, in contrast, is not a minor."[26] Another case saw the defense attorney contending, unsuccessfully, that a 19-year-old soldier was "verging on a minor's age and should thus be sentenced by the same standards applicable to minors." The judges rejected this argument, emphasizing that "the defendant is not and was not a minor at the time of the offense."[27]

On the other hand, statutorily adult soldiers are infantilized in various ways. Traceable back to the early years of Israeli statehood,[28] such infantilization is reproduced by state officials and Israeli human rights activists alike. "The soldiers of the IDF, our children, maintain high ethical values while courageously fighting against bloodthirsty

---

[22] CrimA 3673/15 *John Doe v. State of Israel* (2016), ¶ 27.

[23] Israeli and Rosman-Stollman, "Men and Boys," pp. 67–68; O. Livio, "Producing Soldier Boy: Sperm Donation Discourse and Militarism in Israeli Media Culture" (2018) 35:3 *Critical Studies in Media Communication* 259.

[24] Central Intelligence Agency, *The World Factbook – Military Service Age and Obligation* (n.d., last accessed on February 20, 2020), www.cia.gov/library/publications/the-world-factbook/fields/333.html.

[25] Articles 13, 26b–26x, 36, 40 of Defense Service Law.

[26] CMA 158/98 *Cohen v. Chief Military Prosecutor* (May 10, 1999), ¶ f.

[27] MilA 133/03 *Tubasi v. Military Prosecutor* (May 10, 2004), ¶¶ 5–7 of judge Friedman's leading opinion.

[28] Y. Dekel, "'A World for Itself and for Its Silences': Silence and the Nation in *The Days of Ziklag*" (2018) 59 *Hebrew Studies* 315, 324, 331–33.

murderers," prime minister Netanyahu said in 2016.[29] The Israeli judiciary, too, has depicted soldiers as childish in numerous circumstances.[30] Breaking the Silence, an Israeli NGO whose work I discussed in the previous chapter, has echoed this infantilization. One of the NGO's founding members thus condemned sending "young children" to these territories: "we all know [soldiers are] ... young children... [T]here's no preparation to the army that can make [Israel's presence] ... a more moral situation. ... Controlling men, women, children, old folk, there's no way around it."[31] Other veterans, testifying to the NGO about their military service, referred to combat troops as "19-year-old kids," "20-year-old kids," and even infants. One analogized soldiers' power over Palestinians to that of merciless children over ants: "You feel like a child playing around with a magnifying glass, burning up ants. Really. A 20-year-old kid should not be doing such things to people."[32]

Soldiers' oscillation between childhood and adulthood sets the conditions of possibility for a broad range of positions and practices. Some testimonies of women veterans, published by Breaking the Silence, are an example. When critically recounting misconduct during their military service, they repeatedly attributed it to the childishness, immaturity, and young age of active duty men. Infantilizing the men soldiers alone enabled them to distinguish and thus, to an extent, absolve themselves as mature and composed.[33] The judgments analyzed in the following

---

[29] R. Flood, "Israeli Prime Minister Benjamin Netanyahu Defends Soldier Who Allegedly Shot Unarmed Palestinians," *The Independent* (March 27, 2016), www.independent.co.uk/news/world/middle-east/israeli-prime-minister-benjamin-netanyahu-now-defending-soldier-who-allegedly-shot-unarmed-a6955201.html.

[30] For examples concerning soldiers who stole military weapons, see CMC (Ground Forces) 134/02 *Chief Military Prosecutor v. Dinai* (May 5, 2002); CMC (Ground Forces) 329/03 *Chief Military Prosecutor v. Rami* (October 20, 2003); CMC (North) 118/03 *Military Prosecutor v. Mulla* (February 26, 2004). On defendants' infantilization in non-military Israeli court proceedings, see Y. Eliaz, "Labeling 'Childishness' in Court" (forthcoming) *Law, Culture and the Humanities*.

[31] Quoted in J. Eastwood, *Ethics as a Weapon of War: Militarism and Morality in Israel* (Cambridge and New York: Cambridge University Press, 2017), p. 162.

[32] Quoted in Breaking the Silence, *Soldiers' Testimonies from Operation Cast Lead, Gaza 2009* (June 2009), p. 88, www.breakingthesilence.org.il/wp-content/uploads/2011/02/Operation_Cast_Lead_Gaza_2009_Eng.pdf; Breaking the Silence, *Children and Youth – Soldiers' Testimonies 2005–2011* (2012), pp. 63–65, www.breakingthesilence.org.il/wp-content/uploads/2012/08/Children_and_Youth_Soldiers_Testimonies_2005_2011_Eng.pdf.

[33] O. Sasson-Levy, Y. Levy, and E. Lomsky-Feder, "Women Breaking the Silence: Military Service, Gender, and Antiwar Protest" (2011) 25:6 *Gender & Society* 740, 751–53.

subsections further highlight the ways in which the Israeli judiciary, while professing to hold violent soldiers to "adult" standards and thus protect Israel's image, also depicts and treats them as childlike victims of Israel's control over Palestinians.

In and beyond these contexts, at least three key factors amplify Israeli soldiers' infantilization. The first is their relatively young age. With military service normally being two-and-a-half years for men and two years for women,[34] most active duty soldiers are 18–20 years of age. This has been a source of social concern as well as hope. On the one hand, some, such as court-martial judges in 2004, have warned that young soldiers lack maturity and life experience, and, therefore, are more prone to violence against Palestinians.[35] Voicing a similar concern, a former squad commander once suggested that young soldiers are impulsive and hence wrong to consider themselves adults: "You have 18-year-old guys ... [each taught] to shoot with all kinds of 'tools' he only saw in movies, and now he has the opportunity. And I [the young soldier] hate them [the Palestinians] ... [You] don't think too much, you are 18–19, you are sure you are an adult."[36] For others, on the other hand, it is precisely this immaturity that enables the military to achieve its aims. "Let's be honest," one Israeli publicist wrote in the country's most widely read daily in 2018, "we conscript them very young ... because it is highly doubtful that they would agree to do at a later age what they do at the age of 18."[37] A platoon commander added, in a 2017 interview, that an 18-year-old's "hormones ... ultimately make him a good combatant ... This is the best age ... I think, at the age of 20, 21, you become a bit more restrained, you don't do things, but on the other hand it's a good age, ... sometimes in this job you don't need to be restrained."[38]

A second factor contributing to soldiers' infantilization is the growing involvement of parents in military matters. Over the years, regular

[34] Articles 15–16 of Defense Service Law.
[35] CMC (Center) 300/04 *Military Prosecutor* v. *John Doe* (September 21, 2004), pp. 4–5.
[36] Quoted in E. Grassiani, *Soldiering under Occupation: Processes of Numbing Among Israeli Soldiers in the Al-Aqsa Intifada* (New York and Oxford: Berghahn, 2013), pp. 59–60.
[37] G. Distal Atabarian, "The Sniper's Video: They Exulted, So What?," *Israel Hayom* (April 10, 2018) [Hebrew], www.israelhayom.co.il/opinion/548145. On the unrivaled readership of this paper, see N. Price, "Mid-2016 TGI Poll: Israel Hayom Increases Gap; Haaretz Collapses," *Walla News* (July 25, 2016) [Hebrew], https://b.walla.co.il/item/2982163.
[38] *The Strategic Corporal* (Channel 1 report, A. Binyamin and L. Amir Barmatz directors, A. Rilanger producer, January 12, 2017), www.youtube.com/watch?v=n3hHMenHvO0 (quote appears around 13:20 minutes).

parental visits to military bases have been introduced, parents' complaints to the military ombudsman have mounted, and parent-run political movements on ad hoc issues seem to have had significant success.[39] Protests of bereaved parents have attracted particularly heightened public attention,[40] as have those of parents whose sons or daughters were subject to criminal or disciplinary action. Parental protest of the latter sort arose in a number of cases, including: troops who refused to evacuate unauthorized Jewish settlements in 2007;[41] a soldier (mentioned later in this chapter) who fatally shot a wounded Palestinian in 2017;[42] and a military officer who physically assaulted a Palestinian in 2009. Following the latter's conviction, a group of mothers penned an open letter to the chief of the general staff, repeatedly referring to soldiers as "children": "you ..., who send our children to perform the mission, should provide us as parents with answers ... [about] what happens when our children are faced with borderline situations ... Should we stand along with our children ... opposite the ... [top military command] who have abandoned them ...?"[43] Although subscribing to different political views, parents whose sons and daughters testified for Breaking the Silence have challenged neither the perception of soldiers as children nor Israel's militarism. One parent decried that "service in the territories ... lacerates in our children's souls," while another remarked: "this is not what we send our children to the military for."[44] The relatively low salaries of active duty soldiers (in the range of an eighth to a quarter of the median

---

[39] Y. Bilu and E. Witztum, "War-Related Loss and Suffering in Israeli Society: An Historical Perspective" (2000) 5:2 *Israel Studies* 1, 24; H. Herzog, "Family-Military Relations in Israel as a Genderizing Social Mechanism" (2004) 31:1 *Armed Forces & Society* 5, 9.

[40] G. Doron and U. Lebel, "Penetrating the Shields of Institutional Immunity: The Political Dynamic of Bereavement in Israel" (2004) 9:2 *Mediterranean Politics* 201.

[41] See E. Oshri, "Dad and Mom's Soldiers," *Haaretz* (September 16, 2007) [Hebrew], www.haaretz.co.il/opinions/1.1441808.

[42] See R. Wootlif, "Hebron Shooter Takes Fight for Pardon to the Knesset," *Times of Israel* (March 16, 2017), www.timesofisrael.com/hebron-shooter-takes-fight-for-pardon-to-the-knesset/; Time of Israel staff, "Parents of Hebron Shooter Berate Ex-Defense Minister at Synagogue," *Times of Israel* (July 14, 2018), www.timesofisrael.com/parents-of-hebron-shooter-berate-ex-defense-minister-at-jerusalem-synagogue/.

[43] R. Sharon, "Combatants' Mothers Demand of Ashkenazi: Back the Officer," *NRG* (September 22, 2009) [Hebrew], www.makorrishon.co.il/nrg/online/1/ART1/945/507.html.

[44] C. Kotas-Bar, "This Is Not What We Send Our Children to the Military for," *NRG* (January 21, 2005) [Hebrew], www.makorrishon.co.il/nrg/online/1/ART/859/654.html.

salary, depending on their role)[45] further entrenches their infantilization, especially because of their resultant financial dependence on their parents.

The third and final contributing factor – further explored in Chapters 5 and 8 – is the increased public prominence of mental health. Israeli society, and the military specifically, have placed growing emphasis on psychology, therapeutic models, and, accordingly, soldiers' emotional health.[46] This is evidenced by the judgments to be analyzed shortly, which concern soldiers' violence against Palestinians. Figuring centrally in these judgments are claims about the defendants' "trauma," "loss," "post-traumatic stress disorder," and "psychological fatigue," which are attributed to military service or the loss of fellow soldiers. Usually drawing on psychological evaluations, this language provides a moral grammar for casting soldiers who harm Palestinians into the role of traumatized war victims[47] and thus, potentially, absolving them of responsibility.[48] Indeed, on several occasions, the courts accepted such claims as a basis for mitigation.[49]

In some other instances, however, such claims were dismissed,[50] perhaps illustrating the messiness inherent to any discourse. Nonetheless,

---

[45] R. Zinger, "Approved by the Government: Combatant Salary to Increase to 1,616 NIS Per Month," *Calcalist* (December 6, 2015) [Hebrew], www.calcalist.co.il/local/articles/0,7340, L-3675242,00.html; M. Peled, "4.5% Increase in Median Salary in a Year Not Necessarily Cause for Celebration," *Calcalist* (October 18, 2017) [Hebrew], www.calcalist.co.il/local/articles/0,7340,L-3723025,00.html.

[46] Bilu and Witztum, "War-Related Loss and Suffering in Israeli Society," p. 24; Lomsky-Feder and Ben-Ari, "Trauma, Therapy and Responsibility," pp. 114–15, 120–22; K. Friedman-Peleg, "They Shoot, Cry and Are Treated: The 'Clinical Nucleus' of Trauma among IDF Soldiers," in her *PTSD and the Politics of Trauma in Israel: A Nation on the Couch* (Toronto and London: Toronto University Press, 2017), p. 78.

[47] R. McGarry and N. Ferguson, "Exploring Representations of the Soldier as Victim: From Northern Ireland to Iraq," in S. Gibson and S. Mollan (eds.), *Representations of Peace and Conflict* (Basingstoke and New York: Palgrave Macmillan, 2012), p. 120; R. Morag, *Waltzing with Bashir: Perpetrator Trauma and Cinema* (London and New York: I.B. Tauris, 2013).

[48] Lomsky-Feder and Ben-Ari, "Trauma, Therapy and Responsibility," pp. 121–22.

[49] CMC (Center) 272/02 *Chief Military Prosecutor v. Cohen* (2002); CMC 291/02 (Center) *Military Advocate v. Uzzeri* (2002); CrimC (Jer. Dist.) 157/03 *State of Israel v. Butvika* (verdict September 2, 2008, sentencing April 27, 2009); CMC (Center) 222/03 *Chief Military Prosecutor v. Lieberman* (July 8, 2003); CrimA 5136/08 *State of Israel v. Lalza* (March 31, 2009); CrimC (Jer. Dist.) 2420-05-11 *State of Israel v. Uzeri* (January 12, 2012); CrimA 9507/11 *Sevilia v. State of Israel* (April 4, 2012).

[50] CMA 146/03 *Chief Military Prosecutor v. Rozner* (August 21, 2003); CrimC (Jer. Dist.) 390/04 *State of Israel v. Brier* (April 5, 2005).

while rejecting the claims in relation to the specific defendants, the judges made sure to note the potentially traumatizing nature of combat service more broadly. In principle, recognizing this large-scale trauma could erode support of continued Israeli control over noncitizen Palestinians. However, in mainstream Zionist discourse, this subversive potential seems to remain largely unrealized, since traumatizing military service is perceived as the Jewish nation's fate and hence as requiring further resilience rather than a political change.[51]

The trauma of military service casts violent troops not only as victims but also as children. Vividly exemplifying this is parents' criticism. "My son is traumatized by ... his experiences in the territories," one father complained to the Israeli press, adding: "Children like my son, good kids, are particularly traumatized."[52] The analysis that follows sheds further light on this convergence of trauma, victimhood, and infantilization in Israeli legal and human rights discourses.

7.2.2   Infantilized Soldiers on Trial

Israeli violence and abuse toward noncitizen Palestinians, I showed in the previous chapter, rarely lead to investigation, let alone prosecution; and soldiers who are convicted tend to receive relatively lenient sentences. Given the privileging of video and photographic evidence – another issue scrutinized in the previous chapter – one might expect there to be greater accountability whenever soldiers' violence is caught on camera. Here, I wish to examine the extent to which this has been so and, in particular, what role the perpetrators' infantilization has played in this regard.

The image of armed forces as children persists with no less fervor when their violence is captured on video. Three high-profile cases illustrate this. One involved Leonardo Korea, a soldier filmed shooting at close range a blindfolded and handcuffed Palestinian in 2008. Following his indictment, he argued in his defense that he had simply been following his commander's repeated order to fire.[53] His attorney likewise accused the legal system of "targeting the low-level soldier," whom he infantilized as follows: "This soldier ... was ordered to act as he did. You

---

[51] Cf. K. Friedman-Peleg and Y. Bilu, "From PTSD to 'National Trauma': The Case of the Israel Trauma Center for Victims of Terror and War" (2011) 48:4 *Transcultural Psychiatry* 416, 431–34.
[52] Kotas-Bar, "This Is Not What We Send Our Children to the Military for."
[53] HCJ 7195/08 *Abu Rahma* v. *Chief Military Prosecutor* (2009) 63(2) PD 325.

cannot expect an 18-and-a-half-year-old boy ... to tell his commander ...: 'Your orders are wrong'."[54] In keeping with the lenient trend described in the previous chapter, neither the soldier nor his commander was sentenced to prison. Instead, the former was demoted, while the latter merely had his promotion delayed by two years.[55] The following year, four soldiers videotaped themselves abusing detained Palestinians. They, too, were eventually taken to court. The lawyer representing two of them reasoned that their actions should be treated through "educational action, not criminal charges." Portraying violent soldiers in infantilizing terms, he contended: "This [violence] has been the climate [in the military] since 1948, ... [and resolving it shouldn't be] at the expense of these two kids who are good soldiers."[56]

But undoubtedly the most well-known infantilized soldier to have had his actions caught on camera, and the focus of my analysis here, is Elor Azaria, a military medic who notoriously killed a disarmed and injured Palestinian by shooting him in the head in 2016. Following his indictment, a campaign was launched either to drop the charge or to pardon "the child of us all."[57] Figuring prominently in public debates over Azaria, and contributing to his infantilization, were his parents. A public video asking the public to donate the money needed for Azaria's legal representation featured his mother urging Israeli "mothers, as one mother to another, to please help me get my child out and return him home." The maternal plea succeeded spectacularly: within only a few hours, the donations of around 3,000 people had succeeded in reaching the full amount – 400,000 shekels,[58] the equivalent of five years' median salary.[59] Others in the debate

[54] G. Peled, "Exclusive: Reenacting the Shooting in Naalin," *Channel 2 News* (August 18, 2009) [Hebrew], www.mako.co.il/news-channel2/Channel-2-Newscast/Article-a95dadc897e2321004.htm.

[55] Haaretz staff, "Battalion Commander from Ni'lin Shooting Case, Lieutenant Colonel Omri Borberg, Will Not Be Demoted," *Haaretz* (January 27, 2011) [Hebrew], www.haaretz.co.il/news/politics/1.1159150.

[56] A. Pfeffer, "Kfir Brigade Soldiers Caught with Another Abuse Video," *Haaretz* (September 12, 2010) [Hebrew], www.haaretz.co.il/news/politics/1.1220802. I was unable to trace the court decision.

[57] See, e.g., G. Ben-Zaken, "Elor – the Child of Us All," *Channel 7* (January 8, 2017) [Hebrew], www.inn.co.il/Articles/Article.aspx/15760; S. Bendt, "En Route to Pardon, 'the Child of Us All' Must Convince He Acted in the Public Interest," *Walla! News* (October 9, 2016) [Hebrew], https://news.walla.co.il/item/3003824.

[58] Y. Ofri, "Within 12 Hours: 400 Thousand Shekels Raised for Elor Azaria," *NRG* (July 10, 2016) [Hebrew], www.makorrishon.co.il/nrg/online/1/ART2/797/268.html.

[59] In 2015, the median salary was 6,716 shekels. Peled, "A 4.5% Increase in the Median Salary."

self-identified as parents to soldiers, among them prime minister Netanyahu, who commented, following the publication of the video of the shooting: "I have heard the soldier's father plea [to treat his son fairly]. I must say that, being myself a father to a soldier, his words touched my heart. The IDF soldiers, our children, face ... terrorists seeking to kill them. They are required to make decisions ... in stressful and uncertain circumstances."[60] A few months later, in a highly publicized phone call to Azaria's parents, Netanyahu mentioned again that he himself was "a father to a soldier," while Azaria's father, for his part, voiced concern over "the child being [unfairly] tried."[61]

Apart from Azaria, only a handful of soldiers have been indicted for killing Palestinians in recent decades, as detailed in the previous chapter. For this reason, his lawyers argued that he was the victim of selective enforcement – a claim they tried to substantiate by requesting that they review documentation of all past military investigations into Palestinian fatalities. The lower court-martial refused their request, on account of its supposedly being overly broad and insufficiently substantiated. Subsequently, the defense attorneys presented the court-martial appeal court with 14 cases they had managed to trace, in which soldiers who had shot unsuspecting Palestinians dead had not been prosecuted.[62] This, the appeals court maintained, did not sufficiently demonstrate a systematic and prolonged pattern of selective enforcement.[63] The court made no mention of the overwhelming data available, such as that discussed in the previous chapter, which suggest a clear pattern of non-enforcement. Nor did it note that military investigations into shootings at Palestinians, on the rare occasions that they are conducted, reportedly tend to be far less prompt than Azaria's.[64]

Another argument advanced by the defense attorneys was that, prior to NGO B'Tselem publicizing the video of the killing, Azaria's

---

[60] H. Baruch, "The Words of the Soldier's Father Touched My Heart," *Channel 7* (March 28, 2016) [Hebrew], www.inn.co.il/News/News.aspx/319010. In her recent article on the subject, Renana Keydar comments that depicting soldiers as confused and inexperienced is another form of infantilization: R. Keydar, "'Everyone's Child'": The Challenge of Judging Israeli Soldiers in the Shadow of the Conflict" (forthcoming) *Law, Culture, and the Humanities*.

[61] Ynet staff, "Elor Azaria's Father Cried, Netanyahu Responded: 'Charlie, I Empathize with You.' Listen to the Conversation," *Ynet News* (September 25, 2016) [Hebrew], www.ynet.co.il/articles/0,7340,L-4859388,00.html.

[62] J. Brown, "Azaria's Defense Team Changes Strategy and Claims Selective Enforcement," *Haaretz* (April 5, 2017) [Hebrew], www.haaretz.co.il/blogs/johnbrown/BLOG-1.4002447.

[63] CMA 18, 21/17 *Azaria v. Chief Military Prosecutor* (July 30, 2017), ¶¶ 40, 69–76, 119–26.

[64] Brown, "Azaria's Defense Team Changes Strategy."

commanders had intended only to take disciplinary action. This implied that the motivation for his prosecution was not the killing itself but, rather, its global visibility. Unsurprisingly, the court-martial appeal court categorically rejected this line of argument as well: "[E]ven if the decision to launch an investigation was based on the ... video, there is nothing wrong about that. ... Once the video gave rise to suspicion of a criminal offense having been committed by the appellant, it was the authorities' duty to open an investigation."[65]

Like the few other soldiers prosecuted for killing Palestinians, Azaria, "the child of us all," was charged not with murder, but with a lesser offense: manslaughter. In 2017, he was convicted and sentenced to 18 months' imprisonment, a sentence later upheld by the court-martial appeal court.[66] In response, the UN Human Rights Office described his sentence as "unacceptable,"[67] while the uncle of the killed Palestinian rightly observed: "The sentence given to Azaria is lighter than that of a Palestinian youth who throws a stone."[68] This was not the end of the story. Following Azaria's conviction, the chief of the general staff reduced his sentence to 14 months. Eventually, the military committee handling early release requests ordered his release after nine months in prison.[69] Despite this relative leniency, the prosecutor later cited Azaria's case as an example of Israel's "very effective" deterrence against harm to Palestinians, while another military prosecutor described it as evidence of "the rule of law in the IDF and Israel."[70]

---

[65] CMA 18, 21/17, ¶ 119.

[66] See, respectively, CMC (Center) 182/16 *Military Prosecutor* v. *Azaria* (July 30, 2017); CMA 18, 21/17.

[67] Quoted in Reuters and Haaretz staff, "UN Human Rights Office: Sentence Handed to Hebron Shooter Is 'Unacceptable'," *Haaretz* (February 24, 2017), www.haaretz.com/israel-news/un-human-rights-office-hebron-shooter-s-sentence-is-unacceptable-1.5441568.

[68] Quoted in G. Cohen, "Elor Azaria Sentenced to 18 Months in Prison," *Haaretz* (February 21, 2017) [Hebrew], www.haaretz.co.il/news/politics/LIVE-1.3874976. On the sentencing of young Palestinian stone-throwers, see Chapter 2 (Section 2.2, "The Children of the Stones"), as well as B. McKernan, "Five Children Who Got Longer Sentences for Throwing Stones than Israeli Soldier Who Shot Incapacitated Palestinian Dead," *The Independent* (February 22, 2017), www.independent.co.uk/news/world/middle-east/israel-soldier-sentence-latest-elor-azaria-manslaughter-hebron-palestinian-shooting-wounded-attacker-a7593126.html.

[69] Y. Zitun, "After 9 Months: Elor Azaria Released from Prison," *Ynet News* (May 8, 2018) [Hebrew], www.ynet.co.il/articles/0,7340,L-5254354,00.html.

[70] See, respectively, Y. J. Bob, "Ex-US Military Lawyer: ICC Becoming a Toothache," *Jerusalem Post* (November 11, 2019), www.jpost.com/Arab-Israeli-Conflict/Ex-US-military-lawyer-ICC-becoming-a-toothache-607539; T. Cain, "2016 – The Hebron Shooting

Some of Azaria's critics took issue with his portrayal as a child. Among them was the chief of the general staff,[71] but later, in Azaria's verdict, the court condemned his statements as rash.[72] Moreover, polls found that most Israelis objected to prosecuting Azaria and supported a pardon.[73] On both the Israeli right and left, there were those who shared his lawyer's view that he was "a victim of selective enforcement" who was singled out because his actions were filmed. Some also claimed that this "child" was "a victim of the media" or "a victim of cynical politicians and jurists."[74] The head of the parliamentary opposition described him as "a victim of impossible political circumstances," while others similarly deemed him "a victim of the ... occupation, which cannot always be carried out compassionately and judiciously, especially by youth."[75]

Azaria's image as a victim is made all the more pronounced by the parallels with the rhetoric surrounding the country's other most famous soldier-child in recent times: Gilad Shalit. In 2006, during his military service, Shalit was captured by Hamas and held in the Gaza Strip for five years, which led to him becoming the epitome of victimhood for many Israelis. While in Gaza, he was constantly referred to in Israel as "the

Incident," *The 70 Project – Part A* (MAG, May 2018) [Hebrew], www.idf.il/media/31513/
2016-%D7%A4%D7%A8%D7%A9%D7%AA-%D7%94%D7%99%D7%A8%D7%99-%D7%
91%D7%97%D7%91%D7%A8%D7%95%D7%9F-%D7%AA%D7%95%D7%91%D7%9C-%
D7%A7%D7%99%D7%99%D7%9F.pdf.

[71] G. Cohen, "IDF Chief on Hebron Shooter's Trial: Treating a Soldier Like a 'Confused Little Boy' Demeans the Army," *Haaretz* (January 3, 2017), www.haaretz.com/israel-news/1.762789.

[72] CMC 182/16, ¶¶ 39–43.

[73] B. Taganya, "Mother of Soldier Who Shot Terrorist: 'You Sent My Son and Then Disowned Him," *Channel 2 News* (March 26, 2016) [Hebrew], www.mako.co.il/news-military/security-q1_2016/Article-2f2e33ae6e8b351004.htm; Channel 2 News staff, "53%: Unhappy with Netanyahu's Performance," *Channel 2 News* (March 7, 2017) [Hebrew], www.mako.co.il/news-military/politics-q1_2017/Article-7276d83c7a7aa51004.htm.

[74] See, respectively, D. Zonsheine, "Attorney Yoram Sheftel at the Service of Breaking the Silence?," *Haaretz* (June 3, 2017) [Hebrew], www.haaretz.co.il/opinions/.premium-1 .4141159; 12-Grade Students in Gvanim High School, "Elor Azaria – A Victim of the Media?," *Atzuma* (March 18, 2017) [Hebrew], www.atzuma.co.il/elorazariamedia; Y. Gutman, "They Used Him for Their Own Ends: Elor Azaria Is a Victim of Politicians," *Maariv* (July 31, 2017) [Hebrew], www.maariv.co.il/journalists/opinions/Article-593641.

[75] See, respectively, O. Ravid et al., "Elor Azaria Sentenced to a Year and a Half in Prison," *Walla! News* (February 21, 2017) [Hebrew], https://news.walla.co.il/item/3042389; K. Richter, "Elor Azaria as an Allegory: What Unites and What Separates," *Yedioth Aharonoth* (August 6, 2016) [Hebrew], www.yediot.co.il/articles/0,7340,L-4838139,00 .html.

child of us all"[76] – the exact same phrase later applied to Azaria. Shalit's parents, too, played a key role in the campaign to release him, including their testimony before a UN committee and their meeting with former US president Jimmy Carter.[77] Also involved in the campaign were 40 Israeli mothers who held a protest at the border of the Gaza Strip with signs that read: "We don't have spare children." Their spokesperson added: "Gilad is the child of us all. We are all mothers to soldiers in the past, present or future."[78] Like Azaria, Shalit was infantilized in countless other ways. Two years into his captivity, a story he had written at the age of 11 was published as a children's book, which was later incorporated into the school curriculum and adapted into an award-winning children's play.[79] Upon his release by Hamas in exchange for imprisoned Palestinians in 2011, prime minister Netanyahu told his parents – in a highly publicized meeting – "I've returned your child home."[80]

Throwing into sharp relief the perception of both Azaria and Shalit as comparable victims are statements made by Netanyahu and the chief of the general staff. The former likened his conversation with Azaria's parents to calls he regularly made to parents of dead or captive soldiers, adding: "dozens of parents see their children, the soldiers, in an almost impossible situation."[81] In analogizing a convicted killer with soldiers in captivity, Netanyahu continued his repeated rhetoric of sympathy for the Azaria family. The chief of the general staff, as mentioned earlier, was much more critical of Azaria's actions: "[A]n 18-year-old recruit is not the child of us all, he is not a captive baby, and he wasn't kidnapped near the border. . . . He is a combatant, a soldier, and is required to risk his life to perform the missions we assign to him." However, the references to captivity and kidnapping appear to apply not so much to Azaria (whom the chief of the general staff did not mention by name), but, rather, to

---

[76] R. Rosenthal, "The Linguistic Arena: The Child of Us All," *NRG* (October 13, 2011) [Hebrew], www.makorrishon.co.il/nrg/online/47/ART2/295/455.html.

[77] See, respectively, J. Khoury and Y. Yagna, "Noam Shalit to UN: My Son's Abduction Was a War Crime," *Haaretz* (July 6, 2009), www.haaretz.com/1.5073735; Haaretz service, "Noam Shalit Gives Jimmy Carter Letter to Son Held by Hamas," *Haaretz* (June 12, 2009), www.haaretz.com/1.5063786.

[78] F. Eyadat, "Tie a Blue Ribbon: Israeli Mothers Hold Protest Calling for Gilad Shalit's Release," *Haaretz* (June 29, 2008), www.haaretz.com/1.4997277.

[79] E. Schiff, "Play Based on Gilad Shalit's Book Wins at Haifa Festival," *Walla!* (April 1, 2010) [Hebrew], https://e.walla.co.il/item/1659219.

[80] Prime Minister's Spokesperson, "Soldier Gilad Shalit Met His Parents," *Prime Minister's Office* (October 18, 2011) [Hebrew], www.gov.il/he/departments/news/spokefami181011.

[81] Ynet staff, "Elor Azaria's Father Cried."

Shalit, who by that time had been at liberty for about five years.[82] Indeed, among critics of the deal to release Shalit in exchange for imprisoned Palestinians, there were some who similarly insisted that he "is not 'the child of us all.' He is a soldier [required to] fight the enemy … and, if necessary, to sacrifice his life."[83] Thus, Shalit and Azaria were each the subjects of two interdependent debates: one, over the best way to handle the soldier's situation, and another, on whether or not he was a child.

When condemnations were nonetheless leveled at Azaria's actions, they often followed the pattern, highlighted in the previous chapter, of describing him and those like him as no more than a few rotten apples within an otherwise moral military. "This is not the IDF, these are not the values of the IDF and these are not the values of the Jewish people," the chief of the general staff insisted. Reiterating the sentiment, prime minister Netanyahu and defense minister Moshe Ya'alon remarked, respectively, that the incident "doesn't represent the values of the IDF" and "[is] in utter breach of IDF values."[84] Such framing of soldiers' violence as an exception to the rule also appeared in the previously examined case of Leonardo Korea, whose shooting of a blindfolded and handcuffed Palestinian was likewise caught on camera. This time, it was supreme court justice Ayala Procaccia who characterized "this incident" as "extreme and exceptional," adding that such "exceptional conduct among IDF soldiers and commanders" must be eradicated.[85]

7.2.3 Conflicting Childhoods

During their service, the oft-infantilized Israeli combat soldiers encounter Palestinians under the age of majority. Called forth in these encounters are two potentially conflicting childhoods: that of the Israeli soldier, who is not formally a child yet tends to be portrayed or treated as such,

---

[82] One Israeli commentator indeed picked up on this: R. Alpher, "Eisenkot's Assertion Reveals the Commonality Between Elor Azaria and Gilad Shalit," *Haaretz* (January 4, 2017) [Hebrew], www.haaretz.co.il/gallery/television/tv-review/.premium-1.3195935.

[83] D. Reisman, "Ruled Rather than Ruler," *Channel 7* (October 29, 2011) [Hebrew], www.inn.co.il/Articles/Article.aspx/9950.

[84] See, respectively, G. Cohen, "IDF Chief on Hebron Shooter's Trial"; I. Sharon, "Netanyahu, Ya'alon Slam Hebron Shooting as IDF Vows Probe," *Times of Israel* (March 24, 2016), www.timesofisrael.com/idf-vows-probe-into-hebron-shooting-these-arent-jewish-values/.

[85] HCJ 7195/08, ¶¶ 73, 88 of justice Procaccia's leading opinion.

and that of the young Palestinian, who, by the applicable statutory definitions, is an actual "minor."

Such scenarios appear in state as well as human rights discourses in Israel. A teacher at one of Israel's premilitary academies, for instance, once remarked:

> If you are in battle and [Palestinian] terrorists are hiding in a house behind ... children, there's a very basic moral question here. Whose children are more important? Are their children more important, or [are] my children more important? Because those soldiers fighting are our children ... And I think any sane human being, when ... his children are being threatened, is going to prefer saving his own children.[86]

A veteran interviewed about his military service asserted that soldiers are "children in the end, ... so ... they can't always control themselves when an Arab ..., especially if it's an Arab youth of 18 that says a wrong word, it could be that they will give him a slap in the face." Another ex-soldier recounted to Breaking the Silence: "we chased ... [Palestinian] kids ... [and I thought to myself:] Why did [the kid] ... throw stuff at me? I throw back at him. Really, I think I was acting as a 12-year-old kid, what we did out there. But with weapons. I did whatever I felt like doing."[87]

All the more loaded is the encounter between these childhoods where the soldier-child is charged with abuse or homicide. Contrary to dominant scholarly writing on child law, and as further demonstrated in Chapters 1 and 3–5, such cases exemplify that older people are a key subject of child-centered legal and human rights discourses and practices. These older people, as previous chapters have discussed, are other than those older people whom child law scholarship already has in mind (parents, teachers, and social workers).

One such case, elaborated in the previous chapter, involved four border police soldiers who in 2002, among other things, drove into the West Bank city of Hebron and took onto their military jeep a 17-year-old Palestinian. While driving, they punched the Palestinian and then, despite his attempts to resist, shoved him outside, causing his death. Though one of the soldiers yelled "he is dead, he is dead," they drove away without investigating the matter. They also recorded their actions with

---

[86] Quoted in Eastwood, *Ethics as a Weapon of War*, pp. 146–47.
[87] Quoted in Grassiani, *Soldiering under Occupation*, p. 93; Breaking the Silence, *Children and Youth – Soldiers' Testimonies 2005–2011*, pp. 39–40.

a video camera, but later destroyed the recording upon realizing its potentially incriminating nature. Nevertheless, their actions were eventually revealed, and they were prosecuted and sentenced to prison.[88]

During the trial, the formal legal distinction between the young Palestinian and the older soldiers was doubly blurred. First, the Palestinian, legally a child, was placed in the same terminological basket with his statutorily adult killers. Though the judgments note his age and refer to him twice as a "youth," they more often describe him in terms similar or identical to those they apply to the soldiers: "young" and "a young person" (as well as "a young Arab").[89] Such judicial categorization of both the Palestinian and the soldiers as "young" potentially obscures the child/adult binary set by statute. Second, in its sentencing of one of the defendants, the court took into consideration not only the victim's childhood but also the defendant's own alleged childishness. On the one hand, judge Orit Efal-Gabai noted as an aggravating circumstance the Palestinian's legal classification as a child. On the other hand, based on a psychodiagnostic evaluation submitted by the defense, which characterized the soldier as "childish, with an immature personality," the judge concluded that his "complicity in the offenses is attributable to his weak personality, which made him feel helpless and passive."[90] Further infantilization occurred before and after the trial. While the soldiers were detained as suspects, their parents described them as "good kids" to an Israeli lawmaker, who later echoed this rhetoric in an interview: "these children . . . were sent by the system to the jungle." Similarly, once their sentences were announced, another lawmaker told the press: "I feel that our soldiers and children have been betrayed. Even if they failed, they are still our children."[91]

---

[88] The soldiers were tried separately, due to their different roles in the abuse: CrimC 157/03; CrimC (Jer. Dist.) 907/05 State of Israel v. Wahaby (September 14, 2005); CrimC (Jer. Dist.) 3172/07 State of Israel v. Lalza (April 28, 2008). The State and two of the defendants appealed to the supreme court. For the judgments, see CrimA 10594/05 Wahaby v. State of Israel (May 22, 2006); CrimA 5136/08. I will later discuss how the incident came to light, which is itself telling.

[89] CrimC 3172/07; CrimC 157/03; CrimA 10594/05; CrimA 5136/08.

[90] CrimC 907/05.

[91] See, respectively, Walla News staff, "MP Kara: Release the 4 Border Policemen Suspected of Killing a Palestinian," Walla! News (May 19, 2003) [Hebrew], https://news.walla.co.il/item/389382; A. Glikman, "8.5 Year Sentence to the Policeman Who Killed a Palestinian by Throwing Him from a Jeep," Ynet (April 27, 2009) [Hebrew], www.ynet.co.il/articles/0,7340,L-3707499,00.html.

Culturally, childhood and victimhood are interconnected,[92] and each is associated with innocence and passivity.[93] Therefore, it is no surprise that, just as the child/adult binary was corroded in the trial, so was the distinction between victim and victimizer. Further to its infantilization of one of the soldiers, the judgment also pronounced him a victim: "the acts of violence to which he was part can be seen as a venting of cumulative frustration with being inferior and a victim himself. Out of 'identification with the aggressor,' the defendant was drawn to experience control and strength vis-à-vis an inferior and helpless object."[94] Here lies another parallel between the legal system and some of its Israeli human rights critics (alongside the various parallels revealed in previous chapters). Breaking the Silence publications, in addition to repeatedly infantilizing soldiers (as quoted earlier), have portrayed them as simultaneously victims and victimizers.[95]

Similar infantilization took place in a 2011 trial of another border police soldier. Judge Amnon Cohen convicted her of abusing and threatening a detained and hooded 17-year-old Palestinian, who was repeatedly described in the judgment as "a minor." At the same time, Cohen noted the defense attorney's argument for a light sentence that was predicated on the soldier being just "a 20-year-old girl who served in the border police in difficult locations." Both childhoods, concluded Cohen, deserved consideration in determining the sentence: "The defendant's offenses, committed while entrusted with a subordinate child in custody, should be regarded as severe. ... On the other hand, I am taking into consideration the defendant's ... young age."[96] Though the soldier's appeal was dismissed, it is noteworthy that one of her arguments

---

[92] See, e.g., Holland, *Picturing Childhood*, p. 159.

[93] On this conception of the victim, see, e.g., A. Kleinman and J. Kleinman, "The Appeal of Experience; The Dismay of Images: Cultural Appropriations of Suffering in Our Times" (1996) 125:1 *Daedalus* 1, 9–10. On this conception of the child, see, e.g., P. H. Christensen, "Childhood and the Cultural Constitution of Vulnerable Bodies," in A. Prout (ed.), *The Body, Childhood and Society* (London and New York: Palgrave MacMillan, 2000), p. 38; A. James, C. Jenks and A. Prout, *Theorizing Childhood* (Cambridge: Polity Press, 1998), pp. 13–15; D. Rosen, *Armies of the Young: Child Soldiers in War and Terrorism* (New Brunswick and London: Rutgers University Press, 2005), pp. 1, 7, 122, 124–26, 129–31, 133.

[94] CrimC 907/05.

[95] See T. Katriel and N. Shavit, "Speaking Out: Testimonial Rhetoric in Israeli Soldiers' Dissent" (2013) 116 *Versus* 79.

[96] CrimC 2420-05-11. The defense attorney used the Hebrew word "yalda," which refers exclusively to female children. The soldier was also convicted of recklessness, for lighting her match near detonating caps that she had found in the young Palestinian's possession.

was her being "on the verge of minority" at the time of the offenses.[97] Likewise infantilized were two other border police soldiers, who were convicted in 2004 of assaulting and abusing two Palestinians, aged 17 and 18 years.[98] This time, it was in the media that legal infantilization appeared. Following their arrest, the attorney representing one of the soldiers told reporters: "19-year-old kids are sent to perform impossible tasks and are then expected to follow the norms of soldiers in a lab."[99]

Judicial infantilization of soldiers extends beyond cases involving harm to Palestinians. The Israeli judiciary has called soldiers "children" and "youth" in various other contexts.[100] Court-martial judges also referred to soldiers, in one case, as "youth aged 18 and over . . . [who are] aware of their duty to serve in the military"[101] – a remark later quoted in other judgments.[102] As Chapter 3 demonstrated, such ambiguity of age, and of childhood, characterizes the Israeli legal system's handling of Palestinian defendants as well. However, this ambiguity has conspicuously different effects for each of these populations. Among other things, the exact same terms used by Israeli judges to describe statutorily adult soldiers – "children" and "youth" – are applied by the statutory military law to much younger Palestinian defendants: under-14-year-olds and 14–15-year-olds respectively.

Hence, when presented with soldiers as children on the one hand, and Palestinians who are formally children on the other, courts do two things at once. First, while employing the terms "child" and "youth" in describing soldiers, the judgments I have traced exclude Palestinian defendants over the age of majority from this terminology. Consequently, though the statutory age of criminal majority is now identical for Palestinians and

[97] CrimA 9507/11, ¶ 10 of justice Danziger's leading opinion.
[98] CrimC 390/04.
[99] E. Weiss, "Suspicion: BP Soldiers Forced Palestinians to Chew Sand and Rocks," *Ynet* (June 1, 2004) [Hebrew], www.ynet.co.il/articles/0,7340,L-2925319,00.html.
[100] Examples of references to soldiers as "children" are: HCJ 4550/94 *Isha* v. *Attorney General* (1995) 49(5) PD 859; CMA 12/09 *Tsaig* v. *Chief Military Prosecutor* (February 3, 2009). Examples of references to soldiers as "youth" are: CMA 338/81 *Chief Military Prosecutor* v. *Tsulman* (1981) (quoted in CMA 123/02 *Yishai* v. *Chief Military Prosecutor* (March 17, 2004)); CMC (Special) 1/05 *Military Prosecutor* v. *Zaher* (verdict September 5, 2005, sentencing September 20, 2005); CMA 117/05 *Chief Military Prosecutor* v. *Zaher* (September 29, 2006); CMC (Center) 372/05 *Military Prosecutor* v. *Uzani* (2006); CMA 5/09 *Chief Military Prosecutor* v. *Buzaglo* (February 19, 2009).
[101] CMA 328/96 *Wolfson* v. *Chief Military Prosecutor* (1996).
[102] CMA 30/07 *Chief Military Prosecutor* v. *Tagao* (July 2, 2007); CMC (General Staff) 155/07 *Military Prosecutor* v. *Smorgonski* (verdict July 19, 2007, sentencing August 16, 2007), p. 15.

Israelis, age is nonetheless deployed differentially. As I show in the next chapter, this differentiation is complemented by the dissimilar age categorization of Palestinians and Israelis under Israeli law, as well as myriad other legal disparities along ethnic and national lines. The second characteristic of the judgments is their inclusion of older soldiers within the same age categories as their young Palestinian victims. This potentially allows the soldiers' childhood to somewhat counterbalance the statutory classification of Palestinians as children.

Such counterbalancing can emanate not only from the portrayal of soldiers as currently children but also from an emphasis on their past childhood. Retrospective infantilization of this sort appears in a 2003 judgment concerning two military police soldiers who had physically assaulted two Palestinians, aged 15 and 17 years, while transferring them to a detention facility. Here, too, the court-martial that convicted them, as well as the court-martial appeal court that increased their sentences, referred to the Palestinians as "minors" and regarded this as an aggravating factor. At the same time, both courts described, as a mitigating circumstance, the difficult childhood of one of the soldiers.[103] The appellate court added that the soldier's

> integration into the Israeli military ..., in spite of his difficult childhood ... [is] to his credit. ... Though it is not the court's custom to do so, we allow ourselves to address [the defendant] ... with words exceeding the bounds of law. Despite having sentenced him harshly ..., we are deeply impressed by his past and his ability to overcome the pains of his childhood.[104]

Similar retrospective infantilization can be found in other contexts. As a case in point, the Western media has been shown to systematically paint White domestic terrorism differently, and significantly more favorably, than non-White or foreign terrorism.[105] "He was a good kid," the US media reported about one White domestic terrorist in 2018,[106]

---

[103] CMC 222/03; CMC (Center) 222a/03 *Chief Military Prosecutor* v. *Rozner* (July 28, 2003); CMA 146/03.

[104] CMA 146/03.

[105] See, e.g., K. A. Powell, "Framing Islam: An Analysis of U.S. Media Coverage of Terrorism Since 9/11" (2011) 62:1 *Communication Studies* 90.

[106] K. Macias, "'He Was a Quiet and Normal Kid': The Infantilization of Young, White, Male Domestic Terrorists," *Daily Kos* (March 22, 2018), www.dailykos.com/stories/2018/3/22/1751214/–He-was-a-quiet-and-normal-kid-The-infantilization-of-young-white-male-domestic-terrorists.

exemplifying this bias. Thus, like other issues inspected in this book, the use of a similar rhetoric in Israel/Palestine speaks to a broader practice in need of critical attention.

7.2.4 Infantilization in Military Hazing

Shedding further light on the interplay of abuse and infantilization in the military is a different yet not unrelated issue: hazing among soldiers. This "rite of initiation," involving physical abuse and humiliation, is long-standing.[107] My focus here is on recent years, during which numerous hazing incidents have come to light through sources including soldiers' testimonies, abuse videos, and photographs. Alongside these disclosures, some soldiers have been suspected of destroying potentially incriminating hazing videos[108] (a reminder of the in/visibility of state violence, an issue explored in the previous chapter).

These incidents garnered substantial media coverage and, in some cases, resulted in disciplinary action, suspended sentences, or imprisonment ranging from seven days to five months. Hazing, it was revealed, had occurred throughout different parts of the military: the Armored Corps, the Artillery Corps, the Air Force, the Navy, the Combat Intelligence Collection Corps, the Paratroopers brigade, various infantry brigades (Givati, Golani, and Kfir), the border police, the Duvdevan counterinsurgency combat unit, and the Okets canine special forces unit. Of the abused soldiers, one died, one was permanently disabled (physically and mentally), and some were hospitalized. Among the broad range of abuse practices alleged to have been used were punching, beating and whipping with various objects, defecating on soldiers, verbal abuse, handcuffing the abused soldiers or tying their legs, blindfolding, spraying tear gas at them, and locking them in a room where a smoke grenade had been released. Typically involving only male soldiers, some forms of hazing appear to have tested and revolved around masculinity norms; examples include requiring soldiers to insert objects into their anuses and calling them

---

[107] Examples of earlier hazing cases are: CMA 156/70 *Chief Military Prosecutor* v. *Meir* (1970); CMA 125/90 *Chief Military Prosecutor* v. *Goren* (1990).

[108] The latter issue was reported in B. Fyler and Y. Zitun, "The Hazing in Kfir: Battalion Commander to Testify, Charges to Be Pressed," *Ynet News* (August 7, 2012) [Hebrew], www.ynet.co.il/articles/0,7340,L-4265740,00.html.

"koksinelim," a derogatory term for transgendered women and men perceived as effeminate. For some of the hazing cases, I was able to trace the court documents.[109] In most cases, however, the unavailability of sufficient identifying details meant that I had to rely on media reports.[110]

The military's approach to soldiers' complaints, including those relating to hazing, has been almost a polar opposite to its handling of Palestinian complaints. The latter, as demonstrated in the previous chapter, rarely lead to prosecution, especially if unsupported by either photographic evidence, videos, or Israeli soldiers' testimonies. In sharp contrast, the military ombudsman's legal team assessed 60 percent of soldiers' complaints against their commanders in 2009 (numbering 6,100) as being well founded.[111]

This divergence between Israel's acknowledgment of widespread violations within its armed forces and its dismissal of the overwhelming majority of Palestinian complaints begs two related questions. First, given their long record of internal violence and abuse, how likely are Israel's armed forces to spare the noncitizens their country regards as security threats from violence and abuse? And, second, is the similarity of some hazing methods to the types of abuse reportedly used against Palestinians coincidental? Regarding the former question, a survey in 2020 found that

---

[109] I traced these documents using a keyword search as well as publicly available identifying details. Three examples, in addition to cases cited later, are: CMC (North) 560/07 *Military Prosecutor* v. *John Doe* (July 22, 2008); CMA 497/09 *Chief Military Prosecutor* v. *Bloomenzon* (September 22, 2009); CMA 36/12 *John Doe* v. *Chief Military Prosecutor* (April 4, 2012).

[110] There are too many media reports to cite all of them here. Hence, five examples (other than those cited later) will suffice: Walla! News staff, "Golani: Grave Incident of Soldier Abuse," *Walla! News* (August 19, 2007) [Hebrew], https://news.walla.co.il/item/1156174; Y. Zitun, "Watch the Givati Hazing: Beatings and Kickings on the Floor," *Ynet News* (March 29, 2012) [Hebrew], www.ynet.co.il/articles/0,7340,L-4209966,00.html; Channel 2 News staff, "Hazing in the Paratroopers: Deputy Batallion Commander Locked Officers, Threw Grenade and Sprayed Tear Gas," *Channel 2 News* (July 22, 2012) [Hebrew], www.mako.co.il/news-military/security/Article-0c101625430b831017.htm; M. Hetzroni, "Commander Humiliated Recruits – And Sent to Jail," *Channel 2 News* (August 23, 2014) [Hebrew], www.mako.co.il/news-military/security/Article-373c31616e10841004.htm; Y. Zitun, "Abuse Affair at the Air Force Technical School: 10 Standing Army Soldiers Face Trial," *Ynet News* (July 31, 2019) [Hebrew], www.ynet .co.il/articles/0,7340,L-5561055,00.html.

[111] Y. Azoulay, "Military Ombudsman's Report: Hazing Backed by Commanders," *Haaretz* (May 3, 2010) [Hebrew], www.haaretz.co.il/news/politics/1.1200227.

77 percent of Israelis under the age of 40 support the torture of "enemy combatants" – a higher rate than in any of the other 16 countries surveyed.[112] As for the latter question, soldiers themselves have linked their hazing rituals to their conduct toward Palestinians, though not necessarily in self-critical terms. In 2009, following a commander's conviction for hazing, a former soldier in the same corps told the Israeli press: "Everyone would say [hazing] ... is horrible, but people know this company is the spearhead of the Armored Corps. Whenever there was a need for the battalion to enter Gaza, we were the ones who were sent. It goes to show you that [hazing] ... strengthens, matures, and empowers [Israeli soldiers]."[113]

The image of soldiers as children has governed both the practice of hazing and its surrounding discourse. As repeatedly reported in judgments and the media, hazing involves referring to the abusers as "veterans" and to the abused soldiers as "youth." In addition, among the hazing videos that have come out is one that shows a soldier referring to the younger comrade he was abusing as "my child," while presenting himself as "your father"[114] (bringing to mind, perhaps, the widely held idea of abused children being at a higher risk of becoming abusive parents).[115] Legal and public discourse also frame hazing by an infantilizing rhetoric. One court-martial judgment speaks of the responsibility of a "young commander" charged with hazing toward his subordinates, who are described as "the [country's] best youth."[116] The court-martial appeal court went further by likening recruits and, implicitly, their commanders to "teens":

> The training of young combatants during boot camp is a difficult task indeed. Turning young teens ... into ... combatants ... is no trivial

[112] Times of Israel staff, "Among Millennials in 16 Countries, Israelis Least Opposed to Torture – Poll," *Times of Israel* (January 16, 2020), www.timesofisrael.com/among-millennials-in-16-countries-israelis-least-opposed-to-torture-poll/.

[113] D. Adelson, "The Abuse: 'Even the Brigade Commander Knew, They Shouldn't Play Dumb'," *Ynet* (July 20, 2009) [Hebrew], www.ynet.co.il/Ext/Comp/ArticleLayout/CdaArticlePrintPreview/1,2506,L-3748923,00.html.

[114] Y. Glik, "Report: Revealing Photos of Abuse in the Armored Corps," *Channel 2 News* (July 31, 2009) [Hebrew], www.mako.co.il/news-military/security/Article-ed4e8cd76b1d221004.htm.

[115] See, e.g., J. Kaufman and E. Zigler, "Do Abused Children Become Abusive Parents" (1987) 57:2 *American Journal of Orthopsychiatry* 186.

[116] CMC (GOC) 41/04 *Chief Military Prosecutor v. Soffer* (July 7, 2005), ¶ 7 of the verdict.

matter. Likewise difficult is the duty of squad commanders, who are close in age to their subordinates. ... [The convicted commander] ... violated his fiduciary duty to the soldiers' parents, who entrusted him with their most precious possession.[117]

The country's most watched television channel introduced as follows its report of another hazing case: "You are parents to a child who is a combat soldier. ... When you ask him 'how are things going at the battalion?,' he replies, wearily, 'ok,' because that's what children say, 'ok.' But is he telling you the whole truth?"[118] In another hazing case, the mother of one of the detained soldiers complained to the press: "I sent a well-educated child [to the military] and I'll get him back as a criminal."[119]

Aside from such infantilization, the litigated cases share an additional characteristic: they all ignited disputes over whether these were isolated transgressions. In all cases, the defendants insisted that their actions were part of long-standing traditions. Supporting their claim were abuse photos and videos published in the media, some of which showed them being personally abused as recruits a few years prior to the incidents for which they were being indicted. The top-level command, for its part, consistently denied knowledge of the abuse practices. Such denials continued even after, and thus inadvertently confirmed, a 2010 report by the military's own ombudsman, which found that senior commanders had often denied and turned a blind eye to hazing.[120] The prosecuted abusers, as well as their families and attorneys, repeatedly criticized what one father called this "low-level soldier syndrome," whereby "all blame is placed on the children, [though] ... it is at least a 15-year tradition."[121] Contrary to Israeli authorities' united front in denying Palestinian complaints and depicting the few prosecuted cases as isolated incidents (issues analyzed in the previous chapter), such accusations by soldiers – "our children" – and their families are far harder for Israeli society to dismiss.

---

[117] CMA 87/05 *Soffer* v. *Chief Military Prosecutor* (March 27, 2006), ¶¶ 46, 57.
[118] Glik, "Report: Revealing Photos of Abuse in the Armored Corps."
[119] Y. Zitun and N. Brenner, "Ganz on the Abuse in Givati: 'Not the Last Time'," *Ynet News* (April 4, 2012) [Hebrew], www.ynet.co.il/articles/0,7340,L-4212335,00.html.
[120] Azoulay, "Military Ombudsman's Report: Hazing Backed by Commanders."
[121] Y. Breiner, "Abuse in the Armored Corps: 'The Officers Evaded Responsibility'," *Walla! News* (September 22, 2009) [Hebrew], https://news.walla.co.il/item/1577604.

7.3   Militarized Children

7.3.1   *Palestinian Children as Weapons*

Traceable to at least the Middle Ages,[122] the distinction between civilians and combatants in armed conflict has been enshrined in international humanitarian law.[123] Early into Israel's rule over the West Bank and Gaza Strip, in 1969, a military court undermined this distinction by labeling Palestinian captives neither as combatants nor as civilians but as "unlawful combatants." Those who "have broken ... [the] rules of warfare," the court held, are excluded from the prisoner-of-war status that is afforded to legally recognized combatants. "By [introducing] ... additional distinctions between lawful and unlawful combatants ... it becomes possible to give far-reaching protection to the overwhelming majority of [Palestinians]," whom the court still regarded at the time as either "civilians" and "combatants."[124] The supreme court further eroded the civilian/combatant distinction in its unanimous decision, in 2006, to uphold the lawfulness of Israel's extrajudicial assassination ("targeted killing") policy. Under international humanitarian law, only combatants, not civilians, are legitimate targets for military attack. Citing the First Protocol of the Fourth Geneva Convention, the supreme court held that international law's protection for civilians "does not exist regarding those civilians 'for such time as they take a direct part in hostilities' (§51(3) of The First Protocol)."[125] The reference to the international law of armed conflict in both judgments exemplifies, yet again, Israel's continued reliance on international law to justify its violence – as has been apparent throughout this book.

---

[122] H. M. Kinsella, *The Image Before the Weapon: A Critical History of the Distinction Between Combatant and Civilian* (Ithaca and London: Cornell University Press, 2011).

[123] N. Melzer, "The Principle of Distinction between Civilians and Combatants," in A. Clapham and P. Gaeta (eds.), *The Oxford Handbook of International Law in Armed Conflict* (Oxford: Oxford University Press, 2014), pp. 296–331.

[124] "Case 4/69 Military Prosecutor v Omar Mahmud Kassem and Others," in E. Lauterpacht (ed.), *International Law Reports* (Cambridge: Grotius Publications Limited, 1971), vol. 42, p. 470. On the use of the "unlawful combatant" concept in earlier judgments abroad, and on the impact of this 1969 Israeli judgment on foreign case law, see H. Viterbo, "Export of Knowledge," in O. Ben-Naftali, M. Sfard, and H. Viterbo, *The ABC of the OPT: A Legal Lexicon of the Israeli Control over the Occupied Palestinian Territory* (Cambridge and New York: Cambridge University Press, 2018), pp. 111–12.

[125] HCJ 769/02 *PCATI* v. *Government of Israel* (2006) 62(1) PD 507. For critical analysis, see O. Ben-Naftali, "Combatants," in Ben-Naftali, Sfard, and Viterbo, *The ABC of the OPT*, pp. 60–77.

The international legal distinction between civilians and combatants has often been predicated as much on individuals' identity markers – chiefly their age, gender, physicality, nationality, and race – as on their actions.[126] Thus, the Convention on the Rights of the Child (CRC) affords special protections to "children affected by an armed conflict," the Fourth Geneva Convention refers specifically to "persons under fifteen," and the UN Declaration on the Protection of Women and Children in Emergency and Armed Conflict prohibits attacks on "women and children, who are the most vulnerable members of the population."[127]

Israel's shift from placing boots on the ground in Gaza to remote military control has transferred risk from Israeli combatants – the country's so-called children – to Palestinian noncombatants.[128] While the resultant reduction in casualties among its armed forces helped Israel preserve and even increase domestic support for its military offensives,[129] the dramatic rise in Palestinian fatalities, including those identified as children, attracted considerable international criticism. According to data collated by Israeli NGO B'Tselem, Israeli forces killed more than 6,000 noncitizen Palestinians, mostly from the Gaza Strip, between September 2000 and December 2019, including over 1,300 under the age of 18.[130] Others allege higher fatalities.[131] According to the UN Office for the

[126] Regarding gender and age, see Carpenter, *"Innocent Women and Children."* Regarding all of these identity markers, see Kinsella, *The Image Before the Weapon.*

[127] See, respectively, Article 38(4) of CRC, November 20, 1989, 1577 UNTS 3; Article 14 of the Geneva Convention Relative to the Protection of Civilian Persons in the Time of War, Geneva, August 12, 1949, 75 UNTS 287 [hereinafter: GC IV]; Article 1 of the Declaration on the Protection of Women and Children in Emergency and Armed Conflict, GA Res 3318, UN GAOR, 29th Sess., Supp. 31, at 146, UN Doc A/9631 (1974).

[128] On this as a broader trend in Western counterinsurgency and conscript militaries, see, respectively, M. Shaw, *The New Western Way of War* (Cambridge: Polity Press, 2005); J. P. Vasquez, "Shouldering the Soldiering: Democracy, Conscription, and Military Casualties" (2005) 49:6 *Journal of Conflict Resolution* 849.

[129] Y. Levi, *Israel's Death Hierarchy: Casualty Aversion in a Militarized Democracy* (New York and London: New York University Press, 2012).

[130] B'Tselem, *Fatalities Before Operation "Cast Lead"* (n.d.), www.btselem.org/statistics/fatalities/before-cast-lead/by-date-of-event (referring to September 29, 2000 – December 26, 2008); B'Tselem, *Fatalities since Operation Cast Lead* (n.d., last accessed on January 9, 2020), www.btselem.org/statistics/fatalities/after-cast-lead/by-date-of-event (referring to January 19, 2009 – December 26, 2019).

[131] DCIP, "Over 1,996 Palestinian Children Killed Since Outbreak of Second Intifada" (September 30, 2015), www.dci-palestine.org/over_1_996_palestinian_children_killed_since_outbreak_of_second_intifada.

Coordination of Humanitarian Affairs, 2014 saw the highest number of noncitizen Palestinian casualties since 1967.[132]

To fend off accusations that it indiscriminately attacks populated areas, Israel has accused Gazans of using the presence of under-18s to shield military forces or areas from assaults. This charge offered a pre-emptive legal defense of sorts:[133] the implication that Palestinians aged under 18 were participating in combat purportedly prevents and thus exempts Israel from targeting only adult combatants. This is part of a persistent Israeli narrative, touched on in Chapter 3, about Palestinians weaponizing their young. "We," unlike the Hamas government in Gaza, "know how to give security to our children, . . . not use them as human shields," then-president Shimon Peres asserted in 2009.[134] Similarly, in 2018, following nine years of Israeli forces killing upward of 700 Palestinians under the age of 18,[135] Israel's ambassador to the United Nations placed the blame on Hamas, whom he described as "terrorists [that] hide behind innocent children to ensure their own survival."[136]

At times, allegations that Palestinians use their young as human shields intersect with the previously discussed portrayal of another group as children: Israeli soldiers. "Israel's citizen army – the brave soldiers of the IDF, our young boys and girls – they upheld the highest moral values of any army in the world," prime minister Netanyahu told the UN General Assembly in 2014. These "boys and girls," he contended, were the antithesis of

---

[132] UN Office for the Coordination of Humanitarian Affairs (UNOCHA), *Fragmented Lives: Humanitarian Overview 2015* (June 2016), www.ochaopt.org/sites/default/files/annual-humanitarian-overview_10_06_2016_english.pdf.

[133] On this supposed legal defense, see N. Perugini and N. Gordon, "The Politics of Human Shielding: On the Resignification of Space and the Constitution of Civilians as Shields in Liberal Wars" (2016) 34:1 *Environment and Planning D: Society and Space* 168. On the uncorroborated and disputed nature of these human shields, see Amnesty International, *Unlawful and Deadly: Rocket and Mortar Attacks by Palestinian Armed Groups During the 2014 Gaza/Israel Conflict* (March 2015), pp. 47–49, www.amnesty.org/download/Documents/MDE2111782015ENGLISH.PDF.

[134] J. Khoury, "Peres: Unlike Hamas, Israel Protects Its Children," *Haaretz* (October 26, 2009), www.haaretz.com/1.5317519.

[135] B'Tselem, *Fatalities Since Operation Cast Lead* (n.d.; last accessed June 18, 2018), www.btselem.org/statistics/fatalities/after-cast-lead/by-date-of-event (referring to the period 19 January 2009 to 31 March 2018).

[136] Times of Israel Staff, "Israel Demands UN Condemn Hamas's Use of Children, Civilians as Human Shields," *Times of Israel* (May 14, 2018), www.timesofisrael.com/israel-demands-un-condemn-hamass-use-of-children-civilians-as-human-shields/.

what Hamas did: ... Hamas deliberately placed its rockets where Palestinian children live and play. ... As Israeli children huddled in bomb shelters and Israel's ... missile defense system knocked Hamas rockets out of the sky, the profound moral difference between Israel and Hamas couldn't have been clearer: Israel was using its missiles to protect its children. Hamas was using its children to protect its missiles.[137]

Netanyahu thus juxtaposed young Gazans, whom he portrayed as human shields in the hands of their depraved elders, with Israeli soldiers, whom he extolled as virtuous children. In his account, as in those of others, Israel/Palestine emerges both as a battleground over the nature of childhood and as a conflict between childhoods. Netanyahu's other important rhetorical strategy was to use what he described as Israel's need to "protect its children" as an excuse for its onslaught on the Gaza Strip. Israeli defense minister Naftali Bennett reiterated this image of state violence as a form of child protection in 2019, following another military assault on the Gaza Strip. "Israeli security forces," he proclaimed, "will hunt each and every terrorist, until our children are safe and protected."[138]

However, in accusing Palestinians of using their young as human shields while Israel protects its own young, Israeli officials conveniently ignore two facts. One is that Israel's own armed forces – "our young boys and girls" in Netanyahu's words – have used noncombatant Palestinians, including under-18s, as human shields since at least 1967.[139] In 2005, the supreme court formally forbade this practice. Two years later, a division commander was reprimanded for authorizing this practice on several occasions, but a few years later he was appointed deputy chief of the general staff.[140] In 2010, a court-martial convicted two soldiers who had used a nine-year-old Palestinian as a human shield by ordering him to perform a potentially deadly military task. Both soldiers were spared imprisonment, in keeping with the trend highlighted in the previous

---

[137] Ministry of Foreign Affairs, "PM Netanyahu Addresses the UN General Assembly" (September 29, 2014), http://mfa.gov.il/MFA/PressRoom/2014/Pages/PM-Netanyahu-addresses-the-UN-General-Assembly-29-Sep-2014.aspx.

[138] Y. Kubovich, "Bennett Boasts of Killing Iranians and Changing the Rules, Exasperating the Security System," *Haaretz* (December 9, 2019) [Hebrew], www.haaretz.co.il/news/politics/.premium-1.8233760.

[139] B'Tselem, "Human Shields" (November 11, 2017), www.btselem.org/human_shields.

[140] A. Harel, "Top IDF Officer Censured over Use of 'Human Shields' in Nablus," *Haaretz* (October 18, 2007), www.haaretz.com/1.4987754.

chapter.[141] Despite these rulings, later reports by local human rights NGOs[142] and the UN Committee on the Rights of the Child,[143] as well as Israeli veterans' testimonies,[144] suggest that this practice persists. The other fact ignored by Israel relates to its claim that civilians' proximity to military sites might make them human shields. Such proximity occurs not only in Gaza – one of the world's most densely populated territories[145] – but also within Israel's pre-1967 borders, where large military bases have been placed in or near urban centers.[146]

Israeli officials have accused Palestinians of directly involving their young in combat in two ways. One, discussed so far, is the claim that those identified as children are used as human shields. The other is the allegation that Palestinians are trained for combat from an early age – in violation of international law's aversion toward the active participation in combat of those below certain ages. Thus, the Fourth Geneva Convention and the CRC both prohibit military recruitment of under-15s, the Rome Statute defines such recruitment as a war crime,[147] and other documents seek to raise the minimum recruitment age further to 18 years.[148] In

[141] See, respectively, HCJ 3799/02 *Adalah* v. *Commander of IDF Central Command* (2005) 60(3) PD 6; CMC (South) 150/10 *Military Prosecutor* v. *John Doe* (October 3, 2010).

[142] See, e.g., PCATI, *Prosecutorial Indifference: Systematic Failures in the Investigation of Soldier Violence against Detainees in the Occupied Palestinian Territories* (2014), p. 31, www.stoptorture.org.il/files/Prosecutorial%20Indifference.pdf; DCIP, "Israeli Forces Use an Arrested Palestinian Teen as a Human Shield" (February 11, 2016), www.dci-palestine.org/israeli_forces_use_an_arrested_palestinian_teen_as_a_human_shield.

[143] S. Nebehay, "Palestinian children tortured, used as shields by Israel: U.N.," *Reuters* (June 20, 2013), www.reuters.com/article/2013/06/20/us-palestinian-israel-children-idUSBRE95J0FR20130620.

[144] Breaking the Silence, *Children and Youth – Soldiers' Testimonies 2005–2011*, pp. 24–29.

[145] BBC News, "Israel-Palestinian Conflict: Life in the Gaza Strip," *BBC* (May 15, 2018), www.bbc.co.uk/news/world-middle-east-20415675.

[146] On this location of Israeli military bases, see N. Mann, "General Staff at the Heart of the Metropole | When the Bomb Hits the Kirya in Tel-Aviv," *Haaretz* (June 9, 2012) [Hebrew], www.haaretz.co.il/magazine/1.1724778; Human Rights Watch, *Civilians under Assault: Hezbollah's Rocket Attacks on Israel in the 2006 War* (New York, August 2007), p. 16, https://reliefweb.int/sites/reliefweb.int/files/resources/4C5DA8B7 8DFD3824C1257346004DC02F-Full_Report.pdf.

[147] Article 77 of GC IV; Article 38 of CRC; Article 8 of the Rome Statute of the International Criminal Court (July 17, 1998, entered into force July 1, 2002), 2187 UNTS 90.

[148] Articles 3 and 7 of the Optional Protocol to the CRC on the Involvement of Children in Armed Conflict, May 25, 2000, 2173 UNTS 222; UNCRC, General Recommendation No. 1: Children in Armed Conflict, Report on the Nineteenth Session, UN Doc CRC/C/ 80 (September 1998).

2019, the Coordinator of Government Activities in the Territories (a unit
in the Israeli ministry of defense) released a publicity video in English.
The video juxtaposed what it claimed were Israeli summer camps (represented by images of very young people smiling and holding balloons)
with Hamas summer camps in Gaza (represented by a photograph
showing male adolescent Palestinians holding mock wooden rifles).[149]
That same year, the Israeli police arrested organizers of a summer camp
in the West Bank, while the Israeli media denounced other Palestinian
summer camps for teaching self-defense tactics.[150] Such allegations
against Palestinian education, and summer camps specifically, are yet
another version of the Israeli narrative about Palestinians weaponizing
their young.

As in Israeli allegations about the use of human shields, the double
standard in such accusations is conspicuous. Military service is deeply
ingrained in the Israeli Jewish school curriculum.[151] Israeli law, having
long enshrined conscription, was amended in 2018 to add to the objectives of public education that of instilling the importance of "meaningful
service" in the military.[152] In 11th grade, (non-orthodox) Jewish students
are required to attend a week-long paramilitary camp, where they are
dressed in military uniform, subjected to military discipline, receive
weapons training, and practice shooting.[153] It is no wonder that, in a
recent poll, Jewish Israeli high schoolers expressed a broad consensus on
the prestige of the military and, in particular, its combat soldiers.[154]

As for Israeli summer camps, some have been reported to offer
children as young as three military history education and military-like

[149] Channel 12 News staff, "A Peek into Hamas Summer Camps in Gaza: Teaching Hatred
and Terrorism," *Channel 12 News* (July 15, 2019) [Hebrew], www.mako.co.il/news-
world/arab-q3_2019/Article-95682f31495fb61027.htm.
[150] For a report on both issues, see Y. Porat, "'The Nakba Summer Camp' of East
Jerusalem's Children," *Ynet* (July 30, 2019) [Hebrew], www.ynet.co.il/articles/0,7340,L-
5560089,00.html.
[151] See, e.g., H. Dahan-Kalev, "Officers as Educators: The Ex-Military in the Israeli School
System" (2006) 12:2 *Israel Affairs* 268–83; H. Gur (ed.), *Militarism in Education* (Tel
Aviv: Bavel, 2005)[Hebrew]; G. Levy and O. Sasson-Levy, "Militarized Socialization,
Military Service, and Class Reproduction: The Experiences of Israeli Soldiers" (2008)
51:2 *Sociological Perspectives* 349–74.
[152] Article 2(13) of Public Education Law (1953) (amended on August 17, 2018).
[153] Levy and Sasson-Levy, "Militarized Socialization," p. 354.
[154] Y. Girsh, "Negotiating the Uniform: Youth Attitudes towards Military Service in Israel"
(2018) 27:3 *YOUNG* 1, 6–8.

drills,[155] while children aged 10 and above undergo firearms training and use military aircraft simulators.[156] In summer camps operating within and in collaboration with military bases, children reportedly dined with soldiers, assisted them with their chores, and were lectured by the base commanders on battle history.[157] This leads directly to the next subject: the militarization of Israeli childhood.

7.3.2 Israeli Settler Children as Soldiers in the Making

The inseparability of the ostensibly disparate military and civilian spheres is not unique to Israel.[158] In Israeli society, however, it is far-reaching[159] and complemented by three additional factors: the country's mass conscription, a social sense of a permanent security threat,[160] and, crucially, the prominent (if mutable) militarism of Zionist Israel.[161]

Accordingly, the military and militarism are key social forces shaping Israeli childhood. For most non-ultra-Orthodox Jewish Israelis, military service is a primary rite of passage to adulthood and full citizenship.[162]

---

[155] See K. Elbaz-Aloush, "Tel-Aviv Municipality Presents: Military Summer Camps," *Yedioth Aharonot* (June 27, 2018) [Hebrew], www.yediot.co.il/articles/0,7340,L-5298097,00.html.

[156] See, e.g., D. Bechor-Nir, "Hot Chocolate, a Bun, and Intercepting Enemy Aircrafts," *Calcalist* (July 27, 2019) [Hebrew], www.calcalist.co.il/local/articles/0,7340,L-3766965,00 .html; E. Ben Kimon, "Summer Camp in Samaria: Firearm Training for 10-Year-Olds," *Ynet News* (July 7, 2017), www.ynetnews.com/articles/0,7340,L-4986185,00.html.

[157] See S. Cohen, "A First in the IDF: Summer Camp Within a Military Base," *Channel 7* (July 15, 2009) [Hebrew], www.inn.co.il/News/News.aspx/191887.

[158] See, e.g., C. Dayan, *The Story of Cruel and Unusual* (Cambridge, MA and London: MIT Press, 2007); F. Cochrane, "Not So Extraordinary: The Democratisation of UK Counterinsurgency Strategy" (2013) 6:1 *Critical Studies on Terrorism* 29.

[159] See, e.g., E. Rosman Stollman and A. Kampinsky (eds.), *Civil-Military Relations in Israel: Essays in Honor of Stuart A. Cohen* (London: Lexington Books, 2014).

[160] On these as reasons for Israel's militarism, see Girsh, "Negotiating the Uniform," p. 7; M. Lissak, "The Permeable Boundaries between Civilians and Soldiers in Israeli Society," in D. Ashkenazy (ed.), *The Military in the Service of Society and Democracy* (London: Greenwood Press, 1994), pp. 9–19.

[161] See, e.g., B. Kimmerling, "Patterns of Militarism in Israel" (1993) 34:2 *European Journal of Sociology* 196; G. Sheffer and O. Barak (eds.), *Militarism and Israeli Society* (Bloomington: Indiana University Press, 2010); E. Lomsky-Feder and E. Ben-Ari (eds.), *Military and Militarism in Israeli Society* (New York: State University of New York Press, 2012).

[162] See, e.g., Y. Dar and S. Kimhi, "Military Service and Self-Perceived Maturation Among Israeli Youth" (2001) 30:4 *Journal of Youth and Adolescence* 427; D. Kaplan, "The Military as a Second Bar Mitzvah: Combat Service as Initiation to Zionist Masculinity," in E. Sinclair-Webb and M. Ghoussoub (eds.), *Imagined Masculinities:*

Hence, from the moment of birth until adulthood, most of them are soldiers in the making, as partly intimated in the previous subsection.[163] While preparation for military service peaks during high school, the image of young Israelis as future soldiers already takes effect in utero. For example, one of the country's top hospitals published an advertisement for its maternity ward in 2018, which portrayed a soldier-like fetus wearing a military beret and saluting, alongside the caption: "recipient of the Presidential Award of Excellence for the year 2038."[164]

Before and during the Gaza pullout, such militaristic perceptions informed parliamentary deliberations over the handling of evacuated settler youth who participated in legally proscribed anti-evacuation protests. Some attendees noted to the credit of these Israeli settler youth their future military service. "These are essentially wonderful youths, these are youths who are supposed to go on into serving in the military," a government representative involved in assisting the evacuated settlers told the parliament's Child Rights Committee.[165] "These are the best youths in the State of Israel," MP Gila Finkelstein similarly remarked in one of the committee's later deliberations, adding: "They are in the finest [military] units and are excellent soldiers."[166]

Also blended into this fusion of the child and the soldier was the previously analyzed infantilization of soldiers. Ahead of the pullout, the Constitution, Law, and Justice Committee discussed the potential effect

Male Identity and Culture in the Modern Middle East (London: Al-Saqi Books, 2000), pp. 127–44; O. Mayseless and M. Scharf, "What Does It Mean to Be an Adult? The Israeli Experience" (2003) 100 *New Directions for Child and Adolescent Development* 5, 7, 12.

[163] See also M. Furman, "Army and War: Collective Narratives of Early Childhood in Contemporary Israel," in Lomsky-Feder and Ben-Ari (eds.), *Military and Militarism in Israeli Society*, pp. 141–68; A. Herbst, "Welfare Mom as Warrior Mom: Discourse in the 2003 Single Mothers' Protest in Israel" (2012) 42:1 *Journal of Social Policy* 129, 134, 137; Y. Jacobson and D. Luzzatto, "Israeli Youth Body Adornments: Between Protest and Conformity" (2004) 12:2 *YOUNG* 155, 157–58.

[164] M. Zonszein, "Ad for Israeli Maternity Ward Portrays Fetus as Future Soldier," *+972 Magazine* (May 23, 2018), https://972mag.com/ad-for-israeli-maternity-ward-portrays-fetus-as-future-soldier/135694.

[165] Special Committee for the Rights of the Child, 16th Knesset – Transcript 135 (July 26, 2005) [Hebrew], http://fs.knesset.gov.il/16/Committees/16_ptv_491841.docx.

[166] Special Committee for the Rights of the Child, 16th Knesset – Transcript 142 (November 8, 2005) [Hebrew], http://fs.knesset.gov.il/16/Committees/16_ptv_131202.doc.

of the legislation concerning the planned evacuation on young settlers. The deputy legal advisor of the justice ministry made a remark about the danger of sending troops and police to evacuate settlers, to which MP Yitzhak Levy responded: "we are talking about children now" (not soldiers and police). Instantly, MP Reshef Hen reacted: "Yes. This soldier too, who only yesterday was a child."[167] As in the previously examined cases of soldiers' violence against Palestinians, albeit with radically different consequences, two childhoods came face to face: that of under-18 settlers and that attributed to soldiers. Unlike cases involving young Palestinians, this encounter involved not only two childhoods but also two groups of Israeli soldiers: those currently in military service, on the one hand, and the prospective soldiers evacuated from settlements, on the other.

In and outside parliament,[168] some suggested that these settler youth, in order to ensure their enlistment, should be spared criminal charges, and that those already convicted should be pardoned. Among those categorically objecting to prosecution was the chair of the Constitution, Law, and Justice Committee, MP Michael Eitan. He argued, in the run-up to the Gaza pullout, that "some of them are still minors, are going to the most combative units we have, and should be allowed to do so." In the same parliamentary meeting, a settler mother, whose son had been detained following his participation in anti-evacuation protests, implied that clashes with the evacuating forces might reduce these youths' motivation to enlist: "This would be entirely the military's loss. . . . [O]ur children currently, at this stage, are not interested in serving in the military. But we will recover . . . On the parents' behalf I turn to you [the MPs] . . ., to . . . ask for a general pardon."[169] A few months after the pullout, MP Sha'ul Yahalom likewise proposed to the Constitution, Law, and Justice Committee that charges against all settler youth involved be dropped, apart from cases of proven physical violence. He further suggested that, in any event, "no measures should be taken against [settler]

---

[167] Constitution, Law, and Justice Committee, 16th Knesset – Transcript 360 (December 26, 2004) [Hebrew], http://fs.knesset.gov.il/16/Committees/16_ptv_548587.docx.

[168] For such concerns in the Israeli media, see, e.g., A. Harel, "High-Ranking Military Officers: The Disengagement Caused Youth to Evade Conscription," *Haaretz* (January 9, 2007) [Hebrew], www.haaretz.co.il/misc/1.1377306.

[169] Constitution, Law, and Justice Committee, 16th Knesset – Transcript 579 (August 28, 2005) [Hebrew], http://fs.knesset.gov.il/16/Committees/16_ptv_489700.docx.

minors prior to their recruitment." Other MPs in attendance shared these sentiments.[170]

These propositions eventually bore fruit. In 2009, the Israeli president pardoned 59 convicted anti-evacuation protestors, most (48) of whom were under the age of 18.[171] The following year, a unique statute was enacted, erasing the criminal records of such protestors, terminating ongoing legal proceedings, and nullifying sentences (with the exception of serious charges and individuals with a prior criminal record).[172] This unusual piece of legislation, upheld by the supreme court in 2012,[173] was, according to police figures, applied to no less than 1,483 alleged offenders, of whom 315 were under the age of 18 at the time of their offenses.[174]

Settler youth in other circumstances also benefited from society's perception of their future military service as a mitigating factor. In 2015, a 17-year-old settler was caught on video holding a knife, punching the president of the Israeli NGO Rabbis for Human Rights, kicking him, and hitting him with stones. While his Palestinian peers would stand no chance of avoiding imprisonment for comparable acts, the settler was given a community sentence and was ordered to pay a relatively low compensation. It was his future enlistment, according to the judgment, that warranted such leniency: "the youth's strong desire to enlist in the IDF must be taken into account. Along with his high personality traits, the youth possesses good physical abilities and could easily integrate in a meaningful military course."[175]

[170] Constitution, Law, and Justice Committee, 16th Knesset – Transcript 648 (December 21, 2005) [Hebrew], http://fs.knesset.gov.il/16/Committees/16_ptv_131611.doc.
[171] A. Bendar, "Peres Erased Criminal Records for Opponents of the Disengagement," NRG (June 14, 2009) [Hebrew], www.nrg.co.il/online/1/ART1/903/455.html.
[172] Law to Terminate Proceedings and Erase Records Concerning the Disengagement Plan (2010).
[173] HCJ 1213/10 Nir v. Speaker of the Knesset (February 23, 2012). See also G. Grossman, "Pardon for the Opponents of the Disengagement is Discrimination," Walla! News (February 15, 2010) [Hebrew], http://news.walla.co.il/?w=/9/1643497. For a critical discussion of the Supreme Court's decision, see B. Medina and I. Saban, "On 'the People' Whose Rifts Are to Be Mended: The Judgment Concerning the Pardon Law for Lawbreaking Opponent of the Disengagement Plan," in R. Zreik and I. Saban (eds.), Law, Minority, and National Conflict (Tel Aviv: Tel Aviv University, 2017), pp. 375–88 [Hebrew].
[174] The State Attorney's reply to the petition in HCJ 1213/10.
[175] Y. Berger, "The Court Did Not Convict a Minor Who Assaulted a Left-Wing Activist: He Has High Rehabilitation Chances and Aspires to Enlist in the Military," Haaretz (December 18, 2017) [Hebrew], www.haaretz.co.il/news/law/.premium-1.4729999.

Leniency based on prospective military service is not restricted to settler youth. Illustrating this is a remark made by the then supreme court justice Elyakim Rubinstein in 2010: "[R]egarding minors facing enlistment, the approach is to make every effort to enable their conscription to the IDF, conscription we still regard as ... the most important means of socialization."[176] At the same time, when settler youth are concerned, an additional factor may be in operation: the growing proportion, since the turn of the century, of religious-Zionist soldiers in combat units and officer courses. Accordingly, settler soldiers, often affiliated with religious Zionism, are increasingly viewed in Israel as taking a lead in contributing to, and self-sacrificing for, the country.[177] From this perspective, shielding them from criminal proceedings may be all the more necessary.

Some parliamentary deliberations interwove concerns about prosecuting settler youth with a mental health discourse – a theme Chapter 5 explored in relation to Palestinians. Several months after its completion, MP Yahalom described the Gaza pullout to the Constitution, Law, and Justice Committee as an unprecedented "traumatizing" event. He added:

> prosecuting [minors] can stain them for life. [The State Attorney's Office is] ... now going to destroy the lives of hundreds of young guys, the salt of the earth, who protested against a terrible trauma ... [S]ome of these minors are also not conscripted. [The military says] ...: before you enlist, go to the Mental Health Officer [a military psychiatrist or psychologist assessing suitability for military service]. So they [the military authorities] destroy any motivation to serve in the military.[178]

If evacuation from Gaza was considered a trauma, then willingness to serve in the military was deemed a sign of rehabilitation. Four years after the pullout, the Child Rights Committee convened to review the well-being of the affected youth. A government worker who was invited to present the enlistment rate of the evacuated youth reported an initial decline, but reassured the committee: "in the last year-and-a-half ... [there is] growing motivation, ... [T]his is a rehabilitative process of

---

[176] E. Rubinstein, "The Minor in Law" (2010) 3–4 *The Family in Law* 35, 61 [Hebrew].

[177] Y. Levy, "The Theocratization of the Israeli Military" (2014) 40:2 *Armed Forces & Society* 269; U. Lebel, "Settling the Military: The Pre-Military Academies Revolution and the Creation of a New Security Epistemic Community – The Militarization of Judea and Samaria" (2015) 21:3 *Israel Affairs* 361, 361–62, 384–85.

[178] Constitution, Law, and Justice Committee, Transcript 648.

sorts."[179] Law and the military alike were thus presented as the source of the youths' trauma, but also as helping the evacuated youth carry on with their lives. On the one hand, the law authorized their traumatic evacuation, which the military then executed. This brought many settler youth into conflict with the military (as protestors) and, consequently, with the law (as suspects or defendants). On the other hand, the law was believed to have aided settler youth by pardoning them, while military service indicated their rehabilitation. The dominant narrative eventually emerging in parliament, therefore, interwove two supposed success stories: from trauma to rehabilitation, and from childhood to military service.

For these settlers, past military service was heralded as a redemption of sorts. For other Israelis, it was treated as a mitigating factor. Thus, in 2018, a policeman convicted of assaulting two Palestinian citizens of Israel was spared prison. The court noted to his credit his "full and meaningful military service as a combat soldier and a unit officer," including, specifically, his participation in the 2014 military offensive against Gaza.[180] Military service – past, present, or future – has thus provided grounds for leniency, if not outright unaccountability. In the next chapter, I continue my inquiry into law's shaping of Israeli childhood, with a further focus on settler youth and on contextualization in relation to young Palestinians.

---

[179] Special Committee for the Rights of the Child, 18th Knesset – Transcript 6 (June 23, 2009) [Hebrew], http://fs.knesset.gov.il/18/Committees/18_ptv_138548.doc.

[180] CrimC (Jer. Mag.) 67291-03-17 *State of Israel* v. *Cohen* (October 31, 2018), ¶¶ 17, 22.

8

Unsettling Children: Israeli Law and Settlers' Childhood

8.1 Introduction: Law, Human Rights, and Young Israeli Settlers

Having dedicated parts of the previous chapter to examining issues concerning young Jewish Israeli settlers, I continue this line of inquiry in this chapter. Israeli settlers, a non-monolithic population with enormous sociopolitical weight,[1] have been the subject of a burgeoning body of writing by non-jurists.[2] Legal scholarship, however, has limited its purview to the legal ramifications of settlements and, to a lesser extent, to the settlers' legal status,[3] while paying little attention, if any, to settlers' encounters with the Israeli legal system. With regard to settlers aged under 18, specifically, not only the legal literature but scholarship generally has thus far been limited in scope.[4] This chapter seeks to fill these scholarly gaps while bringing to bear insights and findings from previous chapters.

---

[1] On their non-monolithic nature and their sociopolitical role, see, respectively, E. Lewsen, "Reeled In: The Settlement Project and the Evacuation of an Israeli Fishing Village from Gaza" (2014) 5:1 *Settler Colonial Studies* 66; I. Zertal and A. Eldar, *Lords of the Land: The War over Israel's Settlements in the Occupied Territories* (New York: Nation Books, 2005).

[2] See, e.g., M. Feige, *Settling in the Hearts: Jewish Fundamentalism in the Occupied Territories* (Detroit: Wayne State University Press, 2009); J. Dalsheim, *Unsettling Gaza: Secular Liberalism, Radical Religion, and the Israeli Settlement Project* (2011); vol. 47 *Theory & Criticism* ("The Settlements: New Perspectives") (2017) [Hebrew].

[3] See, respectively, O. Ben-Naftali, A. M. Gross, and K. Michaeli, "Illegal Occupation: Framing the Occupied Palestinian Territory" (2005) 23:3 *Berkeley Journal of International Law* 551, 579–92, 601–05; T. Kelly, "'Jurisdictional Politics' in the Occupied West Bank: Territory, Community, and Economic Dependency in the Formation of Legal Subjects" (2006) 31:1 *Law & Social Inquiry* 39.

[4] Two examples of the existing literature are H. Zubida, M. Miro, and D. Mekelberg, "Kaleidoscope of Framings: The Case of 'Hill-Top Youth'," in H. Zubida and D. Mekelberg (eds.), *Democratic Arrangements in the New Public Sphere* (Tel Aviv: Israeli Political Science Association, 2010), pp. 219–43 [Hebrew]; S. Friedman, "Adversity in a Snowball Fight: Jewish Childhood in the Muslim Village of Sillwan," in D. Chappell (ed.), *Children under Construction: Critical Essays on Play as Curriculum* (New York: Peter Lang, 2010), p. 259. Further studies are cited later in this chapter.

Israeli settlers have had a close, albeit complex, relationship with the two "protagonists" of this book: law and human rights. Like other elements of the Israeli control regime, Jewish settlements owe much of their existence and expansion to state lawyers and legal mechanisms.[5] Having long articulated their views in terms of Jewish particularity and entitlement, settler activists and their allies have also, since the turn of the century, increasingly adopted a universal language of human rights. For example, along with their slogan "a Jew does not expel another Jew," opponents of the 2005 Gaza pullout described it as a "debasement of universal human rights" and themselves as "carry[ing] simultaneously the flags of human rights, freedom and morality."[6]

Laid bare throughout this book are overlaps in the legal and human rights discourses of Israel and its liberal critics. The rhetoric and tactics of Jewish settler activists, though adapted to their own goals, have likewise closely resembled and converged with those long used by the liberal human rights community. In this manner, yet again, law and human rights operate as weapons for dispossessing and exploiting Palestinians. One settler NGO, the Human Rights Organization of Judea and Samaria,[7] has thus filed numerous court petitions against the evacuation of Jewish outposts in Palestinian territories and the "police discrimination and brutality" they entail, practices it describes as putting "democracy at risk." A report coauthored by the same NGO similarly condemned the government for its "extensive violations" of the rights of Israeli protestors against the Gaza pullout, including their "freedom of movement," "the liberty of defendants," and "prisoners' rights and due process." Another settler NGO, Regavim, has complained that the principle of "legal equality," "a basic value in democratic societies," is violated because Israel "does not enforce the law" on Palestinian "illegal building" – claims later cited by right-wing members of parliament. Regavim was, according to its international relations director, consciously created to emulate and thus counter the "lawfare" (legal warfare)[8] waged by liberal human rights organizations. The latter, in turn,

---

[5] Zertal and Eldar, *Lords of the Land*, pp. 333–99.

[6] E. Shor, "Utilizing Rights and Wrongs: Right-Wing, the 'Rights' Language, and Human Rights in the Gaza Disengagement" (2008) 51:4 *Sociological Perspectives* 803, 804, 813–16.

[7] Judea and Samaria are, as noted in Chapter 1 (Section 1.3.2, "The West Bank, Excluding East Jerusalem"), the biblical terms by which Israeli Jews commonly refer to the West Bank.

[8] On the forms of lawfare waged by different political players – Israel, its allies, and its human rights critics – see H. Viterbo, "Lawfare," in O. Ben-Naftali, M. Sfard, and

are aware of this emulation. A lawyer at one liberal Israeli NGO has described Regavim as "basically using the same language [as us while creating] ... a mirror picture of [it] ... They are taking [our] ... petitions and they are reversing everything."[9]

Despite their image as the settlers' foes, liberal human rights organizations in Israel have campaigned against violations of settlers aged under 18, in particular young protestors against the Gaza pullout and evacuees from Gaza settlements. Meetings of the parliamentary Child Rights Committee about the pullout, often chaired by left-wing legislators, were attended by lawyers from two liberal NGOs, the Association for Civil Rights in Israel and the National Council for the Child, with the latter speaking about the "need to remember that these [arrested] minors have rights ... [which] must be upheld."[10] The former NGO also penned an open letter to the police criticizing its prolonged detention of settler girls who, as described later in this chapter, refused to identify themselves.[11] Overall, however, liberal human rights organizations are far more preoccupied with issues concerning noncitizen Palestinians below the age of 18 than with those of their settler counterparts. Possible explanations for this disparity are: the much larger number of Palestinians under Israeli military control (as detailed in Chapter 1); the ever-changing laws concerning young Palestinians (as analyzed in Chapter 4), in contrast to the relatively stable legislation applicable to settlers; and, most importantly, the superior political-legal status and entitlements of Israelis generally, and of settlers in particular, compared with those of Palestinians.

The next section takes as its subject this institutionalized legal disparity between the different populations living under Israel's control. Using an array of primary and secondary sources, I will demonstrate how Israeli Jews aged under 18, and settlers in particular, enjoy far greater rights and

---

H. Viterbo, *The ABC of the OPT: A Legal Lexicon of the Israeli Control over the Occupied Palestinian Territory* (Cambridge and New York: Cambridge University Press, 2018), pp. 246–63.

[9] N. Perugini and N. Gordon, *The Human Right to Dominate* (New York: Oxford University Press, 2015), pp. 101–24.

[10] Special Committee for the Rights of the Child, 16th Knesset – Transcript 135 (July 26, 2005) [Hebrew], http://fs.knesset.gov.il/16/Committees/16_ptv_491841.docx [hereinafter: Child Rights Committee Transcript 135]; Special Committee for the Rights of the Child, 17th Knesset – Transcript 11 (October 17, 2006) [Hebrew] (currently unavailable online) [hereinafter: Child Rights Committee Transcript 11].

[11] L. Margalit, ACRI's letter to the Head of the Samaria and Judea Prosecution Unit of the Police, "Prolonged Detention of Minors Refusing to Self-Identify" (January 20, 2008) [Hebrew], http://ymedad.blogspot.com/2008/01/blog-post_20.html.

a preferential treatment throughout their encounter with the legal system. Following an overview of this issue at both the statutory and state practice levels, I will turn the spotlight on two specific contexts. The first is Israel's handling of settler youth who hurl stones at Israeli security forces or Palestinians. Here, I will reveal several trends, including relative leniency, in the way Israel arrests, prosecutes, and sentences these young settlers, which contrast with its treatment of Palestinian stone-throwers (be they citizens, residents, or nonresident-noncitizens); soldiers' abuse of Palestinian victims of stone throwing; the Israeli judiciary's rejection of Palestinian defendants' selective enforcement claims, contrasting with its acceptance of such claims by settlers; the courts' consideration of settlers' military service as a mitigating factor; and convictions only when Palestinian complaints are corroborated by Israeli witnesses. The second context to be examined is Israel's policy of detaining, along with their older counterparts, settlers aged under 18 who were protesting the Gaza pullout. I will analyze the reasons given for this lack of age segregation while juxtaposing them with Israel's age-segregated incarceration of Palestinians.

At the same time, the relationship between childhood, law, and human rights in Israel/Palestine is not reducible to such legal disparities, as prominent and consequential as they are. Accordingly, the remainder of this chapter will expand the scope of analysis, with Section 8.3 looking at Israel's response to detained settler girls who refused to disclose their identities. My focus will be on the legal system's struggle to cope with young people's silence when asked about their ages, as well as on those who subsequently condemned the legal system for what they described as its infantile approach. Against this backdrop, I will consider broader lessons for thinking about age, voice, and infantilization.

Finally, Section 8.4 will shed light on the operation, effects, and interaction of two modes of representation – a mental health language of trauma and loss, and visual imagery – in parliamentary debates on the effects of the Gaza pullout on young Jewish evacuees. Among other things, I will examine the competing conceptions of trauma and loss at play; the politically contentious nature of drawings by these young evacuees; the elevated status accorded to mental health practitioners as an authoritative source of knowledge about traumatized young people and their drawings; and attempts to render the absence of the evacuated homes visible.

Thus, interwoven throughout the analysis will be themes explored in all the previous chapters: the different modes of control to which Israelis and Palestinians are subjected (Chapter 1); the legal status of under-18s (Chapter 2); stone throwing (Chapter 2); age as a potentially resistant performance (Chapter 3); age segregation in detention (Chapter 4); the mental health discourse of trauma and loss (Chapter 5); attitudes to children's silence (Chapter 5); pictures of young people in times of political unrest (Chapter 6); visual representations of absence (Chapter 6); the preference of Israeli over Palestinian testimonies (Chapter 6); infantilization (Chapter 7); and mitigated sentences based on Israeli defendants' military service (Chapter 7). In revisiting each of these themes, this chapter uniquely contextualizes issues concerning settler youth by relating them to those of young Palestinians.

8.2 Legal Disparity and Discrimination

As described in Chapter 1, Israel operates two parallel legal systems: a non-military one for its citizens and a military system for most non-citizen Palestinians in conflict with Israeli law. Israeli citizens, including settlers, are accordingly put on trial by civil prosecution bodies – the Israeli police and the state attorney – whereas noncitizen Palestinians are usually handled by military prosecutors. There is overlap between these systems, some of which was brought to light in Chapter 4. Nonetheless, Israelis under the age of 18 – who constitute 8.9 percent of those arrested by Israel's police and 7.4 percent of those convicted in non-military courts[12] – enjoy far greater entitlements than their Palestinian peers.

The Youth Law, the main statute concerning Israeli under-18s in conflict with the criminal law, differs significantly from the military legislation that Israel applies to noncitizen Palestinians. Since its enactment in 1971, this statute has been amended several times, including an extensive amendment in 2008 that was designed to bring it in line with international child rights legal standards.[13] Among its provisions, the statute now requires that detention of those aged under 18 be used only as a last resort; that all measures be carried out to protect the dignity of under-18s, in consideration of their age and maturity level, and with due

---

[12] See, respectively, Israel Police – Planning and Organization Division, *2017 Statistical Yearbook* (May 2018), p. 58 [Hebrew], www.gov.il/BlobFolder/reports/police_statistical_abstract_2017/he/shanton_2017.pdf; Central Bureau of Statistics, *Israel Statistical Annual – 2019* (July 29, 2019), p. 154 [Hebrew], www.cbs.gov.il/he/publications/DocLib/2019/Shnaton70_mun.pdf (referring to 2017).

[13] Youth Law (Adjudication, Punishment, and Modes of Treatment), 1971 [hereinafter: Youth Law].

weight being given to their rehabilitation, care, and reintegration into society; that decisions concerning them accord due weight to their wishes; that arrest decisions by the police take into account their young age as well as the effect of arrest on their well-being and development; that under-18s be allowed to express their opinion at different stages of the criminal process; and that the court explain its decisions to them in a manner suitable to their age and maturity level, including explanation of the reasons for decisions taken against their wishes.[14]

None of these provisions exists in the Israeli military law to which noncitizen Palestinians are subject. Conversely, the non-military law spares Israelis from various statutory provisions that the military law applies to noncitizen Palestinians. Two examples, analyzed in Chapters 3 and 4 respectively, are the statutory distinction between three subgroups of noncitizen Palestinians aged under 16 ("child" for under-12s, "youth" for 12–13-year-olds, and "tender adult" for 14–15-year-olds); and the placing of the onus of having a defense attorney's details on young arrested Palestinians rather than on the Israeli authorities. The list of differences in the statutory provisions for these two populations extends well beyond these examples.[15]

At the same time, an exclusive focus on the statutory level might be misleading. As detailed in Chapter 4, young Palestinians are frequently denied their statutory rights, due to inconsistent application, and even their breach, by Israeli authorities; moreover, statutory exceptions enable the authorities to deviate from the formal rules. This is, in fact, not entirely exclusive to noncitizen Palestinians, as exemplified by statutory provisions regarding police interrogations. Under the statutory law, Israelis below the age of majority are generally entitled to have a parent, a relative, or another adult acquaintance present in their interrogation and, as far as possible, to consult with that person prior to the interrogation. This right must be explained to them prior to the interrogation, as too should be their right to legal counsel and representation. Further, as much as possible, the police should notify the designated adult before summoning the suspect to interrogation. Exemptions for that person's

---

[14] Ibid., Articles 1a–1b, 9b(b), 9f(a), 9f(c)(2), 10a, 13a, 17a–17b.

[15] For a comparative table of some key statutory provisions regarding Israelis and non-citizen Palestinians aged under 18, see Military Court Watch, *Children in Military Custody: Progress Report – 2 Years On* (September 1, 2014), p. 23, www .militarycourtwatch.org/files/server/CHILDREN%20IN%20MILITARY%20CUSTODY% 20-%202%20YEARS%20ON%20(1).pdf.

presence in the interrogation are only made when it is deemed harmful to the interrogee's well-being or in certain other circumstances, such as when the adult in question is suspected of complicity in the offense, or when the interrogee is suspected of a "security offense" (a category rarely applied to Jews, as explained in Chapter 2). Even in these circumstances, the adult should normally be notified within six hours of the young interrogee's arrival at the police station. In addition, save specific exceptions, Israelis below the age of 18 may not be interrogated during the night.[16]

In practice, these provisions are often not enforced. Israel's state comptroller sampled 346 interrogations of Israelis aged under 18 in 2012 and found that 73 percent of the interrogees had been informed of only some of their rights; 63 percent received no legal counsel prior to the interrogation; 26 percent did not have their parent informed of their arrest; 64 percent were interrogated without a parent's presence; and 32 percent were interrogated during the night (meaning 20:00–07:00 for under-14s and 22:00–07:00 for 14–17-year-olds).[17] Such violations have resulted in court decisions to release from detention or acquit the young Israelis concerned.[18] As these figures include Palestinian citizens of Israel, who – as detailed shortly – are systematically discriminated against, it is impossible to gauge the extent of infringement of the rights of Israeli Jews. Nevertheless, the latter, including Jewish settlers, are undeniably among those affected: in 2012, for example, an Israeli court criticized the police for illegally interrogating a settler under the age of majority during the night.[19]

---

[16] Articles 9d(a), 9f, 9g, 9h, 9i(a), 9j of the Youth Law. Under Article 9i(b), where the minor is not receiving legal counsel, the public defender's office should be contacted to see whether s/he is entitled to their representation. Under Article 9g(d), the six-hour limit can be extended to eight hours where concern remains that informing the adult would harm the minor's well-being, obstruct the investigation, or substantially harm national security.

[17] State Comptroller and Ombudsman of Israel, *Annual Report 64C* (2014), pp. 404, 419, 423–29, 432–33 [Hebrew], www.mevaker.gov.il/he/Reports/Report_248/e7ec000e-0827-40b9-b5dd-4c3b825cd2fd/209-ver-5.pdf.

[18] See court decisions cited in Public Defender's Office, *Activity Report – 2016* (August, 2017), pp. 35–37 [Hebrew], www.justice.gov.il/Units/SanegoriaZiborit/DohotRishmi/dohot/%d7%93%d7%95%d7%97%20%d7%a4%d7%a2%d7%99%d7%9c%d7%95%d7%aa%20%d7%94%d7%a1%d7%a0%d7%99%d7%92%d7%95%d7%a8%d7%99%d7%94%20%d7%94%d7%a6%d7%99%d7%91%d7%95%d7%a8%d7%99%d7%aa%20%d7%9c%d7%a9%d7%a0%d7%aa%202016%20-%20%d7%a1%d7%95%d7%a4%d7%99.pdf.

[19] C. Levinson, "Court Criticizes the Samaria and Judea Police: Policemen Illegally Arrested Minors," *Haaretz* (January 15, 2012) [Hebrew], www.haaretz.co.il/news/law/1.1617269.

Moreover, as demonstrated in Chapter 4, statutory reforms made by Israel to its military law, which at first sight appear to adopt from the non-military law rights that are granted to Israelis, are in fact carefully designed to be largely tokenistic or even harmful to Palestinians. Therefore, even if Israel amends its legislation so as to seemingly remove some of the statutory differences I have described here between Israelis and Palestinians, this is hardly guaranteed to benefit Palestinians.

Given the partial and potentially deceptive nature of statutory analysis, it is necessary to look at Israel's actual treatment of its young citizens who come into conflict with the law, which sharply contrasts with its handling of their noncitizen Palestinian counterparts (all figures concerning the latter in this section are taken from Chapter 2, unless indicated otherwise).[20] To begin with, Israeli citizens are far less likely to find themselves in criminal custody. In 2011, for example, there were 220 Israelis under the age of 18 behind bars, compared with 1,190 – more than five times as many – noncitizen Palestinians.[21] The hyperincarceration of noncitizen Palestinians aged under 18 is even greater, considering that many others are held in Palestinian rather than Israeli facilities.

Once Israelis under the age of 18 arrive in court, the judiciary devotes much greater time to their cases than it does to those of their noncitizen Palestinian peers. For example, hearings for Israelis aged under 18 in magistrate youth courts take nearly 50 minutes on average for precharge detention decisions and about 41 minutes for authorizing continued detention pending disposition.[22] This is about 14–17 times the amount (three minutes or so, on average) that Israeli military courts spend on detention hearings involving noncitizen Palestinians below the age of 18.

Israeli under-18s standing trial are also far less likely to be convicted than same-age Palestinian noncitizens. According to the Israeli police, the conviction rate of Israelis in this age group is approximately 40 percent, with about 20 percent of cases concluding with prison sentences.[23] Other sources suggest an even lower prison sentence rate of

---

[20] See, in particular, Chapter 2, Section 2.5 ("The Real Trial").

[21] National Council for the Child, *Selected Information from the Annual "Children in Israel – 2012"* (Jerusalem: December 2012), p. 24 [Hebrew], https://web.archive.org/web/20150329055300/www.children.org.il/Files/File/SHNATON/%20%202012.pdf.

[22] K. Weinshall-Margel, "Judicial Workloads in Israel (Case Weights) Dataset" (Jerusalem: Israeli Courts Research Division, June 2013), https://elyon1.court.gov.il/heb/Research%20Division/doc/fw.xls.

[23] Israel Police, *Annual Report 2009* (July 2010), p. 27 [Hebrew], www.news1.co.il/uploadFiles/364513576030732.pdf; L. Yehuda et al., *One Rule, Two Legal Systems:*

6.5 percent in certain years.[24] Moreover, as detailed in the previous chapter, hundreds of young settlers charged with ideologically motivated offenses in opposition to the Gaza pullout were, unusually, pardoned. In stark contrast, of the military court cases I quantitatively analyzed, involving noncitizen Palestinians aged under 18, none ended in an acquittal, while about 94 percent resulted in prison sentences. This reflects a broader disparity in conviction rates: the military courts' 99.76 percent conviction rate is much higher than the non-military courts' conviction rates, which in recent years have ranged from 65 to 86 percent.[25] For Israelis prosecuted in non-military courts for offenses against noncitizen Palestinians, the conviction rate is even lower: 43.4 percent. To this should be added that only 8 percent of police investigations into such offenses lead to indictments,[26] and that Palestinians, as explained in Chapter 6, often prefer not to complain to Israeli authorities.

Israelis who appeal their conviction in the non-military court system stand a greater chance of succeeding than noncitizen Palestinians who do so in Israel's military courts. The success rate of Israeli defendants' appeals (34 percent) is not much lower than that of appeals by the state attorney's office (41 percent).[27] In comparison, appeals by noncitizen

Israel's Regime of Laws in the West Bank (Tel Aviv: ACRI, 2014), p. 73, www.acri.org.il/en/wp-content/uploads/2015/02/Two-Systems-of-Law-English-FINAL.pdf (the latter citing the police 2010 data).

[24] This figure, relating to 2008 and provided by Israeli NGO the National Council for the Child, is cited in DCIP, *In Their Own Words: A Report on the Situation Facing Palestinian Children Detained in the Israeli Military Court System – Reporting Period: 1 July to 31 December 2010* (January 29, 2011), p. 4, https://resourcecentre.savethechildren.net/node/4705/pdf/4705.pdf.

[25] O. Gazal-Ayal, I. Galon, and K. Winshel-Margel, *The Conviction and Acquittal Rates in Criminal Proceedings* (University of Haifa Center for the Study of Crime, Law & Society and Israeli Courts Research Division, May 2012) [Hebrew], https://elyon1.court.gov.il/heb/Research%20Division/doc/Research1.pdf (based on a sample of 1,661 court files from 2010–2011); Central Bureau of Statistics, "Persons Accused in Criminal Trials, 2016" (August 19, 2018) [Hebrew], www.cbs.gov.il/he/mediarelease/DocLib/2018/246/18_18_246b.pdf.

[26] Yesh Din, *Law Enforcement on Israeli Civilians in the West Bank* (December 2017), https://s3-eu-west-1.amazonaws.com/files.yesh-din.org/December+2017+Law+Enforcement+Datasheet/LAW+ENFORCEMENT+Data+12.17+-+ENGLISH.pdf (the indictment and conviction figures refer to a sample of 1,163 cases from the period 2005–2017).

[27] State Attorney, *2015 Report* (August 2016), pp. 28–29 [Hebrew], www.justice.gov.il/Units/StateAttorney/Documents/2015AnnualReport.pdf (figures relating to 2015). The state attorney's office, however, only handles about 10 percent of criminal cases, typically

Palestinian defendants are only half as likely to succeed as military prosecution appeals to increase the sentence.

While my focus here is on arrests, prosecution, and incarceration, the preferential treatment of Israelis extends to virtually all other areas of life. Of the countless possible examples, one is home demolitions. Using various legal mechanisms, Israel has increasingly dispossessed Palestinians from their lands in the West Bank, while expanding Jewish settlements. To apply for a building permit, Palestinians must undergo a costly and lengthy process, in which a staggering 96 percent of applications are rejected – leading to many Palestinians not applying in the first place. Israeli authorities, using an ostensibly neutral rhetoric of "law enforcement," have demolished thousands of "unauthorized" Palestinian buildings over the years. Not a single Palestinian petition against such demolitions has been granted by the supreme court.[28] In 2016, a senior Israeli military official admitted to a parliamentary subcommittee that "our enforcement against [illegal construction by] Palestinians is hundreds of percent higher" than against Israeli settlers, adding: "We simply decided, due to foreign policy implications, to present the full figures behind closed doors."[29]

As part of this practice, Israel has a policy, approved by the supreme court, of demolishing or sealing Palestinian houses if a family member has been convicted of terrorist attacks – an issue discussed in Chapter 3. In 2014, the supreme court dismissed a petition against this policy, which took issue with, among other things, its discriminatory enforcement – the categorical exemption of convicted Jewish terrorists. The petitioners mentioned, as an example of such Jewish terrorists, the three settler youths who, earlier that year, had kidnapped, strangled, and burnt to death a 16-year-old Palestinian from East Jerusalem. The court, rejecting this claim and the petition generally, insisted that such violence was an isolated exception – a framing similar to that highlighted in Chapter 6 – and hence did not warrant applying the house demolition policy to

those involving relatively grave charges, whereas the remainder are mainly handled by the police prosecution. Ibid., pp. 15, 23–24.

[28] Y. Stein, *Fake Justice: The Responsibility Israel's High Court Justices Bear for the Demolition of Palestinian Homes and the Dispossession of Palestinians* (Jerusalem: B'Tselem, February 2019), pp. 7–15, 22, www.btselem.org/sites/default/files/publica tions/201902_fake_justice_eng.pdf.

[29] H. Baruch, "Major-General Mordechai: We Are Taking a Hard Line with Arabs," *Channel 7* (April 6, 2016) [Hebrew], www.inn.co.il/News/News.aspx/319596.

Jews.[30] Three years later, the parents of the murdered Palestinian petitioned the supreme court to have the houses of the three settler youths –
who in the meantime had been convicted of murder and sentenced to
prison[31] – demolished or sealed, as would be done with Palestinian
homes. The court, dismissing this petition too while professing commitment to equality, insisted that there were simply objective differences
between the nature of Jewish and Palestinian terrorism.[32]

In fact, the legal reality facing Jews is substantially different from that
encountered not only by noncitizen Palestinians, as I have illustrated so
far, but also by Israel's Palestinian citizens. The latter, as noted in
Chapter 1, make up only 20 percent of the country's population, whereas
Jews comprise around 75 percent of Israel's population. However, in the
period 2015–17, nearly 12 times more Palestinian citizens than Jewish
citizens were prosecuted for incitement. And although these Jewish
citizens, unlike their Palestinian counterparts, tended to be charged with
violent offenses in addition to incitement, it was the Palestinian citizens
who were kept in detention until the end of trial at a rate 14 times
higher.[33] Between 2011 and 2018, arrests of Jews decreased by 11 percent,
while those of Palestinian citizens increased by nine percent.[34] By 2020,
more than 50 percent of arrested citizens were Palestinians.[35] Between
2011 and 2015, 56 percent of under-18s arrested by the police were
classified as "non-Jews," a classification also applied to 88 percent of
those arrested specifically for "security offenses."[36] The conviction rate of
those classified as "Arab minors" (55.3 percent) is also much higher than
that of "Jewish and other minors" (35.6 percent).[37]

---

[30] HCJ 5290/14 *Kawasme* v. *Military Commander of the West Bank* (August 11, 2014),
¶ 30 of justice Danziger's leading opinion.

[31] CrimC (Jer. Dist.) 34700-07-14 *State of Israel* v. *Ben-David* (verdicts November 30,
2015 and April 19, 2016, sentencings February 4 and May 3, 2016).

[32] HCJ 5376/16 *Abu Khdeir* v. *Minister of Defense* (July 4, 2017), ¶¶ 28–32, 38 of justice
Rubinstein's leading opinion as well as ¶¶ 2–6 of justice Hendel's concurring opinion.

[33] J. Brown, "Since 2015: A 650% Rise in Indictments for Incitement for Arabs," *Haaretz*
(December 19, 2017) [Hebrew], www.haaretz.co.il/blogs/johnbrown/BLOG-1.4730690.

[34] J. Breiner, "More Arab Citizens Arrests, but Fewer Indicted," *Haaretz* (August 7, 2018)
[Hebrew], www.haaretz.co.il/news/law/1.6359920.

[35] D. Dolev, "Police Arrests Fall by Tens of Percent – But Only in the Jewish Sector," *Walla!
News* (November 2, 2020) [Hebrew], https://news.walla.co.il/item/3396245.

[36] N. Rotem, "60% of People Arrested by Israeli Police Are 'Non-Jews'," *+972 Magazine*
(June 1, 2016), www.972mag.com/60-of-people-arrested-by-israeli-police-are-non-jews/
119696.

[37] Central Bureau of Statistics, "Persons Accused in Criminal Trials, 2016."

As a result, young Palestinian citizens are overrepresented in Israeli prisons, making up 57 percent of incarcerated citizens aged under 18 – nearly three times their share in the country's overall population. Jews, in contrast, constitute only 36 percent of under-18s behind bars – less than half their share of Israel's citizenry. On closer inspection, these figures betray inequality based on religion as well as nationality: almost all incarcerated Palestinian citizens below the age of 18 are Muslim. When adding noncitizen Palestinians into the equation, the overall portion of Palestinian under-18s in Israeli prisons is a staggering 85 percent – 6.5 times higher than that of Jews.[38] And this, as I have noted, does not take into account the hundreds, and even thousands, of young noncitizen Palestinians who are annually dealt with by the Palestinian law enforcement authorities. Further, every year, hundreds of noncitizen Palestinians, among them under-18s, are imprisoned as "administrative detainees" without charge or trial. Israelis are very rarely subjected to this practice, and those who are thus incarcerated tend to be released earlier than Palestinians.[39]

Like some previous figures, these last ones reflect a wider discrimination against Palestinian citizens of all ages. Those standing trial are only 65 percent as likely to have their court case cancelled as Jewish

---

[38] On the national composition of incarcerated under-18s, see N. Rotem, "In the Jewish State, Most Prisoners are Arabs," *+972 Magazine* (September 2, 2016), http://972mag .com/in-the-jewish-state-most-prisoners-are-arabs/121686. On the composition of Israel's population, see Central Bureau of Statistics, "Population of Israel on the Eve of 2019 – 9.0 Million" (December 31, 2018), www.cbs.gov.il/he/mediarelease/DocLib/2018/ 394/11_18_394e.pdf. On the religious composition of incarcerated under-18s, see Part II (Table 22) of Addendum: Written Replies of Israel to the UNCRC, UN Doc, CRC/C/ISR/ Q/2-4/Add.1 (May 22, 2013), http://docstore.ohchr.org/SelfServices/FilesHandler.ashx? enc=6QkG1d%2fPPRiCAqhKb7yhsv1txuQys3LgW60cwoE2%2bBXBtcHRoEqMe%2fr% 2brOnX0CgDdc50AuNRpBZ4vz6iUeu6l4igUcn2FviseAtJMJG% 2b7UkbD1kkphZTrDKJffTDpVIh9c2dsdAdjZANis9nh6W9Mg%3d%3d.

[39] For figures regarding noncitizen Palestinians, including under-18s, see B'Tselem, "Statistics on Administrative Detention" (n.d., last accessed on March 29, 2020), www .btselem.org/administrative_detention/statistics. For information regarding Israelis, see O. Feuerstein, *Without Trial: Administrative Detention of Palestinians by Israel and the Internment of Unlawful Combatants Law* (Jerusalem: B'Tselem and Hamoked, October 2009), p. 66, www.btselem.org/download/200910_without_trial_eng.pdf. For an example of a settler "administrative detainee" aged under 18 being released to house arrest, see M. Horodniceanu, "Court Rules: Shin Beit Interrogators Violated Basic Rights of Suspects of Hate Crimes," *Walla! News* (January 9, 2020) [Hebrew], https://news.walla.co.il/item/ 3333991.

citizens.[40] Their conviction rate is higher than that of Jews: 92.5 and 82.6 percent respectively.[41] Following conviction, their chances of receiving, respectively, a suspended prison sentence or a prison sentence are 180 and 228 percent those of Jews.[42] In this area, as in others, court decisions correlate not only with the defendants' identities, but also with those of the judges: court panels that are all-Jewish tend to convict Palestinian citizens at a much higher rate, and impose much longer prison sentences, than panels with at least one Arab judge.[43] Meanwhile, it is Jews who reportedly commit physically violent crime at a higher rate than Palestinian citizens.[44] Further, unlike others convicted of homicide, those classified as "terrorists" – a category generally reserved for Palestinians – are not legally entitled to early release from prison.[45]

The disparity between Palestinian and Jewish citizens in Israel's criminal justice system has been the subject of several academic publications.[46] A handful of studies from the 1980s and 1990s focused on under-18s, but, as one of them acknowledged, "[n]o ... systematic study has been conducted on ... how Jews and Arabs are treated by the juvenile justice system"[47] – an observation still true today.

The next two subsections will further inquire into this disparity, as well as into the Israeli legal system's approach to settlers, with a focus on stone throwing and age-segregated detention. Whereas Chapters 2 and 3

---

[40] G. Rahov, Y. Rabin, and E. Yuchtman-Yaar, "Disparities between Jews and Arabs in the Israeli Criminal Justice System" (2015) 13:1 *Ohio State Journal of Criminal Law* 233, 240–41.

[41] Central Bureau of Statistics, "Persons Accused in Criminal Trials, 2016."

[42] Rahov, Rabin, and Yuchtman-Yaar, "Disparities between Jews and Arabs," pp. 241–42.

[43] G. Grossman et al., "Descriptive Representation and Judicial Outcomes in Multiethnic Societies" (2016) 60:1 *American Journal of Political Science* 44.

[44] Rahov, Rabin, and Yuchtman-Yaar, "Disparities between Jews and Arabs," p. 238.

[45] Article 40a of Counterterrorism Law, 2016 (amended in Counterterrorism Law (Amendment No. 4), 2019).

[46] See, e.g., Rahov, Rabin, and Yuchtman-Yaar, "Disparities between Jews and Arabs"; G. Fishman, A. Rattner, and H. Turjeman, "Sentencing Outcomes in a Multinational Society" (2006) 3:1 *European Journal of Criminology* 69.

[47] G. S. Mesch and G. Fishman, "Entering the System: Ethnic Differences in Closing Juvenile Criminal Files in Israel" (1999) 36:2 *Journal of Research in Crime and Delinquency* 175, 180. Other studies on the subject are Y. Hassin, "Jewish and Arab Juvenile Delinquency in Israel: The Problem and Its Remedies" (1987) 11:2 *International Journal of Comparative and Applied Criminal Justice* 213; Y. Hassin, "Offending by Minority Minors in the State of Israel, and the Social Response to Their Offending" (1997) 17:3 *Society & Welfare* 283 [Hebrew].

investigated these issues in relation to Palestinians, here I will examine
Israel's handling of settler youth who hurl stones at Israeli security forces
or at Palestinians, as well as the Israeli policy of jointly detaining settlers
below and above the age of 18 who were detained in demonstrations
against the Gaza pullout.

8.2.1   Stone Throwing

Israel has taken a hard line with noncitizen Palestinians aged under
18 who throw stones. As discussed in Chapter 3, the military courts have
repeatedly held that stone throwing, being the most common charge
against this age group, warrants harsh sentencing. Also relatively harsh
have been the sentences imposed by non-military courts for this act.
Moreover, Palestinian stone throwing has been met with soldiers'
stones,[48] as well as with sometimes deadly Israeli fire.[49] In 2015, Israel
made two relevant reforms mentioned in Chapter 2: first, its live fire rules
against stone-throwers were relaxed; and, second, stone throwing – a
longtime offense under the military law – was criminalized under the
non-military law as well. The latter amendment, while formally applicable to anyone residing within Israel's pre-1967 borders, was primarily
targeted at Palestinians in East Jerusalem, as was made clear by both the
government and the judiciary.[50] The minister of public security, referring
explicitly to East Jerusalemites, said at the time that "stone-throwers are
murderers in every respect ... and they must not be released on bail or
[merely sentenced to] community service. We would not achieve
deterrence that way!"[51]

While common charges against Israeli under-18s are property
offenses, drug offenses, and knife crime,[52] settlers in this age group have
also hurled stones at Israeli armed forces or Palestinians on multiple

---

[48] G. Cohen and N. Hasson, "IDF Officer Dismissed after Being Recorded Firing and
Throwing Stones at Palestinians," *Haaretz* (June 12, 2012) [Hebrew], www.haaretz.co
.il/news/politics/1.1729824.

[49] See examples in Chapter 3, Section 3.4.1 ("Age in Israel's Open-Fire Regulations") and
Chapter 6, Section 6.3.3. ("Impunity").

[50] See Chapter 2, Section 2.2 ("The Children of the Stones").

[51] Y. Kubovich, "Jews Throw Stones Too, but Arabs Get Harsher Sentences," *Haaretz*
(September 28, 2015), www.haaretz.com/.premium-arab-rock-throwers-sit-longer-in-
prison-1.5402878.

[52] Israel Police – Planning and Organization Division, *2017 Statistical Yearbook*, pp. 54–55.

occasions,[53] sometimes causing bodily injuries[54] and even death.[55] Such incidents, and the non-intervention of soldiers when Palestinians were targeted, have repeatedly been caught on camera,[56] including by Israeli authorities.[57] Nonetheless, Israel has shown far more leniency toward such conduct, compared with its handling of Palestinian stone throwing. Settler stone-throwers are not fired at because, as a military spokesperson once told an interviewer, "I assume you . . . wouldn't expect [soldiers] . . . to open fire at a Jew."[58] Along the same lines, in 2020, a police superintendent reportedly instructed forces deployed in Tel Aviv during the coronavirus (COVID-19) pandemic not to kick anyone under arrest because "we're not in the territories . . . A policeman should only open fire as the very last resort, after being shot at."[59] Often, settlers suspected of throwing stones are not arrested at all[60] or cannot be arrested due to

---

[53] See, e.g., E. Ben Kimon, "Hilltop Youth Shattered a Military Police Jeep Window Near Yitzhar," *Ynet* (September 23, 2020) [Hebrew], www.ynet.co.il/news/article/BybCJJ00Hv; Y. Berger et al., "Evacuation of Amona Completed; Netanyahu: We Will Strengthen Other Settlements," *Haaretz* (February 3, 2017) [Hebrew], www.haaretz.co.il/news/politics/LIVE-1.3591564.

[54] See, e.g., Y. Kubovich, H. Shezaf, and Y. Lis, "Soldier Injured by Settlers' Stones Near Yitzhar, Force Responded with Fire," *Haaretz* (October 20, 2019) [Hebrew], www.haaretz.co.il/news/politics/1.8010099; Y. Berger, "Security Forces Evacuated Trailers from Amona Settlement; 23 Border Police Injured in Clashes," *Haaretz* (January 3, 2019) [Hebrew], www.haaretz.co.il/news/politics/1.6806101.

[55] See, e.g., S. Osborne, "Palestinian Woman Dies 'After Israeli Settlers Pelt Her Car with Stones'," *Independent* (October 13, 2018), www.independent.co.uk/news/world/middle-east/palestinian-woman-killed-israel-stones-aisha-rabi-bidya-attack-a8582616.html. At the time of writing, the settler stone-thrower is currently on trial, and in 2019 the supreme court upheld his release to house arrest: AppR 3313/19 *State of Israel* v. *John Doe* (May 19, 2019).

[56] See, e.g., S. Bendet, "Recording: Masked Residents of Baladim Outpost Hurling Stones at Military Patrol," *Walla! News* (April 15, 2017) [Hebrew], https://news.walla.co.il/item/3057104; S. Bendet, "Recording: Settlers Throwing Stones at Palestinians in Front of Soldiers," *Walla! News* (October 12, 2015) [Hebrew], https://news.walla.co.il/item/2896758.

[57] See, e.g., Y. Berger and Y. Kubovich, "Settlers Hurled Stones at Border Policewoman and Mildly Wounded Her; Three Arrested," *Haaretz* (July 18, 2018) [Hebrew], www.haaretz.co.il/news/politics/1.6290213.

[58] For this quote as well as examples involving Palestinians aged under 18, see J. Brown, "IDF Soldiers More Afraid of Palestinians' Stones than Settlers' Stones," *Haaretz* (April 16, 2017) [Hebrew], www.haaretz.co.il/blogs/johnbrown/BLOG-1.4025222.

[59] B. Peleg, "Don't Kick during Arrest, Policeman Instructs Soldiers in South Tel Aviv. This Isn't the Territories," *Haaretz* (April 2, 2020) [Hebrew], www.haaretz.co.il/health/corona/.premium-1.8734200.

[60] See, e.g., H. Shezaf, "Settlers Hurl Stones at Security Forces Near Yitzhar Again; No Arrests This Time Either," *Haaretz* (October 21, 2019) [Hebrew], www.haaretz.co.il/

being under the age of criminal responsibility (12 years).[61] When arrests are made, the settler stone-throwers tend to be released summarily.[62]

Reports repeatedly suggest that soldiers have, in addition to allowing such stone throwing by settlers to go uninterrupted (for up to hours on end), also harassed, abused, or even themselves thrown objects at the Palestinian victims.[63] In this and other respects, settler violence is informally intertwined with state violence.[64] One soldier was convicted in 2004 for hitting, kicking, and breaking the nose of a 14-year-old Palestinian who, shortly beforehand, had approached the Israeli police for help when settler youths were hurling stones at him. The soldier threatened his comrade not to report the event and, for this reason, was also convicted of witness tampering. Initially, he was given a non-custodial sentence, which the court of appeals increased in 2005 to four months' imprisonment[65] – still far lighter than the likely sentence of a young Palestinian civilian who would physically assault an Israeli.

On the limited occasions when settler youth are taken to court for pelting stones at Palestinians, they tend to be either acquitted or leniently sentenced. In 2018, for example, a settler who, at the age of 17, had hurled stones at a Palestinian journalist's car and hit it, and who had later

---

news/politics/.premium-1.8013351; A. Pfeffer and H. Levinson, "Dozens of Right-Wing Activists Vandalized Base and Assaulted Brigade Commander; No One Was Arrested," *Haaretz* (December 13, 2011) [Hebrew], www.haaretz.co.il/news/politics/1.1589961.

[61] On the prevalence of under-12s among settler stone-throwers, see, e.g., L. Yavne, *A Semblance of Law: Law Enforcement upon Israeli Civilians in the West Bank* (Tel Aviv: Yesh Din, June 2006), p. 43, https://s3-eu-west-1.amazonaws.com/files.yesh-din.org/ %D7%9E%D7%A8%D7%90%D7%99%D7%AA+%D7%97%D7%95%D7%A7/%D7%9E% D7%A8%D7%90%D7%99%D7%AA+%D7%97%D7%95%D7%A7+%D7%94%D7%93% D7%95%D7%97+%D7%94%D7%9E%D7%9C%D7%90+EN.pdf.

[62] See, e.g., Y. Berger, "Seven Settlers Arrested in the Evacuation of Amona for Assaulting Police Released from Detention," *Haaretz* (January 3, 2019) [Hebrew], www.haaretz.co.il/ news/politics/1.6807622.

[63] See, e.g., B'Tselem, "City Center" (October 15, 2007), www.btselem.org/hebron/ 20071015_new_settlement_list_of_events_settlers.

[64] On settlers' close ties with, and influence on, the military, see Breaking the Silence, *The High Command: Settler Influence on IDF Conduct in the West Bank* (2017), www.breakingthesilence.org.il/inside/wp-content/uploads/2017/01/The-High-Command-Shovrim-Shtika-Report-January-2017.pdf. On settler violence as "an informal political mechanism that indirectly reproduces state power through unofficial channels," see N. Gazit, "State-sponsored Vigilantism: Jewish Settlers' Violence in the Occupied Palestinian Territories" (2015) 49:3 *Sociology* 438, 441.

[65] CMC (Center) 276/02 *Chief Military Prosecutor* v. *Elbaz* (July 15, 2004); CMA 84/04 *Chief Military Prosecutor* v. *Elbaz* (January 20, 2005).

admitted to having done so, was acquitted. The previous year, the supreme court upheld the acquittal of two young settlers who, as they admitted, had hurled stones at Palestinian vehicles. In the previous chapter, I examined the view, shared by judges and others in Israel, that a defendant's military service should be considered a mitigating factor. This rationale was also among the grounds for both these acquittals. In the former case, the court noted to the settler's credit his enlistment to a Hesder (a yeshiva program combining military service with Jewish studies) since the time of the offenses.[66] In the latter case, the supreme court emphasized the settler youths' "wish to ... enlist and serve in a combat unit," adding: "It is not impossible that a conviction might hinder [their] recruitment ... to a combat unit ..., and this cannot be ignored."[67] The vast majority of Palestinian citizens, who are not enlisted to the military (as explained in the previous chapter), are ineligible to receive such mitigation (as are noncitizen Palestinians, obviously).

Whereas these two cases ended with acquittals, others have concluded with relatively lenient sentences. As a case in point, in 2017 the supreme court upheld the non-custodial (and hence, as the court acknowledged, "non-severe") sentence of a settler who, at the age of 17 and together with other settler youths, had pelted stones and other objects at Palestinian vehicles. According to the judgment, the youths placed a wooden beam on the road to slow drivers down, targeted and shouted racist slurs at Palestinians, and hurled stones that ultimately hit a car – actions to which some of the stone-throwers later admitted.[68] The sentence – three months' community service and a six-month suspended sentence – is highly unlikely to have been given to a Palestinian in comparable circumstances. In 2009, the supreme court overturned the 45-day prison sentence imposed on a settler who, at the age of 17, was involved in stoning and beating Palestinians, damaging their property, and obstructing Israeli police. Instead, the court gave her only a suspended sentence of eight months. The court upheld the one-month prison sentence of her accomplice, a 14-year-old at the time of

---

[66] Quoted in M. Horodniceanu, "17-Year-Old Admitted to Throwing Stones at a Journalist's Vehicle – But Not Convicted," *Walla! News* (December 24, 2018) [Hebrew], https://news.walla.co.il/item/3209170.

[67] CrimA 3944/15 *State of Israel* v. *John Does* (March 7, 2017), ¶ 13 of justice Danziger's leading opinion. The lower court used a similar rhetoric: CrimC (Jer. Dist.) 39422-06-14 *State of Israel* v. *John Does* (March 24, 2015 and October 10, 2016), ¶ 85.

[68] CrimA 1533/16 *John Doe* v. *State of Israel* (June 29, 2017).

offending, owing to her later involvement in similar offenses; one of the three justices, however, maintained that she should also be given only a non-custodial sentence.[69]

Shedding further light on the subject is a Master's paper written in 2009, which examined 117 Israeli judgments concerning stone-throwers: 76 non-military cases opened between 1991 and 2009 concerning citizens and residents (Palestinians and Jews) and 41 military judgments (the essay does not specify their time period) concerning noncitizen Palestinians. While the cases involved defendants of all ages, 56 percent of Israelis and at least 49 percent of noncitizen Palestinians were under the age of 18 at the time of the offense (some of the remaining 51 percent of noncitizen Palestinians did not have their ages mentioned in the judgments). At least 65 percent of Israelis had no prior criminal record, as had 97 percent of noncitizen Palestinians. In the interest of comparability, only cases with a single charge – ideologically motivated stone throwing at vehicles – were selected for analysis. Several disparities can be extracted from this study. First, Palestinian citizens and residents were overrepresented, making up 62 percent of Israeli defendants. Second, the sentences imposed on Palestinian citizens and residents aged 18 and over at the time of offending tended to be significantly harsher than those of similar aged Jews. Third, Israelis below the age of 18 at the time of offending were usually given non-custodial sentences (without significant differences between Jews and non-Jews). In contrast, noncitizen Palestinians – 95 percent of whom had caused no harm to persons or property – were all convicted, and 97 percent of them were sentenced to prison for up to 13 months.[70]

This Master's paper, while informative, is limited in several respects. Among other things, some data are provided for only one population but not the other, making the comparison incomplete. Another key limitation is that most Israeli stone-throwers are under the age of majority and are hence tried in youth courts behind closed doors.[71] Indeed,

---

[69] CrimA 1939/09 *Jane Doe* v. *State of Israel* (given on December 6 and amended on December 27, 2009).

[70] S. Benkin, "An Examination of the Judicial Policy Regarding Ideologically Motivated Offenses of Object Throwing at Vehicles – A Comparison between Arab and Jewish Defendants," Master's seminar essay, Faculty of Law – Haifa University (2009), pp. 8–18 [Hebrew] (on file with author).

[71] Article 9 of the Youth Law.

notwithstanding some legally permitted exceptions,[72] nearly 85 percent of Israeli defendants aged under 18 are tried in youth courts.[73]

Even a member of the Israeli judiciary – Yuval Shadmi from the Nazareth magistrate's court – once criticized the institutionalized discrimination of Palestinian citizens who throw stones compared with their Jewish counterparts (albeit without acknowledging the even greater discrimination of noncitizen Palestinians). He did so in a 2009 ruling, concerning a Palestinian citizen of Israel who was charged with hurling stones at a police vehicle during a demonstration against an Israeli military offensive in Gaza. According to the charge sheet, the offense occurred while the Palestinian had been 15 years old. The unusual judgment reads:

> [T]he State of Israel is, in effect, ... operating in two parallel and fundamentally different enforcement routes regarding ideologically motivated assaults of security forces by minors. With regard to minors from the Jewish sector, who committed violent offenses against security forces in relation to the [2005 Israeli] "disengagement" [from Gaza] and several house demolitions in the [West Bank] settlement of Amona, ... most proceedings ... are ... either suspended or terminated before [the end of trial]. ... [In contrast,] for Arab minors charged with ideologically motivated assaults of security forces, proceedings are not postponed, charges are not suspended, pardons are not granted, and most of these minors are convicted and sentenced to prison. ... [S]uch group discrimination ... is no longer acceptable. ... [In view of this] selective enforcement, ... I have decided not to convict the minor.[74]

---

[72] Ibid., Articles 3(a), 5a(a), 45b, and 45–45a. In addition, during the Gaza pullout – an event discussed in detail in this chapter – the large number of Israelis aged under 18 who clashed with Israeli authorities led to some of their cases being heard in non-youth courts. See remarks by the president of the youth courts in Special Committee for the Rights of the Child, 17th Knesset – Transcript 32 (June 12, 2007) [Hebrew], http://fs.knesset.gov .il//17/Committees/17_ptv_133925.doc [hereinafter: Child Rights Committee Transcript 32].

[73] Central Bureau of Statistics, "Persons Accused in Criminal Trials, 2016." Settlers aged under 18 can also be tried by Israeli municipal courts in the West Bank, which usually deal with municipal issues pertaining to settlements but are authorized to act as youth courts: Article 138 of Local Councils Regulations (Judea and Samaria), 1981. The inaccessibility of youth court judgments is among the reasons why non-youth court judgments and parliamentary committee transcripts make up most of my primary sources for this chapter. See further discussion in Chapter 1, Section 1.4 ("Methodology and Sources").

[74] CrimC (Nazareth) 6255-01-09 State of Israel v. John Doe (Minor) (November 11, 2009). Instead of convicting the Palestinian, Shadmi ordered him to sign a guarantee and to

Shortly after this "surprising" and "exceptional criticism," as the Israeli media characterized it,[75] the state appealed against Shadmi's decision. Accepting the appeal, a three-judge panel held that the so-called presumption of regularity – the law's assumption that state authorities operate properly absent evidence to the contrary – had not been rebutted. Shadmi's assertions about selective enforcement, the three judges unanimously maintained, were unsubstantiated. Having protected Israel's self-image, the judges nonetheless upheld the sentence, but did so on far less politically controversial grounds: the "loss and trauma" caused to the youth when, during Israel's 2006 war with the Lebanese Hezbollah party, a missile fired from Lebanon killed his two brothers.[76]

Although the selective enforcement argument regarding young Palestinian citizens was thus rejected, similar claims have been accepted as valid grounds for acquitting settlers and other Israeli Jews with comparable charges. This reasoning was, for example, applied by the supreme court in its previously mentioned decision from 2015 to acquit two settler youths of hurling stones at Palestinian vehicles. To justify its decision, the court also cited other acquittals of settler youth who had been charged with stone throwing.[77] Similarly, in 2019, a settler who had publicly justified stoning soldiers if they evicted inhabitants of proscribed settlements was acquitted on grounds of selective enforcement.[78]

In 2016, six adult settlers charged with hurling stones at Israeli forces were all convicted and given what the court accurately described as a relatively "harsh and burdensome" sentence of eight months in prison (though this included time already spent in detention). The judgment mentions their being "young defendants, some of whom were minors on the verge of adulthood at the time of the offenses." As in some of the previously analyzed judgments, it was also noted to the credit of two of the younger defendants their stated desire to enlist and "serve the

---

perform community service, while also banning him from obtaining a driver's license for two years.

[75] See, respectively, H. Einav, "Judge Surprising: 'The State Discriminates between Jews and Arabs'," *Ynet* (November 11, 2009) [Hebrew], www.ynet.co.il/articles/0,7340,L-3803713,00.html; A. M. David, "Judge: The State Discriminates in Enforcement between Jews and Arabs," *NRG* (November 11, 2009) [Hebrew], www.makorrishon.co.il/nrg/online/1/ART1/965/310.html.

[76] CrimA (Nazareth Dist.) 20-09 *State of Israel v. John Doe (Minor)* (June 1, 2010), ¶¶ 23–31, 34, 43–44. On the depoliticizing effect of such mental health discourse, see Chapter 5, Section 5.2 ("The Mental Health Discourse and Its Pitfalls").

[77] CrimA 3944/15, ¶ 7 of justice Danziger's leading opinion.

[78] CrimC (Petah Tikvah Mag.) 41184-12-17 *State of Israel v. Ariel* (July 2, 2019).

country." However, the severity and prevalence of such offenses by "Jewish youth" in the West Bank were deemed to outweigh these mitigating factors, as did the defendants' "ideology . . . according to which the State is an 'enemy'." What makes such offenses so grievous, according to a military official who is cited approvingly in the judgment, is their hindrance to the "activity of the security forces," who instead of handling Palestinians are forced to "dedicate time and resources to deal with hostile actions by citizens, most of whom are teens and youth."[79] Thus, to justify the atypical outcome of imprisoning settlers, the court labeled them as an all-round security threat.

In Chapter 6, I demonstrated how Palestinian complaints against Israeli violence seldom lead to prosecution, let alone conviction. On the rare occasions of convictions, the complaint is often corroborated by Israeli testimonies (though such testimonies hardly guarantee prosecution or conviction). This, I argued, both reflects and reinforces Israel's tendency to dismiss uncorroborated Palestinian allegations. The same trend also characterizes each and every one of the convictions of Israelis discussed in this section. In the case of the soldier convicted of physically assaulting a Palestinian youth who had complained about being the target of settlers' stone throwing, there were corroborating testimonies of two Israeli state agents: a soldier and a police officer. Likewise, in the conviction of the young settler who, together with other settlers, had pelted stones at Palestinian vehicles, it was the confessions of some of his accomplices that ended up corroborating Palestinian complaints. The two settler girls who, among other acts, hurled stones and physically assaulted Palestinians, were likewise convicted based not only on the Palestinians' complaints but also on corroborating Israeli testimonies. The last conviction analyzed here – and the one with the harshest sentence – was of settlers who admitted to hurling stones not at Palestinians but at Israeli forces.[80] This throws into sharp relief, yet again, whose safety, whose lives, and whose accounts are given most weight by Israel's courts.

8.2.2 Age-Segregated Detention (and the Lack Thereof)

In October 2004, less than a year ahead of the pullout from the Gaza Strip, the Israeli government introduced a bill designed to regulate the

---

[79] CrimC (Center Dist.) 38705-07-13 *State of Israel* v. *Cohen* (2016).
[80] See, respectively, CMC 276/02; CrimA 1533/16; CrimA 1939/09; CrimC 38705-07-13.

evacuation, resettlement, and compensation of the Gaza settlers, as well as the aid they would receive from the state. Among other things, the bill made it a criminal offense to illegally enter or stay in evacuated areas. Special provision was made for "minors suspected of [such] offenses ... [to be detained] with adults suspected of committing the aforesaid offenses, provided that the minors have expressed their consent and that their wellbeing is not jeopardized." The rationale for joint detention was clarified in the explanatory notes accompanying the bill:

> [As a rule, Israeli law] requires holding minor detainees separately from adult detainees. ... [However, as regards] detention for offenses under the proposed statute, there is no actual concern that contact between minor detainees and adult detainees would corrupt the minors or introduce them to the criminal world. On the contrary, separation between minors and adults might harm these minors.[81]

Two months later, the parliamentary Constitution, Law, and Justice Committee dedicated one of its meetings to discussing this specific provision. One of the attendees, a police commander from the youth section of the ministry of interior defense, offered to:

> explain how this article was phrased and to place it in its correct context: ... The assumption is that we are ... dealing with minors who, even if they commit severe offenses, are not minors with a criminal record, and we do not treat them with the same tools [used for "regular" criminal offenders] ... In this case there is a different and sensitive background to [the offenses] ..., requiring special treatment. In this situation, all of the reasons underlying the [legally required] separation ... between minors and adults ... are inapplicable.[82]

In a later meeting, a legal advisor to the police likewise told the committee that the bill carved out "an exception" to the legal requirement to separate "minors from adults in detention." As he described it, "our premise was that in this situation of adults and minors being arrested amid the disengagement [i.e., pullout] events, chances are slim that the

---

[81] Article 27(e) of Disengagement Plan Implementation Law draft, 2004 and its accompanying explanatory note (October 27, 2004), in *Government Bills*, vol. 130, p. 2 [Hebrew], https://fs.knesset.gov.il/16/law/16_ls1_517551.PDF.

[82] Constitution, Law, and Justice Committee, 16th Knesset – Transcript 366 (December 27, 2004) [Hebrew], http://fs.knesset.gov.il/16/Committees/16_ptv_548592.docx (the original mistakenly reads: "The assumption is that we are not dealing with minors who ... are not minors with a criminal record"). The Child Rights Committee chair likewise remarked, in 2007, that "the arrests of minors in acts of opposition [to the pullout] were a unique phenomenon." Child Rights Committee Transcript 32.

adults would harm the minors. Detaining minors with adults in this situation would actually help the minors."[83] The bill, including this provision, was passed by parliament in February 2005.[84]

Israel's decision not to separate under-18s from their elders in detention came against the backdrop of demands from the intended evacuees to keep their communities whole. In December 2004, according to reports in the right-wing Israeli media, the Legal Forum for the Land of Israel – a newly established NGO opposing the evacuation of settlers from Gaza and seeking to protect their entitlements – "asked the government ... to do everything in its power to see to it that the communities ... stay together." Using a mental health language akin to that examined in Chapters 5 and 7, the NGO reportedly added: "Every significant study ... indicates that keeping communities intact helps to prevent post-traumatic stress disorder, which can result in serious emotional disability."[85]

These debates and quotes, combined with my findings in Chapter 4, indicate three parallels between anti-pullout settlers and noncitizen Palestinians in conflict with Israeli law. First, both groups have objected to being divided by Israeli authorities. Second, Israel has distinguished both groups from "regular" offenders. And, third, under-18s in both groups, if detained, were seen by their communities as benefiting from being held with their older counterparts. Given these commonalities, it is telling that reasons similar to those cited in support of joint detention for anti-pullout activists were used to justify an opposite policy for Palestinians.

The age-based segregation of noncitizen Palestinians in Israeli custody is among the Israeli reforms critically examined in Chapter 4. Such segregation, I have argued, has deprived Palestinian youth of valuable support, exposed them to greater abuse, facilitated the revocation and narrowing down of older Palestinians' rights, and all of this against Palestinians' own preferences. As I have further revealed, the Israeli legal system strongly pushed for age segregation in the hope of minimizing the ideological influence of older Palestinians and undoing its existing impact on young Palestinians. Without such segregation, Israeli judges

---

[83] Constitution, Law, and Justice Committee, 16th Knesset – Transcript 404 (February 7, 2005) [Hebrew], http://fs.knesset.gov.il/16/Committees/16_ptv_549073.docx.

[84] Article 27(f) of Disengagement Plan Implementation Law, 2005.

[85] Channel 7 staff, "Gush Katif Lawyers Rebuff Gov't Claims," *Channel 7* (August 25, 2005), www.israelnationalnews.com/News/News.aspx/88678.

warned that Palestinians would "capture the soul" of their young, that "minors ... [would] be upgraded in criminality," and that prison would therefore become "a school for many future terrorist experts."[86]

Thus, Israel's reasons for the age segregation of Palestinians are comparable to the reasons for the opposite policy for ideologically motivated Jewish settlers. Not only does this highlight further the wide-ranging discrimination between these two groups, but it also casts serious doubt on Israel's professed commitment – as discussed throughout this book – to operate in young Palestinians' best interests.

8.3   Age, Silence, and Infantilization

Demonstrations against the Gaza pullout, which sometimes involved physical violence and blocking of transport routes,[87] were attended by many settlers under the age of 18. Upon arrest, these young settlers often refused to disclose their personal details, including their ages, to the authorities. As the attorney general would later recount to the parliamentary Child Rights Committee:

> Hundreds of minors refused to self-identify. They said: we wouldn't identify ourselves, we don't care, even if we would have to sit in jail. The State then had the option of succumbing to that demand and releasing them without identification. This would have meant an inability to enforce the law on them, since it's clearly impossible to try an offender who hasn't identified himself. Therefore, our policy, backed by the courts, was that a person who didn't self-identify ... and who according to available evidence had allegedly committed an offense would not be released until he identified himself. ... Most of the minors who had refused to identify themselves were identified within 24–48 hours. The big commotion concerned a small group of girls who could not be identified.[88]

Indeed, although nearly 96 percent of Israeli under-18s in trouble with the law are male,[89] in anti-pullout protests girls were particularly prominent.[90] And while their overall refusal to self-identify baffled the

---

[86] See Chapter 4, Section 4.3 ("Generational Segregation and Its Pitfalls").

[87] S. Friedman, "Hilltop Youth: Political-Anthropological Research in the Hills of Judea and Samaria" (2015) 21:3 *Israel Affairs* 391, 399.

[88] Child Rights Committee Transcript 1110.

[89] Central Bureau of Statistics, *Israel Statistical Annual – 2019*, p. 155 (referring to 2017).

[90] Y. Sheleg, *The Political and Social Ramifications of Evacuating Settlements in Judea, Samaria, and the Gaza Strip – Disengagement 2005 as a Test Case* (Jerusalem: Israel

authorities, it was the inability to ascertain their ages that was especially challenging. The legal system was thrown into confusion by what it saw as the virtually impossible task of placing these girls of undetermined age in the legal array of age-based provisions. Judge Galit Wigotsky-Mor, the president of the (non-military) youth courts, pointed this out to the parliamentary Child Rights Committee, in a meeting dedicated to discussing the prolonged detention of the noncompliant settler youth:

> Regarding detentions during anti-disengagement protests, sometimes we [youth court judges] didn't even know whether the minor was over the age of criminal responsibility, 12 years, or under [that age] . . ., in which case he couldn't even be arrested.[91]

Such conduct was not exclusive to the pullout period. Two years later, in 2007, two settlers aged 14 and 15 were arrested for entering a sealed-off military zone during a protest at a West Bank outpost. Upon arrest, they, like their predecessors, refused to state their ages or any other identifying information to the police.[92]

In Chapter 3, I examined the related practice, by older noncitizen Palestinians, of presenting themselves to Israeli authorities as under-18s, thereby initially receiving relatively light sentences. Once their actual chronological ages were discovered, their sentences were increased. In those cases, the conduct denounced by the legal system was self-association with a supposedly incorrect age group. Presenting no less of a challenge, the settlers' outright refusal to disclose their ages placed what seemed like an insurmountable obstacle before law's desire to ascribe an age to anyone classified as a child. Admittedly, recording and utilizing age are key ways for society and law to know and govern not only those defined as children but people of all ages.[93] But in modern times, the centrality of age to childhood, coupled with society's preoccupation with

---

Democracy Institute, 2007), p. 60 [Hebrew], www.idi.org.il/media/4494/pp_72.pdf. On women's right-wing activism in both Israeli and Palestinian societies, see L. Ben Shitrit, *Righteous Transgressions: Women's Activism on the Israeli and Palestinian Religious Right* (Princeton: Princeton University Press, 2015).

[91] Child Rights Committee Transcript 32.

[92] C. Levinson, "5 Religious Girls Sue Police for Allegedly Strip-Searching Them," *Haaretz* (December 31, 2009), https://web.archive.org/web/20100103095250/www.haaretz.com/hasen/spages/1139049.html.

[93] On the documentation of age throughout people's lives in modern societies, see, e.g., A. James, C. Jenks and A. Prout, *Theorizing Childhood* (Cambridge: Polity Press, 1998), p. 61.

deciphering the child through quantifiable data,[94] makes it especially crucial for the law to establish the ages of society's young members.

Notwithstanding their differences, these acts of Israeli settlers and Palestinians exemplify the potential of both coopting and resisting the utterance customarily directed at young people: "Act your age!"[95] Not only does this dictum express the dominance of age norms, it also constitutes age as a matter of acting and performing.[96] And this performative dimension, as noted in Chapter 3, enables age to be acted and negotiated in different ways, including as a means of resistance.

In the case of the settler youth, this resistance has been in the form of silence. As social theorist Michel Foucault observed, the modern legal system "jams [when] . . . the accused remains silent," especially when "[t]he accused evades a question which is essential in the eyes of a modern tribunal . . .: 'Who are you?'." According to Foucault, "it is not enough for the accused to [admit his guilt] . . . Much more is expected of him. Beyond admission, there must be . . . revelation of what one is."[97] Addressed at young people, the question "who are you?" frequently overlaps with another, ageist and developmentalist question: "how old are you?"[98] The silent settler youths, by leaving the latter question unanswered, frustrated law's efforts to know its human subjects and to enforce on them society's age norms.

In Chapter 5, I called into question prevailing conceptions of voice, including the tendency to equate "voice" exclusively with speech.

---

[94] On the relationship between age and childhood, see Chapter 3. On society's desire to decipher children, see, e.g., J. Hockey and A. James, *Social Identities across the Life Course* (Basingstoke and New York: Palgrave Macmillan, 2003), p. 18; N. Rose, *Governing the Soul: The Shaping of the Private Self*, 2nd ed. (London and New York: Free Association Books, 1999), pp. 135–54.

[95] On this dictum and the social norms it represents, see N. Lesko, *Act Your Age!: A Cultural Construction of Adolescence* (New York and London: Routledge, 2001); P. Alexander, *Schooling and Social Identity: Learning to Act Your Age in Contemporary Britain* (London: Palgrave Macmillan, 2020).

[96] On the performative nature of age, see, e.g., G. Valentine, *Public Space and the Culture of Childhood* (Aldershot and Burlington: Ashgate, 2004), p. 55; R. Bernstein, "Childhood as Performance," in A. M. Duane (ed.), *Children's Table: Childhood Studies and the Humanities* (Athens, GA and London: University of Georgia Press, 2013), pp. 203–12.

[97] M. Foucault, "About the Concept of the 'Dangerous Individual' in 19th-Century Legal Psychiatry" (1978) 1:1 *International Journal of Law and Psychiatry* 1, 1.

[98] On how this question epitomizes society's age-based construction of childhood, see H. P. Chudacoff, *How Old Are You: Age Consciousness in American Culture* (Princeton and Oxford: Princeton University Press, 1989). On ageism, developmentality, and their relation to childhood, see Chapter 1, Section 1.2.1 ("Problematizing Childhood").

A related tendency, in discourses on groups that are viewed as silenced, is to associate silence with powerlessness, whereas speech is seen as an expression of agency and potency.[99] But in certain circumstances (not limited to those examined here),[100] silence offers a way to exercise agency by short-circuiting the power dynamics. Regarding the anti-pullout settler youth who were asked about their ages, what rendered their silence so effective – and in this sense they were not silent at all – was the reaction of the Israeli police and courts: holding them in prolonged detention until they identified. It is due to this reaction that the silence of these youth was loudly heard all the way to the Israeli parliament.

Criticism was similarly leveled at the state's insistence on not releasing the girls from detention unless they signed an undertaking concerning their probation conditions. During a 2006 meeting of the parliamentary Child Rights Committee, the representative of the public defender's office criticized this approach as childish and irrational, adding:

> we would expect the [legal] system to take a deep breath. Just like we sometimes tell children to count to three and think how to get off the tree, here too a creative way to get off the tree was called for ... [As regards] those 13- or 14-year-old girls, minors who cannot even be legally sentenced to prison ..., there should have been created conditions that do not depend on their active participation. Meaning, for instance, not forcing them to sign the undertaking [regarding their probation conditions].[101]

The Israeli legal authorities were thus infantilized by this comparison to an impatient child in need of being taught restraint and reason. This further illustrates my argument in Chapters 1, 3–5, and 7 that childhood,

---

[99] For a feminist critique of the association of silence with powerlessness, see S. Gal, "Between Speech and Silence: The Problematics of Research on Language and Gender," in M. di Leonardo (ed.), *Gender at the Crossroad of Knowledge: Feminist Anthropology in the Postmodern Era* (Berkley, CA and Oxford: University of California Press, 1991), pp. 175–203.

[100] On young people's silence as a form of agency in other contexts, see E. Chase, "Agency and Silence: Young People Seeking Asylum Alone in the UK" (2010) 40:7 *British Journal of Social Work* 2050, 2052, 2059–65; I. Hutchby, "Resisting the Incitement to Talk in Child Counselling: Aspects of the Utterance 'I Don't Know'" (2002) 4:2 *Discourse Studies* 147, 149, 165.

[101] Child Rights Committee Transcript 11. Three other suggestions heard in the meeting were: to impose probation conditions on the girls even if they do not sign the conditions papers; to hold an immediate trial while keeping them in detention; and to release them and possibly even withdraw the charges.

as a legal category, is by no means exclusive to those under the age of majority. Whereas in the previous chapter I investigated the application of this category to soldiers, the quotation here associates it with the legal system itself. That the law itself can, in a sense, occupy this category renders the question of who "really" is a child all the more fluid (further to its fluidity as discussed in Chapter 3).

8.4 Between Mental Health and Visual Representation

Figuring centrally in Israeli debates on the 2005 Gaza pullout were two modes of representing and interpreting the experiences of young settler evacuees: a medical health language of childhood trauma and loss; and visual imagery. Having explored these representational frameworks in relation to Palestinians in Chapters 5 and 6 respectively, I will now turn the spotlight on their operation and effects regarding evacuated settler youth.

The impact of the local political conflict on young Israelis has been a growing source of preoccupation for psychologists and psychiatrists alike.[102] During and following the Gaza pullout, young evacuees were among those whose potential traumatization was at the forefront of mental health experts' concerns.[103] Within the settler community itself, some symbolically placed the 2005 evacuation on a long chain of Jewish traumas, including the Holocaust and, as part of Israel's peace agreement with Egypt, the 1982 evacuation of Israelis from the Sinai Peninsula. Having named a few of their settlements in commemoration of the traumatic 1982 Sinai evacuation, evacuees referenced the Holocaust

---

[102] See, e.g., A. Klingman, "Stress Responses and Adaptation of Israeli School-Age Children Evacuated from Homes during Massive Missile Attacks" (2001) 14 *Anxiety, Stress, and Coping* 149; A. Al-Krenawi, J. R. Graham, and Y. Kanat-Maymon, "Analysis of Trauma Exposure, Symptomatology and Functioning in Jewish Israeli and Palestinian Adolescents" (2009) 195 *British Journal of Psychiatry* 427.

[103] Regarding young evacuees, see, e.g., S. Hen-Gal and Y. Siman-Tov (eds.), *When the Road Continues: Educational Therapeutic Interventions in Relation to the Disengagement Programme* (Jerusalem: Israeli Ministry of Education, 2009) [Hebrew]. Regarding all settler evacuees, see B. J. Hall et al., "The Psychological Impact of Impending Forced Settler Disengagement in Gaza: Trauma and Posttraumatic Growth" (2008) 21:1 *Journal of Trauma Stress* 22; G. Plotkin-Amrami, "'Denial or Faith?': Therapy versus Messianism in Preparing for the Evacuation of Israeli Settlements" (2015) 46:4 *Anthropology & Education* 414.

during the 2005 pullout, including by tattooing their ID numbers on their arms and by talking of "being placed in ghettos."[104]

Possibly due to most non-military youth hearings being conducted behind closed doors, very few depictions of the experiences of evacuated young settlers as "trauma" can be found in publicly available judgments. An exception (in a non-criminal proceeding) concerns three young settlers who, having been arrested during an anti-pullout protest, sued the police for non-pecuniary damages for treating them violently and unlawfully. The court accepted their suit in part, awarded them compensation, and described the police actions as "undoubtedly traumatic for the claimants."[105]

Frequent references to the evacuees as having been "traumatized" can be found in the transcripts I have collected of parliamentary committee meetings. According to information provided by the Israeli parliament, no less than 137 public meetings of its committees, and dozens of its assembly deliberations, were dedicated to the Gaza pullout.[106] Throughout these discussions, the trauma discourse was a common thread. In 2005, for instance, the chair of the Child Rights Committee emphasized the need to ensure that "the [evacuated] children, even if this process entails trauma, . . . be harmed as minimally as possible."[107] Later that year, lawmaker Gila Finkelstein described the young evacuees to the Child Rights Committee as being "in a state of post-trauma."[108] The Constitution, Law, and Justice Committee was warned by another member of parliament, Yuri Stern, that "the trauma has just begun," while the legal advisor to the government referred to the pullout as "this traumatic event."[109]

Four years after the pullout, in 2009, the Child Rights Committee reviewed the well-being of those who in their youth had been evacuated

---

[104] N. Perugini, "The Moral Economy of Settler Colonialism: Israel and the 'Evacuation Trauma'" (2014) 4:1 *History of the Present* 49, 57–60; Shor, "Utilizing Rights and Wrongs," pp. 815–17.

[105] CivC (Jer. Mag.) 4501/06 *Marzel* v. *Bar* (October 7, 2007), ¶ 35.

[106] The Knesset's reply to petition HCJ 1213/10 *Nir* v. *Speaker of the Knesset* (February 15, 2011).

[107] Child Rights Committee Transcript 135.

[108] See, respectively, ibid.; Special Committee for the Rights of the Child, 16th Knesset – Transcript 142 (November 8, 2005) [Hebrew], http://fs.knesset.gov.il//16/Committees/16_ptv_131202.doc [hereinafter: Child Rights Committee Transcript 142].

[109] Constitution, Law, and Justice Committee, 16th Knesset – Transcript 579 (August 28, 2005) [Hebrew], http://fs.knesset.gov.il/16/Committees/16_ptv_489700.docx.

from the Gaza settlements. The committee spent much of its meeting on discussing drawings by young evacuees, thereby bringing into play the other mode of representation I have mentioned: visual imagery. Ahead of the meeting, the committee chair (and later Israel's representative to the United Nations), Danny Danon, arranged for these drawings to be displayed in the parliament's lobby. Soon, these visual images turned out to be politically explosive: on the order of the parliament's officer, the exhibition was removed, but following Danon's intervention it was reinstated. The officer's objection to the drawings stemmed, as Danon described it to the Israeli press, from their "harsh political messages" (one drawing, for example, contained the text "we will neither forget nor forgive").[110]

During the meeting, these drawings were presented as speaking for themselves as well as for their young creators. In his opening remarks, Danon referred to "the exhibition of children's drawings, an exhibition that speaks for itself," and later a representative of the ministry of education thanked him for "the opportunity to make the children's voices heard through the drawings."[111] Their remarks reproduced the belief, popular among child psychologists and others, that young people's drawings can illuminate their inner world, often more meaningfully than words can[112] – a notion that also appears in human rights reports on young Palestinians.[113]

At the same time, the drawings were treated as incapable of fully speaking – either for themselves or for the young evacuees – without a mental health professional to "translate" what it was that they were

---

[110] A. Bendar, "Danon Threatened – and the Drawings of the Gush Katif Children Will Be Displayed in the Hallway," *NRG* (June 22, 2009) [Hebrew], www.nrg.co.il/online/1/ART1/907/087.html.

[111] Special Committee for the Rights of the Child, 18th Knesset – Transcript 6 (June 23, 2009) [Hebrew], http://fs.knesset.gov.il//18/Committees/18_ptv_138548.doc [hereinafter: Child Rights Committee Transcript 6].

[112] See, e.g., S. Elbedour, D. T. Bastien, and B. A. Center, "Identity Formation in the Shadow of Conflict: Projective Drawings by Palestinian and Israeli Arab Children from the West Bank and Gaza" (1997) 34:2 *Journal of Peace Research* 217, 221 and the sources cited there; C. Golomb, "Drawing as Representation: The Child's Acquisition of a Meaningful Graphic Language" (1994) 20:2 *Visual Arts Research* 14.

[113] See, e.g., UN Committee on the Exercise of the Inalienable Rights of the Palestinian People, *Palestinian Children in the Occupied Territories* (January 1, 1981), p. 6, www.un.org/unispal/document/auto-insert-193529 ("the conditions of life under which young Palestinians live are dramatically reflected in their artistic expression, depicted through sombre scenes painted in dark and gloomy colours").

supposedly saying.[114] To this end, the committee invited a therapist, whose participation in the meeting brought into convergence the two modes of representation (visual and psychological) I have been examining here.[115] The therapist, having worked with these young evacuees, explained that she had examined their drawings with the assistance of three other mental health professionals: a developmental psychologist and two other therapists. Deploying the concept of trauma (discussed in Chapter 5), she characterized one of the images presented to the attendees on a large screen as "a traumatized girl's drawing" and another as demonstrating how its young maker "contains the trauma, he contains the evacuation."[116] Visual images were thus presented as necessary for obtaining access to the young people's suffering, while psychological vocabulary was deemed indispensable to deciphering these images.

Like the human rights reports on young Palestinians analyzed in Chapter 5, the discussion in the parliamentary committee linked the trauma in question to the loss of what, for the young evacuees, was their homeland.[117] Among the drawings shown in the therapist's slides was one of two palm trees – a symbol of the evacuated settlements – on which a big "X" was drawn as if to indicate their loss, and above which appeared the unequivocal text "this is absent." "The absence is very visible," the therapist remarked, along lines relating to my discussion of in/visibility and absence in Chapter 6. This absence, she clarified, was of "[w]hat they are missing. And that is mainly home." Such linking of the youths' trauma to the loss of their home emerged on other occasions as well. In an earlier meeting, the Child Rights Committee was told by the director-general of NGO the Israeli National Council for the Child: "These children have been traumatized. [They] . . . left home, their place of living. . . . They had . . . to leave their destroyed home."[118] The supreme court, in a ruling confirming the legality of the evacuation, likewise noted "the psychological effect of the evacuation on minors,"

---

[114] Cf. J. Tagg, *Grounds of Dispute: Art History, Cultural Politics and the Discursive Field* (London: Macmillan, 1992), p. 129 ("To serve as evidence and record, the image had to be said to speak for itself, though only qualified experts could read its lips.").

[115] For an example of such convergence regarding young Palestinians, see S. R. Kamens, D. Constandinides, and F. Flefel, "Drawing the Future: Psychosocial Correlates of Palestinian Children's Drawings" (2016) 5:3 *International Perspectives in Psychology* 167.

[116] Child Rights Committee Transcript 6.

[117] On perceptions of this loss in Israeli debates on the Gaza pullout, see Perugini, "The Moral Economy of Settler Colonialism," p. 58.

[118] Child Rights Committee Transcript 142.

whom it described as having had "to leave their place of residence, ... and to move to a new, unfamiliar place."[119]

Also akin to human rights representations of young Palestinians, speakers at the Child Rights Committee meeting employed the terms "loss" and "trauma" in tandem. However, as I noted in Chapter 5, these and other psychological terms are not mere facts; rather, they are interpretive frameworks susceptible to multiple uses. No wonder, then, that a dispute broke out in the 2009 committee meeting about what psychological concepts best suited the issues under discussion. The committee chair likened the young evacuees to those in "a situation of mourning," but lawmaker Avi Dichter objected to applying the term "mourning" to that context: "There are other applicable ... concepts in psychology instead." Two other members of parliament, Uri Orbach and Orli Levy-Abekasis, defended using this word, describing it as "a term used by professionals. ... This is psychotherapists' terminology ... [and] even if we do not like this term, ... it ... [is] a psychological term." A 19-year-old who had been evacuated from the Gaza Strip four years earlier added his own perspective on the matter by defining "mourning" as graver than "loss": "This term ['mourning'] has been explained to me ... [The evacuation] is much harder than loss."[120] These parliamentary deliberations thus attest to the appealing image of the mental health disciplines as objective and scientific, as well as to the assimilation of psychological vocabulary into popular discourses.[121] It is perhaps the tensions in this dual status of psychology – as both scientific and popular – that brought forth the controversy about the meaning of mourning.

---

[119] HCJ 1661/05 *Coast of Gaza Regional Council* v. *Israeli Knesset* (2005) 59(2) PD 481, ¶ 239 of the majority opinion.

[120] Child Rights Committee Transcript 6.

[121] On these trends in contemporary Western society, see E. Lomsky-Feder and E. Ben-Ari, "Trauma, Therapy and Responsibility: Psychology and War in Contemporary Israel," in A. Rao, M. Bollig, and M. Böck (eds.), *The Practice of War: Production, Reproduction and Communication of Armed Violence* (New York and Oxford: Berghahn Books, 2007), pp. 124–25.

INDEX

48/67 Palestinians, 27, *See also* citizens, Palestinian; East Jerusalem; Gaza Strip, the; West Bank, the

Abu Snima, Muhammad, 128–29

abuse. *See also* border police; human shields; killing; military; police; state violence; torture
  abuse protections in child rights, 201
  child-on-child, 148, 163
  concealment of, 233–38, 250–51
  cultural differences in perceptions of child abuse, 9
  denial of, 239–40
  depictions of abused children as deprived of their childhood, 194
  during Palestinians' arrest, detention, and interrogation, 234–35, 254
  human rights conceptions of, 185, 200, 203–5, 266
  leniency toward abusive soldiers, 244–45
  military hazing, 287–90
  of incarcerated Palestinian children, 150
  privileging of state agents' accounts of, 252–53
  recorded abuse of Palestinians by Israeli forces, 232–33, 276
  soldiers' abuse of Palestinian victims of Israeli stone throwing, 318
  trials of abusive Israeli soldiers, 233, 244–46, 248–51, 276, 282–86
  unaccountability for, 214, 241–42
  visual images of, 261–62

activism, political. *See* resistance, Palestinian; settlers, Israeli

Addameer, 80, 154, 180, 183, 185, 190

administrative detention, 27, 36, 64, 77, 108, 176, 226, 237, 239–40, 260, 314

adulthood. *See also* childhood
  adults as targets of child law and child rights, 17–18, 92–94, 157–60, 201–6, 228, 265–66
  as a perceived indicator of combatant status, 292
  as a social construct, 8–18
  as the opposite of childhood, 8–16, 110, 116, 192, 206, 265–66, 283–84
  its association with independence, competence, knowledge, and responsibility, 8–9, 192, 206, 265–66
  the contribution of child law and child rights to apathy and harshness toward adults, 157–60, 200–6, 265–66

Afghanistan, 265

African Youth Charter, 110

age. *See also* adulthood; ageism; childhood; gender; sexuality
  adult age as a perceived indicator of combatant status, 292
  age assessment tests for young asylum seekers, 95
  age composition of Israel/Palestine, 11, 119–20, 125, 127
  age composition of Israelis in trouble with the law, 307
  age composition of Palestinians in trouble with Israeli law, 60, 64
  age segregation in prisons, 24–25, 140–50

335

For EU product safety concerns, contact us at Calle de José Abascal, 56–1°, 28003 Madrid, Spain or eugpsr@cambridge.org.

www.ingramcontent.com/pod-product-compliance
Ingram Content Group UK Ltd.
Pitfield, Milton Keynes, MK11 3LW, UK
UKHW020402140625
459647UK00020B/2598